C000299986

GUANTANAMO

GUANTANAMO
my journey

David Hicks

WILLIAM HEINEMANN

A William Heinemann book
Published by Random House Australia Pty Ltd
Level 3, 100 Pacific Highway, North Sydney NSW 2060
www.randomhouse.com.au

First published by William Heinemann in 2010

Addresses for companies within the Random House Group can be found at www.randomhouse.com.au/offices.

Cataloguing-in-Publication data available at the National Library of Australia.

ISBN 978 1 86471 158 5

Cover design by Gayna Murphy/Greendot Design
Cover photograph courtesy Getty Images
Internal maps and diagrams by Ice Cold Publishing
Internal design and typesetting by Post Pre-Press Group

Printed and bound by Griffin Press, South Australia

10 9 8 7 6 5 4 3 2 1

Dedicated to those who gave me the benefit of the doubt,
and to those who supported me.

To the individuals and organisations who worked tirelessly
on my behalf, whether openly or behind the scenes; and those
who helped in various ways anonymously.

To those who support the rule of law and the concept of justice,
who believe that abusive treatment and torture is not the
answer and is unacceptable.

To the men, women and children who are detained illegally;
to the human beings who are being tortured at this time;
and to the individuals and families who are still forcibly
'disappeared' around the world.

To my friends in Kosovo; to the people in Kashmir
who continue to suffer and lose their lives; and the
human beings still detained in Guantanamo.

Also to my family, whom I love dearly,
especially my father,
Terry Hicks.

Contents

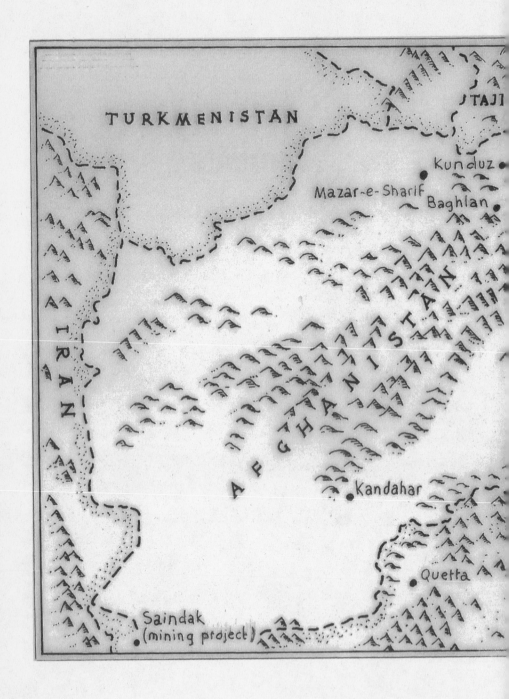

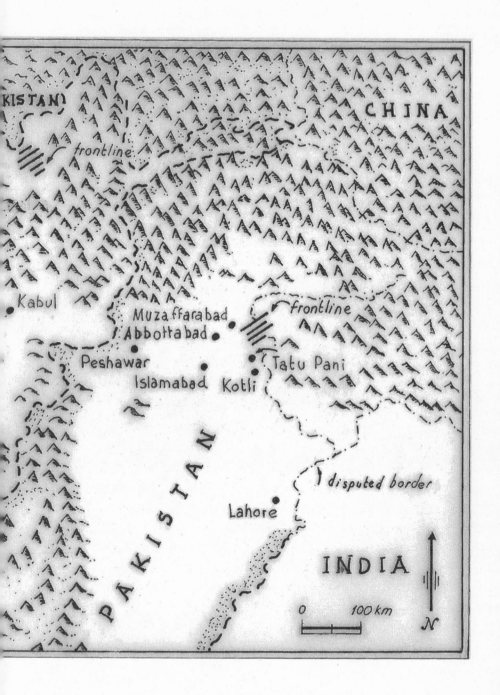

Afghanistan and surrounding area.

Author's note

'Truth is generally the best vindication against slander.'

Abraham Lincoln

The media has long proposed that one of the many questions I should publicly address is, 'What was I doing in Afghanistan?' To those who would ask such a question, I would first answer with a few questions of my own . . . What could I have done to make the treatment I endured acceptable? Is there any situation that would warrant such treatment? For that is what the above question provokes in me. Can selected people be treated harshly – either physically, psychologically, politically or legally – because of the allegations aimed at them based on their actions, intentions, beliefs or myriad other excuses? Should anyone be abused in any form, at any time? Is there a crime or accusation that warrants torture? My own set of questions aside, my book will address how I came to Afghanistan and many other topics truthfully, honestly and in full detail – from my birth, to events leading to Guantanamo, what took place there and beyond.

This is the first time I have had the opportunity to tell my story publicly, despite all the plays, documentaries, magazines, newspaper articles and books claiming to know it. You can now go on *my* journey. It is a view of the world through my eyes, back then as I experienced it. I have not spoken publicly until now for many reasons. A gag order was placed on me, and then a control order. I have been privately threatened with reimprisonment; I have also been waiting for my US lawyers to say that my conviction is now null and void, including the plea agreement that prevented me from collaterally attacking my conviction and publicly discussing my treatment. There are other reasons as well; but, most importantly, I have needed time to recover and heal from my ordeal, to receive treatment for torture and trauma, and generally learn how to adapt to a normal life again after so many years of isolation. This book is my story and my way of simply putting down the facts – how things were and are – after so many years of misinformation. The record cannot be left as it currently stands.

My story and who I am as a person is something so many people have an opinion on already. Whatever you may think of me now, in the past, or after reading this book, you will have a much better understanding of how the following events came to pass and why. You will see that I am not, and have never been, a supporter of terrorism. I am not a public threat. I did not harm anyone – I never attempted or planned to – nor was I accused of such. And I did not break any Australian, US or international laws.

I hope you find that this book is not only a story of injustice, but also a story of hope.

Introduction

NOT THAT IT MATTERS, but I wonder what the time is. Sunlight struggles in vain to penetrate this enclosed room through the few millimetres of gap under the only door. The hue is slightly different, more pure and pleasing than the artificial light that dominates the inside of this enclosure twenty-four hours a day. I am confident that it is daytime.

Another clue to placing myself in the twenty-four-hour cycle is when the food arrives and what the meal consists of. It has been some hours since breakfast was served – different in look but similar in taste to the other meals – so I narrow the time of day down to late morning.

The soldiers' rotation also hints at whether it is night or day. There is a soldier in my room at present, as there always is, and I recognise him as belonging to the day-shift crew. He was sitting in the plastic chair outside the steel mesh cage in which I am housed when I woke some hours ago. He stares, expressionless, saying nothing, keeping his thoughts to himself.

1

He makes a movement, quite the momentous occasion in this oppressive, sullen room. I watch the soldier intently, hoping to see something interesting that will pass a few minutes during this featureless day.

Predictably, however, he reaches for a hardcover notebook bound in green cloth, the only item on the table upon which his forearms rest, his chosen observational position. He makes an entry: 'Detainee 002 sitting on bunk and staring at personnel and base of door.'

Every fifteen minutes the soldier will add similar entries to the endless log about what exciting activities I am up to: sitting, lying down, sleeping and using the toilet. This book of journal entries that divides my existence into fifteen-minute lots is analysed periodically by psychiatrists, psychologists, behavioural experts, intelligence operatives and others who wish to pick my mind apart and make all-knowing assumptions. I have been reduced to an open book for all to read. I feel like an animal sprawled upon a dissection table.

I ask the staring soldier the time. He ignores me. What is the date? The month? The year? The only response from the soldier is another entry into the green book of every word I have just spoken.

This is Camp Echo, one of half a dozen camps that exist on this militarised island called Guantanamo Bay. Some years have already passed. The pain in my back is becoming unbearable. I have received a few heavily redacted letters from my family, but I have not heard their voices or seen them in all the time I have spent here. I was convinced long ago that there is nowhere I can turn for help; there is no-one who can intervene to stop this never-ending nightmare. I often ask myself how I ended up in this bizarre, maddening position. How did I end up in this location and within a program so surreal that I have no faith of leaving with my sanity intact, if I leave at all? How can they treat another human like this? How can they be so cruel? A more compelling question: *how are they getting away with this?* I have lost hope and, at times, the will to live. I keep trying to picture the 'real world', but it becomes more difficult with the passing of time. Even now the memories of my distant life – sun, wind, trees, the ocean, family, friends, love – are vanishing. I don't bother much these days to conjure up that other life. It adds to the depression and, besides, it's becoming more of a fantasy – these four walls are the new reality. It is hard to picture any other way to live. I know my family is out there, fighting for me, but the spell that has been woven by my captors is too strong to resist. Every day, every minute, I wait to be released. I cannot fathom why I will not eventually be sent home. I cannot fathom that this injustice will continue. *Please, do not let it be forever.* But I am tired. Hope is slipping from my grasp.

I do not sleep much because my captors tell me it is not allowed. Yet, even if I do manage to sleep, my fears fuel my nightmares – fear of pain, fear of the beatings, fear of the strange mind games I am subjected to. My captors never sleep. They work around the clock, devising new ways to harm me and the other detainees. In other camps I have listened to the screams of fellow prisoners, watching them being taken away for their 'special treatment', listening to their accounts of what they endured when they were returned. These are the experiences that scare me now. They have not stopped. My captors claim they will always continue. There is no warning of these assaults – any time, day or night, I am never safe.

More hours have passed and I now hear heavy boots ascending the four rickety wooden steps leading to the door of my enclosure. The door swings open and the sudden assault of natural sunlight is blinding. The door is quickly closed and I see two uniformed men holding full-body restraints. The macabre music of the jingling restraints causes my heart to race. I am afraid, very afraid. But there is still the faintest glimmer of hope; maybe I will be taken to the airport, or taken to an interrogation booth where shady government men will inform me of my impending release. I stick my hands through the bean hole of the cage door as instructed. When my hands are secured, I spin around so that the soldiers can padlock my wrist and the chain to my waist. Then, through a bean hole at the base of the cage door, I feel the soldiers' gloved hands secure the chains to my ankles. The cage door is now opened and I shuffle out. They tell me to stop and apply a blindfold. I follow barked orders so that I don't bump into walls or shuffle in the wrong direction. I make my way outside to the back of a waiting van. Forceful hands guide me into a seat and the van door is swung shut as the two military escorts take their seats either side of me. They relay information into their radios: 'The package is en route.' As we drive off we are shadowed by armed Humvees while rifles from guard towers are trained upon us. My thoughts are divided between adjusting to being blindfolded and the pain of the restraints. I am afraid of being struck without warning. I obsess about where I am being taken, and for what reason. I hope the treatment will be endurable, that I will come away intact. But, most of all, I wonder when this will end.

PART
ONE

'The deepest definition of youth is life as yet untouched
by tragedy.'

Alfred North Whitehead (1861–1947)

One

MY MOTHER WAS BORN in the London suburb of Croydon. At around age four she travelled with her family to Australia by ship, arriving in 1953. My father was born and raised in Gawler, South Australia. In those days Gawler was an isolated country community and the first settlement of significance north of Adelaide. The lives of these two young people would intersect in their mutual workplace, culminating in marriage and a move to the newish northern suburb of Adelaide, Salisbury Park. Shortly after, I was born into the new household on 7 August 1975.

Salisbury Park was an enjoyable place to spend my early years. For suburbia, it offered a variety of places to play, beckoning with its creeks, parks and nearby hills. Carisbrooke and Harry Bowey reserves were like an oasis of sorts, with the frontiers being Jenkins Reserve at one end and the hills behind the Old Spot Hotel at the other. It was a huge area, a two-hour trek from one end to the other, where I enjoyed many years of weekend explorations. I found the ecology of the local creek particularly interesting. In the early '80s, two carp lived in a large waterhole at the eastern end of this playland. By the mid-'80s a healthy population of the fish were thriving behind a dam a few hundred metres downstream. In time, the council removed this dam, changing the water's flow, and allowing the carp to migrate deeper into the reserve. A bigger change occurred in the mid-'90s when the council removed a few kilometres of dense bamboo that had clogged the waterway in the central part of the reserve. After that, yabbies appeared for the first time, along with redfin perch – which my friends and I had unknowingly introduced to the ecosystem – and mountain trout. This array of creatures, including the carp, would find their way to the western frontiers and beyond by the turn of the century.

From my earliest memories, frogs abounded in the park, and throughout primary school catching tadpoles was all the rage. Collecting geckos from beneath the bark of large rivergums while avoiding the huntsman spiders lying in wait was another occupation we local youths took seriously. This was not all the wildlife that inhabited the park: leeches were a constant source of fear; turtles fascinated, guppies delighted. As we traversed the overgrown, self-made tracks through the quieter regions, foxes, rabbits, snakes, lizards and many birds helped create an ambience that made us feel like explorers and naturalists in the outback. But the outback it was not.

The park is situated in a valley carved by an ancient watercourse. Salisbury Park, where I lived, was located over the southern side of the valley.

I attended the local kindergarten and primary school until Year Five. Being an only child, I spent the majority of time in my own company at home, but I was never short of activities. Plastic toy soldiers, Matchbox cars, LEGO blocks, Star Wars figurines were some sources of amusement; my mother was another. She patiently taught me the names of plants and animals (or, as she taught me, 'flora and fauna') that could be found in the front and back gardens. She provided me with an assortment of books on various cultural and scientific subjects: Aboriginal Dreamtime, geology, meteorology, palae-ontology and anything to do with the age of the dinosaurs and beyond, but mainly the Cambrian explosion. I still remember her favourite extinct organism: the trilobite. She bought me an insect catcher and an ant farm, and together we assembled three modest collections of stamps, foreign coins and rocks.

Dad, on the other hand, was involved with football. He has served as a volunteer with the Central District Football Club (part of the South Australian National Football League) for over thirty years. I spent every Saturday during the season accompanying him to all the games. The Centrals' footy ground eventually became a second home, while away games allowed me to become familiar with all of Adelaide's other league football ovals. Because I was so young, football only occupied half my attention – the rest of the time was spent exploring the grounds. As soon as I was old enough, I contributed to the games by helping drink stewards, working the scoreboard or being a boundary umpire. I enjoyed the training rooms, with their floor-to-ceiling net to kick footballs into, and all the fascinating exercise equipment. There were lots of social functions in the clubrooms, including the Under-17 and Under-19 weekend parties. All this activity allowed me to get close and familiar with the lads. Some of those young players went on to play league football or pursue AFL careers.

I played football while at school, including a stint with the Central District special squad, now called the development squad. To be honest, I was only an average player. In those days I performed better at cricket. In fact, Dad was the primary school coach. We did well, going undefeated one year, thanks to Dad's expertise.

Those early years in Salisbury Park also included BMX riding. There were some excellent tracks in the area, and we'd fly along them in mobs. The movie *BMX Bandits* came out during that time, and it encouraged us to perform silly stunts. One day, while I was riding my BMX home, a car came around a corner sideways and continued towards me, swerving from one side of the road to the other. As the car passed, the bumper bar clipped my pedal and latched on, dragging me a short distance. I eventually came free and the driver stopped. He asked if I was okay, then got back in the car and took off again, leaving me on the side of the road. The driver, who was later tracked down by the police, turned out to be a drunken teenager who was too young to hold a licence and was joy-riding in his parents' car without their knowledge. I sustained a broken left leg at the knee from the accident.

Books were very popular among my friends and me. We would compete to be the first inside the school library and nag our parents to buy what we thought would give us an edge over our rivals. Dinosaurs were popular, but 'Choose Your Own Adventures' were the coolest. We really loved those books.

I had several playmates nearby. There were twins next door around my age and another kid across the road. Two other friends lived up the street, and my cousin Deanna, whom I was very close to, lived a few blocks over. But I still got into mischief on my own. One night, when I was about five, I snuck out of my bedroom window and wandered to the median strip in the middle of the highway next to our home in my pyjamas and big gumboots. I stripped the bark off the big old gum trees, looking for geckos with the aid of a torch. Dad was not impressed when the police brought me home at three in the morning, asking him if I was his son.

Dad and I spent time together in those early years, occasionally attending the local community club. Saturdays were for football, and then Saturday nights we visited Dad's friends and our family in Gawler. We often returned once more on Sundays to see my half-sister, Stephanie, Dad's daughter from his first marriage to a local girl named Bronwyn, and her side of the family. My nana also lived in Gawler, and she always had fresh chocolate cakes waiting for us every Sunday morning. So Gawler also, over the years, became like another home.

This was basically my early life. But it turned upside down while I was in Year Five. It was at that time that my parents separated. Dad remained in the family home, while my mother and I moved to a different suburb. At first it was Para Vista, then later Ingle Farm. This caused some changes for me. Para Vista was quite different from Salisbury Park. Young children in Salisbury Park were basically isolated by three generalised boundaries: the creek and its adjacent reserves on one side, a main highway on another and an industrial area dominated the last side. The school was small with limited student numbers, which made for an intimate, friendly environment.

At Salisbury Park, all the kids accepted one another, despite differences in dress codes and economic backgrounds. Peer group pressure and the importance of 'fitting in' were almost non-existent, compared to what I would discover once I left that sheltered enclave.

The suburb of Para Vista, for example, was closer to town, one suburb among many. The kids formed groups based on a variety of common social factors. I became self-conscious for the first time, changing my wardrobe, deciding where I could fit in.

At first my mother and I lived in a flat. Our neighbour had a fifteen-year-old son whom I began to hang out with, despite my being several years younger. We wore tight jeans, flannelette shirts, sported mullets and listened to heavy metal bands like Metallica. I began to smoke and got drunk for the first time. I remained in this area with my mother until I completed Year Six, Seven and the beginning of the first year of high school. In the meantime, Dad married his third wife, Bev, and she moved into my boyhood home in Salisbury Park, bringing her sons with her and creating a family atmosphere. I had always wanted to have siblings and experience the type of family that many of my school friends enjoyed. To remedy this, I returned to Salisbury Park to live with Dad and his new family.

However, things didn't turn out the way I wanted them to. I felt like an outsider, like I didn't fit in. I tried hard to be a part of the family, but I didn't feel like a member. We were all experiencing new changes in our lives – new relationships, new address, new schools – but everyone seemed self-consumed while appearing to operate as a unit, a unit I longed to be a part of. This alienation increased as time passed.

Throughout life we tend to wear uniforms, and this plays an important role when we are young because we are judged externally. We tend to gravitate towards those who seem familiar, assuming they share similar interests, and in return we attract a certain type of people to ourselves. The move to Dad's meant I also changed schools and attended Salisbury High School. Within a short time I had sought out a group that reflected my dress code. I was already a smoker and had dabbled with alcohol. To this list of regrettable vices I added pot, skipping school and general rebelliousness.

My attitude understandably caused problems at home. Instead of listening, I rebelled. My place within the family diminished and my isolation increased. In hindsight, I can understand why I thought I had found acceptance among the children of the rougher suburbs. Also at this time, my school marks slipped so badly that I failed Year Nine and had to repeat it.

However, not all was doom and gloom. I boxed during the few years I was in high school and did quite well, winning a state medal. Dad became heavily involved in the gym, even setting up a training system in our home shed. It was one of the last positive activities I was involved in; the last positive connection to the family. But as my behaviour ruined my schooling, it also eventually filtered into my boxing. I lacked motivation and interest, which led me to eventually quit.

I had a busy social life; indeed, it seemed to be the most important thing at the time. I had a lot of friends and a series of girlfriends, but there were times when my loner personality prevailed. More often than not I would jump on the bus, leaving everyone behind for the weekend, and go fishing.

Fishing was the big love of my life, and would remain so into adulthood. The art of fishing was inspired in me by my maternal grandfather. I have wonderful early memories of Port MacDonnell, where my grandparents lived for a time. Port MacDonnell is a little coastal town situated in the far south-east corner of South Australia, not far from the Victorian border. It has four diverse fishing environments: a jetty; a breakwater; huge, rugged cliffs; and long, sweeping surf beaches. Grandad would explain the ecological uniqueness of each environment and fish them accordingly. He was a wise man who knew about many subjects. He passed away some years ago, not long after my grandmother. I am grateful he left me with these two interests – fishing and analysing ecosystems.

This early training from Grandad allowed me to become a good fisherman. During my high school years in Adelaide, land-based game fishing (LBG) was hugely popular, targeting sharks and rays. On many a summer night, the end of Glenelg jetty would be so crammed with LBG fishos that those chasing other species, and casual jetty-walkers, had trouble accessing the end. There would be so many rods out in the water that if one 'ran', dozens of hopeful anglers would jump up excitedly, no-one knowing which rod had made the noise. As the night progressed, a party atmosphere often descended. Many of the LBG fishos were young, so music, pot and drink would keep us amused while passing the long hours between runs. It was not unusual for people to arrive on Friday night and remain until Sunday, camping behind tarpaulins, attempting to escape the ocean winds.

Whereas Glenelg was known for its big rays, the next popular LBG jetty was Semaphore. It was not as heavily fished, but it could match Glenelg on occasion. Semaphore was known for small bronze whaler sharks during the summer months, and the odd ray. If I was not to be found at Glenelg, then I was probably fishing at Semaphore. For a change of pace I would also chase bream and mulloway in the Port River during the winter months.

Sometimes I would disappear for weeks at a time, running away from home – or really just walking away. I would spend that time with the numerous street kids at Glenelg, living the life of a beach bum. A lot of the time when I returned home, no-one would ask where I had been or what I had been doing. I was obviously not attending school. In hindsight, I spent a lot of that time trying to get a reaction. I came home from school once with an earring, another time with tattoos, but neither act elicited a response. I did all sorts of silly things as a kid so that someone would take notice of me, so that I could feel part of something. I think this competition for attention of any kind continued for many years, and is even reflected in the letters I was to send to my family from overseas in the years to come.

After failing Year Nine, I tried to repeat it, lasting two or three months before dropping out of school altogether. I was about fifteen years old at the time. During the following months,

I continued to fish and be a general pain at home. It must have been a real test for Bev, but her love for my father enabled her to persevere with my bad behaviour. Around this time I began to hang out in one of the rougher suburbs, where dysfunctional households were common. It was an environment where the boundaries between adults and adolescents were blurred. I had been brought up to see adults as role models, respectable, authoritative, law-abiding figures to be listened to, their world ordered and in control, their private lives closed to children. This was the first time I had been exposed to negative adult behaviour, to all their problems and vices. To see this raw side of adulthood exposed was a novelty for me at first. But soon enough it disturbed me. I looked at myself, at the adults and how they lived, at their children, who were roughly my age. I could envisage those children following in their parents' footsteps, and then I saw myself as no different from them. I saw my future self, and this insight scared me. It was a wake-up call. Those reflections enabled me to see the road I was on and gave me the determination to get off. My rebelliousness at home had also grown worse, and the chasm widened between me and my new family. Eventually, I did something about it for my own sake.

I stopped fishing and began spending time with only a few close friends who lived in Salisbury Park, no longer venturing to the rougher suburbs. To improve my future prospects, I attended a volunteer eight-week, government-run welding course, learning arc, oxy and MIG techniques. Wearing the blue workman's overalls gave me a sense of satisfaction, of confidence. I felt like a productive and included member of society again.

Those eight weeks were positive in so many ways. In all areas of my life things started to improve, including at home. When the term was completed I was still too young to find employment – and an eight-week course is not much of a qualification. I faltered for a time, unsure how to progress. But I was determined not to lose hope and thought deeply, *what now?*

Unexpectedly, I was taken with the idea of becoming a jackaroo. I still cannot remember where the idea came from, maybe TV? It's hard for a young person to drastically change their life while remaining in an environment they cannot change, especially if they are trying to avoid temptations. Their world can be quite restricted, not having the knowledge or means to escape. For me to change my dress, friends and habits would be no easy feat, so a move – even one away from Adelaide – seemed a reasonable way to execute this long-term plan. A yearning for my earlier life of flora and fauna, the outdoors and adventure, was another contributing factor. A life in the bush appealed to me.

I searched for a way to do this and was eventually accepted into a six-month, live-in farming course at Kersbrook, nestled in the Adelaide Hills. I resided in Kersbrook during the week and spent the weekends at Dad's. About ten of us attended the course, either other troubled teens like myself or city lads looking to improve their chances for a farming career. Working on a property requires one to be a jack-of-all-trades, and for the next few months we were put through the basics: animal husbandry, planting vegetables, basic mechanics and workshop skills and fencing, among other things. The training was designed for working on small properties and dairy farms, more regional than rural. It was not suited for the large cattle properties up north where I wished to work, but at times one must take small steps towards one's goals.

My behaviour and attitude were largely changed for the better; things continued to improve at home. Apart from learning many new skills, I was also learning about life.

My thoughts were always directed to the future, to the time when the course would end. I was determined not to return to Salisbury Park, the old life, with no goals or projects. In anticipation of this, I sent weekly letters to cattle stations all over the Northern Territory, asking for employment. After completing four months of the Kersbrook course, a station owner replied, supplying details about a placement in a three-month jackeroo course at the Northern Territory Rural College, Katherine campus. The training was geared specifically for large cattle stations. I left Kersbrook two months short of graduation to pursue this opportunity. I farewelled my family and friends and travelled north.

Those first few days I spent in the Northern Territory are still an amazing memory. I was greeted by a caressing warmth and humidity as I stepped off the bus. There was a loud, incessant choir of insects. Primitive fruit bats flocked from tree to tree. Everything was green and lush, as I had pictured a jungle would be. I had arrived up north at the tail end of the wet season. It was an exciting time, when everything is humming with life. The alien landscape flaunted majestic, rocky outcrops; deep gorges; strange, ancient-looking trees and a metropolis of termite mounds. At the college in Katherine, I was confronted with the issue of dress once more. The fashion was different. People wore ten-gallon Akubra hats; R.M. Williams longhorn pants, Cuban-heeled riding boots and checked shirts. I remember the majority of students turning around to look at my suburban fashion while lining up for lunch on my first day. Yet, by the time the course had finished, I had blended in and looked as if I had been in the bush all my short years. It was a great college to attend: great food, accommodation and training, not to mention the breathtaking scenery around me.

Other students had also come from afar, ranging from Tasmania to Darwin, with a large contingent from Alice Springs.

I improved on my newly learned skills from Kersbrook, while the college assisted me in learning new ones. I worked with cattle for the first time and, more importantly, horses, because they were to become a major part of my occupation in the years to come. There were lots of places to explore in my spare time: waterholes for swimming and plenty of marvellous wildlife. The other students and I had some crazy times at the pubs in Katherine, the age of fifteen being no hindrance, and at the Mataranka springs, while we did work experience at Mataranka Station. Those three months were a suitable preparation for the years that followed.

When the course at the rural college was completed, I was offered a job on Wollogorang Station. It is positioned on the Gulf of Carpentaria, where the Northern Territory and Queensland border terminates at the coast, on the Northern Territory side. Wollogorang boasts some eighty kilometres of private coastline, a lot of it only accessible by boat or helicopter. It was the dry season when I left the college and there was plenty of tourist traffic, so I was able to hitchhike out to the station with no troubles. I stayed with a family overnight in Borroloola, the last town on Highway 1, before completing the final leg of the trip in the company of a stock inspector.

I love new places, experiencing the many faces the planet has to offer, and arriving at Wollogorang filled me with satisfaction and wonder. I arrived in the middle of a destock, when all hoofed animals are eradicated on a property due to the presence and spread of bovine tuberculosis. It is harsh country, and the men who worked there had been conditioned to the environment. After a week I found it all too much. I was missing home, wondering if anything had changed there during my absence. I thought I might have been missing out on something back in Adelaide. So instead of facing up to a challenge, I quit after a week.

When I returned to Adelaide I moved back in with Dad and Bev and caught up with a few friends. I was unable to find a job and became quickly bored, realising that nothing had changed. After a while I gave up on the job-hunting and made the decision to give Wollogorang another go.

I caught a bus from Adelaide, which delivered me to a restaurant/truck stop named Threeways Roadhouse, on the main Adelaide-to-Darwin highway. The bus continued north to Darwin, while my destination from here was north-east, about 800 kilometres away. My plan was to hitchhike to Wollogorang, but I quickly realised that, unlike last time, it was now the wet season, which is a time of year when there is not much traffic – tourist or local.

From the morning until evening I waited in vain for a passing motorist. During this time I ate the small amount of canned food I had brought with me from Adelaide. Thankfully, just before dusk, I was picked up by a young geologist, who took me to the next town, Heartbreak Hotel (Cape Crawford).

The geologist dropped me off on the side of the road. In the darkness I rolled my swag out beside the one-lane highway, opposite the hotel, and I eventually fell asleep. Hours later, I woke up feeling soaked through. I removed the swag cover from my head to discover heavy rain, a monsoon trough. The bottom half of my swag was under water, so too were my bags. I stared at the hotel, a blurred distant light despite it being directly across the road, abandoned my belongings and ran over to where the patrons were huddled beneath the front veranda admiring the downpour. They must have been surprised to see me running out of the gloomy deluge around 11 pm.

The geologist who had dropped me off earlier was still at

the hotel and was one of those under the veranda. He kindly drove his four-wheel drive to where I had been sleeping, and in the glare of its spotlights I retrieved my belongings, which were now submerged. I spent the rest of the night beneath the hotel's back veranda.

The next morning, I hung my waterlogged clothing and swag out to dry at the back of the hotel. The publican approached, asking if I had any money. When I replied that I didn't, he told me to pack my belongings.

I had received a small payout when my leg was broken by the teenage drink-driver. I tried to access it before leaving Adelaide but was told that, because I was underage, I could only receive funds in an emergency. I now considered my situation an emergency, but I needed to stay somewhere long enough to send a letter to Adelaide and then receive a cheque in reply. I told the publican this, but he remained uncompromising.

I spent a few days hanging around the hotel, mostly on the veranda, which the publican ignored. At night, I slept in my swag away in the trees. I grew hungry, while my rolled-up wet clothes began to go mouldy and putrid. The publican's wife apologised for her husband's attitude and snuck me some food. During one afternoon, a four-wheel drive ute arrived for fuel. As the driver went inside to pay, I spoke with two Aboriginal guys in the back of the vehicle. They explained how they worked at Bauhinia Downs Station, only sixty kilometres away. I explained my situation and they told me to hop in the back.

When we arrived at the homestead in Bauhinia Downs, I related my situation to the station manager. He wasn't pleased with my unannounced arrival and with those who had brought me to his property without his permission. He said I could not stay while I completed my correspondence with Adelaide, but if I worked for my keep, I could remain long enough to wash and dry my belongings.

However, I ended up staying at Bauhinia Downs Station for about three weeks anyway. The station reared buffalo, an animal I had not worked with before. We mustered the buffalo, and chopped down and poisoned trees to clear the ground for a light aircraft runway. I also fished for barramundi with the Aboriginal lads. My swag and clothes were washed and dried. Then the station manager played a trick to get me out of there. He introduced me to a friend of his who worked on a road gang nearby; the team had just finished their job. The friend lived in Darwin and had a truck and four-wheel drive that he needed to get back home. He had arranged for someone to catch the bus from Darwin down to Threeways, the restaurant/truck stop where the bus had first dropped me off, and he offered me $20 to take the four-wheel drive. The friend would take over from there. The station manager claimed he would arrange transportation for my return to Bauhinia Downs. I naively accepted.

I drove the four-wheel drive to Threeways with the guy in his truck close behind for the full day. On arrival, he gave me the $20, then took the keys and handed them to his friend, who had just disembarked from the bus. I waved to the truck and four-wheel drive as they headed north to Darwin. My next step was to ring the station manager at Bauhinia Downs. Unfortunately, he informed me, I wouldn't be returning. He said that my belongings were already on a vehicle heading my way. So, after all those weeks, I was standing in the same spot where my bus had first arrived, having to start again. The only difference was that I was $20 richer, but minus my belongings.

The money kept my stomach full for a few days, but once again things became desperate. Dad offered a solution. He knew the owner (Bronwyn's brother, in fact) of Daly Waters Pub, a township a few kilometres up the highway towards Darwin. I found a lift to Daly Waters and sought out the pub owner. Though he had not seen my dad for years, he remembered him well and offered help when I explained my situation. He extended me the use of a caravan and an account at the pub for three meals a day. This generous offer was on credit, so it could be paid for when the cheque arrived from Adelaide. Even better, he introduced me to the town mechanic, who had an old Ford panel van that had been sitting for some years in a paddock. He gave it to me for a cheap price, so I wrote a request for a cheque to cover the panel van as well.

Two weeks after I had sent my letter to Adelaide, I had a cheque for the panel van and a larger cheque, which I used to pay for my lodging. I was still left with a good amount of change. My situation was improving and the times were quite exciting: I was fifteen and unlicensed, with my first car and more money than I'd ever had. But I hadn't left trouble behind yet. When I was prepared, I drove the first stretch of my trip, heading towards Wollogorang, which took me from Daly Waters back to Threeways. Then I turned east along the highway towards Heartbreak Hotel. The car had baked in the sun for years, and I was about thirty-odd kilometres out of Threeways when a tyre blew. I pulled over and left the motor running while I assessed the damage. Suddenly the radiator cap blew off, with most of the water spraying after it. It had lost the ability over time to withstand pressure. I had no spare tyres, which left me with only one choice: creep slowly back to Daly Waters on one rim, leaving a white line gouged deeply into the bitumen. Back at Daly Waters the mechanic went over the van and ordered new tyres all around and a radiator cap. They had to come from Darwin, which meant another few weeks' wait.

That first night back in town, jackaroos from nearby Kalala Station came to the pub for a few beers. I recognised one of them. We had been in the same course at Northern Territory Rural College. They had two weeks of work left at Kalala Station before going on Christmas break. The head stockman offered me work for this remaining period at an amazingly high pay rate. I accepted without hesitation. It was a good job, and I might have remained there had they not been ceasing work for the wet season, as most cattle stations do. I spent those two weeks in the saddle, moving mobs of cattle to higher feeding grounds in anticipation of the wetlands that would form during the new year.

When the work terminated I was back in Daly Waters a few days before Christmas. The van was now running well and presumably reliable, and I had even more money than before. On the morning of Christmas Eve, I left Daly Waters a second time with renewed confidence and enthusiasm.

I made it to Threeways without incident, had a break, and then continued east. I eventually passed the point where I had broken down on my first attempt. Thankfully, the car kept going. By late afternoon I arrived at Heartbreak Hotel. I fuelled up and made sure the publican saw my vehicle and the contents of my wallet as I paid. Triumphant, I then left Heartbreak and Bauhinia Downs behind. I arrived in Borroloola by sunset and visited the family I had stayed with during my previous visit. I had dinner and a beer with them and then spent a few hours at the pub. Late that night, I drove out of town and slept in the back of the van. I woke up Christmas morning on a dirt track in the bush, surrounded by the calls of wildlife and nursing a hangover. Without breakfast, I continued on my way. After navigating half a dozen shallow rivers and muddy banks, I arrived at Wollogorang, my destination, at lunchtime on Christmas Day. About a month later the panel van would be stolen and wrapped around a tea-tree, but at least it had got me there.

I had left Adelaide in October. It was a long way around to cover a normal two- or three-day journey, with many experiences, changes of fortune and lessons learned along the way.

*

Wollogorang would have to be the most amazing country I have worked on in Australia; it is an untamed, isolated wilderness. There were no ceilings left in any of the rooms, due to the incessant chomping of white ants. I could actually hear them in the walls when the generator was off in the night-time. When I wanted to use the washing machine, I had to stick my hands in among the wiring because it only spun while a particular wire was kept taut. I often did this barefoot, while the entire room was ankle-deep in water.

A few times during my stay at Wollogorang I was able to go up in the mustering helicopter, which was another new experience. For work, we broke in some young colts. I also spent time at the nearby Aboriginal camps. Occasionally, some of the locals would take me on long walks, teaching me about the land and showing me how to track animals, such as wild pigs. There was also a lot of fencing to be done, and I spent the majority of my time in a fencing camp miles from anywhere. Of course, I also fished.

After working at Wollogorang for two or three months, I was the only white employee left. Despite being only fifteen or so, I was placed in charge of half a dozen Aboriginal men in their forties. I found this highly embarrassing. It is ridiculous to place an inexperienced teenager – and a white one at that – in charge of mature, experienced local men, men who have lived in the area since birth and are the true custodians of the land. To add insult to injury, I was paid a wage while they were paid in tobacco and a little food. I had a great respect for these men; they were kind and taught me much. I apologised for the situation and complained to the station manager, suggesting that I was unhappy and might leave.

While on the phone to Dad I mentioned my intention to leave. He asked me to have patience and give him a few days. During our next call he mentioned an ad he'd seen in an

Adelaide paper – jackaroos were needed in the Northern Territory. I called the number Dad provided from an Adelaide paper
and got the job. I arranged to meet my new employer in Ten-
nant Creek and caught the following mail plane there. Once in
town, I went on a week's splurge. I stayed in hotels, ate good
food and had plenty to drink. I bought clothes and an expensive watch. When the day arrived to rendezvous with my new
employer, I realised I had only been told to meet him on 'the
main street'. Once I was standing on the main street, I didn't
know on which *part* to wait. I chose a place and waited all day,
but no-one came to collect me. When it was dark, I called Dad.
He had some interesting news. Someone had placed the job ad
in the paper as a hoax, sending people all over Australia – and
I was one of them. My funds were now low, so I transferred
from a hotel to a backpackers, waited out a week and then
caught a bus back to Adelaide.

I was in Adelaide a very short time when another job offer for
two months' work came my way. This time it was at Numery
Station, a property straddling the western border of the
Simpson Desert. Every station I had seen worked differently,
preferring to use its own techniques, and Numery Station
was no exception. There was no natural source of water on
Numery – the only water available was supplied by bores. I
learned a new mustering technique called spear-trapping. This
is when fences are built around the cattle's water troughs, with
only one entrance/exit: a metal doorway lined with horizon-
tal poles. These poles are locked open with chains throughout
the year. This allows the cattle to wander in and out at will.
During mustering time, however, they are spring-loaded shut,
working like interlocking fingers. The cattle can push their
way through into the drinking yard, but cannot exit again.

Because the cattle must come in for water, every animal in the area must enter these trick doorways within a week or so or perish from dehydration. Every morning a hundred or more are trapped within the yards.

The only problem with this system was the camels: they would ignore the entrances and charge straight through the barbed-wire fences around the water troughs and then make a second hole to get out. The cattle then used the broken fences to enter and exit the water points.

When I worked at Numery it was a dry and dusty place with masses of flies. There was a lack of feed, and the poor cattle had resorted to chewing the bark and foliage off trees as high as they could, resulting in a landscape of uniformly trimmed vegetation.

Only motorbikes were used to move cattle – not horses – and cattle transportation trucks had to make their way across wide, boggy, sandy-bottomed riverbeds that had been devoid of water for years. These new experiences were enjoyable and I found the two months went much too quickly. Luckily, I was able to find another job, on the opposite side of the Simpson Desert, in the south-west corner of Queensland, so I travelled there directly instead of returning to Adelaide.

I caught a bus from Alice Springs to Port Augusta, South Australia. I then caught a mail plane from there to the Queensland town of Bedourie. Sandringham Station is owned by the family of famed pastoralist Sir Sidney Kidman and was once an important link in his chain of stations. Sandringham is actually the second station east out from the Simpson Desert, but it is very different country compared to the Alice Springs side of the desert. The area within and around Sandringham is known as the 'Channel Country'.

The land consists of sand dunes interspersed with blacksoil plains, the larger area fed by the three water sources: Cooper's

Creek, the Diamantina River and the Georgina River. Even in times of local drought, if the rains up north fall into these rivers, they eventually overflow into the south-west corner of Queensland, flooding the blacksoil and producing lush native grasses excellent for fattening cattle. Local lore suggests that Sidney Kidman was the first to truly understand and appreciate this occasional drought-proof system, recognising the security these three rivers provide. Kidman took advantage of his observations by buying up most of the Channel Country and using it sustainably.

I would describe this area of south-west Queensland as traditionalist country, where the practices of the early pioneers are still in use, practices I had heard about in the Northern Territory but had never seen. We went on stock camp for weeks at a time. Only two modern metal yards existed on the entire property; all the other yards were old, wooden bronco yards. We used Clydesdale horses for lassoing and roping calves instead of using metal cradles, while men on the ground threw and held the calves. Having limited metal yards also meant we could not draft in the modern way. Instead, individual cows were separated from the herd out on the flat using 'cutting' horses, that is, horses that can perform rodeo-style campdrafting. When we did use the metal yards for drafting, a mob of a few hundred cattle were funnelled through a series of smaller pens, slowly being separated, until only one or two are led into a round yard. In the centre of this pen is a pole upon which an employee can control the numerous gates, out of harm's way. Each gate leads to a separate yard, and the cattle are divided into calves and their mothers, steers for market, bulls for breeding, and whatever other groupings the manager decides upon.

Stock camp also included night watch, where we would take turns riding around the cattle from dusk till dawn. On stock camp we always had a large plant of horses, allowing each person two horses to perform different tasks, including general mustering and tailing, yarding up, cutting out and night watch. Each technique requires a different set of skills and training. We broke our own horses and trained them accordingly, judging from their early development which job they would be most suited to performing. Sandringham was not the only station that operated in this way; there were other Kidman properties in the area that followed the same practices.

This corner of Queensland had a good social scene. There was a time of year when the rodeo and campdraft circuit passed through the local towns. It was while working at Sandringham that I began competing in the saddle bronc. There were also dances and a seasonal racing circuit. The Birdsville Races was the biggest event, a four-day party with ten thousand people trying to buy beer from a pub built for sixty. Australia's last travelling boxing tent at the time, Fred Brophy's, would often accompany these events. Individuals from the audience could challenge members from the troupe; many would have a go and it was all done in good jest. Those work practices and social gatherings created an atmosphere I had experienced nowhere else in Australia, a remnant of the old days surviving amid change.

The year I spent at Sandringham came to an end, and with it came the Christmas holidays. It was time for me to return to Adelaide. From Sandringham Station I found a lift to Glengyle Station, another Kidman property, and bought a Ford Falcon ute. I drove it to Adelaide via the Birdsville Track, this time with a licence. I was excited about returning to the bush when the Christmas holidays were over: I had a goal to gain more experience before working all over Australia. I was seventeen years old.

Two

I DID NOT RETURN TO THE BUSH after the Christmas break. Instead, while in Adelaide, I met a young woman, whom I would be with for the next three and a half years. Together, we would have two children. She was already the young mother of a two-year-old daughter when we first met. Taking on the responsibilities of instant fatherhood was a challenge at the tender age of seventeen. However, I treated her daughter as my own, and we quickly became a family unit.

Settling in Adelaide brought about a change in occupation. For over a year I stuck with pre-training young racehorses and re-educating general-purpose horses deemed troublesome. There are not too many horses within suburbia, so my days were spent travelling from one side of Adelaide to the opposite outskirts. Tiring of the long travel and increased financial difficulties, I looked for a new occupation. A no-experience-needed butchering job was advertised in the paper, which led me to spend the next few years deboning. It wasn't the best of jobs, but it helped support my family. I was never a 'kangaroo skinner' as the media would incorrectly report in the coming years, nor did I work in a slaughterhouse ('wallowing in blood', as one commentator put it). Friends of mine were self-employed in the building trade, which allowed me to supplement my income through roofing, painting, cornicing, carpeting and landscaping.

During this time I began to fish again. The creek that runs through my boyhood reserve begins a few kilometres up into the hills, where it spills out of the wall of a large reservoir. The public was forbidden to fish in this dam without special permission, which was rarely given. So my childhood friends and I used to walk the one and a half hours up the hill from Salisbury Park when we were twelve years old, sneak inside and catch redfin from among the trees. If we were really keen, we would occasionally lug live specimens back down the hill to Salisbury Park and release them into the reserve's waterholes. So I couldn't believe my luck when, now older and a father, I met someone at work who actually lived at the dam. A childhood dream came true when this new friend gave me permission to fish this lonely stretch of deep water after hours, with whomever I chose to take. The dam was surrounded by bushland and felt deserted. I would find healing in these surroundings after my eventual break-up with my partner, but for the current stage of my life, it provided many memorable, reflective fishing expeditions.

I also began LBG fishing once again. Another workmate, who lived at Middle Beach, bought a small tinny at the beginning of summer. One day, in moderately rough weather, we tried to launch from the St Kilda boat ramp in this modest vessel. While doing so, a larger boat returned from out at sea with a dozen small sharks. The fishermen explained to us that they had taken this catch at an offshore ground called the

Goannas, positioned out the front of Middle Beach. Then they regaled us with stories of large schools of bronze whalers.

One week after that event, another friend and I paid an acquaintance who had a five-metre, centre-console boat to take us to the Goannas. We went out on Boxing Day, and it was a memorable day indeed. The three of us launched from St Kilda, and without an echo sounder or GPS, we had to rely on landmarks to find the fishing ground. We anchored out of sight of the suburban coastline, the mangroves to the north a faint green shimmer on the horizon. From one corner of the boat we floated a punctured two-litre cordial bottle filled with tuna oil. In the other corner, we hung a bunch of fresh fish heads joined together by fishing line. We had anchored at 3 pm, with the intention of changing both the tuna oil and the fish heads hourly. Also, floating at the back of the boat were balloons armed with bait and tackle designed for sharks averaging one-and-a-half metres long.

After the first hour I cut the line holding the fish heads together, allowing them to separate and float down the current. I replaced them with a fresh bunch, then retrieved the tuna oil bottle and emptied it out into the water. We had a spare twenty-litre bottle that was half full, which we used to refill the smaller cordial bottle floating in the water. We would hang over the side, going up and down with the swell, directing the spills so they didn't land in the boat. The owner of the boat was attempting to sleep on the wooden floor while my mate leaned against the outboard motor beside me. As I was pouring oil from one bottle to another my mate leapt back and yelled, 'Shark!' I was expecting a small one, so I had to adjust my eyes to take in the shape that materialised.

I had never seen such an enormous shark before, and with a rush of mixed emotions I threw the larger of the tuna oil containers into the air. It landed on the wooden deck, oil leaking everywhere, causing us to slip around in our excitement. The shark glided up to the back of the boat and devoured the bunch of fish heads. Then it manoeuvred sideways and forward, positioning itself alongside us. The boat was nearly five metres long, and the shark's head reached the bow while its tail stretched to the stern. The other guy and I were half-mad, slipping around in the oil while peering over the side. The water was calm and clear, and the shark appeared to be just below the surface, emanating pride and majesty, strength and beauty.

It slowly turned sideways, its huge pectoral fins like plane wings, exposing a gigantic girth and a white undercarriage with a very distinct line: a white pointer. Its tiny, beady black eye was trained upon us as we hung over the side staring back, speechless. It was an amazing moment. The shark then righted itself and swung its head under the boat, leaving only its back half to view. It then disappeared under the boat. We slid to the other side, but it did not reappear.

After a few minutes the shark returned, circling the boat, its huge caudal tail fin occasionally breaching the surface and slapping the waves as it changed direction. The white pointer eventually became bored and swam away. It was a privilege to have witnessed such an amazing moment.

I attended both my children's births, awed at their entry into this world. My daughter was first, followed by my son a bit over a year later. I remember the early days of sterilising and warming bottles, feeding, changing their nappies and fitting their little arms and legs into their various outfits. I also remember what fun it was to play with them when they grew older, how we went to national parks and amusement parks. We often ate out for lunch or dinner; the two girls loved Chinese, even though their brother threw it at them from his highchair. In the evenings, I would occasionally bake a big chocolate cake dripping with icing and place it on the floor between us. We would eat the whole thing with our hands while laughing at *The Simpsons*. I also continued to ride in rodeos for a while, even though I wasn't very good, and we always went as a family. It was during one of these rodeos that I was bucked off a horse and sustained serious injuries. I broke five ribs on my left side, and one or two of these punctured my left lung. The accident also ruptured my spleen, leaving me in intensive care for two weeks and in hospital for longer.

Injuries aside, I very much enjoyed that period of my life and was perfectly content. I thought all was well between my partner and me, that we would be together forever, so I was heartbroken and disillusioned when I discovered that she was having an affair. With hindsight I can understand why this happened: we were both very young and facing the increasing challenges of raising a family. I had been suspicious for a few months, but the truth was shattering. She then told me to leave the house so her new partner could move in. I left and moved in with Dad and Bev, and then later with a friend.

The next phase of my life was particularly difficult. For six months, the children stayed with me for one weekend every fortnight, sometimes more often. This continued until my former partner moved from Adelaide to a country town with the man she had met. I was not informed of this move, nor were other people I knew who still had some contact with her. My children disappearing with their mother only made things all the more difficult.

It took roughly a year to accept that my family had vanished. I was gradually able to enjoy myself again and look to the future, although I always thought of my children. After

relocating a few times, I ended up in a halfway house of bach-
elors. There were about eight of us living there at one stage,
but there was plenty of space, including a big recreation room
containing a full-sized bar, a lounge, dartboard, pool table
and an entertainment system. My life consisted of staying up
on weekends, going fishing, dirt bike riding and working. But I
grew restless. I had been too idle for too long during my period
of adjusting to the loss of my family. I wasn't getting ahead;
I had no future plans. The only thing I did know was that I
wanted change – and a change I got.

I woke up one morning in the bachelor house with unusual
anticipation. The others were already up before me on this
particular day. I went and joined them in the common room.
On the pool table was the morning's newspaper. I opened it
randomly and, in the employment section, revealed the page
that would change my life: a job advertisement for a three-
month contract for pre-training racehorses in Japan, airfare
included. I did have some experience in this field, so I thought
I would have a chance if I applied. But it sounded too easy
and I wondered what the catch was, and besides, I had never
thought of going overseas before, especially to Japan. In hindsight, the outcome of this job ad was indeed a change, for it
was the beginning of the road to Guantanamo.

With some hesitation I called the phone number provided
and arranged an interview. I met with a Japanese lady, who
explained how things would work. Everything seemed legitimate. I saw photos of the riding track, the stables and staff
accommodation, as well as other locations within Japan for
which she also provided employees. Because of the conversion
rate at the time, I would be earning good money. I decided I
would go if chosen.

I left the interview feeling confident and excited. A few
days later I received a phone call saying I could have the job

if I wished. My next step was to prepare. I spent the following weeks obtaining my first passport and a three-month
Japanese visa. Next, the contract was signed and my airfare
arranged. I had not had contact with my children now for
over a year, which was not by choice. To run off to Japan
would have been irresponsible for a family man.

I flew from Adelaide via Sydney to Aomori in Japan's north at
the beginning of the northern hemisphere summer. I remember how green everything was and the semi-humid weather. For
the first time I was surrounded by an entirely foreign language.
Compared to the more urban settings in Japan, I considered this
first location to be very traditional, and I was able to immerse
myself in the local culture. Besides myself, there was also one
other Australian working there temporarily and two long-term
contracted Brazilians. The remaining staff were all locals.

I was shown to a cosy house, where I would stay for the
term of my contract, sharing with four other people. I became
great friends with one of the Brazilians. We had our own bed-
rooms, but shared a kitchen, sitting area, toilet (with heated
seat) and the biggest bath I've ever seen. Our internal slid-
ing doors were constructed of crisscrossed wood covered in a
material not unlike rice paper. The beds looked like oversized
baby cots. We ate together in a room of polished wood and
shared a laundry. I had to force the prongs of my Australian
alarm clock into the wall socket – there were only two slots
at different angles. It didn't take long to learn that, due to
the differences in voltage, my alarm clock ran at a different
speed.

Every morning before work all the staff, including office
staff, would stand in a circle outside for the exercise ritual. We
performed star jumps and other manoeuvres to the counting

rhythm of *ichi*, *ni*, *san*, *yon*, and so on. It was a bizarre experience. When we had finished the exercises we would disperse to our various jobs for the day.

It had been a few years since I had ridden a horse, so I found the first week testing. However, I quickly found my feet and settled in. Forming a bond with a horse is extremely rewarding, especially when it involves a horse deemed troublesome. Problems may range from a horse's reluctance to 'do as it's told' to outright dangerous behaviour. Such problems are nearly always because the horse has been previously mistreated, whether through general neglect, like being overworked, or physical abuse by aggressive, impatient people. It is a real privilege to earn an animal's trust, to see its health improve and have it perform because it *wants* to. There was a particular small bay filly in Japan, whom I loved dearly. She was already a healthy, friendly horse, and I believe she became just as attached to me as I was to her. She allowed me to ride her bareback, which she had not experienced before. I could also lie along her back while she walked around and ate. She would follow me without a lead rope and gallop over when I called. I would sneak contraband apples to her at night-time. These are the rewards in the horse industry.

I took notice of everything in Japan, fascinated by the foreign culture, including the different vegetation and animals – even the insects. Japanese TV was a novelty also and helped me with my language lessons, which my fellow workmates were kind and patient enough to coach me in. This first trip overseas was so exciting that even a drive to the local supermarket was enough to make me feel high on life. My three months in Japan were spent in a semi-rural location, so unfortunately I only visited a city once, but it was an important, life-changing outing.

*

In the weeks leading up to the Japan trip, I had been waiting for my passport and preparing to leave, hoping that I would receive an idea or an opportunity for the future while in Japan. A nagging feeling had me half believe that I would not return to the bachelor house devoid of ideas or direction. My fanciful mind speculated I would happen by chance to cross paths with an old wizened man while exploring some remote parts on horseback, who would impart some life-changing knowledge, or other such wisdom.

One night, while we were in one of the local Japanese city centres for a Saturday night movie, as we were walking along the streets we passed a street vendor selling rings, necklaces and other paraphernalia. He stood out of the crowd, for he was white in complexion, seemingly European. I said a few words to him as I passed and discovered he spoke English. Two blocks further along we came to the cinema, but we were four hours too early. The group of workmates I was with went to a neighbouring game arcade to pass the time. I returned to the street vendor.

He was young, in his early twenties, and was an Israeli citizen. He was a fascinating, worldly man and shared his many personal tales, such as his current overextended stay in Japan and other travels around the globe. I had never heard storytelling like it before, told with such wonder. He convinced me dreams of travel could easily become reality. If I chose, I could experience similar adventures. He planted a powerful seed in my imagination. Our four-hour conversation was over much too quickly. Before we parted he invited me to accompany him on his next excursion. In a couple of months he was to fly to India to spend time in the mountains, and then slowly make his way overland to Israel. My only obstacle to joining this

journey was my contract and visa expiring a few weeks before
he was leaving Japan.

During the following week at work, I discussed extending
my visa and contract to coincide with my new-found friend's
departure. My request was approved. I was told to wait and
complete the paperwork for the new contract and visa during
the last week of my current contract. I alerted my Israeli friend
to let him know the good news and kept in contact. But it was
not to be.

Sometimes we would give our horses a break from the rep-
etitious track work and walk them instead along a densely
vegetated track dubbed 'the jungle'. Because racehorses are
kept in small spaces and fed high-energy foods, thoroughbreds
can be a handful while riding. Fast work on a track is one
thing, but a slow walk through trees is another. In such situations they like to play the shying game by ducking sideways
quickly at the silliest things, whether it is the sun flickering
through the trees, the sound of nearby birds, gusts of wind or
even their own shadows. One day, shortly before completing
the required paperwork to extend my stay, all our horses shied
while on the jungle track. Three of us fell. I planted my feet,
but the rest of my body kept moving. The left tendon sheath
in my ankle swelled up, and I had trouble walking. I couldn't
ride, and my boss wouldn't allow me to work. After a number
of hospital trips, I was told I would need an operation that they
wouldn't perform in Japan. All these events conspired against
my planned adventure. With great regret, I called the Israeli
man one last time to report what had transpired and that I was
collecting my pay and returning to Australia.

*

Because of my injury I did not return to work upon my arrival in Australia. Instead, I lived off my savings while my previous employer paid for the operation. I returned to the bachelor house to live, but not without direction. Thanks to that chance encounter on a busy Japanese street, my mind was filled with ideas of travel. The proposed trip had been from the Indian mountains to the Mediterranean, via the Middle East. I daydreamed, borrowing as many books as I could read from the local library, covering all the countries within the route. The Indian mountains became the Himalayan mountains, and my reading covered Nepal, Tibet and parts of China as well.

It was the books for independent travellers that appealed the most, such as the Lonely Planet series. They opened up a whole new world, and I read them day and night for months. Within their pages I discovered the old Silk Road and decided I would try to ride that route by horse as it had been done in antiquity. I discovered the old 'hippie trail', which gave me a more modern perspective on the route. One book contained a riveting story of an Englishwoman who bought a horse in eastern Turkey and rode the area independently, experiencing many amazing adventures. In another book, the same lady disguised herself as a Bedouin and crossed illegally into Tibet from Nepal. She then roamed south-west China with roving livestock herders. These types of travel guides and memoirs of the region agreed on two points. First, the biggest challenge for the lone traveller was crossing the border from Nepal into Tibet, though judging from the number of books on the subject, many were willing to try. Second, the other big challenge for all Westerners was getting in and out of Afghanistan, a country described as a romantic last frontier. It was an easy image to conjure up in my impressionable mind at the time.

Now that I was back in Australia, some of my interests were different from those of the people I had lived with. I had felt alone as a kid, and, during this period of my life, I once again felt isolated. My interests were of wild adventures overseas, learning from real-life experiences, exploring the world and experiencing different cultures. No-one else had an interest; they thought I was dreaming. But I thought I had found an exit from the box in which we seemed trapped. One of the guys even nicknamed me 'Constable Kashmir'. 'Constable' because of my many questions and constant search for answers; 'Kashmir' because I mentioned the region often. It had really captured my imagination.

It was hard to study with the twenty-four-hour din of activity around me in the bachelor house. It may have been fun, but it was terribly distracting. To help solve this problem I moved in with Dad and Bev. Back in Salisbury Park I joined a new library and continued my reading. After two months at Dad and Bev's, and a total study period of four months, I had produced a four-inch-thick folder of all the information I thought necessary to attempt my Asian overland trip, complete with hand-drawn maps. Though I now felt ready to leave, my savings from Japan had just run out. I figured I would need thousands of dollars that I did not have. I was impatient – I wanted to leave there and then – but I did not have the means. After some consideration I remembered the Japanese lady who had found me employment in Japan. Back then she had mentioned the opportunity for a one-year contract if all went well the first time. But I had just been to Japan, and I did not wish to return – other lands beckoned. I reasoned, however, that one year's savings would be more than enough to attempt my expedition. Plus, I still had not decided whether to start at the Himalayan end or the eastern Turkey end. I had obtained information about how and where to buy a horse in Turkey, so

starting there seemed feasible. On the other hand, I felt it best
to begin in the most unknown, most exotic land and culture
and head towards something more familiar, namely Turkey,
then Europe. At any rate, a year in Japan would allow me
more time to consider this.

After contacting the Japanese woman, she found me another
job with a one-year contract and a renewable six-month working holiday visa. So, for the second time, I packed my bags,
this time armed with the information I needed for my big
adventure. I said goodbye to my family, and boarded the plane.

I arrived in Japan just before Christmas, 1998. This time I was
sent to Urakawa on the northern island of Hokkaido. It was
the middle of winter, and I was greeted by a sight I had never
seen before: snow. The landscape was blanketed in brilliant
white, and within a week of arriving, more snow fell from a
grey sky.

This location was unlike my previous job. More than a
hundred foreigners worked here. A small number of these
foreigners were from Australia and New Zealand, but the
majority had come from Ireland and the UK. There were not
many locals, so unfortunately I was not exposed to their culture. We were housed in small but nice units, a lone compound
on a snowy flat.

It was very cold at that time of year. Night-time temperatures
could drop to minus fifteen degrees Celsius. The temperature
would rise in the mornings to minus two degrees Celsius, and
then peak with a daytime temperature of two degrees. This
slight warmth would be enough to melt some patches of snow
during the day, which would refreeze at night, leaving ice sheets
the following day on which the horses would slip and occasionally fall over. Because this part of Japan was blanketed by

snow half the year, two massive indoor training arenas had been constructed. One was a straight track with two opposing directional lanes. The other was round, with all horses working in the same direction. The area in which we worked was a few kilometres back from the coast. Between us and the ocean the land was flat, mainly farms and paddocks for livestock. The rest of the complex was encompassed by mountains rising above us on three sides, like being inside a high-sided, very wide V. On a few occasions I climbed among these peaks, spying various animal tracks in the snow. One time I attempted a shortcut across a frozen stream. The ice cracked and I fell through – luckily, the running water beneath was only ankle deep. As spring approached the streams thawed. Large salmon entered these awakening waterways from the sea, and on two occasions I caught them on paternoster rigs using worms for bait. The warming weather also allowed us to begin riding on outdoor tracks in the crisp spring sun.

I bought a TV in the spring, and it was at that time that I first saw on the news the events taking place in Kosovo. Kosovo was a province of Serbia before it declared its independence in 2008. Kosovo Albanians made up ninety per cent of the population before Serbian forces mounted a horrific campaign of genocide and human rights abuses. I found the broadcasts deeply disturbing. I watched the updates daily, learning of the ethnic cleansing, the oppression, the brutality, the refugees and the injustice. As the weeks passed, the Allied spokesman, Jamie Shea, became my main source of information. He addressed the media daily, giving the people of Kosovo a voice and informing the world of what was happening. As images of the atrocities flashed across my screen, I felt it was important to do something to help. Jamie Shea spoke of the Kosovo Liberation Army (KLA) and the thousands of volunteers who were swelling its ranks. I interpreted his choice of language as an invitation to anyone capable of volunteering their services for Kosovo to come.

The compulsion to go and help was a strange experience. It built up over weeks, without my being conscious of it. By the time I was aware of these growing thoughts, I was already quite resolved to go. The inner conflict I experienced from this decision was short-lived. The travel adventure I had been focused on for so long would need to be placed on hold, or abandoned altogether as the message on TV was too strong, the Kosovo people's suffering too great. So the decision was made.

The next step was to put this decision into practice. I called my family and friends to inform them of my decision. They expressed deep concern, and some thought I was nuts. They advised me to leave the people of Kosovo to sort out their own problems, despite my informing them that we and our allies were the biggest players in this struggle for freedom.

The KLA (UÇK in Albanian) was supported by NATO. The KLA performed as the ground forces, while the Allies conducted their air campaign. At the time I left Japan, the number of Kosovan refugees had climbed above the one million mark. I do not remember what the death toll reached.[1] The refugees tended to escape, or were marched at great peril, into Montenegro, Macedonia and Albania. The Albanian military under NATO command set up training camps under the KLA name. The recruits largely came from the refugee camps and comprised men, women and teenagers. Some of these unfortunate people had witnessed a family member raped or killed by Serbian forces, maybe both. They were all victims of loss and witnesses of atrocity in some way. The second-largest recruitment came from within the population of Albania, and those who had been living abroad, many of whom had family or some other close relationship with Kosovo – the countries' language and culture is very similar. The other group of recruits were foreigners who had arrived from various countries, mostly Western nations. I was surprised to learn that this group was represented in the thousands.

I didn't know all of this when I first made the decision in Japan to go. I knew that the KLA had training camps to the north of the Albanian capital, Tiranë, and around the border with Kosovo. But I did not know how to find or join them, the simple logistical things.

I formed a plan, however. I would buy a one-way ticket to Tiranë. On arrival, I would stay in a hotel and walk the streets during the day, asking where I could join the KLA, and hope that I would receive answers before I ran out of money. This may smack of stupidity, and it does to me in hindsight, but years ago with the confidence of youth and the passion associated with injustice, it did not. The psychological preparation for my first adventure, riding across Asia, which in itself seems reckless when I think of it now with a few more years to my name, would have made my new plan seem not so impossible.

At the local flight centre in northern Japan I learned that I could not obtain a ticket to Tiranë because of the war. Instead, I was given two choices: I could travel to Greece or Italy. Italy sounded difficult, considering the amount of water that would stand between me and Albania. Instead, I chose Athens, the capital of Greece, with the aim to take a bus or taxi to the northern border. I would then cross over and continue to Tiranë. (I would later learn that Italy would have been the easier of the two choices had I attempted an overland route from Athens.)

My contract up, I left my job in Hokkaido and flew to Tokyo, where I learned that I could not enter Greece with a one-way ticket and was asked whether I wanted to travel on to another location. I mentioned that I wanted to get to Tiranë. To my pleasant surprise I was told, contrary to the advice of the previous flight centre, that Tiranë would not be a problem, so I was booked on a small plane for Tiranë, departing from Athens, with an open ticket. It was a lot cheaper than I had budgeted for an overland trip, and the worries of a border crossing no longer applied. A big difficulty in the trip had been dispelled in an instant.

I boarded a plane at Tokyo International Airport and began the journey towards Athens. On the way to Greece I changed planes in Singapore, which resulted in a few hours' layover. During that time I chatted with a young German woman in the smoking area who was living in Greece. We learnt that we were on the same flight.

After hours of flying, I stepped out of the airport and into the early-morning light of an Athens street. My intention was to go directly to the domestic airport with my open ticket in order to arrive in Tiranë as soon as possible, but standing next to me was the woman I had spoken to in Singapore. She talked of the beauty of the Greek islands and persuaded me to experience them before I moved on. We caught a cab together, and it dropped her home. Before disembarking she gave the driver instructions, and we said goodbye. I next found myself at a wharf. I hesitated for a minute, considering whether to ask the taxi driver to take me to the airport. Instead, I bought a ferry ticket and spent the day on the water. The ferry stopped off at various islands, picking up and dropping off passengers. The young German woman had been right – the islands of Greece were stunning.

It was close to nightfall when I made it back to the domestic airport, only to learn that I had missed three planes that day. I retired to a hotel for the night. I was late in returning to the airport the next morning, which meant I'd missed the first plane of the day. When the time approached for the lunch-time plane to leave, I made inquiries about its exact departure at the counter. I was told there was only one seat left, and they couldn't guarantee it until everyone else had checked in. When the time came, I found myself in a race to the counter with another person. They got there just before me and were rewarded with the last seat. I was guaranteed a seat on the next plane, however, which would be the last one for the day. In hindsight, there was a reason for that.

I had nearly reached my destination, but I knew the real difficulty would begin upon arrival. Fortunately, that uncertain future was cleared up by the young man I sat next to on the plane, an Albanian returning home after working in Greece. He was able to speak just enough English for us to communicate. He asked why I was travelling to his country. I answered that my intention was to secure a hotel room and find the KLA. He told me to forget the hotel – I would be welcome to stay at his mother's with him – and that he himself would take me to the KLA. I was suspicious. I asked him straight out if he planned to kill me and take my money. He laughed and produced his wallet, displaying more money than I had. Satisfied, I accepted.

The Tiranë airport came into view, its runways lined with US military hardware. As we descended I noticed airborne Apache helicopters not far from the plane. We landed and the young man took my suitcase and delivered it into a waiting taxi. We travelled to Durrës, a coastal city. His family was lovely and welcoming. We spent several nights with them and, true to his word, we wandered the streets during the day while he gathered information on the KLA. This led us to various locations and cafes.

On the third or fourth day, we arrived at a restaurant that the KLA were using. I spoke to a commander, who jotted down my information and then took my passport for safekeeping, explaining I would get it back when I had finished with the KLA. This was standard routine, and I felt comfortable and trusted the agreement.

We had a meal and boarded a bus, which was filled to capacity, and drove to a nearby beach house. All the people at this location were the KLA's new recruits. Three times a day we would all climb into the bus, travel to the same restaurant, eat our meals and then return to the beach house. There were Germans, French and Italian citizens in this group. Some of them had arrived individually, like me, while others had come in groups. Most had travelled by ferry from Italy. The young man who had befriended me said goodbye, having fulfilled his duty. I gave him half the money I had and, with a wave over his shoulder, I watched him disappear into the crowded streets.

Every few hours our numbers increased until eventually there were enough of us to fill two buses. We were then told that we would leave the city and travel to a training camp near the border. The next stage of the adventure had begun.

Three

WE TRAVELLED THROUGH AN IMMENSE GORGE, skirted the edge of an angry, fast-flowing river and drove in the shadows of rugged mountains. We passed a huge dam, among other man-made and natural wonders. Cement domes with slitted windows dotted the countryside in the thousands, and I was informed that these structures served as bunkers in the event of a war.

The bus came to an eventual halt in an area thick with natural vegetation, and we were told to disembark. We hastily assembled on the side of the road in two disorderly lines. A stony, dirt path wound its way through a gate and down into a valley, and we were told to march in this direction.

At the bottom of this track was a KLA training camp in what appeared to be old army barracks. It was here that I was to spend the next month. Having never been in a military environment before, I felt intimidated, scared, hesitant and curious. I had jumped into the deep end. Names and nationalities were taken, and we received our uniforms. Then I was sent to one of a number of large barracks.

As we entered, we were peppered with questions in various languages from several scattered groups. In answer, our group dispersed in various directions, joining fellow countrymen, or at least picking out the language we recognised from among the jumbled masses. I answered to an inquiry, 'Anyone speak English?' and found myself with American and British citizens. 'From the military, mate? SAS?' I was asked. I had to answer no and admit that I was inexperienced. I was a clueless observer as these confident young men and women broke down and reassembled weapons with ease while discussing past exploits and contemplating the current conflict. It was at this stage, while feeling out of place, that we newcomers were called to assemble outside.

Standing in the Albanian summer sun, we were asked by a German volunteer what previous military experience we had and whether those with past experience wanted to go directly to the frontlines. Everything around me on this day was bewildering, but now something even more unsettling occurred. One of the Germans in my group began demonstrating his past experience and what he wished to do in this current conflict. He clenched the imaginary handles of an anti-aircraft gun, shaking his fists violently, displaying the recoil with added sound effects. His facial features were distorted into a scowl and his lips pursed, spittle and slobber spraying everywhere, as if the imitation flak clearly explained his message. At the end of this show of animated enthusiasm – and I thought madness – he was taken away to the frontline.

Later that day an assembly was called, which everyone attended en masse. We filled a parade ground at one end of the camp, forming orderly lines in separate units, and faced the Albanian flag: a double black eagle on a red background.

A commander addressed us in a language I could not understand, but apparently the others did, for his remarks elicited a roar from all around. Order disintegrated into chaotic action as ten or more large military trucks appeared, their squat cabins sporting camouflaged canvas draped over metal frames. With song, laughter and lots of bravado, the young soldiers climbed into the cabins of the waiting convoy and departed in a cloud of dust, leaving the camp almost deserted and eerily silent.

The main body of remaining volunteers were those with whom I had recently arrived, plus some left over from the original group. Out of this motley crew a new unit was formed. I did not commit myself to a group straight away because I wanted more time to get my mind around what was happening. Instead, I spent the next two or three days with other Westerners who were still milling around, and I did what I am now told is an annoying habit: I interrogated them.

These guys were mainly French and German, plus a sprinkling from the Netherlands. I attempted to glean any information I could on the current conflict – who exactly were these foreigners and what motivations brought them here?

I categorised the KLA volunteers into four groups. The first consisted of men who were in their forties at least. They had served out their contracts in their respective European militaries but had never been to war. They saw this conflict as a last chance to experience what they had spent years training for. The second group hated Serbia, or Russia, or both. They hated communism in general and saw Serbia as a political disease that needed to be purged from Europe. The third group was made up of the young men who were hell-bent on adventure and adrenaline, pleased to partake in a war that their governments would not look upon as illegal. One such person explained war to me as being on the outer limits of extreme sports. The ultimate game of 'hunt and be hunted'. I found a number of these guys to be crazy and more than a little scary. They made up a good percentage of volunteers.

The fourth group went to Kosovo because they were disturbed by what they saw and heard in the media concerning the country's people and their plight. They had a belief that all people have the right to independence, freedom, peace and security. They believed that all people should be free from violence and oppression. I would place myself in this last category, with adventure an added motivation. This resolve strengthened as time passed.

Apart from asking a lot of questions, attempting to absorb as much as possible about this new world I had exposed myself to, and learning some basic infantry manoeuvres one-on-one from the French, those first few days were not overly productive. Each morning I saw the people I had arrived with train in their newly formed unit. Seeing them grow together – witnessing their determination, strength of will, suffering, heartbreak and the emotions they shared – made me feel like an outsider. Among those who had not yet joined a unit, I spent the most time with the French. They did not seem to be emotionally involved with the cause. As for the training, it did not really matter for them – they already had military experience. On the other hand, I knew absolutely nothing, yet I intended to enter the zone of conflict. To resolve this dilemma, I left the foreigners to their own devices and joined a unit.

The unit comprised locals, many of whom had arrived on the same group of buses as me. Admittedly, some were Albanians who had little else to do and were influenced more by movies than reality, but many had come from within Kosovo after having suffered themselves, either personally or through their loved ones. There were others in the camp, as well as my own unit, who had family members in Kosovo who were reported as missing or dead. They had now returned home after living abroad, to find their family and friends, and assist in any way they could.

Due to the language barrier, I initially befriended those who had previously spent some time in the UK. Another group who could speak English were those returning from Germany, where apparently a large Albanian community resided. What I found most surprising about those with the German connection was that they claimed to have come from German prisons. According to them, they had been serving their sentences when they were offered the choice of freedom in exchange for joining the KLA. True or not, I don't know, but they seemed serious nonetheless.

We shaved upon waking in the early morning and then went to the toilet in the area behind the barracks. It was like a virtual minefield. I had never seen anything like it. Hundreds, if not thousands, of people had passed before me in this camp. Those early crowds had obviously spent their time soiling the ground as close to the barracks as possible. By the time I had arrived, this polluted area had radiated outwards a few hundred metres so that one was forced to tiptoe quite far up a hill to find an area devoid of waste. Not a fun track at any time, but especially in the dark.

Breakfast consisted of dry biscuits and tea, and cigarettes were handed out to those who wanted them. We then ran as a group. The smokers jogged with cigarettes hanging out of their mouths, myself included. Needless to say, it made the training all the more difficult. While in the camp I was told that some NATO members had donated various goods to the KLA. Our uniforms were German, our boots British. Cigarettes were donated by the Netherlands and Denmark. The weapons came from Albania and, on a very small scale, from the US. Modern communications equipment had arrived from France.

I understood that the food had come from many sources. One day it was announced that a lunch of rice had been supplied by China. I would think that unlikely, considering the US 'accidentally' bombed the Chinese embassy in Belgrade. That tragedy, resulting from incorrect intelligence, was the last event I had seen on the news before leaving Japan.

Apart from simultaneously jogging and smoking in the mornings, we spent the rest of the day learning and performing basic infantry manoeuvres. Even though the camp had been emptied soon after my arrival, it refilled just as quickly. As time passed I settled into a routine. I was constantly sick, however, due to the lack of food and basic hygiene, and I suffered aches and pains, especially in my left knee as a result of my earlier bike accident.

It was after a month in the camp that I grew close with my fellow comrades. I began learning words in their language, Shqip. I endeavoured to observe their customs and behaviour, and even learned a patriotic marching song in Albanian by heart. This attempt to see the world through their eyes, showing respect, regardless of our different cultural upbringings, and sharing in their pain earned me respect in return. They opened up to me and invited me into their world.

It is difficult to describe what I felt during this episode of my life. I had been brought up without any knowledge of politics; it had played no role in my life as a young person. When I think about it, I hadn't been brought up to believe in anything in particular, whether the matter is religion, politics, corporatism, family history, a particular tradition or culture. The same seemed true of those I had grown up around. The closest culture I would have come to experiencing was the rural tradition while working as a jackaroo, where there were rules, codes of conduct and beliefs steeped in history. But this did not compare to the cultures I found myself surrounded by now.

These new friends had strong traditions, family ties and a loyalty I had not known or experienced before. There was also another level to the experience which was new to me: witnessing people brought together by war, oppression, injustice, homelessness and politics. I had not met people before who had been subjected to such abominable circumstances and who, through necessity, had emotionally banded together for a single cause, a cause that I considered noble and just.

These individuals would openly shed tears as they told me their sad tales in English or by way of a translator, and as I listened I could not help but share those tears. I heard the most heart-wrenching stories from teenage boys and girls to grandparents. Those stories explained how they used to live, socialise, work and spend time with family – then how certain events had horribly altered their lives.

From some, I heard the history of the region, right back to the seventh century. A large portion of the blame for the political unrest in the Balkans was placed on Russian colonists from this distant historical time. I also heard rumours about the current conflict as well, as all conflicts are plagued with rumour and speculation.

Those rumours suggested that before NATO began its air campaign and gave its support to the KLA, equipping the KLA as a capable ground force, the fatality rate of the KLA as they tried to infiltrate the border averaged seventy per cent. This astonishing rate was due to the border region being heavily guarded by Serbian forces; snipers and ambush accounted for this massive loss of life. In an attempt to change the high death toll, NATO commenced bombing, or punching out 'corridors'. It concentrated on strategic points along the border until it had cleared narrow areas for KLA soldiers to enter safely. The KLA then took control of these corridors and cut off the Serbian forces from behind, blocking their supply routes. This continued until large numbers of Serbian forces were isolated along the border regions. The KLA's change in fortune was due to a combination of the aerial strategy, better equipment and support, and a boost in morale. I would not say the training improved – the average preparation time for inexperienced KLA volunteers was a two-week crash course. Nevertheless, by this stage in the conflict the statistics had reversed so that the fatality rate was now thirty per cent. This was apparently how things stood upon my arrival in Albania.

Those isolated Serbian forces, said to be in the thousands, low on fuel and vital equipment, with only ammunition in plentiful supply, cracked under the pressure. Those forces were made up of two distinct groups. The first consisted of young conscripts, barely eighteen years old, a large majority of whom were forced into service. The other group consisted of older veterans, patriots, some of whom belonged to paramilitary forces and had fought previously in the Bosnian and Croatian wars. When the situation turned against them and the young conscripts attempted to flee, their older comrades shot them. This infighting was the catalyst that contributed to the collapse of the Serbian border defence, allowing the KLA to enter and leave Kosovo at will, and to conduct a more conventional war with trenches and artillery deep within the province. It was the beginning of the end for the Serbian military. But all this was supposedly occurring in a neighbouring country.

Back in Albania, I continued to train and adjusted to the food and camp lifestyle in general. Despite the physical and emotional difficulties, I found time to admire the many land tortoises and fireflies, which I had never seen before. We also occasionally swam in a creek behind a rock dam we had built ourselves. US jet fighters and large bombers flew over the camp daily on their many sorties into Serbia. At times, we would observe the smaller fighters hooked up to the much larger refuelling jets by an umbilical cord, seemingly hovering way up in a blue sky.

It was in this camp that the now notorious picture of me with the empty rocket-propelled grenade (RPG) on my shoulder was taken. I was standing with a group of other young guys in that particular shot. There were many of us who went into the storage room and took out unloaded weapons to be photographed with; it was only a silly trophy shot. It was just unfortunate that years later a friend from Adelaide who asked me for the photo sold it to the Australian media for two or three thousand dollars. He told me that he regretted his actions afterwards and, in banter, claimed he should have asked for more money.

I was surprised by the large number of young women who joined the KLA; some even arrived wearing make-up and high heels. You know a situation is bad in a country when the women take up arms. Joining the KLA was not a career move, like joining a government's armed forces: it was a crash course in infantry matters. As in all wars, the women were treated appallingly by their enemies. Men and boys I had spoken to described being forced to watch their sisters or mothers being raped, then sometimes killed. The most horrifying story I heard, which was very widespread and told in earnest, was of pregnant women having their stomachs ripped open and their babies removed by those acting on behalf of the Serbian forces. Sometimes the babies were replaced with something else, such as a dead animal. Examination of these women's bodies showed only wounds to the stomach, suggesting they would have been alive when these horrifying procedures began.

Women entering the zone of conflict were at risk of more than just being shot. Hearing this made me feel sick, and I dislike writing it, but such things should be known. Disgusting acts, like rape, are not uncommon in our modern conflicts and must be stopped.[2] The stories also strengthened my resolve to protect these people from something so evil.

During my time in the camp, on at least half a dozen occasions, bandits attacked our position late at night. They either fired at us from atop a ridge, or even came into the actual camp. Exchanges of fire rang out during these incursions, sometimes just outside our sleeping quarters. I found this baffling and inquired about these attacks. I was told that poverty ravaged the surrounding areas and that those lands were virtually lawless. Gangs of brigands often committed violent crimes and attacked us, knowing we were largely young, inexperienced and unarmed. Their goals were to obtain food, weapons from the storage rooms, clothing and anything of practical value. The bandits were always successfully fought off.

I may have been in this camp for a month when a US helicopter flew over very low during the day and released a number of flares. Those around me cheered and celebrated. One rumour claimed that the flares signalled the end of the war, another suggested they meant it was time to go to the frontline. Shortly after the flares we were called to an assembly. With a full parade ground, we all faced a table, upon which stood an Albanian flag alongside the NATO flag.

A commander stood to attention by the side of the table, while another sat behind it. We approached them one at a time. When it was my turn, I stood before both officers and saluted. A translator then said something along the lines of, 'You hereby agree to enter Kosovo under the command of NATO, to abide by their orders, rules and laws.' He had read from the top of a form that had been placed on the table. I then signed this paper, with all the other signatories, beneath the written speech and the NATO flag. I shook hands with the standing officer and returned to my unit while the next volunteer marched up. When we had all completed the ceremony, we were told to pack our gear and board the buses that would take us to the frontline. It was the moment we had been waiting for. It is hard to read another person's thoughts in such a situation, but I tried. I do not know if my thoughts betrayed me, but I was bloody scared.

We boarded the buses and drove for a number of hours. Some people chatted incessantly, others were quiet. I was among the latter. We thought our destination would be Kukes camp, apparently the last destination before crossing the border into Kosovo. We had heard that, while the Serbian military still held positions along the border, Kukes camp was regularly subjected to artillery fire. But instead of Kukes camp, the buses came to a stop at Burrel camp. It was not a final destination, just another training camp, so it did not seem to us that we had progressed further along the line. But it did signify a change in policy. This new location was a very large facility. We were told our previous camp had been closed down, along with many others, and that all volunteers were being centralised in this new location. Within days our numbers swelled to around two thousand.

The training in this new camp was much more rigorous and disciplined, with low-ranking Albanian army officers present, such as lieutenants and captains. The food was a massive improvement, with more variety and quantity, and my health rebounded. And there were toilets. While my memory is not perfect, I believe it was at this stage that an announcement was given: the war was officially over (hence the flares from the chopper). Milosevic had signed on the dotted line to end the conflict.[3] The Serbian military was withdrawing, and some NATO ground forces were actually entering Kosovo for the first time.

Then there was some added speculation. The north of Kosovo contains natural resources, and we were told that the Serbian forces had only retreated to this point. It was said they had stopped, turned around and entrenched themselves for the long haul. Russia had still not signed the treaty and Serbia was relying on Russia to help them defend this northern area. If this situation held, then NATO was going to use the KLA, which was well equipped by this stage to fight a conventional war, to uproot the Serbian military and push them over the border into Serbia. This news unsettled a lot of the people I was with; they had a great fear of the Russian military. However, after two weeks in this camp, we were all summoned to the parade ground for another announcement.

Russian troops were currently dissatisfied with the long period of little or no payment from their own government. As an alternative, they were being offered to serve under NATO as peacekeepers in the newly liberated Kosovo, where they would receive the same pay as other NATO soldiers. Whether this was the reason or not, Russia eventually agreed and allowed its forces to serve in Kosovo under NATO command, and not independently as they had previously requested. The war had finally ended; Serbian forces had completely retreated from Kosovo.

I was told privately that a condition that the KLA had agreed to with NATO was that all foreign volunteers would immediately relinquish their uniforms and depart. I was still in parade when I learned of this, along with the others. It was suddenly time for me to go, but first I was summoned to speak a few words in front of the gathered crowd. I would not have minded had just my unit been present, but I was standing in front of around two thousand people, most of them strangers.

I felt embarrassed. I was a foreigner, an outsider who had come from a nation that was peaceful and prosperous. I found it hard to look these people in the eye, people who had suffered unspeakable horrors. Though the war had ended, I knew that they would now return to a country in ruins: ruined homes, ruined families, loved ones dead or missing. They would still have the laborious task of rebuilding their homes, their nation and society, the entire time haunted and tormented by the horrors of the recent past. For some, I was sure that worse news was still to come.

With a translator, who was also a friend, beside me, I congratulated them on a victory and expressed my heartfelt sorrow for what they had endured and lost. I then wished them well for the future. As I finished, my friend convinced me that I must sing the song I had learned in their language. I apologised in advance for any mistakes and sang. I thought I might offend some people, because I was about to walk away from their harsh reality back into my safe world. Instead, they all joined in and we sang together. It was an extremely emotional experience and I finished with tears in my eyes, unashamed.

After I had finished addressing the assembly, I climbed into the back of a troop carrier and was driven to the Ministry of Defence in Albania's capital, Tiranë. As I had been told, foreigners from all over were being called back to the same place. I had an opportunity to meet a number of these foreigners, but unlike me, these individuals had come from inside Kosovo, where they had been involved in the conflict. I was to spend the next few days with about ten of these characters, who were citizens of Italy, Germany and Finland.

Apparently German NATO troops had entered and secured Pristina, the capital of Kosovo. However, in rural towns and villages throughout the province, disgruntled mercenaries (rogue Russian officers or individuals from Bulgaria, Hungary and other places), who had been promised pay by the Serbian government upon victory, had refused to leave with the

Serbian military and were violently roaming the countryside, killing and looting while high on drugs. Heavy drug use seems to have been widespread on both sides during the conflict. We were told that the KLA was going to send small teams into Kosovo to take care of those violent individuals in order to clear the way for other NATO forces. The group I was with agreed to go, and so did I, but within a day or two this proposal was cancelled.

During my time at the Ministry of Defence, I listened to the foreign volunteers speak among themselves. Some were great linguists, as one German displayed by acting as a middleman between two or three others of different nationalities. It fascinated me to watch this man's mind tick over as he translated four languages simultaneously, without, I assume, making a mistake. Germany had quite an influence within Albania, probably because of the two countries' relationship during World War II. German is the second language in Albania, and in many instances the Deutschmark was the number one currency. Many of the cars were of German make; talk of anything German was done with respect; and, of course, there were signs of German support throughout this conflict.

The foreign volunteers I was with at the Ministry of Defence did not fit the description of mercenaries under the International Laws of War in this conflict, mainly due to a lack of payment.[4] However, outside this conflict I would regard them as such. I was able to overhear bits of information from these foreign volunteers. Some had served in the earlier Bosnian and Croatian wars, in various locations in Africa or throughout scattered parts of Asia. They also discussed their future prospects, which mainly concerned Central America.

Once the proposed operation into Kosovo was cancelled, the Italians in my group discussed catching a ferry back to Italy, where they would approach the Spanish embassy. They

hoped to be sent to a conflict in a Central American country. I remember them saying it was a twenty-year-old civil war
involving communists. They would spend a month or two in
the jungle, then two weeks 'R and R' at a paid hotel where
booze, drugs and prostitutes would be free of charge. But the
one conflict they all spoke of in awe was in Venezuela. They
claimed that the then Venezuelan government had been logging in the Amazon in the far south of the country for years
until the indigenous Indians, whose home is the jungle, fought
back. The locals killed the logging teams, using such methods
as poison blow darts. The government first responded by sending in their own professional commandos, but these soldiers
also quickly met their fate.

I sat listening as the men claimed the Venezuelan government was paying mercenaries a handsome sum to go on stints
in the jungle for up to a month at a time. Their mission was
to subdue the Indians. It was apparently the highest-paid job
out there for a mercenary – but also the most dangerous. The
government could afford to offer such a large sum because
the chance of mercenaries lasting long enough to be paid was
low. This mission was spoken of as being the last frontier in
the world for these people, a place where only the most experienced and burnt-out mercenaries went. It was referred to as
the 'ultimate challenge'. None of the foreigners I listened to had
claimed to have been there, nor did they claim they intended to
go. Whether this story was true or not, these volunteers, strangers from different countries, discussed such subjects seriously,
and they were all familiar with the information. Personally, I
found it fascinating – and horrifying – listening to such tales.

Meeting these seasoned travellers had exposed me to a whole
new world, but not one I could understand or agree with. Even
so, being a mercenary did sound like a popular occupation.
Many European, US and some Australian citizens participated

as mercenaries. In fact, so many people were apparently willing to volunteer their services for free that it was not easy to find a paying job any more, unless you were an expert in a demanded field. The foreign volunteers further claimed that certain publications discussed which conflicts were looking for recruits and gave details on how to find the relevant organisations, even if you had to read between the lines.

I believe the US has always taken advantage of this market, especially in its current conflicts. Today, however, recruiting mercenaries is disguised under the new phenomenon of 'security contractors'. The employment of wartime security contractors is just a loophole as far as I am concerned, to legalise or soften the word 'mercenary'. Under international law, mercenaries are not classed as lawful combatants.[5] The US is not a signatory to the *International Convention against the Recruitment, Use, Financing and Training of Mercenaries*. If another nation apprehends a mercenary of US citizenship, they appeal to that nation not to prosecute them and to surrender the individual to the US.[6]

One of the definitions of a mercenary to fall under scrutiny is if the combatant receives a higher salary than a soldier of equivalent rank of the nation or group they are fighting for. Years later in Guantanamo, many US soldiers would complain to me about the security contractors in Iraq being paid in excess of US$150,000 per annum – much more than a US enlisted soldier. There was nowhere near the same amount of discipline in the contractors' ranks. If there was an incident, such as a civilian being killed, the chance of disciplinary action was much less. Because these security groups are relatively new in their modern form, no-one is sure where they fall under international law.[7] The Blackwater incidents have highlighted this.[8] Members of this group – and other security contracting firms – have been described as gun-toting cowboys by

Iraqis and US military personnel.[9] We have seen these groups accused of civilian deaths in the media, yet they continue to get away with such acts, despite a US Congressional hearing on the matter.

At the time I was overseas, Australia had legislation concerning its citizens partaking in conflict abroad for other parties.[10] As long as the person was engaged in a conflict that was only about liberating a province (Kosovo and Kashmir) or supporting a government (Afghanistan) then it is legal. Only the involvement in a conflict that was about the overthrowing of a government was illegal. Ironically, if I had fought for the Northern Alliance in Afghanistan it would have been illegal under Australian law, even if some people thought it was a good thing.

I listened to such tales from the volunteers I was with at the Ministry of Defence; I also asked a lot of questions about their experiences inside Kosovo. I was relieved that the conflict had ended for the Kosovars, and also for myself. Until that moment, I had been afraid the whole time, but now I had no reason to fear because I knew I would not see conflict – I would be going home instead. Listening to their experiences gave me an idea of what it would have been like to have faced those fears and what situations I would have been confronted with. As I listened I also took notes, gathering their tales into a diary.[11]

After a few days had passed, we were called into the office once more and given our passports, tickets or cash for our fares back to our respective homes. I was given a ticket for my home town of Adelaide. We were also given certificates detailing our services and a welcome to return to Kosovo when it received its future independence.[12]

I had a few other memorable experiences before I boarded the plane back to Australia. While at the Ministry of Defence, I once entered a room full of hard-featured KLA veterans, some displaying combat wounds, who were there on sentry duty. They looked mean, tough and intimidating, but they were all nodding their heads to a pop song. Surprisingly, that song was 'All That She Wants (Is Another Baby)' by Ace of Base. The bewildering thing was that the song was kept on repeat. After what felt like half an hour, I gathered the courage to ask what this was about. They could not wipe the hardness from their expressions, but with surprisingly soft voices they claimed to love the song – and the TV show *Home and Away* as well. I left the room confused and bemused by such a bizarre incongruity.

I had also met a young Turkish man who was waiting for his fare home like the rest of us. He invited me to accompany him back to Turkey. I was reminded of my original intention to follow the Silk Road, having dragged my folders of research along with me from Japan. I had decided to start my Asian overland route from the Himalaya, travelling west, but there was a time when I thought I could start in eastern Turkey due to the books I had read. I wondered if that was how it would work out. I considered travelling with this Turkish man to Istanbul and then continuing east on my own. After a day's consideration, however, I decided otherwise, thinking I might never do it – it was time for me to go home, anyway. I boarded the plane at Tiranë Airport, which by then looked like one big US military base. After a night stopover in Milan, I landed back on Adelaide soil.

Four

I RETURNED TO ADELAIDE IN JULY OF 1999. I spent the first few weeks living back at the bachelor house. Now that I was back where I had started – back in the box – after all these experiences, especially Kosovo, the suddenly familiar isolation was much more intense.

I had become very interested in international politics and world affairs, namely the causes of conflict, and this deepened my isolation. I was curious about the political reasons behind why some people were made to suffer and how societies broke down. Such events were so different from our stable, structured lifestyle and society here in Australia. I wanted to know *why* these atrocities happened and how I could be a part of preventing them. Because my family and friends had no interest or knowledge of such things, I felt alienated.

Travelling overseas and expanding my mental horizons contributed to this isolation – not just from my family, but from friends as well. To an extent, I even felt isolated from society.

Only having access to a limited group of people, I felt that there was no-one I could spend time with who shared my interests or empathised with my thoughts. Unfortunately, I didn't know any politically aware people or any progressive political organisations. I even began to sense that I was the only one who felt the way I felt, who thought the way I thought. But that would change.

My stay in the bachelor house was short this time as I moved back in with Dad and Bev. I did not return to work straight away. Instead, I processed what I had learned and seen in Kosovo. My time there had been eye-opening, life-changing. It was at this time that I thought about joining the Australian Defence Force. My reasons were much the same as going to Kosovo: to help people in foreign lands achieve freedom, peace and security. When I put my application in to the Australian Defence Force, the recruiting office refused even to consider it because of my lack of schooling. At a minimum, a pass in Year Ten was required, but I had not even completed Year Nine. I was told that despite my ability to read, write and perform basic arithmetic, let alone having undergone some basic training and other experiences in Kosovo, there was nothing they could do for me. I had imagined that keenness alone would have got me through the door.

The setback of not being accepted into the army did not deter me, especially when I saw on TV the conflict brewing in East Timor.[13] The East Timorese struggle for independence was the main media focus on my return from Kosovo. I was ashamed and frustrated by the criticism from abroad towards Australia for not leading an international peacekeeping force into East Timor. It inspired me to give a stirring speech – at least it was stirring to me – to Dad and Bev. I proclaimed I would volunteer and go directly to East Timor, proudly holding an Australian flag high to show the world we weren't cowardly or any of the other accusations hurled at us. Once again, however, my experiences since have led me to believe that this scenario may have been no more than media disinformation and hyperbole. Watching John Howard and others discuss that point in time in the documentary *The Howard Years* in late 2008 painted a different picture,[14] a scenario that blamed the United Nations, and not Australia, for our inability to quickly mobilise and lead in East Timor. In the end we did intervene.

After my initial excitement, I briefly tried other means of becoming involved. A short documentary on East Timor was screened in Adelaide's CBD, and during that evening I obtained the address for the Adelaide office of a humanitarian organisation that worked in East Timor. The following day I went to this address, only to find the office unlocked but unstaffed. This allowed me an opportunity to browse through leaflets and other reading material that described the atrocities in East Timor. I found a lot of it disturbing and spent the following week on the phone networking. This eventually led to my submitting an application form to volunteer on a humanitarian mission. But time passed without a response. By then an international peacekeeping force had entered East Timor, and I directed my thoughts elsewhere.

I began factory work again and watched as much news and read as many papers as I could, but finding quality coverage of international affairs is not easy. Even so, I noticed that there did seem to be some recurring themes at the time. First, conflicts inflicting the most oppression against civilian populations were in the poorer parts of the globe. Second, many of those populations were predominantly Muslim.

I had come across Islam while reading travel guides but, as far as I knew, I had never met a Muslim person. What I had read was more of a romanticised version, more like *One Thousand and One Arabian Nights* type of stuff. Contrary to what the media has reported, I did not convert to Islam in Kosovo. As far as I was concerned back then, and still today in hindsight, Islam had nothing to do with the conflict in Kosovo. I never saw any indications of the religion, or even heard it mentioned. Islam was the last thing on my mind in Kosovo.

I had a lot of questions swirling around in my head about why disadvantaged people – Muslim or not – were being targeted, but I had no-one to put those questions to. I had also noticed that I was becoming even more disconnected from my friends, an estrangement that deepened each time I returned to Adelaide. I wanted to discuss global issues because that was where my mind always drifted. I needed to process the things I had been exposed to in the areas of politics and conflict. I had travelled outside the circle I had always lived within, thinking beyond the limited scope my friends and I were used to operating in. It was not my friends who were different; I was changing. I felt alone, unsatisfied and frustrated at what was happening overseas, and by the lack of interest from those around me. I knew there was much more to life.

Not knowing who else to turn to, it occurred to me that I might have a lot of my questions answered if I could meet and speak to a Muslim person for the first time. I had read about the Middle East, had planned to travel across the region, and it seemed to be Muslim populations caught up in the trouble spots. I didn't know where to start, so I reached for the yellow pages and looked for the closest mosque, which back then I thought was pronounced mos-que (as in pool 'cue'), having only read the word.

I spoke with a man on the phone, who invited me to attend the mosque that afternoon. On arrival, I was placed in a room with numerous magazines and was asked to wait for five

minutes. I passed that time perusing the publications. They
were of an Islamic nature and contained dozens of articles
regarding various strained political situations throughout the
world. They were comprehensive international bulletins – the
type of literature I had long been searching for. I finally felt
I was in a place where I could learn about and discuss world
affairs – so much so that when the man returned I said, 'I want
to be Muslim', taking him, and myself, by surprise. He led me
to another, larger room, which was used as the mosque, and
declared my previous statement to two or three others who
were sitting cross-legged on the floor. They were very friendly
and congratulated me. Then the man, who played the role of
part-time imam (mosque leader) had me recite a few words
before declaring me a Muslim. And that was my first day's
introduction to Islam.

Each day after work I travelled directly to the mosque, where
I would spend the evenings. This location was only attended
by about ten full-timers, most of whom were new Australians
with a poor grasp of English. On Friday, the holy day in Islam,
the mosque was bursting with a hundred or more people.

Through broken English, or with the help of a translator,
these new Australians kept me entertained with their stories
of foreign lands. During their prayer time I sat and watched.
I found this new environment interesting and exciting. However, after a week, a Pakistani man who spoke English well
said that, since I was now a Muslim, I should start observing
some of the practices, like praying. The next few days were
quite a struggle as I internally debated whether to pray or
quit the mosque. I decided to give it a go, and actually didn't
mind it. My attendance at prayer was sporadic at first, but I
slowly improved until I prayed the compulsory five times a
day. I spent the majority of the first month or so at the mosque
with a young Australian-born and bred Afghani, which helped

ease the cultural adjustment. However, he became busy and the older Pakistani who had first recommended prayer became my main tutor.

This Pakistani man belonged to a movement known as Tabligh, whose adherents would doorknock and engage in general preaching. During that period of 1999, I came to know Tabligh as the largest global Islamic movement. They were very friendly people with kind personalities. Their ideology was to preach, nothing more. They were almost extreme in their insistence to remain non-political, refusing to be involved, even verbally, in the multitude of issues plaguing the Muslim world. Their motto was that prayer would fix all. It was a good introduction to Islam, for I quickly learned the fundamentals of the faith. However, this individual and I did not see eye to eye. At first I had many questions of a political nature that he would dismiss or ignore. I soon learned not to bother asking him such questions, which became easier with the passage of time, for my Kosovo experience began to fade and my original intention to engage in adventure was inflamed once again.

I also didn't agree with his insistence that I had a responsibility to talk to other white Australians about Islam and bring them to the faith. I had no interest, because I did not feel entirely connected to the spiritual side of the religion, not enough to preach to others about it. Instead, I wanted to travel again, this time in Islamic lands, absorbing the new, fascinating culture I had stumbled upon. Of course, he was disturbed that I wanted to go gallivanting abroad with no purpose other than adventure. He saw this as a waste.

An opportunity presented itself during this period that could have sidetracked me. I had left my phone number with a Frenchman I had met in Kosovo, and he rang to ask if I was interested in a job. By 'job' he meant mercenary work. Of course, I declined. Ironically, in years to come, my nickname in Guantanamo was the 'Australian mercenary'. If I had wanted just to shoot guns, there were many conflicts I could have become involved in, but I was never interested in fighting for 'fun' or material gain. Contrary to what has been claimed, religion was not the motivating factor behind my receipt of military training and intent to engage in hostilities as a soldier against other soldiers. It was seeing communities suffer that led me down that path. The oppressed people and injustice inspired me to go to Kosovo. I had not even met a Muslim before then. East Timor was the next theatre of oppression that motivated me to contribute – again, without religion playing a part. And religion obviously played no part when I tried to enlist in the Australian Defence Force. The besieged communities of Kashmir, which I was to experience in the years to come, was the first conflict where religion played a role – geopolitically and personally.

Between August and November 1999, I learned as much as I could about Islam. I had also been working full time during these months and saving every cent, leaving me with over two thousand dollars after airfare, which I considered more than enough for another overseas trip, especially to a country where Australian currency is worth so much. Similar to the trip from Japan to Kosovo, I did not consider a return flight. *Just do it and all will fall into place*, was my motto in my youth. Pakistan was the closest Islamic state to the beginning of my previously planned Asian overland route, and also the home of Kashmir, so I settled on that country as my destination. My short-time Pakistani friend from the mosque made one last attempt at convincing me to stay when I announced my decision. Accepting defeat, he wrote down an address of a Tabligh centre in Raiwind, Pakistan, just beyond Lahore, and little notes in Urdu, the national language of Pakistan, with English translations. I was to present these notes to taxi drivers once in the country. He also included a letter of introduction for the Tabligh centre. I agreed to this, for it gave me a destination to start my trip. Until then I had no plan for where to go upon my arrival.

I left Adelaide on 11 November 1999. I spent a night in Singapore before disembarking at Karachi. It was early morning when I stepped out of the airport; the air was warm and dry. It reminded me of dawn in a desert, with an added exotic element. It was exciting to arrive in a new part of the world, with a whole country before me to explore. Unlike last time, because of the previous few months I had spent at the Adelaide mosque, I already felt like 'one of the people'. I had even arrived wearing the national dress.

I remained at Karachi Airport until noon, then boarded a domestic flight to Lahore. Outside the Lahore airport, I was surrounded by taxi and rickshaw drivers. This large and noisy crowd attempted to pull me in different directions, each hoping to relieve me of my money.

One individual pushed his way through the throng and addressed me in English: 'Where are you going?' After I supplied an explanation, he led me through the crowd and directed me to a white mosque across the road. The crowd dispersed as quickly as it had appeared, and I crossed the road and entered the mosque with relief.

One of my first lessons about Pakistani culture was how slowly and casually people conduct themselves, and this would remain a constant frustration for me throughout my stay. I entered the mosque bubbling with excitement and impatience, showing my notes in Urdu to anyone who would look, but the response was the same: 'Relax, sit down, have a tea, you'll get there.' With impatience subsiding into disbelief, then accept-ance, I resigned myself to a corner and quickly became bored.

As the hours passed, I grew frustrated that nothing would be done without decisive action, when I was unexpectedly offered a lift to Raiwind. As the driver negotiated the car through potholed streets, I was able to observe the bustling activities that make up daily life in Pakistan. I saw children playing cricket, hawkers shouting their wares, men squatting in groups drinking tea, and individuals relieving themselves in the open. Grey-bearded men herded goats through the throngs of people, pausing at the numerous mountains of rubbish where they rummaged through what looked to be plastics and papers. I saw buses, rickshaws and trucks, all tinkling with the sound of hundreds of suspended bells and loudly flaunting the most bizarre colour patterns, like some hippie interpretation of a paint job.

I could only shake my head in wonder at the lack of road rules and concern for personal safety. Buses were literally packed with people, and so many more clung precariously onto any available hand- or foothold on the outside that you could not tell what colour the bus was. It looked like a rectangular lump of people magically bound together, moving down the road on four wheels. And of course there was the ever-present dad, mum, and three or four children, all astride a little 100 cc motorbike; I don't believe I ever saw a helmet. It was loud and pungent, and the streets pulsed with life and poverty. Such were the sights that fascinated my senses on that hour-long drive from Lahore to Raiwind.

I was dropped outside the Tabligh centre's monstrous double-door iron gate, which contained another smaller iron door. At either side of this entrance a mud wall of equal height stretched beyond my view. I rapped on the small door, and it swung open, revealing an elderly face sporting a suspicious countenance. I passed the man my letter of introduction. It was accepted and the door closed, leaving me with enough time for a cigarette before it swung open again, admitting me inside.

The first thing I noticed was the mass of people and the countless traditional costumes reflecting the centre's diversity. Then I noticed the size of the mud structures – I was standing within a citadel, a city enclosed within a city. These structures were three or four storeys high with dozens of little enclaves, all surrounded by the mud wall. A few steps in from the iron door brought me to the edge of a swept mud floor covered with bamboo mats. Surrounding these mats was a sea of shoes. I removed my own, placing them into my bag – I did not relish the effort that would be required to locate them again. I then found myself seated in front of another grey-bearded elder, who spent some time reading the letter of introduction that had somehow been delivered into his hands. He finished with a welcome in English and released me into the bowels of the citadel.

The number of people around me and the endless list of countries they hailed from were mind-boggling. It was not just the cultural diversity but the whole spectrum of social standing and education: people ranged from the poor and virtually homeless to academics, doctors, lawyers and Pakistani military officers. The unique thing was that they could not be distinguished; all went barefoot and wore similar threadbare clothing. Only national dress and physical features hinted at differences. Everyone was equal and humble during this time of religious duty. I found this impressive, not having mixed before on a personal level with those outside my social status. I was to learn that nearly every country was represented among this conglomerate, which numbered in the thousands, though the majority were Pakistanis.

As Mormons are encouraged to leave home for two years to spread the Good Word, Muslims involved in Tabligh also leave home to do similar work and encourage other Muslims to do likewise. How much time a Muslim devotes to this practice is optional. It may be three days or a few weeks, with four months usually being the maximum. In Pakistan, the centre at Raiwind is used as a home base for this activity. Food and accommodation in the citadel are free. We paid for our train tickets and food, however, while travelling in the field. Groups ranging from five to twenty individuals will travel to an elected town or village, where they will spend one or two nights in a mosque before travelling to the next mosque in town, and so forth, until a week or more has passed. They will then return to Raiwind before travelling to a new location, not necessarily with the same people.

The five daily prayers are conducted in the mosque in which the group will spend the night, and most meals will be consumed there also. After prayers, one person from the group will deliver a sermon to the congregation before they all venture out onto the streets together, encouraging those in nearby homes or small businesses to join them – or at the least to join the prayer in the mosque if they have not been attending. The sermons are very basic, usually revolving around the Five Pillars of Islam.

On hearing about these expeditions upon my arrival at Raiwind, I felt reluctant to participate. I had just arrived in the country and was happy just to remain where I was. How could I talk about Islam to Muslims when I knew nothing about it myself? It was a ridiculous notion, and I made my thoughts known. Though the people at the Raiwind centre protested, they accepted my decision not to preach or give a speech. However, I was told that the centre was not a hotel – if I wished to stay I would need to spend some time in the field doing the work of Tabligh. Nevertheless, using the justification that I was new to Islam and Pakistan, and needed time to adjust, I was granted a few weeks' grace.

I had sufficiently learned the prayers by this stage. They had become second nature and part of my daily routine. I was also able to observe Islamic etiquette so as not to offend those around me. My outward behaviour and appearance allowed me to blend in, even my first beard was gaining length, but they were superficial changes: I gave the game away once I engaged in conversation. As I previously mentioned, throughout my childhood I was somewhat experienced in changing 'uniforms', having gone from one environment to another, and this skill now assisted me. Even here fashions were followed, and by close observation I adopted them like a chameleon: pants rolled up past the ankles, a stick called a *miswak* used to brush one's teeth sticking out of the chest pocket in the correct manner. I was able to wear the various head adornments (caps, scarves and turbans) according to the accepted manner. However, in other areas I failed.

Each morning we were woken by the *azan* – the call to prayer. Thousands of bodies spread about on various levels would rise, prepare themselves and pray in unison. After prayer, an hour-long educational or inspirational speech was delivered. The place was so big and there were so many people that loudspeakers were spread throughout the facility. The speeches were always in Urdu, though translators were present for all the various non-Urdu-speaking listeners. There were dozens of these people spread about. They absorbed the speech via an earphone and then translated to the group sitting at their feet in a nominated language.

At first, I returned to my sleeping bag directly after prayer, seeing it was 5 am or so, to gain an extra hour of sleep before breakfast. I was horrified when I was woken and told to attend the compulsory morning sermon. Every morning after prayer a group of elected people went searching through the sleeping areas, looking for truants like myself. I thought it was madness. I tried resisting, but every morning they returned – friendly, patient, determined – and always found me, no matter how many times I changed my sleeping location or whatever ruse I deployed.

I reluctantly had to start attending these speeches that lulled me back to sleep anyway. Some topics discussed were good and made sense: there is only one God, without partners, and we don't need any intermediary between us and God, whether it is Mohammed, Jesus or the saints. They spoke of the need for unity among mankind, the importance of love for one another, the promotion of tolerance and forgiveness in all situations, and giving charity with one hand so the other hand is unaware.

I had never been religious, nor was I brought up with religious instruction, but I had been exposed to Christianity through school and society at large, so I knew the basics. I was surprised then to find that Islam was not completely foreign. The Islamic God is the same God worshipped by Christians and Jews, and Satan is the same fiend recognised by all. We all go to the same heaven or hell. We also share the same prophets (besides Mohammed) and historical stories, albeit with some differences. I did like to think, back then, that I believed in religion. But the faith I required, whether it be in Islam or otherwise, clashed with some of my secular beliefs, especially in natural science. It was a massive struggle to accept religion in its entirety, and though my capacity to believe went up and down over the three-year period that it played a part in my life, I failed to completely grasp it deep down. I did try very hard though.

My first Ramadan began during the second week at the Tabligh centre. Being new to Islam, this was another challenge, because it was like jumping straight into the deep end. I had no choice in this environment but to participate. However, I was determined to succeed and did not mind the challenge. For one full cycle of the moon I would not eat, drink, smoke or have sex (not a real possibility considering the environment) during daylight hours. To my surprise, I did not find it difficult. I only succumbed twice to cigarettes. While fasting, I spent the days reading. I had access to an English Qur'an and some translations of other religious literature. I spoke with people from around the world, asking them questions about their homelands as a second-hand way of experiencing the atmosphere of such exotic foreign places.

After I had been at the centre for two or three weeks, I was told once and for all that I would need to go out into the field. I was still reluctant. What I really wanted was to spend time with Pakistanis in their homes, a background observer to their everyday lives, in order to truly experience the culture and travel the country. I wasn't sure how to go about this yet – I had been shut away in this city within a city since my arrival in Pakistan. I recalled the books I had read about the mountains, the isolated back country, the history, a nation teeming with adventure. It was at this stage that the elders, if I may call them that, sent Ikram to me.

Ikram could speak English exceptionally well and had received a good education. He was an engineer at a government mining project located in the north-west corner of Baluchistan Province near the Iran and Afghanistan borders. He had become religious in recent years and was nearing the completion of a four-month stint with Tabligh. He was very friendly and we got along well. He had already been briefed on my reluctance to actively participate in Tabligh, and gave me the benefit of the doubt by putting it down to my being new to the religion. However, he did inquire about my feelings. I had to beat around the bush a bit; I didn't want to offend him regarding my faith and ideological struggles with the Tabligh. I did say that I would much prefer to travel and see the country as I pleased, not following the timetable and strict discipline of Tabligh. Ikram was very diplomatic with his answers. He explained that Tabligh would be a great way to see the country – I would not be disappointed – and we would be able to travel together. I agreed to go with him, thinking that once I had learned the ropes and gained confidence I could branch out on my own to explore Pakistan.

Another factor that influenced my decision was that the next location on Ikram's schedule was the city of Peshawar. Peshawar conjured romantic visions in my mind as the gateway to Afghanistan and the North-West Frontier Province, both places on my must-see list. It is a city that had featured in nearly all the literature I had read, from the hippie trail to historic conquests. I also had wrongly assumed it was at the base of a mighty mountain chain. I had an obsession with mountains, especially the Pamir, where five major mountain chains converge in this part of the world: the Himalaya, the Karakoram, the Kunlun, the Tian Shan and the Hindu Kush. Even during the flight from Karachi to Lahore, my eyes were glued to the view outside my window, searching for any hint of a mountain – all I saw was a blanket of smog. But my time in the mountains would come later.

Five

IKRAM WAS RIGHT. I did enjoy Peshawar, despite being under Tabligh tutelage. Like most places in Pakistan I found it large, noisy and exciting. There were huge bazaars selling rugs and everything imaginable, alongside fruit and vegetables I had never seen before. It had a different atmosphere from the other places I had briefly seen in Pakistan, for this area is dominated by the Pashtun people who call eastern and southern Afghanistan and western Pakistan home.

Peshawar's local mosquito community gifted me with malaria. I consulted a doctor while I was there but was misdiagnosed and carried the disease with me for some months to come. During our ten-day stay in this city I was sent with two others from our fifteen-man group to the nuclear institute to remind the employees to pray. We were allowed into the facility because, even though they aren't keen on Tabligh, the people of Pakistan have an almost reverent respect for the group.

With many institutions, if foreigners are present, Tabligh

is even more welcome. As we entered the nuclear institute I was greeted by a huge framed photo of Pakistan's first successful nuclear explosion lovingly placed on the wall. As I walked down the passageway I glanced through open doors to my left and right to see filthily dressed men squatting on their haunches. They were stirring the contents of big metal cauldrons with wooden spoons. We spoke for a while with the CEO, and I asked what the men were doing. He explained that they were stirring apple sauce. He also explained that they were using atomic technology to genetically manipulate apple trees, and they had succeeded in creating a few new varieties. This announcement was followed by a tour of the orchard. Afterwards, back in the office, he opened a cupboard, exposing rows of glass jars containing apple sauce. We politely declined as he offered as many as we liked.

When our time in Peshawar was finished, Ikram and I caught the train back to Raiwind. I was more enthusiastic now and looking forward to our next journey, especially when I learned it was going to be in the actual mountains, to a town named Abbottabad. After three days in Raiwind we were on the train again. It was wonderful to be in the mountains at last. They were majestic and high enough to support alpine peaks. There was a distinct vegetational boundary where trees gave way to grasses, mosses, craggy outcrops, and a cool summer breeze. These peaks that would hold snow in the winter were now carpeted in small flowers.

The locals in the area reflected the variety of distinct features that could be found throughout Pakistan, Central Asia and beyond. In one village, we came across young men with blue eyes and white skin, wearing clothing similar to highland kilts. Ikram said that in the isolated valleys far to the north were communities who had still not heard of Islam, where modern history had overlooked them. They still retained their own languages, customs and religion – elements strange to mainstream Pakistan. Ikram went on to say that there were many theories on the origins of such people, that the culture of one valley could be very different from another, and that those theories did not explain all communities. The only plausible explanation he was aware of was that some, like the people we had seen in kilts, were said to be descendants of past invaders, such as Alexander the Great.

We stayed in Abbottabad for less than a week. Though I was still with Ikram, the other group members were different. One was a surgeon, who was a major in the Pakistani army. There are a lot of Pakistani military bases in Abbottabad, and the major took us on a tour. We also visited a school and technical college. One time, while we stood on the side of an anonymous stretch of road, the major informed us that it was, in fact, the Karakoram Highway. I savoured the experience, because it had also featured in the many publications I had read. The Karakoram Highway is classed as an engineering marvel, one that reaches all the way into China.

During one afternoon, as Ikram and I strolled along a street, we came upon two men in combat fatigues sitting at a table. They were surrounded by posters depicting military scenes, weapons and picturesque mountain vistas. Ikram agreed to translate for me as I asked them what their display was about. They said they represented an organisation named Lashkar-e-Taiba (LeT), or Army of the Righteous, and were involved in the freedom struggle in Kashmir.[15] They asked me to accompany them to a nearby office to hear more, and I agreed.

We all sat on the floor in their office while they handed me horrific pictures of Indian troops committing atrocities against Kashmiri civilians. There were some leaflets in English explaining the situation in Kashmir, though most were in Urdu, a translation job for Ikram later. We did not stay for long but the impression I received about the Kashmiri struggle reminded me of Kosovo's situation before the liberation. I expressed an interest in learning more. They supplied an address in Lahore and we bade them farewell.

We returned to Raiwind once more before visiting a town on the Indian border in Punjab Province. We stayed there for only three days, and it was to be the last destination for most people in our Tabligh group before returning home, including Ikram.

Since the meeting in Abbottabad, I had not been able to get Kashmir out of my mind. I asked Ikram about what I had been told, and he agreed that horrible atrocities took place there. But he did not agree with LeT or any of the other dozen organisations operating at that time. When I asked Ikram's opinion about the people of Kashmir defending themselves against violence, he refused to answer, instead saying that there is no such thing as 'jihad' today. 'Jihad' has various meanings in Islam, and has been taken largely out of context by the media. Jihad literally means 'struggle', which can refer to defence against aggression, such as the case in Kashmir; or jihad can refer to the struggle against personal desires in the attempt to become a better person. There is also a jihad with the tongue, meaning exercising non-violent action to bring about change. Jihad with the tongue is what I considered the Tabligh's mission. Before leaving Abbottabad, I had asked the army major the same questions and received similar negative views on the conflict in Kashmir in general.

Once back at the Tabligh centre, I asked a number of random people questions about Kashmir. The non-Pakistanis expressed a lack of knowledge on the subject, while, on the other hand, the Pakistanis were well aware. Most of them said, 'We do not get involved in politics', or showed no interest. Occasionally, some did say that Kashmir was a terrible situation and that the Kashmiris had a right to defend themselves. Some believed that there was an obligation to support them in any way, but such views were rare and often expressed covertly. The Qur'an and other religious texts I was reading spoke of self-defence, so at the time I found these mixed attitudes baffling and frustrating. I think this had a lot to do with what I saw in Kosovo and the thought that, while we were sitting around talking about what to do in Kashmir, people were being killed. After asking so many people at Raiwind for their opinions, my own views within the centre became widely known, and these views were clearly not in line with Tabligh's views.

In my opinion, if a society is occupied and systematically killed, tortured, illegally detained or raped, then the citizens have a right to defend themselves, their families and their country, and it is the responsibility of those outside the country who have the means to help restore peace to do so. Our own government, as well as others, engages daily in various military programs to subdue aggression.

By this stage Ikram had now finished his four months with Tabligh. He was scheduled to return to his family home in a Punjab city for the remainder of Ramadan before returning to his place of employment. He invited me to go with him. This was a great relief. At last I could travel, be myself and follow my own routine, spending time with Pakistanis in their homes, and truly experience the culture. I had grown frustrated with some of the restrictions placed on me and was looking forward to moving on.

Overall, my experiences in Pakistan to that point had been exciting and educational. The Tabligh people were nothing but kind, welcoming and patient, especially about my differing views. I had seen a satisfying amount of the country, but there was so much more to see and do, and I wished to venture off the beaten track. During that time in my youth, I could not understand people who went on holiday to places like Egypt, for example, and stayed in a hotel, visiting the pyramids with a tour guide. In my view, they may have been to Egypt but could not have come away with an understanding of the nation or its peoples. I, on the other hand, did not wish to be such a tourist.

Six

FIRSTLY, AFTER LEAVING TABLIGH, Ikram and I travelled from Raiwind to the LeT address in Lahore. I wanted to learn more about Kashmir before we left the city and travelled to Ikram's boyhood home. The Lahore address turned out to be LeT's main office. We were told they did not cater to foreigners in that location, so they supplied us with the address of another LeT office within Lahore. We caught a taxi to Yateem Khana Chowk, which translates as 'Place of the Orphans' because there was a large orphanage in the area. We climbed three flights of stairs in a pocket of shops and came to two doors on the top level. One was labelled Computer Centre, the other was unmarked. Behind this anonymous door was the LeT foreign office. We were seated in one of the rooms with the person in command. He was a tall, fit-looking Pakistani with a long, bushy beard.

He launched into a basic geography lesson, producing a large map of Central Asia. He pointed out the Line of Control

(LoC), the disputed international border between Pakistan-controlled Kashmir and India-controlled Kashmir. He spoke of the plight of the Kashmiri people and the aggression of the Indian military that had been impacting on their lives for years. He also showed me information about the schools, hospitals, humanitarian projects, refugee centres and military training camps that LeT ran or was involved with. These military camps were designed for people to learn basic tactics that could be used in Kashmir to assist in defending the civilian population from the Indian army. The information was brief and general. I was still interested when the meeting concluded an hour later. The person in command invited me to visit one of the training camps and their other facilities, such as the hospitals and schools. I declined at the time but said I would think about it. And with that, Ikram and I left.

We caught the train to Ikram's home town, which was as big as an Australian city. His boyhood home was located in a pleasant, suburban street. His father, his mother and two sisters lived there. It was the first time I had seen the inside of a family home in Pakistan. There were two front doors. One was strictly for the family to use; the other was for guests, like me, and gave direct access to the guestroom, which also acted as a dining and bedroom. There were another two doors within the guestroom. One led to a toilet, which also had a second door into the main house. The centre of the main house consisted of a large, open courtyard surrounded by all the rooms one would expect to find in a home. I considered it very cosy and practical.

The guestroom allowed me to be comfortable while keeping me separate from the family, namely Ikram's sisters. In this part of the world it is common for the women to be kept separate from the men. I found this disappointing, as surely the women must, being isolated in such a manner. I was really interested in hearing their views and opinions, but unfortunately they are rarely heard.

Once I found the toilet door locked from the inside and received an apology from one of these mysterious sisters. This gave me an opportunity to exchange a few words through the locked door, a very rare and unusual encounter, and a first for me. One day, I was surprised when Ikram's mother came into the guestroom and kissed my forehead. Obviously the rules did not apply to the elderly women. On the occasions when the sisters were out, I was allowed into the main house to look around, watch TV or sit up on the roof among the chimneys and plants. There was not much more I was allowed to learn about life in a Pakistani family home.

I observed the last four days of Ramadan in Ikram's home town. When it was close to sunset, Ikram and I would venture down the road to break the fast. The multitudes would gather in the street where plastic cloths had been laden with food. In the minutes leading up to breaking the fast, an eerie silence would pervade the crowd. However, that would quickly change when it was time to feast – it became a very jovial atmosphere indeed.

During the first night at Ikram's home, I broke the fast with five ice-creams bought from a street vendor. I was very sick the next day, and I'm not surprised, considering that the offending ice-creams may have been a year old. I wish Ikram had told me before I had eaten them. They may have been okay for a local, but not for an unconditioned new arrival like me.

Apart from these outings, I didn't see much of Ikram's town. We prayed at a mosque on the same block where he lived, and we played cricket. Night-time cricket matches were serious affairs. The local men and boys would block off Ikram's street at both ends, and it seemed the males from every household spilled onto the street. Dozens of light bulbs were illegally wired into the overhead electrical lines and strung back and forth across the street, brightly illuminating it for the matches.

On one occasion during my stay, LeT visited me at Ikram's address and dropped off reading material. This time it was an expensive set of religious books, not just more information about the situation in Kashmir.

Once Ramadan was over, it was time for Ikram to return to work. As previously agreed, I was to travel with him. We caught the train from his home town to the city of Quetta, the capital of Baluchistan Province, a journey of nearly twenty hours. The ride through the Punjab is interesting. It has lots of heavily populated centres and lush natural vegetation interspersed by rural villages elaborately constructed of mud and surrounded by thriving farmland. The mangos are truly delicious.

Then the landscape changes abruptly as the train enters Baluchistan, Pakistan's western province. It becomes dry, barren and rocky, but has a beauty all its own. Quetta, if it must be compared to another Pakistani city, is similar to Peshawar. Both are gateways to Afghanistan and dominated by Pashtun people, but, as with any city that evolves in isolation, it has its own distinct characteristics.

Once we had arrived in Quetta, we travelled to the home of Ikram's cousin, where we would spend the next few days. His name was Kaleb and he was in his thirties. It didn't take Ikram long to bring up Kashmir, informing Kaleb of my interest in assisting the people there and my previous discussions with LeT. They worked in tandem: once Ikram had concluded his usual spiel on the subject, Kaleb began in a similar vein. Kaleb's main theme was alerting me to the hypocritical politics that dominate Kashmir. I did not understand the history or the situation at the time, so both Kaleb and Ikram were rebuffed with my usual stubborn resistance.

After a few days with Kaleb, Ikram and I bade him and

the city of Quetta farewell, and caught a bus to the Iranian border. At the desolate border crossing most of our fellow travellers proceeded into Iran, whereas Ikram and I hired a driver to take us north along the border. We bumped along a stony two-wheel track for several hours until we came to a military checkpoint. Beyond this point was the Pakistan–China mining consortium project, known as the Saindak project. It was a large, open-face mine, which grudgingly surrendered its principal treasure: copper, with a little gold as a by-product. I am not sure why Ikram thought it was a good idea to have taken me there; scenic trips were rare since he was away all day working while I was left behind in the living quarters.

To keep myself amused during the day I would watch smugglers from a distant mountain peak. They had long strings of camels, upon whose backs they smuggled goods, principally fuel, back and forth across the border. Otherwise, my time there was boring. Within a week, however, I became very ill. It was the third or fourth time I had been sick since Peshawar. I shivered with cold chills, then sweated feverishly. I could barely move and honestly thought I would die. It was during this bout of sickness that Ikram suspected I had malaria. To seek an answer, we had to travel all the way back to Quetta, where a doctor confirmed the diagnosis. I was prescribed medication and improved rapidly. Ikram needed to hurry back to work, so he left me in the care of his cousin Kaleb, who was happy to help. Ikram departed and, other than a five-minute catch-up months later, I would not see him again.

Once I was alone with Kaleb, he made a confession. He said he did not hold Ikram's views about Kashmir and LeT. He claimed he had actually been involved in Kashmir when he was younger. Though he was not very clear, he explained how he used to have something to do with Pakistani intelligence. He considered himself now too old to be involved in Kashmir but still sympathised with the people. He admitted that Kashmir policy was highly politicised in Pakistan, and that was disappointing, but he had been too long out of the loop to know the current climate, despite having the odd acquaintance still involved. He went on to say that his speech about Kashmir while Ikram was present was premeditated – he agreed to talk me out of having an interest – and asked me to disregard what he had said.

Like most Pakistanis, Kaleb was an amazing host. He operated a business with a friend, supplying wholesale medicines to pharmacies within Quetta and along dusty rural roads. He had little money but still took countless days off work to show me around. We ate out and bought imported foods from places known as the 'Western shops'. I knew he could not afford such luxuries, yet he often refused to allow me to pay. Besides his generosity, he was a lovely man and we got along fantastically well.

As part of my adventure, again due to my past reading, Afghanistan was a place I really wanted to experience, and Kaleb encouraged me to go. Now that I was in Quetta and so close to that country, I raised the subject. Along with independent travel in Tibet, Afghanistan was known as the hardest place for a Westerner to enter and explore; it was truly off the beaten track. I had no interest in its civil war, but to me the whole archaic country sounded intriguing; to traverse that land would be to experience another age. I attempted to obtain a visa to enter the country from the Afghan embassy while I was in Quetta, but I was refused. Because of this, and due to my finances, I began to resign myself to the fact that I might not get to experience Afghanistan or any other country besides Pakistan during this trip. Pakistan had so far consumed little of my funds, but I expected that, unlike Pakistan, I would have to fully support myself in Afghanistan if I attempted travel in that country. I had no contacts or knowledge.

On the odd occasion, Kaleb took me to the LeT office in Quetta, where we chatted and drank tea. It gave me a chance to further understand the politics of the conflict in Kashmir by reading their monthly magazine, which not only covered Kashmir but also organisational affairs and current world issues. I had been reading about these horrific abuses for months now, becoming more and more frustrated. It was at this point that I decided to go to Kashmir and view the situation first-hand and see if I could assist. To do this, I arranged with the LeT staff in Quetta to travel to Muzaffarabad to attend a basic military training camp there and be introduced to the region.

LeT had offices all over Pakistan that were used by local members and non-members with internal connections as places to drop in unannounced at any time for a meal or to socialise, or even sleep for a few days. They operated as twenty-four-hour hotels. Foreigners were seen as guests and, whether involved in Kashmir or not, they were treated as such. On occasion, LeT also allowed people to travel the country for free, using their own transport network, or provided them with small amounts of travelling money; they paid for my plane ticket so I could return to Lahore. Kaleb wished me luck as I departed Quetta and had his brother meet me at the other end at the Lahore airport. His brother then drove me from the airport to Yateem Khana Chowk, back to the LeT foreign office, where I had been previously with Ikram.

Seven

Throughout my time in Pakistan I inquired from countless individuals and read various publications about the history of Kashmir, trying to pin down the reasons for the current conflict. The escalation of violence seemed to have coincided with the end of the Soviet war in Afghanistan some years earlier, when many Afghan veterans flooded over the border into Pakistan. They were unemployed, restless and harbouring new political views, as many other combatants did who had served as mujahedeen in the conflict. Instead of cracking down on them as other nations did, the Pakistani government embraced them. To keep them occupied and onside, the government employed them in the conflict in Kashmir. 'Don't judge us. India is your enemy. Fight them not us. We'll support you. We're on the same side.'

There have always been intermittent clashes in Kashmir since the birth of modern-day Pakistan and India. Though the Pakistani government had always been involved, during the

1980s the Inter-Services Intelligence (ISI), which is Pakistan's version of the CIA, began to influence a group called Jammu and Kashmir Liberation Front, comprising mainly intellectuals who initially followed a non-violence philosophy and whose goals were to achieve independence from India *and* Pakistan. The Indian military responded with violence and the ISI took advantage of the Liberation Front's grievances and manipulated them to use more violent strategies to defend themselves and to achieve their goals. This of course only escalated the violence.

By the late 1980s, the ISI was creating new groups of irregular forces, trained to be more effective militarily, better organised and equipped, and more pro-Pakistan. By the late 1990s, Kashmir was suffering a full-scale guerrilla war. The Pakistani government was using them to serve its own political agenda. It was a conclusion I did not reach until the end of my stay in Pakistan, but one that would always be on my mind afterwards. During my time in Pakistan the people of Kashmir were in serious trouble, but all my theories led back to the conclusion that they were being used as pawns in a game, which left me disillusioned.

It seemed that from the beginning the ISI played a part in creating the various Kashmir freedom-fighting mujahedeen groups. They controlled their policies, growth and activities, while on-the-ground military training was coordinated by the Pakistani army. Whenever one of these groups became too large and influential, especially if they publicly espoused policies and views not in the government's interest, the ISI would dilute their power by taking one large group and re-forming it into five or six smaller, more easily controlled groups. This was the explanation I received when I asked why a dozen or more such groups existed during my time in the country.

*

LeT was an organisation that had been around for many years and had offices in all major Pakistani cities, including many smaller regional centres. In an interview with ABC America, the head of LeT at the time I was there reinforced its main goal by saying that LeT has 'no interest in fighting America . . . Lashkar-e-Taiba is engaged in fighting against the occupying Indian army in Jammu and Kashmir'. He stated that LeT was about fighting for the 'rights of all oppressed human beings: Muslim, Sikh, Buddhist, even Hindu'.[16] This is also what I was about: fighting against oppression through standard military means. This was the LeT that I joined, which is something quite different from what has evolved during my time in Guantanamo Bay and what is reported today.[17]

Structurally, LeT had connections to two larger organisations. One of those organisations was the ISI and the other was Markaz al-Dawa wal-Irshad. The ISI controlled all the major military groups within Pakistan connected to Kashmir and split, recreated and controlled those various military groups. The groups differed in size and popularity, and, from my understanding, in 1999 LeT was the largest and most dominant. The ISI made sure it was also the most patriotic. LeT often printed pamphlets instructing its members and the public to stand behind the government.

The other organisation, Markaz al-Dawa wal-Irshad, ran many projects. LeT was actually Markaz al-Dawa wal-Irshad's military wing. Markaz al-Dawa wal-Irshad also ran about forty schools throughout the country. I visited their largest school outside of Lahore and observed only ordinary school subjects being taught, plus sports like soccer, cricket and horse riding. They had a chain of madrasahs, Islamic institutes of learning, and I also visited their main madrasah in Karachi. Students in the Karachi madrasah learned to recite the entire Qur'an by heart. Once memorised, such a person is known as a *hafiz*. Becoming a *hafiz* is an important and popular achievement in Islam. Learning to read the Qur'an in Arabic was something I wished to do, but I would not find the opportunity until later. There were three bachelor degrees on offer: Islamic jurisprudence, *Hadith* (sayings and actions of the Prophet Mohammed), and *Da'wah* (preaching techniques in which one would learn the teachings and philosophies of major groups within Islam and other religions). I did not witness any political teachings or militant philosophy in these madrasahs.

Markaz al-Dawa wal-Irshad also ran a few homeless shelters and orphanages. They had a housing program and hospitals for refugees who came from the India-controlled parts of Kashmir. The hospitals were also used by injured combatants. I visited one of these hospitals in Pakistan-controlled Kashmir. For the country's standards, it was very modern and clean, with professional staff and female nurses. Most of the patients during my visit were inhabitants of villages who lived along the LoC and had stepped on Indian landmines. These unfortunate victims had access to prosthetic limbs and rehabilitation services not readily available in Pakistan. Markaz al-Dawa wal-Irshad also ran refugee centres for those fortunate enough to make it into Pakistan alive. I also visited one of these centres and spoke with people of various ages, listening to their stories and hopes for the future.

Upon entry into Pakistan, refugees recovered in one of these centres for weeks or months before moving on further into the country. They were supplied with food, shelter, bedding and clothing. Those below twenty years of age usually went off to school, while adults were found housing. Some of the refugees who were concerned about others left behind in Kashmir went off to the military training camps then returned to their homelands as combatants, or 'freedom fighters' as they are referred to by the civilian population of India-controlled Kashmir.

One thing that was not readily available for the refugees was employment, unless it was working within the refugee centres, hospitals or housing construction. But opportunities were limited – though the operation was large, it was also expensive. From my understanding, funding for the various projects came from the Pakistani government or the private sector, namely citizens from various Arab states and elsewhere around the world. There were many people who felt strongly about Kashmir and gave generously to the cause. From what I observed, the military wing received the least amount of funding and was often on the verge of collapse. But I would learn these things slowly and over a period of time.

As previously arranged, Kaleb's brother dropped me at the LeT office in Lahore. I then surrendered my passport, spare money and important documentation, such as my birth certificate, in a safe where it would be looked after. I remained at the office for two or three days and then left for the mountains of Kashmir in a van with a few others. It was half a day's travel to our destination, and at one point the road ascended so quickly and wound about in such a manner that I was close to being physically ill.

Kashmir is a truly breathtaking place. The further we infiltrated the mountains, the higher they climbed and the deeper the valleys plunged, gouged and eroded by wind, rain and snow melt. The town of Muzaffarabad, our final destination, was located in such surroundings, the furthest point motorised transport could take us. Just outside of Muzaffarabad, our van dropped us at the base of a painful-looking climb. I was the first in line behind the guide as we began the ascent. When I lit a cigarette he turned around and snatched it from my mouth, stamping it into the ground. He asked for my packet, which I surrendered. Then he asked for the rest. I sighed and retrieved the four or five packs that were wrapped in the bottom of my bag. He apologised then informed me that there was no smoking where we were going. A good thing, for I was ill prepared for the level of fitness required in the coming months – smoking would have made it nearly impossible. Not once did I feel like a cigarette, despite being forced to go cold turkey.

We marched in single file, zigzagging our way up a goat track. The valley floor fell further away; the raging brown torrent of a river that skirted one side of the valley below took on the appearance of a thin, brown ribbon, no longer a powerful force of nature. Even the town below became just a point of reference in an unfolding landscape. Hours had passed and we were in an entirely different world. We had reached the summit of our first peak, the valley floor now lost to view and forgotten. The panorama from our summit exposed yet another new vista of even loftier summits. On the horizon, majestic mountains pierced the sky, ancient sentinels covered in thick snow. It was a frozen wilderness that did not look inviting to man.

This first summit we had climbed sported a training camp, but this was not where we would stay – it was for Pakistanis only – but it did provide us with a drink and a rest. Once we had revived and admired the view, we continued on our way. For a while the track was level with slight inclines and declines as it hugged the sides of ever-larger mountains. Eventually, we were reduced to almost vertical climbing, which I found petrifying, before the path levelled out again to expose another training camp. These mountains amazed me. Every time we reached a summit, and what I expected to be the last, we were presented with other, higher peaks. Though we had already climbed for hours, most of it uphill, this second training camp was in a valley surrounded by the ever-present taller summits.

It was at this second camp where we would stay and train.

Like the previous camp, there were also a lot of Pakistanis, but there was one large room elaborately constructed of rocks, which was used as the sleeping quarters for foreigners. We trained in our own group, separate from the Pakistanis, and even had our own instructor. Our food was prepared and served separately – not all foreigners can tolerate the spice and heat of Pakistani food, especially me. The local Kashmiri people ate big, mild raw chillies for breakfast and used salt instead of sugar in their cups of tea. Apparently, this diet gave an advantage to the people who lived at such high altitude.

There were only about thirty of us foreigners at one time in this camp, representing about ten countries, and roughly two hundred Pakistanis. This camp in Kashmir was similar to the Kosovo camp in one respect: both were targeted on a particular conflict within a unique environment. Otherwise, they were quite different. For example, these were largely religious people, and even if they weren't they still participated in the routine observations. I was isolated with foreigners, who were not closely linked with Kashmir. This meant that, unlike in Kosovo, I was not able to spend time with those who had been directly affected by the atrocities. This does not mean I felt less strongly on the subject.

The training element in Kosovo was a mixture of standard guerrilla and conventional warfare, whereas Kashmir was only guerrilla tactics, including an urban element. Years later in Guantanamo, the Australian government would consult experts from within different divisions of the Australian Armed Forces, commissioning them to produce statements regarding all the training I received in Kosovo, Kashmir and Afghanistan. To the government's disappointment (they claimed there were terrorist strategies in my training) the conclusions were the same: it was standard, basic military training, poor in quality to that which our own forces receive. It contained no techniques that could not be found in libraries or on the internet. I received no training in how to make or operate bombs, hijack planes or target civilians, nothing that falls outside the scope of infantry training or could be regarded as terrorist activity. Had there been such training, I would not have been there in the first place, for I do not – and never have – supported terrorism.

Besides this training, there were theoretical lessons, morning sports and walks – lots of walks. The camp was already positioned at about four thousand metres above sea level, and any walk usually ascended even higher. For those who wished to enter India-controlled Kashmir, they had to be able to traverse those mountains with ease, fully laden. Night walks were the hardest at first. Torches, talking and other noise were not allowed. On my first night walk, the path we were following curved around the face of a mountain, and I was assaulted by a strong wind. The lights of Muzaffarabad twinkled so far below that they could have been as far off as the stars above. It was pitch black. I was two paces behind the man in front. I could not see the half-metre-wide path at my feet, so I relied on the barely visible sneakers in front of me to guide my way. But, with the wind and lights below, I hesitated, losing sight of the guiding sneakers. I was too afraid to place one foot forward, so I squatted down and refused to move, holding the line up behind me. In the end the instructor had to hold my hand and lead me until we were off the mountain face.

We would often go for two or three days continuously, as well as night trips with little food and water. By the time I left the camp I was able to jog along those paths, but it was a difficult and sometimes scary road to get there.

The most amazing sight I have ever seen in my life is still emblazoned on my mind. We had walked all night, ascending the never-ending slopes. Ten minutes before any hint of daylight, I eventually reached the pinnacle of our last summit before we could turn around to begin the descent. While on this peak, I turned to the north-east, facing China, gasping in the thin air. The sky paled from the darkness of night into an inky blue. Silhouettes appeared and for once I could see that there was nowhere higher to climb, no loftier summits – I had finally reached the top. Quickly, the horizon's colour morphed into a maroon red then an intense orange. Displayed before me was an impenetrable line of rock walls, ancient bones of the earth thrusting out of an abyss, containing not one peak but a long, craggy serrated edge. To my amazement, there was another wall behind this one, then another, and another. The peaks of these stone fortresses flowed parallel to one another, marching off to my left and right, separated by deep, unseen valleys, advancing all the way to the far-off horizon.

The light of this new day was followed by a brilliant glow that spilled from peak to peak, bathing myself and the land-scape around me. But the true beauty of this scene was how each unseen valley released clouds of dense fog, which rose just above the mountains' edges. The sun's rays penetrated the misty clouds, transforming them into a kaleidoscope of revolv-ing colours, until the horizon became blurred by the rising sun itself. It was magical, and I could almost hear Near Eastern music playing in my head, a buried memory from the docu-mentaries I had watched in the past, portraying similar scenes. But in person it was incomparable. On the odd occasion in Kashmir, I was able to reflect that the place where I stood and the majestic scenery before me used to be only a fanciful dream when I was trapped in the 'box' in the bachelor house. I took solace that a dream had come true. I had achieved what had seemed impossible to me only a year before, and was humble and thankful to have stood in that part of the world.

An example of the extremes in elevation was our ascent of a slope one morning in heavy rain. As we climbed, the rain froze until it had become snow by the time we reached the summit. During the descent, I observed how the snow changed consistency until it was raining again.

During my time in the camp I had an opportunity, and found the time, to learn the written Arabic Qur'anic alphabet. Many Qur'ans have been written with non-Arabic speakers in mind. Being able to read the Qur'an in Arabic does not mean one can read Arabic, let alone write, speak or understand the language. It is totally different, lacking particular symbols signifying how to pronounce letters. At the peak of my Arabic, which was while I was in Guantanamo, not before, I had learned about one hundred and fifty words, but without any knowledge of grammar I could only string those words into two- or three-word sentences. On a scale of one to ten, I was told my ability to read the Qur'an was a three – nothing to be proud of, and far removed from the ridiculous allegation that I was an Arabic-to-English translator in Afghanistan. This lack of skills was something the authorities were well aware of. Many non-Arabs memorise the entire Qur'an in Arabic yet do not speak or understand it. I did not memorise the Qur'an. I remained in this camp for a maximum period of three months. By then, I had learned my ABCs in preparation for reading the Qur'an. A fellow student from the UK taught me in exchange for my teaching him sit-ups and push-ups. That may sound bizarre, but he had never done a day's sport in his life, and he wasn't the only one.

I also found time in this camp to befriend a cheeky goat. He was black and had a long, white beard. He was a person; there is no other way to describe him. He would bellow somewhere in the camp and I would imitate his call, both of us repeating these strange sounds until we met. He was always ready to greet me, rearing up on his back legs, poised to bash heads. After the headbutting I would sit and relax, my legs hanging over a high ravine, while he would sprawl out alongside me, resting his head in my lap. After a good scratching between his stubby horns, he would leap up quickly, threaten me good-naturedly with a parting headbutt, and wander off to other amusements. We became good friends.

The lessons taught throughout the training were limited. It was mostly sport-oriented, for there was very little funding for ammunition. All up there was about three months' worth of unrepeated training, and this three-month selection ran in a circuit, so that when someone began, they joined in with the group wherever the selection was up to. If someone stayed the full three months or less, they would avoid a lot of repetition. The students always differed in what lessons they had completed and came and left at different times.

Around the time that the lessons started to repeat themselves, I wanted to move on. Though I was hesitant, I decided to progress to the next level towards entering India-controlled Kashmir. To do this, I had to travel back to the office in Lahore, Pakistan.

Eight

IT HAD BEEN WINTER when I first ascended the mountains but spring when I set foot back onto the valley floor at Muz-affarabad. I was waiting for the LeT van when I noticed a five-centimetre seedling at my feet. I bent to examine the plant, and was astonished to identify it as hemp. Due to its small size, I thought I must be wrong until I looked around me – it was growing everywhere, over a metre-and-a-half high. Observing from the van window, I noticed it grew all the way back to Lahore, anywhere from out of cracks in footpaths to dominat-ing unkempt spare blocks. I had never seen anything like it.

Once I was back in Lahore, I visited the zoo and museum. The zoo and its treatment of animals was disgusting. The museum housing the nation's treasures, however, was enchant-ing. I also went to visit popular landmarks, such as the grand structures left behind by the Mogul and British empires.

I saw people sharing needles in the street. Apparently, cheap heroin was still being imported from Afghanistan at the time.

I was told twenty cents Australian would buy a syringe full of the drug, the needles often pre-used, pulled out of the street corner rubbish heaps. I felt sad for the children, professional beggars who would relinquish their takings to the adults they were forced to work for.

I went on such observational forays while waiting for permission to progress further along the line to enter India-controlled Kashmir. The procedure when a combatant crossed the border from Pakistan into India was called 'launching'. The ISI allowed about five thousand combatants to operate inside India-controlled Kashmir at one time. Each individual muja-hedeen group based within Pakistan chose or allowed trainees from their own camps to go on a list for launching. Lists from each group were then sent to the ISI, who then granted permis-sion to individuals from all groups to proceed.

These individuals were then sent from their respective locations within Pakistan to a village or town near the point along the LoC where the ISI had determined they would cross. Once individuals were stationed at their border positions, they waited for final permission from the ISI to advance to a Paki-stani military bunker. From the bunker, they then launched across the border under the cover of darkness, entering India. A guide was employed to lead them across the border at night, around the time of a full moon to take advantage of its light. Depending on whether there is cloud cover, this allowed a one-week window per month for launching. The guide was used to navigate Indian minefields, armed checkpoints and bunkers.

Once inside India-controlled Kashmir the combatants made their way to towns or villages where they were sheltered by the locals, usually in secret cellars of their homes. The people of Kashmir were largely united in this, and even though the majority of combatants were Muslim, they were often shel-tered by people belonging to faiths other than Islam. No more than a week would be spent in one home before relocating to another, so as to keep one step ahead of Indian security forces. The Kashmiris did this at great peril, for the punishment inflicted upon the people of Kashmir by Indian troops for entertaining independence in any form was severe – often an entire community would be punished for the activities of just one individual.

Indian government agencies would place agents in marketplaces as a means to discover if locals were sheltering individuals involved in the resistance. They would look for signs, such as households that suddenly began buying extra food, especially out-of-the-ordinary products like Pepsi, or those who were simply spending beyond their means. Crackdowns and house searches would then be conducted, not just of the suspected household, but of the entire village. Sweeps of neighbouring areas were not uncommon. Abuses of one kind or another nearly always accompanied such operations.

Years before, while I was still working on cattle stations in outback Australia, the conflict in Kashmir was allegedly almost exclusively between Muslims and organisations involved in the independence movement and reforms in governance on one side and Indian government security forces on the other. As the years passed and the movement for independence grew (especially when non-Muslims became involved), the Indian army stopped discriminating against selected members of the community and inflicted their aggression on the population at large, including the women and children. I was told that all citizens suffered and that this was the catalyst for all peoples, regardless of faith or political views, to demand a stop to the oppression and insist on the right to vote for their independence.

Alcohol was said to have played a large part when the Indian military turned acts of violence and rape into some sort of

drunken, gruesome game. Another alleged factor that helped
unite the people of Kashmir was a program implemented by
the Indian government where agents would disguise themselves
as mujahedeen and attack non-Muslims and Muslims during
public events, such as at a Shia mosque or Hindu festival. The
plan was to divide the people and give the independence movement a bad name. But these activities were often exposed,
infuriating and uniting the people instead, and increasing the
movement's number of supporters.

By the late '90s the Indian military was engaged in an
all-out intimidation campaign against all Kashmiri people,
designed to subdue their spirit for independence and support
for the freedom fighters. However, the policy had spiralled
into a vicious conflict, with the Indian side of Kashmir being
closed to tourists. Some of the pamphlets I read from LeT were
accounts written by Western journalists and non-government
organisations (NGOs) who had somehow got inside, even into
some detention facilities, and recorded what they saw. They
interviewed victims of the aggression, then broadcast their
findings to the world – if it chose to listen. Those reporters
were brave and admirable people.

The fighters emerged from the cellars at night to scout and
collect information about the operations they believed would be
effective, then they would send it to their respective groups. The
organisations then passed the information along to the ISI, who
collated it and decided on which operations could be carried
out, giving so many green lights to each group. Among the five
thousand operatives there was a lot of activity, but, on an individual scale, apparently weeks or months could be spent living
from cellar to cellar without being involved in any hostilities.

There were two main types of operations the combatants
were involved in. One was to counter the Indian soldiers'
intimidation tactic known as 'crackdown'. The Indian soldiers

would surround a village and violently harass the occupants, such as ordering the men away and raping the women, who had been ordered to stay behind. Or they would search houses for signs of its owners being involved in supporting the resistance, taking men away who would not be heard of again. Then there were the beatings, torture and murders.

As a protective measure most villages had elected a young boy or teenager to act as a runner. As soon as a village was suspected of facing an imminent crackdown, the boy would be sent out to make contact with nearby mujahedeen before Indian security forces enclosed the village in a secure perimeter. The mujahedeen would then mobilise and use force to drive the offending military away from the besieged village.

The other operation involved the general harassment of Indian soldiers by ambush, attacking such targets as posts and garrisons. The purpose was to demoralise the soldiers and have them protest against their deployment. Apparently, troops from the far south of India did refuse to deploy to Kashmir, and many went AWOL on arrival. Reports indicated that desertion was common. The number of Indian troops in Kashmir would have numbered 700,000, more than all of Australia's armed forces put together, such was the scale of the government-sanctioned terror campaign.

India-controlled Kashmir is known as Kashmir in the north and Jammu in the south. A lot of the northern region is five thousand metres above sea level and higher. Only Pakistanis may cross over into Kashmir along this part of the northern border because of the cost, information and effort needed to get someone into that area, as well as the high elevation and inaccessibility of a landscape that is frozen most of the year. Once inside northern Kashmir, it is twelve months before someone can return via the northern LoC.

Among Pakistanis involved in Kashmir, non-Pakistanis

had a reputation for impatience, fickleness, disobedience, general lack of physical fitness and fortitude when faced with hardships and rough conditions – and sometimes cowardice. Because of these perceived attributes, non-Pakistanis were only allowed to launch further south in Jammu, such as the Poonch District, where the mountains are tamer and the border can be passable six or more months of the year. The Pakistanis become extremely annoyed when a foreigner begs to return two or three weeks after launching.

When it was time to depart Lahore and begin the launching procedure, I crammed into a public transportation van with some volunteers and made the half-day journey to the outskirts of a town named Kotli. I knew this would be a launching point, but didn't know what else to expect. We were based in a housing complex by a raging river encompassed by high cliffs. The scenery was spectacular. This part of Kashmir was adorned with large swathes of manicured-looking, lush green lawns, punctuated by tall pyramid-shaped weathered rocks. It looked as though a giant had rammed the points of his Stone Age spears up through the ground. Strange animals scuttled stealthily across the lawns; long, sleek, furry mammals whose species I could not identify.

In Kotli there were about ten of us foreigners awaiting further instructions, finding ways to pass the time. We helped one another with food, taking turns to cook and buy groceries. Almost daily we made the trek to the river, where we swam and whitewater rafted in car inner tubes that I had bought from Lahore.

At other times, I spoke with the refugees in the housing complex, most of whom were in their early teens. Many were traumatised and did not wish to discuss their experiences in

India or their journey to Pakistan. They preferred to ponder their future and relegate Kashmir to the past. Any sentiment they expressed about their homeland was a desire to return when it was independent and there was peace.

A month may have passed when the ten or so of us were separated into twos and threes then summoned to the commander's office. I was teamed with a British friend, whom I had trained with in Muzaffarabad. The commander alerted us that it was time to move on and gave each group its new location and supplied travel fare. We wished the others luck and left.

As the crow flies, distances in Kashmir are not far, but the terrain makes for long travel when winding your way by road. Thankfully our new location was only about four hours away. Instead of a camp, we were actually housed in a three-storey building that served as the local LeT office on the main street of a small town closer to the border, named Tata Pani. Once we settled in, the waiting period began again, but this time we received some information: a guide would arrive to coincide with the next full moon. There had been a full moon just after our arrival, but no guide, so we were guaranteed another month's wait. The only other occupants in this building besides the British man and me were the commander, his wife and their ten-year-old daughter. We passed the time eating at local restaurants. It had been some months since we had undergone training at Muzaffarabad, and the fitness we had achieved was long gone. To rectify this, we began to jog in the mornings and took the occasional night walk, another essential skill we had practically lost. Eventually, we harassed the commander to allow us to visit the LoC where we would be launching. It took a few days, but he granted us permission.

Nine

To reach our launching point on the LoC from Tata Pani required half a day's drive up, down and around plump mountains blanketed in short, light-green grass. We passed through deep, narrow ravines decorated with birds' nests and across one wide, shallow river before our vehicle stopped. We were on the summit of a lofty mountain. Below, a large valley snaked off to our left and right, with more mountains rising from the other side. The valley and our side of this rocky fortress were marked by mud villages, dirt tracks and animals, the landscape devoid of grass and trees. The opposing side was heavily vegetated, the only sign of life being squat stone buildings with small slits or holes in their walls. The mountains on our side represented Pakistan, and the mountains on the opposite side represented India. The valley separating these sovereign nations was the LoC itself.

We entered one of the buildings pointed out to us by the driver and met Captain Ali of the Pakistan army, who was expecting us. He directed a couple of enlisted soldiers to show us our sleeping quarters, then we spent the rest of the day with him in conversation. Just before dark, Captain Ali led us on a tour of the bunkers via the network of trenches closest to the office, the first set down from the summit. Looking hundreds of metres across to the opposite summit, we could see a corresponding Indian bunker. These bunkers were placed at intervals down the mountain slopes so that on the valley floor, Captain Ali explained, some Indian bunkers were only fifty or so metres away from the Pakistani ones. Captain Ali led us along a trench that was deep enough to protect our heads. There were only a few trenches in some areas along the summit, allowing safe passage. On this occasion we were able to use a trench to travel from an above-ground building to one of the forward bunkers – a solid stone hut with walls a metre thick. We were being introduced to the soldiers manning this position when the firing began.

The captain asked us not to be concerned, explaining that a constant trickle of fire was normal. It was a way of letting each other know 'we are here'. He told us only to be suspicious if there was a lot of firing – or none at all. We stayed for a week, and during that time a lot of fire was exchanged, at times quite heavy, while at other times an hour or two would pass without event. But as the captain said, it was steady, including occasional stray rounds that whizzed past one's ear. The Englishman and I participated in this exchange, under the orders and supervision of Captain Ali. We did not fire upon Indian soldiers or any other people. We only participated in the symbolic exchange of fire. Both sides remained safely housed within their stone bunkers, so we knew we were in no danger of actually hurting anyone (or being hurt ourselves), nor was that our intention.

However, due to Indian military aggression, there were

innocent civilian victims on our side of the border. Throughout the day, the occupants of the mud homes that littered the
valley floor and extended up the face of the mountains on the
Pakistani side to the summits went about their business, even
during these exchanges of fire. Captain Ali explained how the
Indian military occasionally pointed their weapons directly at
the civilians and their homes, resulting in casualties. I was to
personally witness one instance on a quiet, peaceful, sunny
afternoon, when you could listen to the birds if you ignored
the occasional gunshots.

The captain's radio crackled with news that a civilian had
been shot down in the valley. The captain, a military doctor,
the Englishman and I skirted our way down the face of the
mountain. I could hear something whacking through the leaves
and thought nothing of it until the captain recommended that
we continue out of the line of fire. We reached the village on
the valley floor to find forty-odd civilians – some were mothers
with babies in their arms – pinned behind a slight rise. They
were crying and afraid, unable to reach a boy of about twelve,
who was writhing on the ground out in the open.

The perpetrators had followed our progress down the mountain and released a volley of fire as we reached the victim. The
number of rounds passing just above us was, for me, surprisingly loud and, not surprisingly, scary. It was only a slight rise in
the ground that prevented the Indian military from a direct hit.
The four of us crawled out to the victim. A bullet had entered his
skull just behind an ear but had not exited. The doctor cut away
the hair from around the entry wound then applied a bandage.
We then lifted him and, using a steep, narrow gully between
mountains, were able to leave the valley and deposit him into a
waiting vehicle and safety. He was still alive at that stage, but
the closest hospital was four to five hours away by road. We
received the news later that he had died in transit.

Later, when we were back in the bunker, the captain noticed I was shaken up by this event and mentioned that such incidents were common. I heard that out of the nearly four hundred kilometres that is the LoC, fifty such incidents per day were reported to the UN. They were either murder, as I had witnessed, or the result of villagers having stepped on landmines that had slid down into the valley. Representatives from the UN investigated the site of each incident (or were at least meant to). The captain said that, even though they clearly distinguish their identity on their bulletproof vests and hard hats, the Indian military occasionally fired at them as well. I then asked the captain about the civilians' predicament, living between warring parties. He explained that the people used to live on the Indian side of the LoC. The Kashmir LoC was regarded as the second-most heavily fortified border in the world following the North Korea – South Korea border. The Indian military had drawn a line running parallel with the LoC, ten kilometres into their own territory, resulting in a 'military-only zone'. Previously, this area was occupied by civilians, and all were forcibly removed during the creation of this zone, producing many refugees in the process. Most, if not all, of these people did not wish to leave their homes.

When they reached Pakistan, for that was the direction in which they were forced to flee, they found the valleys already occupied. Though the Pakistani government offered assistance, many of these displaced people wished to remain as close as possible to their previous homes, so they built villages or re-tenanted previously abandoned homes along the LoC itself and the opposite mountain slope, sometimes in the vicinity of a Pakistani bunker. They faced daily risks living in this location, and though the Pakistan army tried to reason with them to move further into the country, they refused.

Due to the high density of people living in a small area

on the Pakistani side of the border, the resources had been exhausted, such as grass used for animal fodder and trees used as building material. However, those resources were abundant on the Indian side of the valley. Despite the risks, this situation forced the people to go further afield to obtain those valuable resources. Women went collecting the long grass on the Indian side of the border, close to soldiers in their bunkers, even though they knew the risks of rape and other degrading harassment. Yet through desperation they continued to wander across the LoC. Captain Ali said that even those they knew to have been raped still collected the grass.

The men who shepherded their animals where the grass was still long risked beatings or worse, but they persisted. The captain said they were working hard with the people and had various programs in place, but they would not move. The Indian military occasionally expanded this military zone, engulfing more civilian homes, creating more homeless refugees who had no choice but to leave.

The Indian military zone was manned with trenches, bunkers and posts. It was a large area to patrol. To help conserve manpower, the Indian military chose large areas to lay down minefields, which would then be all but forgotten about for possibly months at a time. Some of those minefields were on the mountain slopes above the LoC valley. Over time, erosion caused some mines to slide down the mountain face and settle on the valley floor, where they were occasionally stepped on by unsuspecting people and animals.

But those unpatrolled minefields within the military zone served a purpose for infiltrating combatants. Guides were employed to painstakingly pick a path through the mines, a high-risk occupation, which did occasionally leave people maimed or injured. Guides then led combatants over the border into India and back via these secret paths, some of which would be used for months before coming to the attention of Indian security forces. At one stage, Captain Ali asked rhetorically, 'Which houses do the guides own?', pointing to the various structures around us. His answer: the houses worth the most money. Such people were paid handsomely by the Pakistani government to find and keep pathways open and to guide combatants back and forth over them. Captain Ali also told stories of how guides would accept payment from both Pakistan and India, leading combatants into the military zone only to abandon them to be ambushed and killed. These stories were not encouraging.

Combatants generally launched in the first half of the night, allowing themselves enough time to cross the ten-kilometre-wide zone and reach civilian areas before sunrise, where they would be sheltered by the local people.

The day before we left the LoC, an eight-year-old girl was shot and killed instantly. She was a few posts away along the valley, so other army personnel retrieved the body. My experience at the border strengthened my resolve and corroborated all the pieces of information I had collected about Kashmir since my arrival in Pakistan. I could not, and still cannot, get my head around how a professional soldier, whose job is to protect vulnerable people, can shoot a civilian, especially a child, for what appeared to be no reason – not that there could ever be a reason. I wonder how those soldiers who committed such murder felt? Only they would know.

We returned to Tata Pani where we were to wait for another full moon, a guide and our launching. During that time I thought about some of the Pakistani government policies that Captain Ali had described. He admitted that Pakistan could not sustain a conventional conflict with India. Pakistan had

learned through experience that around five thousand combatants operating within ISI limits in Kashmir created enough
incidents to reach the international media's attention, but were
not quite enough for India to retaliate with all-out war. Pakistan continuously requested that the international community
send a third party to Kashmir who would create a stable environment for the people of Kashmir to vote for independence
and safely decide their future. The Indian government refused,
saying it could take care of its own internal issues – Kashmir
was a part of India, and would remain so.

Captain Ali claimed that the ISI were involved in various
ways of inflaming independence movements that were taking
place in many of India's provinces at the time. He described
these provinces within India as a bomb, and Kashmir the fuse.
If Kashmir was to receive independence via a third party, then
the other provinces would follow in a way that would see
India disintegrate into smaller independent states, as Russia
had years before. It was a lesson the ISI had learned from the
Soviet war in Afghanistan, in which it had played a prominent
role, and it sounded like they hoped to repeat those circumstances. I was uncomfortable to hear of such divisive political
activities, and I started to question the Kashmir dilemma. I
became confused; each week I was presented with new, conflicting information that shaped my evolving ideas and views
about the region.

My English friend and I continued to eat once a day in the
restaurants along the street until the ISI visited and ordered us
never to eat in public places again. We were to remain in the
house, or else the Indian intelligence could learn of our movements and intended launching point. Neither of us appreciated
the lecture. We had been told that, when it was time for launching, a member of the ISI would collect us from this address. He
would then drive us to the LoC under the cover of darkness

and remain with us in a Pakistani military bunker – in our case, the one we had already visited. The ISI employee would remain with us for that first night and the following day. He would be the last person we would see as he waved us over the border on the second night. It would also be a member of the ISI who would retrieve us at a Pakistani bunker when we re-entered the country some months later.

After some time during our second stint waiting in this town, we boarded a van and returned to Captain Ali's section of the LoC. He had given us an open invitation to return when we chose, and we decided to take him up on this offer.

We returned to the border post to find that Captain Ali had gone on leave. The captain who had replaced him was not so forthcoming or friendly. Except on odd occasions, he preferred to keep us by the office. A new event during this second visit was the firing of flares. From sunset until about 10 pm, the time that combatants must launch across the border, the Indian military was firing the flares almost continuously up and down the length of the valley. They were white and extremely bright, hovering high above for thirty seconds, like a fireworks show, illuminating the entire area. With special-ised vision, the Indian soldiers scanned the valley floor, firing on moving shadows. We were instructed that if we were ever caught in the glow of such a flare in a target zone, to remain absolutely still – we would be mistaken for shadows.

The captain had explained that more civilian deaths had taken place during my absence as a result of hostile Indian fire. He further stated that such deaths were often due to rogue bunkers or, more specifically, rogue soldiers who might be alone for weeks at a time in a particular bunker. When this occurred, the Pakistani military responded by ordering all bunkers within range – up to ten or more – to direct their fire at the one rogue bunker until its occupants stopped targeting the civilians and quiet returned. The bunkers are sufficiently fortified so that the occupants are usually safe, even through such a barrage. But with enough harassment, the rogues usually ceased their murderous behaviour.

The Indian bunker responsible for the death of the boy whom I and the others had attempted to save was also responsible for these new deaths. After we had left, Captain Ali had ordered daily assaults on this bunker once it was identified, but the occupant continued to take shots at the civilians. The rogue was still posing a danger. To tackle this problem, the new captain had sent men within close range at night, armed with rocket-propelled grenades. They launched a quick attack before retreating. He did not know whether the rogue occupant had perished in this assault, but he commented that they had achieved their goal – the LoC in his sector had returned to a more normal level of fire. Most importantly, there was no more reported firing at civilians or civilian deaths.

The British guy and I stayed for another three or four days with this new captain at his post, then we decided to return to Tata Pani.

I had been in Pakistan for a year by that stage and I was still waiting to launch into India-controlled Kashmir. I felt I was not helping the situation, and the internal politics were starting to get to me. The involvement of the ISI in the region was disconcerting, and so were stories of their tactics. At times the ISI would order operations against Indian troops, and then those troops would retaliate against nearby villages, the Indian military blaming local civilians for supporting those involved in the attacks. From what I could understand, if the Pakistani authorities really wanted independence for Kashmir, and if they had given the people the freedom to pursue this, then the conflict would have been over quickly. Instead, their policies seemed counterproductive and sometimes contributed to the people's suffering. I decided to leave and travelled back to Lahore.

I needed some time-out to get my thoughts together. I wanted to go back to Australia and see my family before returning to Kashmir. I was to learn in the near future that, a few weeks after I had departed Tata Pani, my companion had been given the go-ahead to launch. He was ambushed and killed while crossing the ten-kilometre-wide military zone. If I hadn't left when I did, I would surely have met the same fate.

Throughout my time in Kosovo, and now Kashmir, I had often been anxious about where I was and what I was doing, always having to internally push myself along. I constantly grappled with fear and, at times, such as at the LoC in Kashmir, I needed to exercise a measure of effort to be there. I tried to overcome these emotions in various ways, but no love of country or patriotic slogan helped me. The only resolve that encouraged me to continue on my path was hearing about the abuses that were occurring on the other side of the border. What the people of Kashmir had to endure infuriated me. I also attempted to utilise the one subject that those around me shared as a motivator to overcome fear: Islam. I tried during this period to deepen my faith, as is reflected in the letters I sent home to my family, where I believe I preached more to myself than to them. But it was little comfort, for I lacked a spiritual connection to the teachings of Islam, and so failed to find it a source of strength.

In the letters I wrote to my family, I see a young person who is poorly educated and un-researched – insufficiently informed and ill-prepared for his location, company and activities. I was impressionable, naive and, on occasion, full of bravado and exaggeration. To read those letters today makes me cringe. They are regrettable and embarrassing and, looking back over a decade ago, I do not recognise the author. To begin to understand why I wrote my letters, it would be helpful to have an understanding of the environment in which they were written. Such political views as seen in my letters were the norm and mainstream in the country I was in. People openly expressed their contempt of the US and the Israeli governments, denouncing those nations' foreign policies to crowds of eager listeners in busy marketplaces and street corners. These sentiments were also expressed in the Pakistani English newspapers I read, on national TV by community leaders and politicians, and discussed often over the family dinner table.

There was anger about Western companies extracting resources from many locations within the Middle East and talk about Western influence and control over the media, and how it infiltrated and interfered with their own cultures. There was anger about US foreign policy, the long-term US military bases and action in the Middle East. There was anger and sadness about the conflicts in Kashmir, Kosovo, Bosnia, Palestine, Chechnya and the oppression of the Uighurs in south-western China. However, the most powerful influence on my views at the time was hearing the stories of people who had been the direct victims of these conflicts. I heard about people's lives being torn apart, and such foreign policies were almost always to blame – policies based on greed, power and wealth.

Despite my shoehorning people into national groups in the letters I had sent to my family I was referring to governments and not the citizens. I held no ill will towards peaceful, innocent civilians. Instead, my intention was to help such people. It is ironic that I would eventually be labelled for entertaining thoughts to do the opposite. Explanations aside, I wrote those letters, and for that there is no excuse. Today I am older and, I hope, wiser.

Ten

AFTER HAVING MADE THE DECISION to return to Australia for a while, I attempted one last time to see Afghanistan. I was interested in the country rather than in its internal politics and ongoing civil war. Back in the LeT office in Lahore, I mentioned my interest in Afghanistan and asked them how I should plan my trip. They wouldn't help, insisting that I shouldn't go. They said that the Taliban were dangerous and the general situation wasn't safe. Despite their warnings, and due to my limited knowledge of the region, I made up my mind to see the country for myself. My naïve mind still envisaged the romanticised Afghanistan of the many books I had read in the days before I travelled abroad. I packed my bag and passport, and made my way to the train station on my own, where I boarded a carriage to Quetta.

It is a twenty-four-hour trip from Lahore to Quetta – slow, hot and, after a few times, boring. Snacks can be bought from ten-year-old vendors who sneak aboard for a few stops before disembarking. Proper meals, however, can only be found at station platforms, providing the train stands idle long enough. Buying anything can be a challenge for foreigners. Prices are extremely low in Pakistan, even when they quadruple for foreigners. Still, I did not have a sustainable source of money, and as a matter of principle I did not want to pay inflated prices.

As the hours passed I grew extremely hungry, but I was hesitant to attempt to buy a meal. This was the first time I had truly travelled on my own in Pakistan and fended for myself. I could not go the entire trip without eating, however, so I devised strategies of how I could obtain a meal at local prices. I was not concerned about being recognised as a foreigner, because my outward appearance and skin colour allowed me to blend in well – I had a beard, wore the national dress and, until I spoke, locals often assumed I was Afghani. I was worried about communicating because I could not speak Urdu. When it was announced that our next stop would be for half an hour, I emerged from my carriage hungry and cautious. I strolled along the platform, examining the various meals on offer. I settled for a particular rice dish and stood with my back facing the vendor while glancing over my shoulder, watching how much customers paid for their meals.

Once I had discovered the locals' price, I turned to face the vendor and confidently announced 'Eck plate'. (Eck meaning 'one' in Urdu, 'plate' having the same meaning in both languages.) Before the vendor had time to scrutinise me, I had turned my back again. I waited until I heard the vendor say something in Urdu that I hoped meant, 'It is ready.' I turned back around and paid the exact amount with the correct note and received my plate of food without question. I boarded the train with a satisfied stomach and a contented mind. Hours later I attempted this again, but with a kilo of mangos. The difference this time was that it was going to be more expensive than the previous plate of food, and I only had a large note that would require change. Plus, no-one else was buying mangos, so I could not observe any transactions. Again, I did not have to engage the vendor in conversation and judged the change I received to be sufficient. It was satisfying to feel that I was becoming independent in this foreign land.

I arrived in Quetta exhausted and covered in dust. I was looking forward to catching up with Kaleb again and caught a rickshaw directly to his house. We exchanged pleasantries and news before I mentioned my intention to check out Afghanistan for a while. Kaleb questioned my plans, only to find that I did not have any. My idea was to travel to Kandahar and ask passers-by where foreigners congregated and then find accommodation. Kaleb said I was being too hasty and suggested that I at least attempt to speak to someone at the Afghanistan government office before I embarked on my own. We travelled together to the office and Kaleb spoke to someone in Urdu on my behalf.

That conversation turned out to be an example of how translations between different languages can go terribly wrong. From what I understood, the amir at the office said that I could go to Afghanistan in the company of a government official. Kaleb thought the proposal sounded legitimate and considered it much safer than simply going alone. I was told that a bus would be leaving from that location in a few days and that I should travel to Afghanistan with the government officials on that bus. The amir would alert the passengers of my situation. However, as the following days would prove, the amir had obviously not understood what Kaleb had said, and what had been translated back to me was something very different from what the amir had actually intended. Until then, I was excited that I would finally see the country I had read about. I was finally going to see the Hindu Kush and Pamir mountain ranges to the north.

At the designated time, I boarded the bus outside the Quetta office. It was full of Afghanis, who all greeted me in the cheerful, boisterous, Pashtun way, yet no individual took responsibility for me or introduced himself as a government representative. Concerned, but not overly worried, I settled back and watched the dry, forbidding landscape pass by. Occasionally, we passed large fruit orchards enclosed by high mud walls, fortified structures and clusters of four or five houses surrounding a common well. The road eventually wound its way through rugged, sun-baked hills. Dozens of well-camouflaged military bunkers stared down at the road from the eroding cliffs above. Their purpose was to defend this road, and ultimately Pakistan, from any army who wished to invade via this route from the north. In time, the hills sloped away, revealing a flat, shimmering plain as far as I could see. The bus bumped its way down to this plain, and some time later we arrived at a town called Chaman, right up against the Afghanistan border.

This was when I realised that the conversation back in Quetta may have been misinterpreted and misunderstood. The bus came to a halt and everyone disembarked. I was expecting the bus to travel non-stop to Kandahar, but apparently this was as far as it was taking us. All the passengers began walking along the road towards the border post not far away. A few of the passengers I was seated next to encouraged me to follow them. We walked straight over the border into Afghanistan and then caught a taxi a short distance up the road to another town called Spin Boldak, the first settlement once having crossed the border. It was a commercial centre with lots of transport vehicles and the hustle and bustle of any border town. We then caught a bus from this town that took us all the way to Kandahar along a dusty, potholed road.

I was too worried about my next move to pay attention to the city of Kandahar as the bus entered and stopped down a side street. As I expected, all the passengers alighted and quickly dispersed. I was left standing on my own until one of the passengers turned around and came back to me. I tried to communicate with him but, as with everyone else who had been on the bus, we could not understand each other. He took my hand and led me to a complex of houses that were nestled behind a surrounding wall, where he left me with a group of people. I was able to make out that this housing complex was a government compound, and the people around me were Taliban. I had not heard much about the Taliban at the time, except that they were the government and they were dangerous. I was about to learn a lot more about them, however.

They seemed to find me amusing as I struggled in vain to be understood. I was shown to the room where I'd sleep, and as the days passed I only stayed in this one particular house. There were about twenty of us. We sat down together for meals and the rest of my time was frustratingly spent trying to communicate. By about the third day, while we were seated for lunch, one of the Taliban officials asked me a question I could understand: 'What group do you belong to in Islam?' Many Muslims follow one of the four main schools of Islam – Hanafi, Hanbali, Maliki and Shafi'i – all of which are considered orthodox Islam. The Taliban are Hanafi, and in their view one should follow at least one of the four main schools.

I was at the head of a plastic mat laden with food, while the amir was at the other end. I answered that I did not follow any particular school of thought. To the people I was eating with, my response meant that I was wandering about aimlessly, picking and choosing what is most convenient from within Islam. My answer was not well received. The official who had asked the question and was sitting closest to me then asked why I did not follow a particular school. Innocently, I answered that the Sahaba (the companions and followers of Prophet Moham- med) were not Hanafi. This is correct because Imam Hanafi came after that period in history. However, I could not have said anything more offensive to the people I was with. I had discredited Hanafi, and the very roots of their beliefs.

The official sitting to my side picked up a knife from among the food and placed his other arm around my shoulders. The hand brandishing the knife was positioned threateningly. Strangely, I did not move, which was probably the right course of action. I had a feeling that he would not follow through with his threat. The amir laughed and dismissed the knife-wielding man with a wave of his hand. The man obeyed and removed his hand, drawing his finger across his throat, cursing me in his language, his facial expression matching his rage. I glanced at the twenty-odd people around me. I guessed half were inclined to harm me in some way, while the other half seemed amused by the whole situation. I nervously carried on eating.

Once lunch was over, I told the amir that I was going to return to Pakistan. I wanted to get away from these people. I was thoroughly concerned. He ordered me not to go anywhere. I was panicking now. Early the next morning, I again pleaded with the amir to let me go. He looked about us, then signalled that I could leave – but quietly and quickly. I grabbed my bag and left as fast as I could, expecting to hear a 'he's escaping!' ring out from behind me. It was a massive relief to reach the bus without incident and my fear eased with each kilometre that passed between me and Kandahar.

The first thing I did back in Quetta was go and see Kaleb. I spent a few days with him before deciding to return to the LeT office in Lahore. The staff there used my knife story to support their negative statements about the Taliban. I also had nothing positive to say about the Taliban.

An opportunity crossed my path while I was in Lahore: learning the Qur'an in Arabic. As mentioned previously, it's a huge achievement in Islam, yet I couldn't even read the text, so it was something I really wanted to do. LeT offered a place in their madrasah in Karachi, so once again I was off on the train, travelling across the country, but this time to see and explore somewhere new. The route followed what was for me a new part of Punjab Province before entering the southern province of Sind.

I made my way from the Karachi train terminal to the madrasah. The city was like a breath of fresh air after coming from Lahore. Although it had the air of being rundown, it is big, much cleaner than Lahore and has a hint of a sea breeze. Food and accommodation was free on campus, and I found a spare bed in the student quarters and unpacked. On my first morning, I joined the students in a classroom but quickly discovered that all the lessons were in Arabic, so I couldn't understand what was said. The students in these classes were completing bachelor's degrees, and many of them had already memorised the Qur'an. Since I could not participate, the only option I had was to join the children in the mosque. These children, from between five to twelve years of age, were learning to read and memorise the Qur'an simultaneously.

The teachers in the mosque were too strict on the children for my liking, using wooden rulers to 'encourage' them. I knew it would be a waste of time if I complained, so I avoided these teachers, not bothering to have them check my reading. I also knew what my reaction would have been had they chosen to use a ruler on me. Instead, I glowered at them each time I heard the slap. This left me in a position where there was no-one to teach me how to read the Qur'an. Luckily, I met a fellow student from the Zanzibar Archipelago off Tanzania who lived on campus and offered to be my tutor.

During his lunchbreaks, in one of the empty classrooms, he would teach me how to read half a page. Then between sessions I would repeatedly go over the previous lesson. If he was happy with the way I read that half of a page, we would progress to the next part. If I could not read the lines articulately, I would have to continue with the lesson from the day before until I could pronounce the words to his satisfaction.

For the next four months, my daily program consisted of breakfast and then practising my allotted Qur'an lesson among the children in the mosque for an hour or two. I would then walk down the road to the business sector to buy the daily English-language paper and return to my room to read it back to front. If I finished the paper an hour or two before lunch, I would practise my Qur'an reading lesson some more. After eating, I would meet with my Tanzanian teacher and commence my next lesson for the remainder of the lunchbreak. When all the students returned to their lessons, I would return to the mosque and continue with my new lesson until I became fatigued. I would then usually go for walks, exploring the nearby parts of the city, or catch a bus and go further afield.

On the weekends I would go on daily excursions around Karachi with my friend from Tanzania or some of the other students. I would take great interest in the various fish for sale at the markets. They were fresh from the trawlers, and I was surprised to recognise many species from home, allowing me a visual image of the offshore ecosystems. The fruit and vegetable markets were also interesting to me. A market is a microcosm of the larger country – it's like the country visiting you. Different produce from many different surrounding environments are all laid at your feet. Every Sunday there was a medium-sized market right next to the madrasah, and I would spend the afternoons there, enjoying the exotic sounds and smells around me.

I often thought about Kashmir and how I had become disillusioned and confused. I was still unsure about the politics surrounding the conflict.

Despite this confusion, I could not ignore the suffering of the Kashmiri people. I could not turn my back on them. I believed in the cause and planned to continue assisting. However, I also judged that some of the people attracted to LeT and the other Kashmir liberation organisations did not have honest intentions. Instead of thinking of the people in Kashmir, the cause was seen as a means to personal gain. I suppose that is not surprising. In a country with so much poverty it is inevitable that any flow of money would attract people with insincere motivations. There were sections of the Pakistani community that, while supporting the people of Kashmir, did not support the Kashmir liberation organisations.

Some of the leaders were accused of greed and misusing funds meant for refugees and other humanitarian projects. I was told to observe who drove the expensive four-wheel drives in the main cities – those vehicles had been bought with donated funds meant for Kashmir by members of Kashmir aid groups. I was also asked to observe the massive stomachs of such men – on whose income did they grow fat and live well?

Apart from such observations, my life at the madrasah followed the same routine. I wrote to my family in Australia, mentioning my intention to come home. It was around this time that I received a phone call from the LeT office in Lahore, requesting that I return there for a few days. I agreed and caught a train for the long ride back to the Punjab.

When I arrived at the Lahore office, I was greeted by an ex-student from the LeT Muzaffarabad camp. We had become good friends in those days, and I was glad to catch up with him once more. Since we had parted ways he had been busy operating inside India-controlled Kashmir. He was now about to go into Afghanistan and, unbeknown to me, LeT had asked him to take me along. Now they wanted to use me, unlike last time when they had recommended that I not attempt to go. Once we had spent some time catching up, LeT asked if I was interested in going into Afghanistan. It was the last thing I was expecting, and I wasn't keen on the idea at first. LeT was interested in the guerrilla and urban warfare training that was apparently being conducted at that time in government-sanctioned camps in Afghanistan.

My previous attempts to see Afghanistan had failed – the last time spectacularly. Even so, I still entertained the idea of exploring the country. I knew this would probably be the last chance I would have to visit Afghanistan before returning to Australia. I thought I would do the training, see some of the country, report back to LeT, then go home and see my family, and then consider how best to help the Kashmiri people before returning to Kashmir. I was highly concerned about the Taliban, however. LeT assured me that although these camps were Taliban controlled I wouldn't need to go anywhere near the Taliban – they would neither harass me nor make inquiries concerning me. Also, unlike last time, I would not be abandoned; there would be people who would assist me. Standard accommodation and food would be provided. I was also told that I would have the freedom and find the time to explore and see the country. Otherwise, I could just train and then leave. Unsure whether I was making the right decision, I agreed to go to give Afghanistan one last chance and then returned to Karachi to prepare.

Eleven

AFGHANISTAN HAS A FASCINATING and complex history. The major historic trade routes of the central Asian regions are found within modern-day Afghanistan, which attracted countless travellers from faraway lands. Exotic goods, ideas, customs, religions and philosophies all came together at the large, colourful bazaars, with people exchanging news and information.

Afghanistan is also a land that has unfortunately suffered its share of invasions. The urge for foreign powers to defeat and occupy a submissive Afghanistan is interesting – the US is now the third major power to attempt this over a two-hundred-year period. To the Afghani people foreign interference has always been a rallying cry to resist.

During the Cold War, the Soviet Union was accused of having designs to occupy Afghanistan and then capture a warm-water port on the Indian Ocean, allowing it access to the Arabian oilfields. To counter that plan, the CIA under

President Reagan funnelled billions of dollars to provide arms and strategic military supplies to the mujahedeen, funds matched by Saudi Arabia and reportedly surpassed by private donations, encouraging those whom they now deem terrorists to fight for their freedom against the Soviets and participate in jihad.[18]

The result of that support is today's phenomenon of jihad and the mujahedeen. The definition of mujahedeen has ranged from 'freedom fighters', as expressed by the US and others in the 1980s, to the present-day meaning, 'terrorists'.[19] During those years, thousands of young Muslims from around the globe travelled to Afghanistan. The bulk of these young men received military training upon their arrival, while other, more high-profile figures, received training abroad. After this training, they engaged the Russian military in hostilities.

During the decade-long conflict, a handful of Muslim scholars and others among these multitudes began to spread their influence, preaching that the conflict was not just any war, but a *holy* war. They believed that their intention should not just be to liberate Afghanistan and defeat the Russians, but to also rule a free Afghanistan by Islamic law, the Sharia law. So what may have started out for some as a nationalistic cause, or one based on an array of other intentions, became very much a religious one, where combatants did not separate religion and state, where combatants intended to become politicians upon victory.

The US, some of its allies and a lot of the Islamic world at the time did not help this situation, because they used the word 'jihad' in their recruitment drives and as a motivating philosophy, despite the term not having been used on such a scale for some years. Governments, such as Egypt, arranged travel plans and paid the airfare for their citizens who wished to fight the Russians in Afghanistan. On behalf of governments, influential scholars issued fatwas (Islamic rulings) stating it was legal for all Muslims to fight the Russians.

The Taliban movement holds its origins in the displacement of around four million refugees who were seeking stability in Pakistan after the Afghan war.[20] Some of those refugees ended up in the countless madrasahs that existed in Pakistan. Taliban literally means 'students'. These madrasahs were influenced by the Islamic party Jamiat-ul-Ulema-e-Islam, or JUI. This party became a junior partner to Benazir Bhutto's government in 1988, the Pakistani government that is attributed with giving birth to the Taliban.[21] The madrasahs were further influenced, financially and ideologically, by Saudi Arabia and Pakistan's ISI. Pakistan, Afghanistan and other local entities preached a Hanafi, Deobandi style of Islam, while Saudi Arabian influence spread a different Salafi, Wahhabi school of thought.

The madrasahs were primarily used as centres for religious instruction. Later, as they filled with Afghan refugees, selected individuals were chosen for military training. Some training camps were funded and run by the CIA and Britain's MI6,[22] but many other individuals and organisations, including states, had interests in the numerous other camps that existed over the years. The students, who were few in number at first, became furious at the exploits of the Afghan warlords and the general suffering and destruction of their homeland and fellow countrymen that continued after the Soviets had left. Encouraged and supported by the ISI, a small and new group of men named the Taliban crossed the southern border of Afghanistan in 1994 and participated in their first known military operation. The area at the time was virtually lawless, ravaged by Mansur Achakzai, a warlord renowned for rape, pillage and general violence. He surrendered Kandahar without a fight and the Taliban quickly established authority. Once Kandahar and its surrounding areas were secure, the US began to back

the Taliban, the Taliban being just one warring group out of
the many that existed at the time, viewing them as a possible
means of securing a sufficient amount of territory to establish
an oil pipeline from the former Soviet Republic to the coast
of Baluchistan.[23] The US was concerned that such a pipeline
might otherwise end up going through Iran.

America's plan of backing the mujahedeen with weap-
onry and training to remove the Soviets throughout the '80s
worked. Historians have claimed that the most important
US contribution that changed the course of the war was the
provision of surface-to-air missiles called 'Stingers'.[24] These
weapons enabled the mujahedeen to shoot down transport aircraft and helicopters, inflicting serious damage on the Soviets
for the first time, providing the resistance with an adequate air
defence system. Russia crumbled.

In Central Asia, what had formerly been the USSR became
independent states. The oilfields were secure and the US pock-
eted a hefty sum in Russian assets. There was a side effect,
however: the fraught US presence and messy war against the
Taliban that we are trying to deal with today. As current Secretary of State Hillary Clinton recently remarked, 'The problems
we face now to some extent we have to take responsibility for,
having contributed to it.'[25]

With the vacuum of power left by the Russian with-
drawal, a massive stockpile of weapons and, in some cases,
interference from foreign nations pursuing different agendas,
the veterans of the resistance re-formed into new political
parties – and so began the bloody civil war, or the 'war of the
warlords', which lasted until the birth of the Taliban nearly
ten years later.[26]

US support of the Taliban was considerable during the
group's early days, even up to the highest levels of government. In 1995, Assistant Secretary of State for South Asia

described the Taliban as 'supporting a peaceful political process'.[27] In 1998, the Vice-President of International Relations
at the Union Oil Company (Unocal), spoke at a congressional
inquiry, saying that 'the Taliban does not practise the anti-US
style of fundamentalism practised in Iran'.[28] Of course, it was
in Unocal's interests to back the Taliban – they had already
signed a contract to build a $3 billion dollar pipeline from
Turkmenistan to Afghanistan and Pakistan and transport
$8 billion dollars worth of natural gas.[29] After two or three
years of supporting the Taliban, however, the US reversed its
attitude from support to hostility. Self-interest no longer was
an issue, the pipeline was secured and pressure was building
in the US due to the Taliban's treatment of women and other
human rights abuses.

Despite the US's reversal, by 2001 the Taliban was in control
of ninety-five per cent of the country with revered mujahedeen
leader Ahmad Shah Massoud in control of the remainder,
though in the north-east the frontline continually shifted back
and forth with some towns changing hands on a weekly basis.

During their continued expansion in 2000, the Taliban captured a major supply route in the north of the country that
linked Massoud's forces to their northern neighbours, boosting
outside support for the Northern Alliance. For years, Afghanistan had supplied sixty to seventy per cent of the world's
heroin.[30] Once the Taliban was in control of the majority of
Afghanistan, its leader, Mullah Muhammad Omar, fulfilled
an earlier promise and banned the growing of poppies and the
operation of processing laboratories. By the second year of this
ban, official poppy growing and heroin production was almost
non-existent. Only in Northern Alliance territory did it grow
in a commercial quantity.

This was the state of affairs when I entered Afghanistan
around the beginning of 2001, though much of the situation

I did not learn about until many years later. I did not have an opportunity to observe life under Taliban rule, and I only had my first discussion with someone about what that was like near the end of my stay. However, from what I have heard and seen since, their legacy is a sad and often brutal one. I think the women have suffered the most under Taliban rule, being subject to violence and brutality with no chance of holding accountable those who have caused them such anguish.[31] The human rights abuses in Afghanistan are widespread, and I hope one day life improves for the people of Afghanistan.

When I arrived in Kandahar for the second time, I was able to relax and observe my surroundings. Judged by the vivid impressions I had gathered from books and stories, this southern Afghan city did not let me down. It was different from any other centre I had seen so far in the region – it truly felt like I had stepped back in time.

My friend led me to a large, white mansion where a hundred or more non-Afghanis were staying. It was like a hotel or a halfway house, full of people leaving and entering the country. Others used it as a temporary dwelling while in transit within the country. It was a meeting place for friends, somewhere to sleep and eat for free. The hotel also acted as a general information centre, where people involved in various freedom movements, such as the Uighurs, could find out information about the state of affairs in a particular country and how they could assist.

Some of the foreigners who passed through this hotel organised charity for the country's innumerable poor. Others sought investment in Afghanistan's underdeveloped resources or built wells, schools, mosques and other such projects. There were people on pilgrimages and tourists on holiday. One day I met a group from the Arabian Peninsula who were capturing hawks, which would then be sent to the Arab countries to be trained in the sport of falconry, a pastime of the rich. Religious courses were on offer, as were the location and times of military training.

Some came to train as soldiers, with the intention to use those skills back in their respective homelands where military struggles of one sort or another were under way. In this respect, quite a lot of different organisations and nationalities were present, from the Philippines to African nations and everywhere in between, such as in Kashmir, or other provinces under siege. Combatants from China's south-western Muslim province were present, as were a group of Kurds from northern Iraq who were involved in hostilities against Saddam Hussein, demanding independence on behalf of the people in that region. From my experience, Saddam was extremely disliked by the Muslim community, whether they were of a military bent or not, Shia or Sunni. This ran contrary to how some in the media, and the US government, portrayed such sentiments.

I know it might sound strange to some people, but some of the young men who came for military training thought it would make an interesting holiday during their time off from work or uni. They left the camps without any intention of getting involved in any conflict; they just saw it as a travel experience. Others trained for the personal challenges, such as getting physically fit. There were also those who believed it was their religious duty to take training that would protect vulnerable communities and fellow Muslims, whom they saw as oppressed and on the defensive. Some young men wanted to protect their families. Then there were those who were simply curious and wanted to know what military training was all about, or experience what their kin had during periods of violent invasions and occupations. Apart from those people actually representing a freedom movement organisation, most of the people I met never seemed to have any intention of joining a military force and engaging in a combat situation. The mere receipt of such training should not lead to an automatic assumption of hostile intentions. Many went, trained, then returned to their respective countries and resumed their daily lives. The intentions for engaging in military training were varied, just as it is for Westerners who join the military.

I did meet some unsure and confused individuals. They tended to be young men, some of whom had only left their mother's home for the first time in their lives. They had been bombarded with daily media images of injustices aimed at Muslim people around the world. Shocked and horrified, they travelled to Afghanistan to receive training but were unsure how to right the injustices they had seen. From what I saw and heard, these young men were not motivated by an intention to commit violent acts and, no matter how angry they were at what was taking place, they never spoke of committing *terrorist* acts. On the contrary, they wanted to help their fellow human beings, not harm them. They were driven by a deep belief in justice. This signifies a good heart to me. I could understand their frustration. I was also disturbed by images of civilians, the innocent and the vulnerable, being targeted in inhumane ways. That's what motivated me in Kosovo and Kashmir. I had wanted to prevent injustice. Of all the people I met on my travels, whether in Kosovo, Kashmir, Afghanistan or the US soldiers in Guantanamo Bay, there was one thing they all had in common: they all thought they were doing a good thing.

Defining a legitimate cause differs from person to person. Some may believe a cause is just because their government has sanctioned it through the media, for others it may be more personal. Dismissing the historical pretext for a conflict and the ever-present politics, I look at those who are participating in the fighting and those who are affected by it. Young men and women calling for arms may be fuelled by the emotions that come with youth, while the elderly males in a society may be nostalgic, reliving dreams, thinking how things 'could have been' or aiming to settle scores. But to me, when the elderly women of a community cry for arms, there must be a serious reason. They seek stability and comfort and take pride in seeing grandchildren grow up healthy and safe. I believe our grandmothers are the last members in a community who want to see or risk having the underlying fundamentals of a stable society undermined and break down into violence and anarchy. Even a community already exposed to injustice may opt for the status quo, instead of inflaming the situation into something worse. Those grandmothers' voices were present in Kosovo and Kashmir.

Twelve

UPON MY ARRIVAL AT THE KANDAHAR HOTEL, I followed the same standard procedure I had followed in Kosovo and Kashmir: I handed in my passport, important identification, surplus money and valuables for safekeeping in a secured environment. No-one had to carry such items and risk losing them or having them stolen. My friend, who accompanied me to Afghanistan, only stayed at the hotel for a day or two before leaving to attend basic training at a camp a few hours outside Kandahar. I didn't join him because I had already completed basic training before and wasn't keen on putting myself through the hardships of an introduction level again. LeT had asked me to take courses relevant to the terrain and combat situations in Kashmir. For example, the courses contained strategies to defend villages from hostile soldiers and deter them from entering, or strategies for mountain warfare. These courses are considered standard military training similar to what our Australian troops undertake. None of these courses included bomb-making, hijacking planes, targeting innocent civilians or other such terrorist activities. Since I wasn't interested in participating in any basic training again, I stayed at the hotel and used the opportunity to see a small part of the city.

During that period, Ramadan ended and the Day of Eid was celebrated, marking the end of the fasting period. Across the road from the hotel was an Islamic school that occasionally ran language and religious classes. On the Day of Eid, the school's inner courtyard was used to host lunch and midday prayers. I crossed the road and entered in the company of someone who had a sufficient command of English. As we entered, we passed five or six visiting Afghan and Arab scholars sitting on chairs. We followed the example of others who shook the hands of these scholars, then we sat on one of the numerous mats spread about on the courtyard lawn. After a few minutes, my acquaintance pointed to the seated scholars and asked if I recognised one in particular. When I replied that I didn't, he informed me that his name was Osama Bin Laden.

I had heard of Bin Laden while I was in Pakistan. I had scant knowledge of him at the time, and what knowledge I did have was derived from the odd conversation, newspaper report and rumour. I knew him to be a wealthy man. His family owned the largest engineering and construction company in the Middle East. It is said that he donated much of his considerable wealth to fund the mujahedeen when he worked alongside the CIA during the Russian invasion of Afghanistan. As I understand it, when the relationship with the Americans soured, he became critical of what he saw as US interference in the Middle East. He was particularly critical of the military bases on the Arabian Peninsula (especially in Saudi Arabia where the oil reserves are vast), the sanctions against Iraq, the Israeli–Palestinian conflict and other conflicts that he saw as fuelled by US aggression. I had come across him in Pakistani newspapers where they said that he was being unfairly targeted by the US and made out to be a scapegoat. His name was one of many portrayed in such a manner, and thus didn't have a meaningful impact on me. Talk on the streets in Pakistan mentioned nothing ominous about him, and the Muslims in general often considered themselves the target of US aggression or interference.

While there were some who held him in high esteem, there were also those who claimed that Bin Laden was not a scholar and not worth making a fuss over. They viewed him in the same light as everyone else, despite his wealth and profile. As the months went by, Bin Laden did visit the camps on a few occasions. He often travelled about the country, sometimes giving talks as a guest speaker. I don't know exactly what he said – he only spoke in Arabic and live translations were not allowed. He was very quietly spoken, and at the time I did not have any reason to think there was anything evil about him – of course that has all changed now. Even though I did see him on a few occasions, we never met, nor did we ever converse. Whenever I saw him, I was just another person in a crowd.

The camp I was to attend was only one out of thirty or forty similar camps that existed in Afghanistan at the time I was there, a situation I found not unusual because of my time in Pakistan. I have come to learn since my release, through books and other sources of information, that the actual terrorists based in Afghanistan had only a few very small and highly secretive camps.[32] I attended the big, very public, mainstream camps, administered by the local Afghan government, although the trainers and students represented many countries and peoples, nearly all of whom were non-Afghanis. They were very casual camps – any Muslim off the street was welcome – and involved basic military training, namely infantry training, designed for those who wished to volunteer for Kashmir, Chechnya, or other such locations where armed forces were involved. They offered a crash-course for those with no previous experience. Because the terrorists and their very different style of training were tucked away from all this mainstream, open activity, I am not surprised in hindsight that I did not witness terrorist training, hear of terrorist activities, or any plans to commit acts of terror, including hearing about a group named al-Qaeda. Bin Laden did travel openly and visit these mainstream camps; however, he was not involved in the running of these camps, nor did he have any say on what went on in them. If he did covertly recruit from the mainstream camps, I was not aware of it at the time, nor was I aware of any small, secret camps. I do not find this surprising, because I presume the world's best intelligence was also unaware, which I suppose is how the terrorists were able to prepare undetected and commit acts of terror.

It is easy to forget in hindsight that hardly anyone had heard of al-Qaeda prior to September 11. The world learnt of this only after, though these days there are many self-styled experts on the topic. My conclusion, and I have seen nothing to the contrary, was that Bin Laden was not a leader of a global army of thousands of violent men, their tentacles stretching around the world.[33] However, the US labelled every foreigner and every camp in Afghanistan at that time as being a structured, single entity named al-Qaeda. Nothing is ever so simple.

I spent my first three weeks in Kandahar sitting around the hotel, trying in vain to arrange where and when to begin the training. In the end, I was presented with two choices: enrol in basic training first or leave and go elsewhere, which for me meant leave the country. Accepting that I had no choice if I wanted to see more of Afghanistan, I reluctantly signed up.

To get to basic training, I travelled by bus with an

assortment of other newcomers. We travelled for two or three
hours through terrain that looked as if it had undergone a torturous upheaval in the geological past. The land was littered
with tall, twisted, jagged peaks and deeply gouged gullies. It
looked like the artist responsible for this archaic landscape had
used an eon of blasting winds and torrential floods. Elsewhere,
tall, isolated peaks jutted skywards from a barren desert floor.
Their heights were uniform, as were the old eroded rings
engraved fifty metres below their summits. It was easy for my
mind to conjure up the ancient sea that once filled the plain:
the desert floor an ocean bed, the eroded rings the tide mark
and the exposed peaks islands in a shallow sea.

The camp was situated beyond a stone doorway, where a
wall of mountains parted to reveal an enclosed flat area. At the
back of the camp was a brooding stone wall, almost impenetrable except for the gullies and creeks, which glowed red as
the early-morning sun crept along its many faces. I remained
in the basic training camp for about seven weeks.

After completing that training, I returned to the hotel in
Kandahar, where I stayed for a week, eating and sleeping as
much as I could. I then returned to the camp and participated
in an eight-week mountain warfare course. When it was completed, I returned once more to the hotel. It was then that I
applied for the urban warfare course that was held in a different location, not far from the Kandahar airport outside town.
This course dealt with such situations as found in Kashmir,
where hostile soldiers would have to be evicted from an urban
environment, or when a village would need to be defended to
deter soldiers from entering.

The final course I took was in Kabul. By that point I was so
tired and fed up with training that I just wanted to go home. It

was mid-August 2001, and I decided that as soon as the course finished I would take two weeks to explore the city and then leave.

Kabul was an interesting and intriguing place – not what I was expecting at all. It was quite different from the other cities in Afghanistan – even Pakistan. It had a slightly European feel. There was a show of wealth with impressive houses built upon the sides of the large hills and mountains that surrounded the city. I had expected to see buildings displaying scars of war, but I had to look closely to see any evidence of rocket damage or bullet holes. The markets were bustling and banks operated out in the street, their stacks of money in view for all to see. Being in Afghanistan allowed me for the first time to be a millionaire – for $20 or $30 Australian you would get 1.2 or 1.3 million Afghanis, thanks to the inflation. A thick stack of notes was needed to buy a can of Coke, if you could find a can of Coke.

By the time the course had finished, I had seen more than enough of Kabul and Afghanistan to satisfy me. I had now been overseas for two years and I went about organising my trip home to see my family before returning to Kashmir. However, I had two problems: an expired Pakistani visa and no money for the return airfare. I considered asking LeT in Pakistan. I knew they could organise a visa for me, being a virtual branch of the government.

When I was personally present with LeT back in 2000 and the time had come to renew my original visa, they told me not to bother – they would sort it out the day I was ready to leave the country. I knew this to be true, because I had seen them do this for others. Being involved in Kashmir gave foreigners a lot of latitude; one did not need to produce a visa or passport to police or other inquiring bodies or have to pay road tolls while travelling. Uncertain about how I was going to return home, I decided to go back to Quetta, pay Kaleb a visit and ask LeT if they could offer any monetary assistance.

Before leaving for Pakistan, I rang Kaleb to let him know I was coming and then caught a taxi to Quetta. I had not seen Kaleb in close to a year, and it was great to catch up. It was also great to be out of Afghanistan. To hear music again and not see women shrouded from head to toe made me realise how intense it had been back in Afghanistan – the atmosphere in Pakistan was relaxing by comparison. Kaleb and I exchanged news and I told him of my intention to return to Australia. We made contact with LeT and arranged to meet with them over the next few days to discuss visas and possible airfare.

I stayed at Kaleb's the following day, watching TV while he returned to work. Coincidentally, I watched the movie called *The Siege*, about terrorist attacks in New York leading to a declaration of martial law. When it was finished, I flicked through the other channels to see what else was on. I came across footage of a plane crashing into a building, but I thought it was just another military thriller. Finding nothing to watch, I flicked back to the channel with the plane and realised it was not a movie at all, but the real thing.

I didn't know what to think as I watched the horrific events of September 11 unfold. I couldn't believe my eyes; I was in shock as I watched the Twin Towers and Building Seven fall in on themselves. In the early hours I heard commentators blame the state of Afghanistan for the terrorist attacks. One of the first Islamic political activist groups to publicly condemn the attacks was LeT. It had always rejected the ideology of terror. LeT's philosophy was expressed in a US ABC interview with then LeT leader, Professor Hafiz Muhammad Saeed, when he said, 'We condemn all acts of violence against civilians and those who commit such acts, whether Muslim or non-Muslim.

Islam does not allow the killing of peaceful, innocent, unarmed civilians'.[34]

It was a tremendous loss for those whose friends and family died that day. As a human being, I felt truly sorry for that loss. There were so many victims, and I hope for all involved that one day they will receive justice.

Thirteen

THAT NIGHT, KALEB AND I discussed how I would return to Australia. It was becoming obvious that my return home would not be as simple as it should have been. My passport and identification documents were still in Afghanistan, along with my collection of local clothing that I wanted to take back to Australia. I couldn't leave the country without a passport, so I had no choice but to go back into Afghanistan. Kaleb had heard through his contacts that the border between Quetta and Kandahar would be closed within days. The border did close occasionally, as standard policy, but for no more than a week or two, due to the amount of trade going back and forth. It was speculated that foreign nations would pressure the Pakistani government to close the border and maybe even make arrests of foreigners in border cities like Quetta, or at the least create problems for those people trying to move about between the two countries.

Because of this, Kaleb thought that it would be best if I

returned to Afghanistan before the borders closed to pick up my belongings and then wait in Afghanistan until things calmed down. We assumed that it would only take a month or so. I had also considered going into the main centres of Pakistan, away from the borders, to begin my quest for home. But that would have been difficult without my passport and other belongings that I would be leaving far behind. At least while I was in Quetta, Kandahar was only a few hours away by car. Ironically, I was too afraid of getting in legal trouble back in Australia if the Pakistanis provided me with false documents. I needed my passport back.

I regret making the decision to go back into Afghanistan now, but at the time I couldn't have known the events that were about to unfold. I went by taxi back to Kandahar. The border was closed on 12 September for most of the day, and it was very late when I arrived in the city. The hotel was shutting down, so I gathered all of my belongings, including my passport and birth certificate, and then went across the road to the school with a small group of others. The news of the terrorist attacks in the US had only just reached Kandahar, and the place was abuzz with rumours. There was confusion, no-one seemed to know exactly what had happened or who was responsible. There was no cheering or celebrations, no claims of victory. If anything, people were angry that Afghanistan was being blamed for horrendous acts that they were only just learning about a day after they had taken place.

The people around me were aware that any location within the country was a potential target for air strikes. Things had changed, and everyone's plans were disrupted by an unknown and troubling future. It was then that I first realised how serious the situation was for me and the part of the world where I found myself.

Speculation was that there would be an air campaign

but no ground assault, based on how the US had dealt with Afghanistan a few years before. People were on the move, changing location in anticipation of bombing. I had no plans and was too apprehensive to make any decision other than to stay where I was until I could learn what choices I had and where the safest place would be to wait until the chaos blew over.

As the days passed, people kept leaving the school until only a few of us remained. We knew we were expected to move on and were eventually told the school was going to close. Still, we made no effort to leave, until some time later when we were forced out. A van came to the school, its driver threw our bags into the back and ordered us to leave with him. None of us spoke Arabic, though his meaning was clear. He couldn't answer our questions asked in English, so we continued to remain in the room, pleading ignorance, until he placed guiding hands on our shoulders and directed us to the van. We were taken to a suburban halfway house where we were given three choices: go to Kabul, go to an abandoned village near the airport or go to the mountains. We all ignored this request as well.

After two or three days, an Arab man who spoke English well explained the situation. He said that many centres were closing down due to anticipated air strikes; people were moving to safer areas. We were told that the chance of a ground assault was slight and that things would resume to normal after some time. He then added that the borders were closed and no-one could get into or out of the country. He gave us a few hours to decide – or we'd have to fend for ourselves.

At first the English speakers and I, five of us in total, discussed a way we could leave the country, which seemed futile. We then discussed leaving the house. We knew the hotels had closed in Kandahar and that we had nowhere to stay. None of us relished trying to make it on our own if we remained in Kandahar, or the country for that matter, which none of us had done before. We pooled our money and discussed making a push to the border, but doubted we could find a way across. There was also talk that, since the Taliban had become preoccupied with the defence of the country, highway robbers had begun to operate again, making travel a dangerous affair. The whole atmosphere of the place had changed; nowhere seemed safe.

We thought about going to Kabul, which may have presented us with more options on arrival, but it was the last thing we felt like doing after having just travelled from there only a few days earlier. It is a long and uncomfortable two-day journey. The mountains represented hardship with little food and water, and inadequate warmth in the night. We then discussed seeking refuge in the abandoned village outside the city near the airport. This option sounded better – we would have access to food and a relative degree of comfort – and we made the collective decision to wait it out there. Still not knowing how things would play out, we placed faith in the rumour that whatever happened would blow over soon, and we chose what we thought would be the safest and most comfortable way to pass that time. As the impending assault grew imminent, none of us wanted to get involved in this conflict. I just wanted to go home.

Instead of staying within the complex by the airport, we slept and stored our belongings around the perimeter. There were horse stables nearby, and throughout the day I would ride. For eight days or more, we sat around waiting for news. Then one night, around 8 pm, I heard a strange noise above, which I knew was not the Taliban helicopters that flew occasionally from the airport nearby. I was sitting in my sheltered position, my mind still trying to decipher the sound, when the answer came as an explosion. The ground shook. Two jets whizzed by, unseen in the night sky, dropping their deadly payload. Then the airport lit up as more bombs rained down, setting off an ammunitions dump. For the remainder of the night, every hour or so, the pair of jets swept by overhead, lighting up the night as they destroyed the airport and surrounding area. I was petrified and sat tight until dawn crept over the eastern horizon, brightening the sky and ending the bombardment for a time.

In the light of the new day, I saddled a horse and rode about, inspecting the damage. Craters big enough to swallow cars pocked the landscape and jagged bits of shrapnel, their edges tinged blue from heat, were strewn about. Some of these dangerous projectiles were the size of dinner plates and could be found hundreds of metres from the craters. They would have whizzed through the night air, maiming, if not killing, anyone in the vicinity. My body was still in shock as I caught up with the others who had spent the night in nearby locations. Scared and vulnerable, we reassessed our situation. Many areas of the country had been bombed that night. As the day progressed, armed Afghanis and foreign volunteers came out to inspect the damage and view the airport, which was close to completely flattened. Once again, rumour suggested that no ground assault was expected and the bombing would only last a few days. However, the bombing triggered a new mobilisation of Afghani ground forces. It was obvious that a new phase had begun.

Some Taliban troops came to inspect the area we were in after the bombing and, although I had been worried for my safety in their company before, I used the opportunity to ask questions. We wanted to know where we could safely wait until the bombing campaign was over and, more importantly, how we could get there without any transport. We gained no information of value and resigned ourselves to the fact that we would be spending another night there. We were scared and wanted to arm ourselves in case a ground force attacked, but the troops told us we couldn't. It seemed unnecessary because there were no troops on the ground, but we all thought it would at least make us feel better, a type of false security.

We ignored what we had been told and collected what arms we could find, even though some of it was old and rusty. I also had my Kashmiri military uniform in my bag, which I now wore. The others collected what uniforms were available and also dressed themselves as combatants. Under international law, to be considered a lawful combatant one must carry arms openly, wear a uniform, fixed emblem or distinctive insignia identifiable from a distance, be subject to an internal disciplinary system, and comply with the customs and laws of war.[35] Also, if you are under a sovereign nation's armed forces, then you automatically become a POW if captured.

My decision at this point was not about supporting the Taliban – I had no allegiance to them. A survival mechanism was triggered in me: I wanted to live. When the bombs started to fall and the people of Afghanistan were being attacked, I felt I had no choice but to defend myself, prepare for the worst and hopefully make it home in one piece.

The Taliban was the sovereign ruling government of Afghanistan at the time. There were thousands of foreign combatants. Under international law they were classified as serving in 'foreign volunteer militias', such as LeT, which was not listed as a terrorist organisation at that time. These thousands of foreigners represented dozens of nationalities and languages, from organisations to freelancers. For the sake of order, the Taliban had these militias split into their language groups. Each of these language groups had leaders who took orders from the Taliban. They then relayed those orders to the soldiers under them. Because Arabic is spoken in multiple countries, that language group was the biggest. Many of the Arabic speakers had travelled widely and thus spoke the most languages and had a greater understanding of other cultures. Whenever any miscellaneous foreigners were in Afghanistan, such as Westerners, they were always placed with the Arabs because someone would eventually be found who could understand their language and background.

The planes returned as darkness fell on the second night. We huddled together, cursing ourselves for not leaving when we had the chance. We were showered with sand and small stones from the blasts. Not all bombs were delivered by unseen jets. Some were missiles that had been launched from ships or submarines off the coast of Pakistan. They streaked across the sky with fiery tails and landed with such impact that, even though some of them looked to have landed roughly two kilometres away, we were assaulted by a wall of hot air that felt as if it would strip the flesh from our bones.

With the rising of the sun on the next morning, we once again emerged from our nightly shelter: a large irrigation channel that had served as an open-air bunker. The destruction was even more pronounced, with most of the buildings now flattened. As we walked about, an unexpected cloud of dust rose into the air, followed by the now-familiar sonic boom. Terrified, we glanced up to see two low-flying jets going about their sorties in the full light of day. That was the last straw – we had to get out of there. That decision was about to be taken care of for us. Someone came over to gather all of us together. We were informed that it had become too dangerous to remain; we were going to be assigned to new locations. At the same time, all remaining undamaged vehicles were being removed from the nearby airport.

For some reason, the planes were ignoring the tanks and other clearly visible military vehicles, concentrating their fire on immobile targets instead. The new group I was allocated to did not include any of the others I had been with up until now. I was told to go with one of the tanks that was crawling its way back towards Kandahar. Halfway to town, it pulled off the main road and parked at the foot of some small mountains beside an old, abandoned village. None of the structures had roofing and some didn't even have four walls. I refused to ride on the tank, seeing that there were jets above us freely dropping bombs. I walked instead, keeping some distance between the tank and me, and caught up later on.

This new group of people consisted of six or seven young men from the Philippines and a guy in his late twenties who had recently left the Australian army. Our assignment was to make sure that nobody drove off in the tank. The location and its surrounding environs were not subjected to bombing, which was quite a relief. The bombing was either five kilometres away in one direction at the airport or five kilometres in the opposite direction in and around Kandahar itself. Unlike the last location, we now had someone who came frequently from town, who brought news, food and supplies.

The tactics of the air campaign changed while I was with the tank. First, the jets, which always flew in pairs, started to target vehicles on the road – military and civilian, including taxis. Unmanned drones began hovering above Kandahar so low they looked vulnerable to small-arms fire. Indeed, they would suddenly swoop at times, as though individuals *did* take pot shots at them. These drones obviously collected target information because, not long after they left the airspace above Kandahar, precision bombs would fall on cars within the city, and even individual people in crowded marketplaces.

The man who brought us food and news informed us that the US had recently created and backed anti-Taliban Pashtun insurgency groups in the south of the country where we were.

These groups were to be used to fight the Taliban and act as a ground assault force for the US, who had supposedly promised these groups the right to govern and form a provincial body as an incentive to defeat the Taliban. Their orders were apparently to kill all non-Afghanis on sight – a category I fitted into – regardless of who they were or what they were doing. For the first time there was someone on the ground who posed a threat and, by the sounds of it, would shoot first and ask questions later. It was unsettling, fearful information.

I managed to get hold of a radio and was able to tune in to the BBC. I learned that the Northern Alliance had stepped up its activities in the north of the country and they planned to sweep down on the capital and other centres as a ground assault force on behalf of the US. For the first time, I also heard that Bin Laden was being blamed for the terrorist attacks in the US. I do not remember any mention of al-Qaeda, and in fact the first time I would hear this word would be from the lips of an interrogator in Guantanamo.

It was now obvious that a large-scale ground assault was imminent, conducted by local groups opposed to the Taliban, not the US or its allies themselves. I spoke with the guys from the Philippines about this. They were distraught, and looked barely sixteen. They told me they were currently studying at a school in Karachi, Pakistan, and that they had come to Kandahar to visit some friends during their school break. They had been rounded up and sent out of the city at the time I had and were now trapped in the country. Recently, with news of hostile groups approaching Kandahar, they had been given arms to help protect themselves as had many others. Some of them refused to accept these weapons, while others clumsily handled them, having no knowledge or experience in such things. I felt sorry for these guys whose holiday had gone terribly wrong.

My anxiety was immense. To hear of impending doom – but

not when, where or how that doom would arrive – was unsettling. Apart from the planes above, things could have been normal. The birds still sang and the sun still shone. It was an illusion of tranquillity that drove my stress levels higher. I could hardly stand not knowing what would happen next. I had no control and felt vulnerable. It was unwise to remain where I was, to keep sitting there without preparing for the coming storm and my own possible death. I realised how easy it is for the brain to refuse to accept news it does not want to hear and pretend that what is happening all around is not happening at all. I believe we could have tricked ourselves into viewing the planes as just an unusual novelty – that all else was normal – until an attacker was on top of us with weapons pointed.

I was not prepared to sit and wait. I left the group and travelled the short distance back to Kandahar. At first I went to a hospital that non-Afghanis used, which I had heard was still open. At this location I learned of a new hotel that had opened and made my way there. I wanted to go to Kabul, but it took two or three days to find enough people heading in that direction to fill a taxi. Finally, I did. Kabul is a two-day journey from Kandahar. We were still on the road as darkness approached, hours from the town where we planned to stay the night.

Our driver grew concerned because highway robbers had been out in full force again since the commencement of the air campaign, so this threat was a new situation for me. We were following close behind another taxi when tracer rounds came out of the dark and shot across the path of the taxi we were following. The taxi in front had no choice but to stop, blocking our progress as well. The occupants of both cars got out as more fire whizzed over our heads. Some of the taxis' occupants were armed, and they attempted to fight off the would-be robbers, while the rest of us lay flat on the road. A small village nearby must have heard the firing because in a short space of time two pick-up trucks filled with Taliban fighters arrived and fought off the robbers. We were then able to recommence our travels.

Once in Kabul, I went to the hotel where I had stayed previously. It was still operating and extremely busy. I met someone there I had not seen for a long time, whom I recognised from LeT. He and a handful of others were on their way to a frontline in the far north, outside the town of Kunduz. I was curious about this because LeT was a strong opponent of Taliban policy and conflicts, despite their using the facilities and resources in the country to train, as did many other groups and individuals. They explained that, although LeT did not agree with the Taliban, they had put their differences aside for the sake of Afghanistan and its people. Unrest seemed guaranteed with the coming invasion, even an occupation was possible. They said it was not about defending the Taliban, but about the defence of the people.

Ending up at one frontline or another seemed inevitable, so I asked if I could accompany them. My reason for choosing the Kunduz frontline was because I wanted to be with my friend from LeT. I did not enjoy the feeling of being among strangers in a foreign land at war – if I was going to be injured or worse, I wanted to be with someone a little familiar. And so, within a day or two, we filled three four-wheel drives and headed north.

It was a two-day journey to Kunduz, and on arrival we went to the place where foreign volunteers gathered. The heaviest fighting had been at the next larger town to the west, Mazar-e-Sharif, and on the day we arrived it fell to the Northern

Alliance. As a result, thousands of soldiers began retreating to the city of Kunduz. The day after arriving, we travelled to the frontline, a few hours' journey to the east, positioned against a river that served as Afghanistan's northern border. It was a hilly area, but between the river and those hills was a flat, one-kilometre-wide, dusty plain. A four-wheel track traversed the plain, linking Taliban-controlled territory to that of the Northern Alliance.

The frontline began at the river's edge and headed south into the country, dividing the flat plain and then the hills. We drove along the road until the frontline prevented us from going further, then turned off the road and up into the hills. We stopped about three kilometres in from the river, at the backlines of one section where food was prepared and supplies stored. It was mid-afternoon and we were told that we would progress up to the forward lines under the cover of darkness. However, there was a heavy, sustained attack by the Northern Alliance that afternoon. As darkness fell and we were preparing to move forward, the lines collapsed and out of the dark it seemed hundreds of people were running towards us. Chaos and confusion reigned. Out of the raised voices of mixed languages I heard someone yell, 'The frontline has collapsed, run!' So I turned around and followed.

The number of people in the retreating group would have been around two hundred. Within half an hour we crossed over the hills and came down onto the flat area by the river. We found the road and followed it in the direction of Kunduz in a tight bunch. We had not been walking for long when, from behind us, in the direction of the trenches, we saw headlights approaching. This was another example of when the mind can dismiss news too terrible to accept, even though it is obvious your fate cannot be avoided. In this case, that frame of mind cost lives. Collectively, everyone ignored what those headlights portended and just kept walking in a tight-knit group. I was waiting for a reaction from the others; it was obvious that in a moment the headlights would be upon us.

No-one bothered to move until the two or three pick-ups driven by the Northern Alliance were among us, large 50 mm-calibre guns mounted on the back. They started firing randomly at point-blank range in all directions, killing many. The group suddenly snapped out of its daze and split in all directions. Everything was a blur, people firing in all directions, too confused amid the mayhem to know who was who.

The hills were about three hundred metres off to my left, and I ran to them as hard as I had ever run before. I was not the only one who chose this particular route, and a group of us ran up the first rise, down into a valley, over the next hill and down into the second valley. Some struggled; some couldn't even make it. In the shadows of a rocky outcrop, about twenty of us stopped to catch our breath and absorb what had happened. We huddled in the dark, listening to the gunfire that slowly abated. An hour later, all became silent. Around midnight, thanks to a two-way radio, we discovered that a significant number of people had regrouped another three valleys in from the road behind us. Taking a guess at the right direction, we left our position and climbed out of the valley. It was dark and eerily silent as we reached the first summit, when suddenly a jet screamed down and bombed the peak beside us. The earth shook and I squatted down for stability. The sound of the jet then faded away into the distance and silence returned.

Eventually, we reached the main group, and I was presented with a sight I would not like to witness again. I looked at the horrors of war in the face. Moans of agony helped us pinpoint the others in the dark. Slowly, I was able to make out the shapes of people sprawled about two pick-ups. However, I discovered that not all were alive as I attempted to communicate with various individuals. Others were groaning in pain from wounds that were obviously serious. Everyone had separated into small groups based on nationality and language. I went from group to group, desperately trying to find someone with whom to communicate. I was panicking and wanted to know what was happening. I was afraid we would be attacked at any moment. The worst part of the experience was the moaning and agonising cries for help. I felt terrible not being able to do anything for those who desperately needed medical assistance. The people with stomach wounds clearly suffered the most. I could only look at them, knowing that they were dying a horrible, slow death.

The only person I was aware of who could speak English seemed to have disappeared. I gave up and turned my attention towards the two vehicles. The first appeared to be undamaged. The second, when I looked at it closely, was riddled with bullet holes. I looked in the passenger window and was sickened to see a badly damaged corpse. I then went around to the other side and forced myself to look in the driver's window. There was a man sitting upright in the seat; I could not tell if he was dead or asleep. I peered through the window but could see no signs of wounds. It was dark and the dull moon cast shadows over the body. I wanted to open the door and give him a shake, to see if he would wake, but I could not ignore the number of bullet holes in the vehicle.

I had finally collided with the absurdity and cruelty of war. I saw such needless violence and waste of life. It was all too much. Despite the cold, I curled up in a hole I had roughly scratched into the soft ground and fell asleep from exhaustion. My last thoughts were of being bombed, or killed some other way, on top of that hill at first light.

Unfortunately, I could not sleep forever, pretending it was a dream. I woke with the coming dawn, the moment I most feared. Light filled the sky, exposing our position, but it also allowed me a clear look at my surroundings. I first noticed the driver still behind the wheel; my fears of the night before were justified. Then I noticed the moaning had stopped – more people had passed away while I slept. During the night the dead had been collected and placed in a long line, which comprised about thirty people, some displaying sickening wounds. I then saw that the back of the other pick-up was filled with the remaining wounded, and it was preparing to leave. Then, to my relief, all who could walk began to file out.

There looked to be about a hundred people or more who set out for the march, but the line quickly became thinly stretched into smaller groups. After about one hour, those groups became separated from one another. At first, I was in one of the front groups, comprising soldiers from Uzbekistan. As we walked along, I listened to the BBC on my radio. The news reported an eventful night: not only had our frontline fallen, but many others had as well. Even Kabul, along with all the other major centres, had been captured. Only nearby Kunduz and Kandahar in the far south remained. This meant that I could not get back to Kabul, a lifeline I did not expect to lose. I could not even get back to Pakistan, let alone home. I was trapped.

When the Northern Alliance had captured the frontline the night before, they continued to advance until they reached the first occupied villages before stopping. We knew it was going to be a two-day walk back to Kunduz, but this first day would be through an area newly captured by the Northern Alliance. We were now at serious risk.

We stuck to the hills where there were no roads for several hours, until we came upon a large plain, in the centre of which sat an expansive village. I could hear the sound of fighting in the distance. Northern Alliance troops had entered the village, and the occupants were attempting to fight them off. Because of the situation, we decided to skirt the edges of the plain and avoid the village by sticking to the foothills and the creased contours of the land. When we were about halfway around, we unknowingly passed behind a group of villagers. They were armed and had positioned themselves a little way into the hills. We were only alerted to their presence when they opened fire. They pinned us behind a slight rise, but at that stage we did not know who they were: friend or foe, armed villagers or soldiers. Some of the Uzbekistanis moved forward to have a look and reported back that they were civilians from the village. To my surprise, the rest of the people I was with just stood up and walked away from our protective cover, exposing themselves to fire. Thankfully, we were recognised, and the locals turned around and faced back into the mountains, waiting for the Northern Alliance.

The Uzbekistanis were a lot stronger than me, and after that incident I began to fall behind. For a while I was on my own. We no longer stuck to the base of the hills, instead walking openly across the plain towards the other side. I turned around, and in the distance I could see the bulk of the others starting to emerge from the hills behind. However, from the way they were reacting, it looked like they, too, were being fired upon. Before I made it to the other side, I once again disturbed another group of civilians. They had enough time to recognise me and, like the others, turned to face the other way. But then, for some reason, one of them started taking pot shots at me. I did not remove the weapon from my back but yelled out instead, making sure he could see my headwear – but he didn't seem to take notice. He was squatting, arms and weapon stabilised, a position allowing the best accuracy. He was only a short distance away with no obstacles between us. I instinctively looked behind and down and saw dirt kicking up only inches from my heels. He raised his aim, and I could then hear his rounds impossibly near, barely missing me. I began a slow jog, expecting to feel pain any moment, but thankfully he ran out of ammunition. While he was reloading I was able to put more distance between us, and by the time he was ready one of the many stragglers behind me had taken my spot in his sights. Moving as fast as I could, I did not look back to see the outcome.

I eventually made it back to the safety of the hills and stopped to catch my breath. I met others who were already there debating which way to go. I teamed up with two or three guys and spent the remainder of the afternoon journeying through a maze of hills and valleys, occasionally joining up and parting ways with other small groups. By dusk we were on another rise, at last looking down at the main road to Kunduz. The people I was with rested, but I could hear the occasional indication of fighting approaching from behind and did not want to stop. I continued down to the plain below on my own as the sun set and another night began. By the time it was dark I came to a fork in the road, and while I was deciding which path to follow a group of local horsemen appeared. They were kind enough to share their water and showed me the right direction. One road offered slim hope, the other held potential disaster. Grateful and trusting, I accepted their advice, but not long after I collapsed from exhaustion on the side of the road and fell asleep.

Fourteen

I AWOKE SOON AFTER to the rumble of a number of military trucks – it was the rescue team from Kunduz. I boarded and guzzled as much water as I could. The trucks continued a little further in the direction I had been fleeing from. At the fork in the road, a large fire had been lit, and many of the people I had spent the previous night with had gathered there. A lot of them had not made it, however. Some had been killed back at or near the frontlines, and others had been killed in the subsequent gunfire and confusion. Some had become lost, while others had become too exhausted to continue and died of various causes, such as dehydration or from being overrun by the Northern Alliance. If it hadn't been for some children who ran out from villages with bottles of water along the way, I might not have survived myself. Those of us who had made it as far as the fork in the road, however, all boarded the trucks bound for Kunduz.

Within a day of returning, the city was surrounded by the

Northern Alliance and bombs fell constantly. The US had deployed B-52 bombers in the north of the country, as well as fighter jets. It was in Kunduz that I first saw B-52s being used in the conflict. Their main targets were the defence lines that had been established around the perimeter of Kunduz. For a week I listened to the bombing and artillery on the outskirts of town and knew it was only a matter of time before the defences fell and it would all be over.

Bombs continued to fall within the city itself, forcing civilians – sometimes whole families with children and babies – to flee, carrying what few possessions they could. Unfortunately, many civilians did not make it. They were killed in their own homes or on the run. Much of the bombing was random and no place offered refuge from death above. Targeting the innocent occupants of Kunduz, as well as infrastructure, was a strategy deployed by the US to pressure the Taliban into surrendering.[36] I was outraged. What had these families done to anyone? Targeting civilians is not an uncommon technique. It is either employed directly with military might or more subtly by implementing sanctions, for sanctions always cruelly harm a nation's civilian population much more than it harms the offending government or regime. I do not understand why either technique is not officially recognised as a form of terrorism.

We moved location and were ordered not to wander about town randomly. Rumour suggested that certain individuals within the city were gathering information for the Northern Alliance on soldier positions and numbers in preparation for their assault and occupation of the city in the very near future.

It was around this time that I went to the market and bought a warm jacket. I was down to my last dollars, but I had lost my only cold-weather jacket during the earlier retreat, and a snowy winter was approaching just as fast as the impending invasion. The man who sold me the jacket, Mustafa, invited me to stay after the transaction for a glass of tea. Communicating through his nephew, Mustafa told me the takeover of the city would soon occur and I was welcome to take refuge in his home. He was afraid for my safety and said it would be the safest option. I was overwhelmed that he would put himself at risk to protect me, but many people in Afghanistan were selfless in their generosity. I didn't want to fight anyone – this was not my war – and I finally had an opportunity to get out of harm's way.

When I returned from the market, I heard that the leader of the Taliban had ordered all Taliban soldiers and foreign volunteer militias to lay down their arms. Under no circumstances were they to continue fighting within towns, villages, cities or any other built-up residential areas. This was to save lives and infrastructure. He announced that the Afghani people had already suffered twenty years of conflict. Enough was enough. This is why the Taliban, as a defending military force, seemed to disappear overnight. Negotiations between the US and Taliban forces also took place at this time. The US agreed it would stop bombing within urban areas, and the Northern Alliance would allow all Afghanis and some Pakistanis to surrender their arms and pass through the lines, providing they returned immediately to their homes. All other nationalities, however – the majority of the foreign volunteer militias – would have to surrender.

There was a dispute among the non-Afghanis on this subject on the day I returned from the market. Some were willing to surrender to a body like the United Nations or ICRC (International Committee of the Red Cross), as long as it was not to US forces. Others claimed they would never surrender but fight to the death. I was not keen on either choice. I just wanted to return to Australia and forget about the whole predicament I had become embroiled in, so I seriously considered Mustafa's offer. I returned to the markets a day later, but this time I went to Mustafa's nephew's shop instead, because he could speak a little English.

We discussed staying at his uncle's place, and I asked a lot of questions – I could not help being suspicious at first, considering the circumstances and the fact that I did not know them. When we were finished, we went to see Mustafa, whose shop was only six or seven premises away. I eventually decided I would hide in Mustafa's home until it was safe for me to leave the country. It was mid-afternoon when I left to walk back to where I was staying. I grabbed the few things I could carry in a backpack, such as my passport, identification and a few pieces of clothing. I decided I would leave my larger bags behind, for I was already wearing full civilian clothing under my military uniform due to the cold weather. I then wrote a note in English explaining what I was going to do and addressed it to the person I knew from LeT whom I had travelled with from Kabul.

At the facility's front door, I gave a guard my note, guessing that he and the person whom it was addressed to could not read English. I hoped this would give me enough of a head start before they could find someone capable of reading English and realise I had left. I didn't want them to come looking for me. I was worried about causing my LeT friend an inconvenience. I also wasn't sure if the guard at the gate would let me pass, because upon my return I heard that we had been ordered not to go out on the street any more. Fortunately, though, the guard did let me leave. I walked as quickly as I dared until I was around the corner and out of sight, then hurried to Mustafa's nephew's shop.

I arrived without incident, and was greeted by Mustafa's nephew wearing a grave expression. He stressed the seriousness of what we were doing, which did not help my nerves. He instructed me to follow him without being obvious, allowing about fifty metres between us. Keeping the requested distance, I followed him through side streets and alleys, while he had someone follow me the same distance behind. It did not take long for my guide to disappear through a front door of a whitewashed, two-storey house positioned by a lane. It was a relief to pass into the shadows of the foyer, and for the first time in a long while I felt safe and had a glimpse of hope. For days, weeks in fact, I had felt nothing but fear and anxiety. The guy who had followed me entered last and noted that we had not been followed. Only then did I relax and settle into my new lodgings.

Time passed quietly until the third night, when I was kept awake by heavy artillery and the droning sound of a large plane. It sounded as if projectiles were being fired over the top of the city. I later heard that the Pakistani government had attempted to land a transport plane to evacuate its citizens. The Northern Alliance, however, had continually bombed the airport from a distance and was successful in preventing the plane from landing. The next morning, the takeover occurred.

At about 7.30 am, I looked out of the window of the guestroom I had been staying in on the second storey of Mustafa's house and saw Northern Alliance soldiers up close for the first time.

Almost as soon as they were in the city, fighting began. I could hear gunfire from various directions around me, sometimes close, other times a number of blocks away. It would last for thirty seconds to a minute in one direction, then in another direction for a similar duration. These short skirmishes took place every half hour or so until about lunchtime. I mentally pictured Northern Alliance troops flushing out desperadoes, who quickly emptied their ammunition belts until they were killed.

I was barely able to summon the courage to look out of the

window. On one occasion I saw kids and adults down on the street. They were casually standing by the kerb, some pointing, directing the Northern Alliance to an enemy. Even though RPGs and assault rifles were being used, none of the civilians ducked for cover or even looked concerned. The sound of stray bullets scared me back from the window.

It was a terrifying time from that day onwards. Houses were searched; people were dragged out and killed. The Northern Alliance had lists of people suspected of hiding combatants or being sympathetic to the 'other side'. These suspicions were based on flimsy evidence, or none at all. Only those who sucked up to the occupying force or offered their services were immune from the violence.

In the days leading up to the takeover, jewellery stores had boarded up their windows and businesses had closed. Fathers feared for their daughters. Even my host, who was Farsi, the same ethnic identity as the occupying force, was afraid for the safety of his daughter. I heard stories that the Northern Alliance soldiers looted and took what food and items they pleased when they first entered the city. The Northern Alliance in general has a terrible reputation for violence against civilians.[37]

Within a day or two of the takeover, journalists were allowed to enter Kunduz. The marauding soldiers were made to behave and begin the business of policing and governing. Businesses slowly reopened and, despite the ominous, tense atmosphere and suspicions, the city began to operate once again. My host had taken in another combatant, an Uzbekistani, and we sat together in the upstairs guestroom. This caused some problems for our host. Someone had noticed the glow of our candle in the window during the night and inquired who was staying in the guestroom. One day, soldiers came asking such questions, but thankfully Mustafa persuaded them to leave. We could hear the yelling and arguments downstairs and were fearful that they would come up to our room, our ears straining to hear the telltale sound of boots on the stairs.

From that time on, we stayed in the main part of the house, which was very unusual for non-family members. Bizarrely, Mustafa had relatives who were officers in the Northern Alliance and part of the Kunduz occupation force. He took a risk and met with them, explaining how he was hiding us in his home. He sought protection for us and asked their advice on what we could do. They refused to help and would not agree to offer any protection. However, his relatives had given their word that the secret would remain with them.

After a week or so, when the city was firmly under Northern Alliance control, I decided I needed to leave Mustafa's home. The Uzbekistani was content to remain for as long as it took, but I was afraid for our host's safety – he was taking a massive risk by housing us and I felt guilty for eating his food. I knew he had a modest income, but I had completely run out of money. One day he went to the market with my weapon and ammunition and sold them for about 2500 Pakistani rupees, just enough to pay for a taxi and food for the return trip to Pakistan, where I would seek out Kaleb. This brave man had already risked his life and family for me, something for which I will always be grateful. I did not want to endanger him and his family another day. Mustafa did not want me to leave but, when I persisted, he invited his nephew over to discuss plans. Unfortunately, even with an interpreter, we all misunderstood each other.

I thought I was to catch a taxi with an uncle or nephew to Kabul. This family member was currently visiting Kunduz and about to return home. Once in Kabul, I would remain in his house while he organised transport to take me to Pakistan, either with him or someone else. I would then arrange my trip back to Australia. It was settled I would leave the next day.

When I first entered Mustafa's home, Kunduz was under the control of one government, and now a couple of weeks later, as I stepped forth for the first time since the takeover, the city was under the control of a new government. It might as well have been a different country. It was a scary experience as Mustafa and I walked to the taxi stand, but it was a relief to find the mid-morning streets deserted. The taxi stand was a hive of activity, however, with soldiers patrolling every corner. Mustafa kept me company for half an hour while we were thankfully ignored. He then directed me to a taxi, said good-bye and left. I was the first passenger, and for the next half an hour other passengers filled the taxi one at a time until the car was full. As each person entered, I tried to make eye contact with them, wondering which one was 'the family member'. To my horror, by the time we departed I had reached the conclusion that none of my fellow passengers knew who I was.

The next problem confronted me when the taxi reached the first town. I was expecting the car to go directly to Kabul, but when we arrived at Baghlan everyone disembarked. I realised I had to find a new taxi and start again. One of the younger passengers, who had helped me pay the taxi fare with my Afghani currency, signalled for me to follow. I was unable to figure out if he was 'the family member' because we couldn't understand each other, but I followed, desperately hoping it was him. We walked down the road to another taxi stand. He indicated for me to stay in one spot off to the side. While he went from taxi to taxi, presumably looking for one going to Kabul, an armed member of the Northern Alliance approached and attempted to engage me in conversation. Not knowing Farsi, I didn't attempt to answer him. After yelling directly into my ear, he took me by the hand and began to pull me away. I went to resist, but he made a gesture to go for his gun. I stole a glance at the young guy I had followed, who was still talking with taxi drivers. He saw what was happening and turned his back, leaving me on my own. With dread, I resigned myself to the situation and allowed myself to be led away.

This was the beginning of six years of hell.

PART
TWO

'An eye for an eye only ends up making the whole world blind.'

Mahatma Gandhi

Fifteen

'No physical or mental torture, nor any other form of coercion, may be inflicted on prisoners of war to secure from them information of any kind whatever. Prisoners of war who refuse to answer may not be threatened, insulted or exposed to any unpleasant or disadvantageous treatment of any kind.'

Geneva Conventions

THE NORTHERN ALLIANCE SOLDIER who had taken me from the taxi stand led me to a post down the street. I did not know at the time, but I was about to be sold for around US$5000.[38] It was manned by a bunch of kids who looked barely fourteen years old. I still had not spoken, but I could not hold my tongue any longer after they searched me and pocketed the little money I had. They cheekily wagged their fingers at me as I cursed them in English. After they had had their fun, my escort led me further along the street to the centre of town. We entered a rounded, glass building that seemed to operate as a police station. A number of senior officers gathered about us and began firing questions at me. A doctor was brought in as an interpreter. They wanted me to agree that I was a soldier, but I would only request to meet with someone from the United Nations or an NGO. One of the officers was furious and threw my shopping bag of belongings across the room.

They gave up after a few hours and moved me to a more permanent position in a house consisting of two large rooms. The soldiers used one room and detained people in the other. They chose to house me in the soldiers' quarters, which gave me some hope. On one occasion I was shown the prisoners in the next room – a mixed, forlorn bunch. At least half were old enough to be fully grey in hair and beard. I felt sorry for them. Several of the soldiers glowered at me; the other soldiers were fine and I did not fear any of them. It was those soldiers in whom I placed my hopes.

I spent every day waiting to be thrown into the other room as a prisoner. Yet I could not help believe that I would be allowed to move on and leave the country. On two separate occasions visiting troops left their loaded weapons in the room, leaving me alone with them for up to half an hour. As each day passed, my belief of being allowed to leave faded, but once again the mind can be stubborn with its illusory hopes. After five days or so, I was woken at dawn and told that someone from the United Nations had come to collect me and was waiting outside. For days, I knew what the outcome would be, but as I got ready I reserved hope that they spoke the truth.

My morale began to wane as I stepped outside and saw the large crowd of young men gathered on the street. I was led into this crowd and through to the centre. They parted, created a space, then hemmed me in. I had nowhere to go. In a pathetic voice, I asked where the United Nations was. A voice in English with a Russian accent answered, 'There is no United Nations.' My arms were painfully restrained from behind, bent back as far as they would go without breaking, and then string was used to tie my biceps together so that they were almost touching.

I was pushed to the outside of the crowd of people, some of whom were cursing at me, and pushed into the back of a waiting car. There were two people in the front and one in the back with me. I kept asking where we were going and what they were going to do, until a verbal threat silenced me. I then pleaded with the guy sitting next to me to loosen the string locking my arms together – I was in so much pain. I was surprised and grateful when he actually did.

We drove for about an hour to the town of Mazar-e-Sharif, the town that had been captured on the day I had first arrived in Kunduz. We pulled over somewhere in the centre of town. The front passenger got out and I watched him organise some papers before he disappeared into a building. I saw that among the papers was my passport, which I had not seen since the kids rifled through my pockets. We left this man behind and drove for a few more minutes before stopping again. This time we were in a side street, outside an unassuming rundown house. I was taken out of the car and led inside. A man opened the door to a room and I was assaulted by an awful smell unlike anything I had experienced before. It made my stomach reel. I glanced into the room and saw a sorry sight.

Eight or so men were chained together at the ankles by some heavy, rusted clasps. They were looking extremely unwell, encrusted by weeks of filth. I had one of the rusty clasps locked shut around my ankle, joining me to the human chain. After the first day, my clothes were full of lice, and I was shown the source of the stench, a smell I had become somewhat used to. One of the prisoners had a badly infected arm wound. A bullet had gone through his bicep and bone, leaving his arm attached to his body by only his triceps. What made it worse was that it had been left untreated for a week or more, exposed to the elements, and it wriggled with maggots. The poor guy kept crying every time he looked at his arm, and cursed the maggots. Within a day my dejection, fear and lack of hygiene quickly had me resembling the others.

On the first or second day, the door to the room swung open, revealing an American Special Forces soldier dressed in black. He yelled at me not to look at him and to put my hands on top of my head. He then shut the door. A short time later he was back, this time with the Afghanis who were watching over us. The Afghanis unlatched the clasp from my ankle, and the soldier ordered me to follow him. As I moved out of the room a number of other US soldiers moved in behind with their weapons drawn on me. I was led into an empty room and told to kneel on the ground with my hands on my head.

Two or three of these soldiers stood in front of me while four remained behind. They told me to take a good look at them as they displayed various weapons hanging from their mostly black uniforms. They then began launching verbal threats, scaring the life out of me. I was practically shaking by the time one of them asked the first question. I began to run through my story. I was interrupted, told I was lying and then the violent blows descended. They employed open-handed cuffs to the back of the head, but the soldiers took big swings and put a lot of force behind the impact.

At first they would let me get a sentence or two out before hitting me, but as time went on they discarded the verbal interruptions and the blows became more frequent. I kept restarting my story at their orders, but I came to the conclusion that nothing I said would make any difference – they weren't listening. This activity was purely a display of physical intimidation.

By the end, I had at least one of the soldiers behind me, striking continually with great force. I was then sent back to the other room and secured as before. It had all happened so quickly in a flurry of pain and fear. They had acted unreasonably and I was afraid they would never listen, that in their mad quest for whatever they were looking for they would end up torturing me. Back in that fetid, lice-riddled room I kept thinking of the saying, *like trying to get blood from a stone*. I was afraid of becoming that stone.

Later that day, I was taken out of the room again and led to a different part of the house. In this room, one wall was dominated by a large window with a wide sill. I was told to enter the room first, and as I did my attention was drawn to maybe six US personnel standing outside the window. Again, they were mostly in black, looking like CIA-types or at the least some brand of Special Forces. As was becoming customary, they had their weapons pointed at me through the window. A voice from behind advised me to move very slowly or I would be shot. It then instructed me to walk to the window, turn around and sit slowly on the sill with my back to the window. As I turned around I saw the voice belonged to a US soldier, unarmed I think, who sat beside me. He first told me to turn around and look out the window, to look at the weapons, pressing the point that I would be shot if I made the wrong move.

He then directed my attention to a particular soldier who was brandishing a shotgun. He said the shotgun was especially for me, that it could maim my legs or other body parts, but they would not give me the pleasure of death. Just in case I was thinking of using death as a means of escape, he added. He then offered me a cigarette. The procedure was time-consuming and nerve-racking because he kept commenting that one of the soldiers outside the window could misinterpret any move. He passed me the cigarette and then lit it, ordering my hands away. He continued with his insistence that I could be shot any time, as if the men outside were mad, trigger-happy, paranoid killers.

He produced a pen and notebook from a pocket, and I

began relating my story. This time he listened and made notes as I spoke for an hour. He then thanked me and ordered the Afghanis to take me back to the room with the others.

I think it was first thing the next morning when a group of armed Northern Alliance soldiers came and led me outside, placed me into the back seat of a car and slipped a hood over my head. We drove for a short distance to a house the Northern Alliance was using as a base. I was taken to a room. The hood was removed but two lots of cuffs, one metal and one plastic, were left on my wrists. In front of me were several US soldiers. Two remained in the background with their weapons pointed at me while the third introduced himself as Cliff. He said I was moved to this new location for my comfort and that he would be asking me a series of questions over the next few days. He also said that if anyone else attempted to question me, I must let him know. He then launched into the spiel I was coming to expect: his comrades in the background were there for his safety, they would not hesitate to shoot and they would be present at all times.

Cliff was tall, blond and dressed like all the other US soldiers I had seen so far – black uniforms, no headwear that I can remember. He showed a high level of control, which I had not seen in the others. When he said that as long as I cooperated I should not be physically hurt, I believed him . . . at least I wanted to. He began by asking about my citizenship, family, home address and other such details, then he left. The Afghanis were ordered to chain me to a table in the room, which they did. However, once the US soldiers left, the Afghanis not only unchained me from the table but they also removed all the restraints. I then guessed from some of the comments they made that they were ridiculing the US soldiers for their safety precautions.

Later, the Afghanis came into the room flustered and in a

hurry to put all the restraints back on me. They then walked out as an M16-wielding US soldier entered with his weapon trained on me. Then Cliff entered and said, 'Good news, your government has acknowledged you. We now know who you are.' He then questioned me for some time and left. After that, Cliff would come at 2 am over a few days to question me, except for one occasion when he came during daylight hours to tell me that someone else was there to speak with me and I was to cooperate. He left, and another US soldier I had not seen before entered the room.

This soldier projected a very hostile energy. With a no-nonsense attitude, he grabbed a seat and positioned it in front of mine so that we were face to face. He held a pistol in one hand, sideways, hovering out in front of his chest. His arm was not stretched outward yet he was sitting so close I could have reached out and touched the pistol. He rested an elbow on his knee. He began yelling at me in foreign languages, and he only grew angrier when I indicated I could not understand him.

The hand that held the pistol started to shake so violently that I thought he would accidentally squeeze the trigger. I knew it was loaded and the safety catch was off. He was obviously there to test my knowledge on various languages, place names, and other details that would have indicated a deeper understanding of my environment. Because I only spoke English and did not pick up on key foreign words, he was furious. I had the impression he thought I was wasting his time and that he might have even been a little insulted to have exposed himself to such an amateur as me. I was sure he was going to do something drastic, and I was so relieved when he eventually gave up and left. Cliff did not come back in and I was left in the room alone.

On a different day, I had my wrists cable-tied behind my

back and was led outside to the middle of the backyard. Two foreign white men approached from around the side of the house. One held a video recorder towards me while the other identified them as representatives of an NGO. He then started asking why I had come to Afghanistan and a few other similar questions. I could not tell if they were friend or foe until they asked my occupation and I told them that I had been a horse trainer. One answered sarcastically with a hint of anger, 'Yeah, you were training horses for Bin Laden.' They then turned the camera off and became polite, asking if I was all right and saying that things would be okay. After they had left, a Northern Alliance guard then tried to remove the plastic cuffs from my wrists but was unsuccessful. He tried using a knife but applied so much pressure that he accidentally cut my forearm. He was aggressive and didn't apologise, but I knew it wasn't intentional. It's funny in a way, because these guys had the capacity to torture – and a robust reputation for doing so – yet this man went to some effort to avoid cutting me.

Back in the room, one of them told me in English that the guys who claimed to be from an NGO had done some filming out the front before filming me, accrediting me with an array of incriminating allegations. They basically painted me as a killer and a terrorist. He also told me that the men were, in fact, American and with the soldiers. *Arseholes*, I thought. I have never heard of the tape since, despite all the investigation done on my behalf by defence lawyers, let alone the prosecution.[39]

That night I was hooded and returned to the other house. I was chained to the others as before and again became infested with lice. The same prisoners were still there, and the wounded man with the maggots had still not been treated. From my understanding, the next morning I was to be interrogated by the person who had first questioned me on the windowsill. On a number of occasions, preparations to move me were begun and then put on hold.

I was eventually transported back to the other house instead to be isolated. Cliff made an appearance and complained about the other interrogator, leaving me with the impression that two different agencies were competing to get at me. He then said he was finished with me and that I would be going on a little trip. The boys would be a little rough with me where I was going, he said, but they would be all right once they got used to me. *Great*, I thought. With the US involved, I thought I would have been treated responsibly and sent home to Australia. I expected to be treated according to the law. After all, I had nothing to hide from them and told them all I knew. So far I had been treated unprofessionally, and I now feared for my life.

Sixteen

'They will not be treated as prisoners of war. They are illegal combatants.'

George W. Bush, 28 January 2002

WITHIN HOURS I WAS HOODED and transported to a make-shift facility that the US was using within Mazar-e-Sharif. The procedure of 'hooding' consists of slipping a rough, itchy, hessian-like material, shaped like a pillowcase, over the head. Duct tape is then wrapped four or five times around the head at eye level on the outside of the bag and then another four or five times around the neck, securing the bag tightly. Even though some of the bags used were of a lighter material similar to an actual pillowcase, breathing could be difficult. This hooding occurred every single time I was transported.[40]

Once I was housed within this facility, and the hood removed, the first interrogator from the window sill incident came to see me and again asked if I wanted a cigarette. I said I did and he returned with a packet. I was sitting cross-legged on a makeshift bed while he sat on the floor with his pen and paper, his back to the wall. I was in a higher position and unrestrained. The guard with the gun was initially told to keep his aim trained on us from the outside hallway, and then eventually to be at ease – the most reasonable suggestion so far. He finished the interrogation quite abruptly around sunset, and then I was hooded and transported once more.

This time it felt like I was being moved in a van. I can say this because when one sense is taken away the other senses compensate for the loss. It is a skill that sharpens from necessity. I also believe that the heightened sense of fear complements the ability to assess one's environment, even when blinded – a true survival instinct that comes from a deep place. At first I relied on physical senses, like the sounds of conversations, which bounce off surrounding objects. Then later you begin to 'feel' different objects and their relative distances from you, and even envisage your surroundings in the mind's eye. On the other hand, that could be a sign of going mad, which is also possible.

In the van I could hear and feel a number of US soldiers seated around me. They would talk among themselves about things at home. Then they would curse at me, calling me a 'scum bag' and a 'terrorist', threatening to harm me, describing the punishment I would receive where I was going. From the time I was picked up till we reached our destination, my surrounding companions switched back and forth between these topics. We stopped and disembarked at the local airport. I felt my feet touch tarmac, and I could hear the blades of a helicopter idling nearby. I was facing the direction of the chopper and asked if I was going to board it. 'No, you're going into the kitty bag,' I think the reply was. At the least, they intimated that I would be hanging in a bag from beneath the chopper.

Unexpectedly, my feet were suddenly kicked out from under me. I landed with full force upon the tarmac. No sooner than I had time to comprehend what had happened, I realised that someone had taken hold of my head and was repeatedly ramming it into the tarmac. I think by then my body and mind were too exhausted; the beating I was getting seemed to be taking place in slow motion. It was a strange experience. It hurt, but there was no pain. It was like my body had shut down, and it was all a bad dream.

Time sped up to a more normal pace, and I felt more aware when I was picked up and literally thrown into the helicopter. I landed heavily on my side. Hands quickly worked around me. A strap was placed over my arms beneath the shoulders and across the chest. While I was still lying on my side I could hear a ratchet noise then felt the strap tightening until it pressed me hard into the floor. The helicopter roared into the air and we were off. Someone beside me took the cuffs off my wrists and replaced them with new ones, both metal and plastic. They made sure the plastic ones were very tight. I could feel fingers periodically rest on my neck and wrists, checking my vital signs. I was also given the odd slap on top of my hands. I could feel my head bleeding into the hood. Only then did I begin to feel a throbbing from the assault on the airport tarmac.

However, as time passed the plastic cuffs started to feel tighter. Soon the pain in my wrists dominated all of my senses. Eventually, I lost feeling in my hands – I could not even tell if I *had* hands, like they had been severed with a blunt knife. The cuffs were not removed until fourteen hours later.

It felt like forever until the helicopter finally landed. I was unstrapped from the floor and marched into the bowels of a large plane, which I guessed to be a C-130 Hercules. For some reason I can't remember now how I was transported in that first plane. Some incidents I remember clearly, including some things that were said to me and conversations I overheard, while other things I cannot. But I will never forget the agony of the cuffs digging into my wrists.

The plane ride was not as long as the one on the helicopter. After we landed I was removed from the plane and told to

sit in a small, open cart, like a golf buggy, and driven away
from the tarmac. We stopped briefly once; I believe we were
going through a checkpoint or gate because I heard someone
on my buggy yell to someone further away, 'We have a POW
coming through', and then more quietly, 'We're transporting
this POW.' The next time we stopped I was ordered to get out.
I was grabbed roughly, hurried inside a building and told to
stand in a hallway. This may have been the first time I was
aware that plastic cuffs were also around my ankles.

I could hear a TV in a nearby room and someone very close
to me clear their throat occasionally. I started appealing to this
unseen individual to loosen my cuffs. A male voice answered,
claiming there was nothing he could do. I continued to plead
until I pissed him off and he threatened to show me what real
pain was if I didn't stop. I stood in this place for what felt like
an hour or more, unable to sit down. At one stage, however,
the tape around my head was removed and the hood lifted up.
A water bottle was placed to my lips, and I was allowed a few
small sips. Some time later the hood and tape were completely
removed and replaced by a more conventional blindfold.

Then I was marched out onto the tarmac once again and
into the belly of another plane; it could have been the same
one, but the soldiers and procedures were different. They
placed me facedown on the floor of the plane. Once we were
in the air I could feel my body rise with the turbulence, but
then the floor would fall away and I would quickly land with
a thud. At times the floor would already be coming back up to
meet me, intensifying the impact. Generally, the fall was slight,
but on occasion the plane would drop sharply, leaving a bigger
gap and creating a more violent impact. I quickly learned to
hold my face to the side – it was less painful when my cheek
smacked the floor compared to my nose and forehead. Soldiers
were sitting on seats along the plane walls, and the one closest

to me would sometimes press his boot into my lower back and hold me onto the floor. I was grateful when he did this, he just didn't do it very often. By their whoops and yells it seemed they made sport of the turbulence. This plane, like the others I would be transported in, seemed to lack insulation. The inside temperature felt similar to what I imagined the outside temperature would be – bloody cold at high altitude. The soldiers were probably rugged up for it, but I was not. Between the turbulence, tight cuffs and freezing cold, this was a very challenging and painful experience.

By 'challenging', I mean learning the ability not to break down and completely lose hope. I was forced to mentally adapt, looking to a future time when the agony would cease while trying to ignore the pain and fear of the present. When you cannot change the situation, you have no choice but to endure. In a way, this was like mental training, which would help me later when things were much worse.

This plane trip felt slightly shorter than the one before. Once we had landed, I was picked up off the floor, marched out of the plane and straight into another waiting helicopter. I was positioned upright in an actual seat, though my hands being restrained behind my back was an issue. By now my pain was at its peak – any bumping of my arms caused extreme pain where the cuffs were. This chopper ride was the shortest trip yet compared to the three previous stages. When we landed and I was made to walk, I could see under the blindfold that the sun had risen. I could even see my own feet. I had left Mazar-e-Sharif at sunset and by the light I estimated the time now to be roughly 9 am.

They made me walk more quickly than I was able. I had to shuffle more than walk because of the short plastic cuffs about my ankles. I was watching my feet and trying to ignore the pain when they made me shuffle so fast I actually snapped the plastic. I was so relieved to hear one of my captors comment to forget about the restraint and keep going. I lifted my head enough so I could see a large, green-painted corrugated shed from under the blindfold. Along the front stood a line of armed soldiers watching me approach, a large word painted in white behind them on the wall. I suspect it was the name of the location. Unfortunately, I can only remember the first letter, 'P', but I am confident that if I saw that word today I would remember it. From memory, the name would contain between ten and fifteen letters.

I was marched into this complex and thrown upon a cement floor. A group of people approached and gave me a quick medical examination. At long last the cuffs on my wrists were cut off and I was left with only standard metal ones. I was then picked up, walked back outside, made to turn right, then walked a little further until I felt myself enter a narrow corridor and descend a flight of metal mesh steps.

At the bottom of the stairs I could hear new soldiers, and my present escorts handed me over. The door closed behind me, and I was standing in a small, empty room. My blindfold was removed and I was surprised by the size difference between the two African–American soldiers in front of me. One was nearly the tallest man I had ever seen, while the other was shorter than my 163 centimetres. I was still looking from one to the other when they yelled to pay attention and remove my clothes. By the tone of their voices, I knew they meant business, and their demeanour suggested something unpleasant was about to take place, which made the next event almost amusing. They told me they were about to take photos of me, and I said, 'What, of me naked?' For a second, I saw a softening of their hardline attitude. The short one answered, 'Nah, man. Shit, man, just of your face, man.' How could I have thought otherwise? There was an informality in his tone, like he would address a friend in this manner; I relaxed and smiled. They saw this change and quickly resumed the standard, threatening attitude and the moment passed. I was again tense and nervous.

After the photos were taken I was given a pair of blue overalls to wear. The door of the room I had been in was opened, and I stepped into a larger room with adjoining cells for prisoners. There was a large cell, which held eight or nine beds and two small one-man holding cells without beds. I was put into the larger one, where a lone prisoner was asleep. Some hours later, enough prisoners were brought in so that all the beds were taken. I was kept here for about ten days.

I noticed that the room was moving up and down; I could feel it swing about as a ship at anchor. On the outside of the cell, where two soldiers played the role of guard, and further back where a high-ranking soldier sat, I saw coffee cups with USS *Peleliu* written on them.[41] When medical staff came to treat one of the prisoners who suffered from a gunshot wound to the thigh, I saw USS *Peleliu* on their caps. None of the other prisoners would agree with me at that stage that we were on a ship, but it seemed obvious to me.

During those first days I was told I had a visitor. I was taken out of the cell and stood near where the one in charge sat. My visitor appeared and through the bars he identified himself as a member of the Australian navy. He went on to say that he was just there to confirm that I existed. He could now report back that he had seen me with his own eyes. I tried to ask him questions, but he informed me that he was not allowed to answer them and left.

The next day I was taken out of the cell, hooded, and again told someone was there to see me. As I was marched along corridors, I began to plead with the escort not to harm me and did not want any more trouble. The bastard played on my fears and said nothing to dispel my certainty that I was off to be tortured. I could feel myself shaking, and I knew he could feel that too. We entered a room and I was seated in a chair. The hood was removed and I saw two men at a table opposite. They said they were there to ask a few questions, and I relaxed, feeling foolish. They introduced themselves as ASIO (Australian Security Intelligence Organisation) employees.

I thought they were there to help, but they would not answer any of my questions or give me information about what was happening and what was to come. They spoke with a tinge of hostility in their voices as they asked the most outlandish questions: Have you ever been in charge of prisoners? Have you ever tattooed prisoners? Have you ever dismembered someone under your care and responsibility? Have you been involved in genocide or in the making of nuclear weapons? I couldn't believe the bizarre situation I was in. The questioning made me feel helpless; they are serious and scary questions to be asked in that environment. What did these people think?

I expected professionalism from my own countrymen, for them to be sensible and realistic. I had a hard time accepting that they were serious. And when I reported how I had been treated, they firmly replied that it was not their business – they were only there to collect information on the many evil crimes I had committed.

Devastated, I was returned to the cell, only to have to repeat the procedure the next day. I was absent-minded and depressed during that next interview. A bad dream was becoming a reality. The abuse, the threats, the asinine questions, the indifference of my own government's representatives when I mentioned the mistreatment, the feeling that no-one could

help me or really cared – it was all a horrible, daily reminder
of this bizarre new life forced upon me.[42]

One of the other prisoners was an American, another was
from Saudi Arabia and the rest were Afghanis. Apart from
the American and one Afghani, the rest did not speak English. While on this ship, we were given numbered wristbands
for identification. We must have been the first, because the
American was 001 while I was 002. One day an Afghani was
moved to one of the small holding cells. Only the front wall
of the cell was made up of bars; the other three walls were
sheetmetal. Once the Afghani was placed in there, a blanket
was hung up over the bars so we could not see him. Not long
after, four or five soldiers entered the outer area. They made a
great show of putting on plastic gloves, stretching and letting
them go so that they snapped into place. Then they entered
the cell. Because we could not see what was happening behind
the blanket, the rest of us in the larger cell listened intently. At
first we could hear voices spoken in a normal, conversational
tone. As the minutes passed, those voices were raised in anger.
Then the banging started. It sounded like an object – a head,
perhaps – being rammed against the metal wall. These thuds
were followed by pained cries, we assumed of the Afghani.
This went on for some minutes, and it was horrible and sickening to listen to his screaming, loud and eerie in that cavernous
chamber. I am sure the other prisoners shared my thoughts:
when will it be my turn? The soldiers emerged from behind
the blanket wearing satisfied expressions. A short time later,
the Afghani was sent back to the larger cell with us. He displayed no visible marks of abuse, unless they were hidden by
his clothing. However, the man was a mess. I had never seen a
person so scared or heard a fellow human being cry out with
so much anguish. He was teary and whimpering, flinching at
the slightest motions. The other Afghanis attempted to speak

with him, but he did not reply. He curled up into a ball and fell asleep. I felt so sorry for the broken man, but I was also scared for myself, as I'm sure everyone was for their own safety.

Then, within the day, they took the same Afghani out and performed the whole routine all over again. This time he was kept in the solitary cell overnight, where he had been beaten, before he rejoined us. Again, there were no visible marks on him. Then it was someone else's turn. The lone Arab was moved to the holding cell and, as we feared, the plastic-glove-wielding soldiers entered the brig and disappeared behind the blanket. There was a lot of banging against walls but not a sound from the prisoner. At one stage a soldier came out and grabbed a chair with anger and re-entered. The noises of objects being struck against metal and the angry voices of the soldiers reverberated loudly. There was no escaping that dreaded racket – yet we never heard the prisoner. The soldiers came out looking angry, a different expression from when they emerged after dealing with the Afghani. They left him in there overnight, and a day later the terror started all over again. It is as if you are the one being beaten when the torture is happening to a fellow prisoner right next to you, and there is no reason to believe that you will not be next.

During one of those occasions, the officer came over to the bars near the American prisoner and said, 'Don't worry, that won't happen to you. You're an American.' The high-ranking soldier, I do not remember his exact rank, was the same one who escorted me on both ASIO visits. During his shift he would point his pistol at us from his chair in the outer area. He would act as if he had fired it and silently mouth the word 'pow'. I assume the gun would have been empty and the safety on. He was just a young smart-arse, but that doesn't make it all right.

To be clear, the one Afghani and the Arab were the only two who were beaten aboard that particular ship. Neither I nor the others were physically beaten while I was aboard the USS *Peleliu*.

One day, as I was sitting with my back up against the cell wall, I noticed one of the marines who was to keep an eye on us had a pack strapped to his back as he paced the outer chamber. I further noticed a thin hose protruding from the base of this pack, which rested in a position for quick and easy access. I was such a frightened mess by this stage that I was horrified that the pack contained a harmful liquid, to be sprayed on us at any moment. All I could think was, *What now? What next? What will that do to us?* How relieved I was, despite feeling completely foolish, when, after hours spent staring in fright at this new stratagem, I watched the marine take a casual sip from the end of the hose. I had never seen a CamelBak before.

After about ten days, extra soldiers came down to the brig and laid out enough hoods for the seven of us. We were called out one at a time, had those horrible plastic cuffs fastened on our wrists and the hoods taped onto our heads. When it was my turn, I pleaded with the soldier who was about to apply the cuffs not to put them on so tightly. He put the first one on loose but unfortunately secured the last one tight. He then picked up the hood. I felt it slide down over my head. It suddenly became dark, my vision restricted to the inside of the bag, and my ability to hear became slightly muffled. It's always a little bit scary when you take those first few blind steps, being led and having to rely on hostile people.

With my whole world reduced to the few centimetres of space inside the hood, I was made to climb a number of stairs. When I stepped outside, my 'personal space' brightened a little and I could feel a breeze tugging at my overalls and hood. I could even smell the fresh air as it permeated the fabric about my face. I then stepped up into a helicopter with three of the other prisoners. We flew for only about fifteen minutes and landed on the deck of an aircraft carrier called the USS *Bataan*. I was glad for the short flight because my right wrist was beginning to hurt from the plastic cuff again. We were marched down ramps in single file, and I could feel a huge space around me, unlike the *Peleliu*, which was always cramped. Eventually, we began to navigate corridors, bringing us to our destination. We were placed together in the one cell, very similar to the previous ship. The first thing I noticed was the sound of aircraft landing and taking off above our heads. There was also a speaker on the wall, constantly announcing information about what was happening aboard the ship. It didn't take them long to turn it off once they realised we were listening.

I found the diet aboard this ship difficult. Three times a day, we were served literally a handful of rice and five or six single, purple grapes. Not long after our arrival, we were made to strip naked as a group and form a line outside the cell. We were told that a doctor wanted to examine us one at a time. As he did, he declared the most ridiculous conclusions into a hand-held tape recorder.

For example, one of the Afghanis had a prosthetic limb and was overweight. The doctor's conclusion was that he was a very important figure, 'a big fish', and that he had abused his power and oppressed others in order to live a life of luxury, thus explaining his weight – not that having one leg for many years probably prevented him from exercising. Another Afghani had an old immunisation scar on his shoulder. He explained to the doctor that an international aid organisation had given all the children in his village a common vaccination about twenty years before. Instead, the doctor dictated into the tape recorder that this individual had left Afghanistan in recent years to receive an injection in Iraq that would help immunise him from biological weapons – a shame that the poor guy had never left his village, let alone the country. From my naked body he somehow reached the conclusion that I was a leader.

I was interrogated aboard this ship once for a brief period by an American in civilian dress. He was interested in the detained US citizen. Because I did not know him, the interrogator asked what he had spoken about over the last two weeks while we had been incarcerated together. He even had the nerve to ask me to put certain questions to the American and report back to him, which I didn't do. I did not see that particular interrogator again, anyway.

After a few days another lot of hoods were laid out. I interpreted this to mean we were about to be transported again. I counted them and concluded that one of us would be staying behind. That prisoner turned out to be the US citizen. The rest of us were hooded and restrained as usual and led up the stairs to the deck of the ship.

We were again split between two helicopters and flown back to land, about twenty or thirty minutes away from the ship. We landed at an airport, but I didn't know where. We were then led into a large, empty hangar. From listening to the others and from where the soldiers barked orders, I knew we had been positioned in a large half circle, and I had been placed at one end. We were made to kneel and lean slightly forward, though at other times we were able to sit back on our haunches. Our hands were restrained behind our backs.

As I have said previously, when robbed of your vision, all your other senses are heightened. I heard a thud and one of us, about four along in the half circle, moaned from the blow. Then someone closer to me gasped; then I was struck in the back of the head. It was unexpected and powerful. I received a few more hard blows and could hear the others being struck as well. These blows were serious, much more aggressive than my earlier experience in Mazar-e-Sharif. Numerous cameras took photos continuously, the flashes lighting up the inside of my hood. They held weapons while they placed a foot on my shoulder, posing as if for a hunting trophy shot. Unseen hands delivered open- and closed-fisted blows to the back of my head. Boots executed multiple kicks to my thighs and my back. Many of them spat on my back and into my hands, which were crossed over each other behind me.

I was called a 'kangaroo fucker', a general US slang expression for an Aussie. Others verbally threatened to rape me, while one African–American said, 'You're fucking with a New Yorker now.' It was very hard to endure. I had to gather every ounce of willpower not to feel the pain, yet at times I felt dazed and unaware of what was happening, pain translating into a numbing throb in some distant background.

This went on for an hour or two until it sounded like only one soldier slowly walked around us, whereas before there seemed to have been quite a few. Sometimes he would sneak up on me so I could not hear him, and then I would receive an unexpected vicious blow. At other times only a boot or hand striking one of the others, followed by a groan, would give away the soldier's position. A hand would occasionally slap down, gripping my thigh, and violently spin me so I would face another direction, making it very hard to visualise my surroundings. I would become disoriented. Other times he would walk heavily, and hit us so hard that it was impossible not to make some noise, whether a yell, moan or expulsion of air.

Each prisoner made a different noise when struck, and I could hear the soldier approach me along the half circle until I was hit. Then the distressed chorus would travel back away from me. I desperately attempted to detect the soldier's whereabouts, and dreaded the sound of his approaching boots. I would hear them stomp in my direction and stop right in front of me. I would brace myself to receive the blow, which would be delivered instantly before he stomped off.

One of his other intimidation methods was to approach loudly and stop next to me. My ears strained at the silence while I remained tense, but he was patient because the blow would come just as I allowed myself to relax, thinking he had snuck away. Then there were times when he did just that. I would be waiting anxiously for the blow, thinking he was standing beside me, but I would hear one of the others receive it instead.

During one of the quieter times, after I had been kneeling there for around three to four hours, I heard what sounded like multiple helicopters landing outside the hangar. After the blades had wound down to neutral, I heard a small group enter the hangar amid whispers, murmurs and shuffling feet. At first they stood just within the entrance, but then walked directly towards me. It was a horrible feeling to hear them all stop right behind me. I was nudged in the back of the head with what felt like the butt of a rifle – it then slammed into my head so hard that I fell forward onto my face. I picked myself up and was knocked down to the ground a second time. The third time I rose I heard the group turn around and walk back out the way they had entered, not bothering the other prisoners. The blades picked up and I heard the helicopters depart.

Sometimes the abuses were more ferocious when several soldiers were involved, and would then settle back to the more stealthy techniques when only one soldier was overseeing us. This treatment must have gone on for about seven hours. It felt like I had webbed fingers by this stage because of all the spit that had accumulated and dried there. They had also been rubbing spit into my back and hood. I was picked up, led outside into the sun, pulled to a stop and had the tape removed from around my neck. The hood was lifted and someone shoved a water bottle into my mouth. The tape was removed from around my eyes and the hood was lifted even further so that I caught a glimpse of a few soldiers.

I was told to 'look down' and 'piss into the hole'. I saw that I was standing at the edge of an earthen well. Once I had finished, the hood was again fitted and I was taken to a building across from the hangar. We were walked through a back door and to the front of the building, so that the tarmac was just outside the room, and individually seated around on the floor. The abuse wasn't as intense in this spot: the odd kick to the thigh, being spun around and disoriented. At one stage I heard a male soldier saying, 'He's all over the media,' and I had a feeling they were talking about me. Then he said, 'Let's have some fun with him.' A female answered in a very sarcastic voice, 'We can't, the Geneva Conventions . . .' I was grateful to hear that answer, but dumbfounded at the request. *Haven't they done enough?* I thought. After what I had experienced so far, I hated to think what they would have done with me had I been singled out for 'special treatment'.

We were probably in this room for an hour when I heard a large plane land and taxi up to our building. I heard one or two of the other prisoners being moved before I was also yanked up and dragged along. I was led right to the plane, the noise of the engines was deafening, and I felt the steps leading up in front of me. I was directed around to the other side of the plane instead, and put into a helicopter. I was too confused to know if any of the other prisoners were with me.

We did not fly for long before we landed and I was led down a flight of stairs. I couldn't believe what I saw when the hood was removed: I was back in the USS *Bataan* – the same cell – and all the others were there as well. Our blue overalls were covered in fine, white dust from when we had been knocked to the ground. We were bruised and bloodied and looked a general mess.

I was infuriated at what had taken place – and only to end up back where we had started. They did not mind telling us the time on this ship, so I knew we had left about 10 am, and we now returned at around 8 pm. If you subtract an hour for travelling, it meant we had been beaten and taunted for about nine hours. The doctor just happened to be there, and I was very vocal about what had been done to us. He didn't care and refused even to give me any pain relief – not even a Panadol – to ease the pain in my head. I continued to protest to the soldiers guarding us about what had happened until they punished us all by refusing to feed us until I shut up. The other detainees told me not to worry about it, let it go.

I made sure the American prisoner heard all the details of what he was lucky enough to have missed out on. He had actually received a letter from his lawyer, which was news to him. His parents had arranged it and said they were working on his behalf. Again, I kicked up a fuss, demanding that I also be given access to a lawyer, but they just ignored me, saying something about not being an American, and threatened to punish us with food deprivation again unless I dropped the subject. This rage and bout of defiance was good: it gave me some strength and an ability to endure the injustices that just kept on coming. It was the first time I had truly stood up for myself and found courage during this ordeal – but it would not last for long.

Within no more than two days, the dreaded hoods were laid out once more. It was déjà vu: we were escorted up to the same deck and boarded helicopters as before. To my horror, we even landed at the same air base and were taken into the same hangar. This time as I entered, an unseen fist struck me on the right side of my face. I thought, *Great, it's begun before*

I've even been made to kneel. I was placed in the same position within the half circle. The abuses dished out on us were
also no different from before, except we only suffered through
about five hours instead of nine before we were moved to the
next building. The plane landed and taxied to where we were
being held and, as before, I was marched to the base of the
boarding stairs. This time, however, I was actually taken up
the stairs and into the plane.

I was made to sit on the floor with my legs stretched out in
front of me. A rope was tightly wrapped around both my biceps
and then tied to the upper arms of detainees on either side of
me. Other ropes or straps were then used to fasten me to the
floor. I could tell that there were quite a few other detainees
around me. Some of them would complain in English about
the cold until I heard a boot or hand lash out and an angry
order to shut up. The plane landed for two or three brief periods, taking some detainees off and bringing new ones aboard.
I later learned that one of those stops was Bagram Airbase.

We had left the unknown airfield where we had been beaten
while it was still light, possibly late afternoon; we landed at the
Kandahar airport around 3 am – though I had no idea at that
time that it was Kandahar.

Seventeen

'A place [where] even dogs won't live.'
  Interrogator describing Guantanamo to a detainee in Abu Ghraib

BEING UNLOADED FROM THE PLANE was a tricky operation. I soon discovered that I was still bound to two others, and we were only a small link in a long line. As we shuffled blindly across the tarmac in the rain I listened to guards screaming orders while moving from one end to the other. I estimated the length of the line and guessed that there were about thirty of us marching in single file. Some of the detainees were exhausted and collapsed to the ground, pulling two or three others down with them from either side. The rope then tightened, digging deeper into the others' arms. Unfortunately, this happened numerous times, making the walk slow and painful.

Once we were off the tarmac, we were made to lie face-down in the cold, wet mud. We were tied together by the upper arms. Our hands were restrained behind our backs with both the plastic and metal cuffs, and we were ordered to hold our fingers out flat. A soldier then stepped from one lower back to the next, placing his full pressure on our hands. He yelled that if we held them correctly there would be no pain, but if we curled our fingers or made fists then we could only blame ourselves.

He was right about that. However, as the cold seeped in and the cuffs became tighter, I started to lose feeling in my hands and could not tell if my fingers were curled or not until he stepped on me – and it was painful. I was kicked a number of times in my hands and yelled at to hold them out flat. I felt a sharp, shooting pain as my right hand fractured under one of their heavy boots. I could hear a very vocal smart-arse kid who sounded too young to be in the army. He never shut up, hitting us on the head with a piece of hollow plastic pipe. Other soldiers went about yanking on the rope between our arms.

This walking across our backs and hands, among other things, continued until light began to fill the sky. I was the first to be lifted out of the mud by two soldiers with great urgency. They were yelling and extremely hyper, carrying me away hurriedly, stopping once to throw me on the ground, yelling things I could not understand. It all happened so fast; I was confused and disoriented, which I'm sure was their aim.

After being dropped, I was picked back up and carried to a covered area. Without removing my restraints, the overalls were ripped and cut off me with scissors in a quick, skilful manner. The hood was removed and I saw that I was standing naked in front of a large group of people in civilian dress. Most of them seemed to be pointing cameras and taking photos. A soldier screamed a bunch of questions, roughly removed the restraints, told me to put on a new pair of overalls and then secured the restraints once more. I was made to run, ripping the skin off my ankles, to a hangar where I was placed without restraints into one of eight cells made of razor wire. I was alone in the razor wire cage; but some cages within the same hangar contained half a dozen prisoners. At each end of the hangar US soldiers armed with M16s kept watch from elevated platforms.

I was actually glad to be here – out of the rain, limbs free – and I could rest in any position I wanted. I was exhausted, having been on the move for a day and a night. I slept until lunch, when I was woken by a ration pack thrown into my enclosure. The word MRE – Meal, Ready-to-Eat – was printed across the front of the plastic wrapper. I read what the package was meant to contain (black bean burrito, minestrone, pasta, etc.) and found that the single-use heater and at least half the food items had been removed. I would eat a lot of MREs in the future, and they were only ever half full.

No sooner had I finished lunch than I was ordered out of the enclosure. I was partly restrained and blindfolded and made to join a long line of prisoners. It was demoralising to half stand and half crouch with chests to backs and bums to crotches. There was no space between any prisoners. We were ordered to shuffle along as one body – move, then stop, move, then stop. It was weird and seemed to have no purpose. Suddenly, a soldier yelled, 'Where's kangaroo?' Guessing it was me, I stuck my head up and heard, 'Go get him.'

I had my arms stretched up behind my back and was made to run as fast as I could with ankle restraints across an open area. By the outside of a long tent, my overalls were once again cut straight off me with a pair of scissors. They shaved my head and removed all my body hair with razors. The recently shaved areas were sponge-washed with a whitish liquid in a silver bowl. Next, I was escorted into the tent, still naked. Every few steps into the tent, a US soldier was doing something to a detainee, and I could see detainees exiting at the far end. It was like a production line.

I was pushed towards the first of these medical personnel, subjected to general inspection and examination, then moved along to the next station. I also saw a Northern Alliance soldier who was playing the part of translator. Three-quarters of the way down the tent, I was bent over and held down by the two soldiers who were escorting me. The soldier at this station held a large piece of white plastic and shoved it up my anus. As this was done, I heard a nearby soldier say, 'Extra-ribbed for your pleasure.' Years later my defence team was told that this practice was standard operating procedure but offered no further explanation when the lawyers requested a reason for this demoralising and pointless action.[43]

Eventually, I stepped out from the other side of the tent and was given orange overalls to wear instead of blue. The Arabs in this prison camp were convinced that the orange meant they had been selected for execution, as is the practice in some Middle Eastern countries. For the US, orange was just a handy coincidence, but the chain of command were delighted to learn this information and used it to their maximum benefit. Throughout the day I heard the occasional grenade-sized explosion just outside the camp perimeter. When this happened a soldier would yell, 'There goes another of ya buddies.' The ICRC later told me that the military was staging mock executions, convincing a large number of detainees that they were randomly taking prisoners outside and killing them. This was no half-hearted game – they treated it as a serious and purposeful operation.[44]

Once I had the overalls on, painted-over ski goggles were placed on my head instead of the hood. Then industrial-style earmuffs were fastened over my ears and orange oven mitts taped onto my hands. I was then made to sit on the ground, all rugged-up, and wait. I sat there for a few hours until my goggles, mittens and earmuffs were removed. I was escorted through the camp, able to see for the first time. My escorts sat me down next to three civilians, and I felt such joy to see the

ICRC identification on their shirts. They recorded everything that had happened to me up until then and said they were working on improving the way detainees were being treated upon arrival. They told me I was at the Kandahar airport, which was a huge surprise. Up until then, I did not know where in the world I was, thinking I'd left Afghanistan far behind. Our fifteen-minute chat finished with their registering me into their system as a prisoner of war, which they said would help prevent me from 'disappearing'. An identification number was written on a card and placed in my pocket. Then they took my family details and mentioned that I would be transported out of the country but they did not know where. (They really did know, but were not allowed to tell me, I later found out.) I was led back to my waiting spot and saw there were twenty or thirty other detainees spread around me. The soldiers rugged me up with all the sensory deprivation accessories – goggles, earmuffs, mittens – and I again waited.

After nightfall I was moved and told, because I understood English, that I would be leading a line of restrained detainees. It was cold and windy as we shuffled along in the dark. I concentrated on the voice giving orders, but it became more difficult to hear him as we approached a nearby plane, its engines roaring. I was led up a ramp and, surprisingly, pushed into a real seat. I was restrained, but not as painfully as I had been on past flights. Listening to the noises about me, I learned I was in a row of chairs arranged down the length of the plane. There was another row between me and the wall behind. During the flight I was kept restrained and blindfolded, taken to a toilet and fed the odd peanut butter sandwich.

We flew for a long distance and landed in a cold location, so I guessed we were still in the northern regions of the globe. We changed planes in this location, and when the soldiers handed me over to new escorts, I heard one of them say, 'Shit, he ain't six-foot-four, he's four-foot-six!' I had heard other similar comments and was wondering what rumours were circulating about me. Back at the airport, I had heard a soldier ask another, 'Have you seen his file?' in a tone that suggested my file was some damning, over-embellished document, more closely resembling Hollywood than reality.

The next leg of the trip was so long that I fell asleep a number of times and guessed we had been in the air long enough to have made it to the US mainland. I was awake but extremely exhausted when the plane began its descent, when, without warning, a needle was stabbed into my thigh through the overalls. I learned later it was morphine intended to disable us for the coming landing, and it exaggerated my exhaustion to near delirium.

Winter was just beginning in the Northern Hemisphere, so I decided that if it was cold upon landing then we were probably in the US. So I panicked when the door of the plane was opened briefly and I was hit with a wall of humid, tropical air. I had the sudden, terrifying thought that the military must be making us 'disappear' into the jungles of Central America.

A short time after we had landed, a soldier said angrily, 'What did you do it for?' I knew this disembodied voice was probably addressing me, though I hoped not. He asked, 'Was it for the money?' Then he pulled my goggles away, and I could see he was wearing a black beret and he said, 'Don't you forget this fucking face!' He then stared at me, as if undecided on what to do. He grunted and snapped the goggles back onto my face.

We all remained in place for an hour or so before a voice boomed over a megaphone: 'You are now the property of the US Marine Corps. You have reached your final destination. Welcome to Cuba.' I'm told I remember the last sentence incorrectly – that it was never spoken – but I swear I heard it. Those words are burned into my brain. It also made sense because of the humidity. After the announcement it was quiet in the plane, which made the next thing that happened all the more dramatic. The door opened with a boom, and in flooded a racket of screaming soldiers and barking dogs.[45] The bright glare of spotlights wove through the hold. With a sigh, I felt myself taken out of the plane and into the centre of the chaos.

I must have passed out because I was then transported by both ferry and bus, but I have no recollection of any of it what-soever. When I came to, I was kneeling and leaning forward, trying hard to keep my balance. Someone kept hitting me in the back of the head and yelling, 'Head down!' At times I was so groggy and weak that I could not tell what position I was hold-ing my head in, and I kept being hit for not following orders. I was not allowed to sit on my haunches, so my thighs and knees had to take the full weight as I leaned forward on sharp gravel. I had to fight to keep from falling forward. Whenever my legs gave way and my backside came to rest on my feet, I was hit and screamed at until I sat up again.

I was eventually made to get up and move, and I was taken through a medical tent. When my blindfold was removed briefly, I saw a sticker on an X-ray machine that read 'Cuba'. I was then led to a little wire cage, where I would live for the next three months. I was so out of it and disoriented, my state compounded by the effects of the bright floodlights and lack of stars, that I could not tell if I was in a large, covered area or actually outside. These were my last thoughts as I passed out for a much-needed sleep.

Eighteen

'We have indicated that we plan to, for the most part, treat [the prisoners] in a manner that is reasonably consistent with the Geneva Conventions, to the extent they are appropriate, and that is exactly what we have been doing.'

Former Secretary of Defense Donald Rumsfeld[46]

'See, in my line of work, you got to keep repeating things over and over and over again for the truth to sink in, to kind of catapult the propaganda.'

George W. Bush

I AWOKE ON A CONCRETE SLAB with the sun in my face. I looked around and saw that I was in a cage made out of cyclone fencing, the same as the boundary fence around my old primary school. Internal fences divided the cage into ten enclosures, and I was in one of the corner-end cells. Around me, I saw five other concrete slabs with what looked like birdcages constructed on top. A fence covered in green shadecloth and topped with rolls of razor wire was wrapped around these six concrete slabs, able to house sixty unfortunate human beings. Hanging on the inside of this fence were signs saying, 'If you attempt escape, you will be shot', complete with a featureless person with a target for a head.

All around the outside of the shadecloth, civilian and uniformed personnel cleared and flattened grass and trees. They
poured cement and assembled the wire cages, calling them
'blocks'. There was nothing much else around us except guard
towers boasting large, painted American flags and manned by
armed marines.

My block was only the second to have been built, but that
would change over time. As this prison grew out of the grass,
more 'detainees', as they liked to call us, rather than POWs,
arrived. About a month later, around three hundred and sixty
of us lived in these outdoor enclosures. They were open to
the wind, sun, dust and rain and offered no respite. The local
wildlife was being disturbed as their homes were bulldozed
to make room for the concrete blocks, and scorpions, snakes
and nine-inch-long tarantulas tried to find shelter in what were
now our enclosures.

My cage, like all the cages, was three steps wide by three
steps long. I shared this space with two small buckets: one to
drink out of, the other to use as a toilet. There was an 'iso-
mat' (a five-millimetre-thin foam mat), a towel, a sheet, a
bottle of shampoo that smelt like industrial cleaner, a bar of
soap (I think), a toothbrush with three-quarters of the handle
snapped off and a tube of toothpaste. When I held this tube
upside down, even without squeezing, a white, smelly liquid
oozed out until it was empty.

This bizarre operation was called Camp X-Ray. Our plane
was the first to arrive on this barren part of the island, and we
remained the only detainees for the first three or four days. We
had been spaced apart because of the surplus of cages. Every
hour of the day and night, we had to produce our wristband
for inspection, as well as the end of our toothbrush, in case we
had 'sharpened it into a weapon'. These constant disturbances
prevented us from sleeping. We were not allowed to talk, or

even look around, and had to stare at the concrete between our legs while sitting upright on the ground. If we did lie flat on the concrete, we had to stare at a wooden covering a foot or so above our cages, which served as some type of roof. Apart from blocking the sun for about two hours around high noon, the roof offered no other benefit.

Sitting or lying in the middle of the cage, away from the sides, were the only two positions we were allowed to assume. We could not stand up unless ordered to, while the biggest sin was to touch the enclosing wire. If we transgressed any of these rules, even if innocently looking about, we were dealt with by the IRF team, an acronym for Instant Reaction Force.[47] The Military Police (MP) nicknamed this procedure being 'earthed' or 'IRFed', because they would slam and beat us into the ground.

I first witnessed the IRF team a day or two after my arrival. An MP stopped outside the cage of an Afghani, my closest neighbour at the time. He was the detainee with the prosthetic limb, who had been on the two ships with me. The MP demanded to know what the Afghani had scratched into the cement. He had not scratched anything and could not even speak or understand English. I heard the MP read, 'Osama will save us.' The detainee had no idea what the guard was on about, yet the MP was furious when he did not respond. 'I'll teach you to resist,' the MP threatened and stormed off. Suddenly six MPs in full riot gear formed a line outside his cage. The first one held a full-length shield. He entered the cage first, slamming the detainee, pinning him to the cement floor with the shield, while the others beat him in the torso and face. The last to enter the cage was a military dog handler with a large German shepherd. The dog was encouraged to bark and growl only centimetres from the Afghani's face while he was being beaten. In later cases, the dogs bit detainees.[48]

When they had finished, they chained him up and carried him out. His face was covered in blood. A few hours later an MP washed the blood off the cement with a scrubbing brush and hose. To add to that injustice, an MP told me some weeks later that he himself had scratched that statement into the cement before any of us had arrived at Guantanamo, while they had been training and awaiting our arrival.

Every two or three days another planeload of detainees would arrive. They were always made to kneel and lean forward on the gravel while being yelled at and struck in the back of the head. They had to balance in this position while one detainee at a time was picked up from the line, escorted into a block and deposited into a cage. Those who were moved first were lucky not to have to endure the stress position for hours. When all the cages in our block had been occupied, detainees began to fill the other newly built blocks around us.

It was around this time that helicopters hovered above and very large groups of civilians walked through the camp to view us in our cages – specimens in an international makeshift zoo.

The first two weeks of Camp X-Ray was a blur of hardships: no sleeping, no talking, no moving, no looking, no information. Through a haze of disbelief and fear, pain and confusion, we wondered what was going to happen. To pass time and relieve the pressure on my ailing back, I chose to lie down rather than sit up. During the day I would look slightly to my right, focusing my vision just beyond the wooden roof, and lose myself in the sky beyond. It was an escape, so peaceful, so blue and full of sunlight. I gazed at the odd cloud and spied big, black birds circling high above, called vulture hawks. It was never long, though, before a hostile face blocked the view, screaming, 'What are you looking at? Look up at the roof.' All I could do was sigh and avert my gaze from the infinite, blue sky to a piece of wood.

I noticed after my arrival in Guantanamo that the guards took a special interest in me. I soon learned what the curiosity was about. MPs would come up and ask questions like, 'Are you an expert in multiple martial arts?' Another would ask, 'Are you an expert in small-arms weapons?' Am I this? Am I that? Others would walk past, winking and saying, 'You're hardcore; you're high-speed,' and other such nonsense. They should have been embarrassed, approaching me googly-eyed, clearly believing what they were asking. I was dumbfounded and asked where they had heard such rumours. 'I've heard about you . . . Our superiors inform us during our briefings . . . I read about you in *Soldier of Fortune* magazine.' Someone was filling these soldiers' heads with nonsense, which showed in various ways. Some were scared, some were in awe, and in those early days many thought that their government had captured hard-core professional terrorists responsible for the tragic events in the US. The main theme preached about detainees, especially me, was to be wary.

Though they had fooled their soldiers into believing such things, as time passed the guards began to doubt what they had been told. From what I observed over the years, the higher-ups went to great lengths to preserve their troops' cautious frame of mind, but it was a campaign in which they were never fully successful. I believe they were concerned that their troops could relate more easily to me, an English-speaker, than to other detainees, which would erode the layers of propaganda when they realised not all was as they had been told. I believe this was why I was being singled out and attributed the most elaborate claims. If the MPs were afraid of me, they would be less inclined to let their guard down and chat. They were also told in their briefings that we detainees were experts in psychological manipulation and expert liars – if they engaged us in conversation, we would be able to convince them of our innocence, extract information, manipulate them into doing our bidding and, most dangerous of all, talk them into opening our cage doors so we could kill them. Every day these impressionable minds were told we would kill them the moment we had our chance, that we were lethal. Beware the detainees!

Amusing as such stories may be, there were two rumours circulating that I took personally. During their briefings, MPs were told that 'the Australian mercenary' had promised to kill an American before he left Guantanamo. No matter how many times I told inquiring guards that it was not true, they still believed I was drooling to murder them. To back this up with an example of how 'dangerous and capable' I was, the top-brass also invented a story about how I escaped out of my handcuffs on the plane between Afghanistan and Cuba, while we were over the ocean, and tried to bring the plane down by chewing through electrical wiring. When I asked an interrogator about this fabrication he actually produced a news story reporting the same thing. It was so frustrating not being able to contest these ludicrous allegations. Typical MP deployments to Guantanamo varied between six months to a year, and each group of newcomers were fed such stories, officially in briefings and unofficially by the departing MPs. The legends would grow over the years through this pass-the-parcel medium until some guards asked if it was true that I could do 10,000 push-ups and kick the ceilings of the cages. It was amazing to me that these people who did push-ups as part of their occupation actually believed it might have been true. By then, I usually just agreed. If they were that gullible, that was their problem. Explanations were a waste of time.

In the years to come, I wouldn't be the only detainee to have this problem. We would compare such legends about ourselves as a form of amusement. We also created our own experiments, further exaggerating these fictional stories to see how much the MPs could be made to believe before they evaluated the information. The higher-ups had somehow been able to make these soldiers believe almost anything. To be fair, from my observations some had their heads stuck in the movies while others were independent, critical thinkers who kept their eyes and minds open and knew what was really going on – they just kept quiet and followed orders. The ability of MPs to disregard the nonsense and ask questions improved over time.

After we had been in Camp X-Ray for around two weeks, the ICRC arrived and interviewed most of the detainees over a one- to two-week period. It gave us a chance to discuss our treatment and the camp rules, in addition to telling our stories and detailing earlier abuses. The ICRC was the first group to confirm that we were, in fact, in Cuba. I will never forget one of the things they said to me on this first visit: 'The most dangerous thing to do is adapt, because you will keep adapting until there is nothing left.'

One of them was a doctor, and he examined my wrists. They were still sore from the plastic cuffs that had been secured on me weeks earlier, and when I lightly tapped the side of the wrist below the thumb I experienced shooting pains, not unlike electric shocks, through the entire area. He said it was to be expected and that it would pass in time. Thankfully, he was correct. On that occasion they even brought Camel cigarettes and biscuits, something the US did not allow ever again. In fact, I heard many US personnel cursing the ICRC among themselves; they clearly did not want them there.

In those early days, the ICRC was very effective in improving our conditions. By the time they had left after that first visit, the quantity of food improved. We were able to look around and talk to each other. We were actually allowed to move around within our cages and exercise. The only restrictions were that any exercise should not look like some form of self-defence and that we did not touch the wire. We were given lids for both the drinking and toilet buckets. Stools dissolving in urine in the full Cuban sun smelt awful, and it was revolting to keep the drinking bucket right beside the toilet bucket. The guards usually emptied these buckets once a day, and prior to the lids I heard one of them refer to the stench by saying, 'Ah, the smell of victory.'

Before the ICRC came we were chained up and 'rough-handled' to the showers; now we were able to wrap a towel around ourselves instead of having to go about naked. We were offered fifteen minutes of exercise outside our cages in a small fenced-in area twice a week. However, the restraints had to stay on and we were forced to walk so fast that the ankle restraints cut us and we bled. Our chins were pushed into our chest by one or two hands; the extreme pressure applied the whole time hurt the neck. The hands that gripped the chain around our waists were used to rip us violently about from side to side when they directed us to change direction. They performed their duties so recreation resembled a punishment. It was payback for the ICRC persuading the officers to allow this small freedom. The soldiers could not be bothered and did not want to give us 'rec'.

However, high praise and recognition must be given to the ICRC for what they did for us, and I cannot forget the personal sacrifice of one of these brave individuals in particular. They visited a second time a few months later while we were still in Camp X-Ray. Around lunchtime a gang of MPs forcibly removed a detainee from his cage in the block opposite me. I had a clear view of them throwing him against a fence, boxing him in, then standing around, kicking their boots into him. It looked like some violent street fight – there just happened to be an ICRC visitor in the block at the time of this assault. He ran over, forced his way in between the soldiers and threw himself on top of the detainee. He shielded the beaten man with his body, exposing himself to the hard boots. The ICRC employee raised one hand in the air and pleaded for them to stop kicking, which they did.

Some of us, myself included, received letters from home. The ICRC, accompanied by military escorts, personally delivered them. Had the ICRC not been present, I would not have believed the letters to be genuine. I read them sitting down, memories of another life and the real world teasing my senses for that fraction of time. They gave me hope in those early days when my spirit had not been completely broken: my whereabouts were known; I had not been forgotten; I had not 'disappeared'.

The first few letters were great, but lift in spirits fades. Once I realised no-one could help us, whether family, government, ICRC or international law, I became disillusioned and bitter. All detainees wanted – *needed* – information. We were consumed with our daily treatment and the outrageous things they did to us. We were consumed with being released before we lost our sanity. It's hard then when letters of home talk about the weather or going out with friends, for example, and I've just been tortured or am about to be. Interrogators used the letters to their benefit, blacking out entire sections, even 'I love you'. To censor in that way is very personal – they are not just interfering with me, but with my family. Very quickly detainees refused their letters after initial contact with family, including myself. We wanted to discuss law, our current and past treatment, what the future might hold, but that was not allowed. Letters became a source of pain and anger. Our captors' ability to control, manipulate and cause pain knew no bounds. We were not even allowed a moment of privacy with our family. We were not allowed love, hope, positive encouragement – anything that would help us survive or give us strength to resist. The interrogators wanted us to remember at all times that they were all powerful, in total control of our fate. They wanted us to feel like neglected animals that no-one cared about. The letters were always photocopied and stamped with 'approved by US forces'. If any photos were approved, they were just a black smudge. We were better off without letters; they brought no joy. The old life is forgotten, including loved ones, in a way that can't be explained. The real world is replaced by this bizarre, never-ending hell where reality is warped.

Interrogations began after we had been in Camp X-Ray for a week or two.[49] Portable wooden rooms had been constructed just outside the camp for this purpose. We were transported to these rooms strapped down on medical stretchers. The interrogations in those early days were simple affairs compared to the more elaborate techniques used in the purpose-built facilities in later times. My first few interrogations were conducted by people in civilian dress, as was the case with other detainees. However, military personnel quickly took over; they were the ones who would show the most interest in me over the years. Other detainees were interrogated mostly by civilian branches, such as the FBI. Over the years several civilian and military agencies conducted interrogations in Guantanamo, as well as some foreign intelligence organisations.

After a while, the stretchers were scrapped as a means of transporting us to interrogation.[50] Instead, we were made to run to the portable units while wearing what in Guantanamo was called a 'three-piece suit'. A three-piece suit begins with normal handcuffs, which are directly joined in the front to a chain that wraps around the midsection. A chain then goes from the midsection down to the ankles, where they are restrained by modified handcuffs. This was our running attire. Everywhere we went, we were escorted by two guards who kept a constant four-point contact: one MP held the chain at my back while their other hand was used to force my head down so I could only see my feet and not where I was going or my surroundings. The other MP did the same thing. This was in accordance with their Standard Operating Procedures (SOP). Later, thanks to the intervention of the Muslim chaplain, the hand that forcibly held our heads down was used to grip our triceps instead. They would arrive at the cage and say, 'Exhibition', which meant it was time for interrogation. Later, they changed the word to 'reservation'. Over the radio they said, 'The package is en route,' then we quickly shuffled to the portables, watching the skin rip off our ankles. I swear some cuffs felt like they had been sharpened. After a while, so many detainees had to have their ankles bandaged that the medics complained. But their concern was not for our treatment; it was just that these injuries caused a lot more work for them. So the MPs began placing the ankle cuffs over the top of our pants.

Most of my early interrogations in this camp were spent having to repeat my story. My main interrogator for the time I spent at Camp X-Ray was a uniformed officer. Other detainees saw a different interrogator each time they were interviewed. In hindsight, it seemed that during the period at Camp X-Ray only those detainees who were talking were taken to interrogation, while those detainees who did not cooperate were left alone, for the time being anyway. Their time would come in the different camps later on.

I talked and was up-front about my activities from the beginning. I knew I had not committed a crime, and as far as receiving military training for a cause like Kashmir, I expected these people, being soldiers, to understand my motives. In fact, I thought this was why I might have been assigned just the one military interrogator. Despite everything that had happened to me so far – and was still happening – I expected them to be professional and reasonable if it came to accusations and legal proceedings. I could then forgive them for the poor treatment during this early stage of forced abduction. I also did not know of anyone else having committed a crime, though I could not speak for the hundreds of us at Camp X-Ray. I was confident of being released in the near future, of even being one of the first to go. When the interrogator told me he knew I had done nothing wrong, that there *were* some terrorists in the camp but I wasn't one of them, I was all the more confident that reason would prevail. I trusted him when he said I had nothing to worry about, despite the fact that I had no access to a lawyer. Such matters did not concern me, he said; I did not need a lawyer, I had no reason to disbelieve him. He also advised me to have patience as he explained how the Geneva Conventions did not apply to us in Guantanamo. False hopes, false security – but in those early days I had faith. Besides, I was an Australian, the laws protecting prisoners would apply to me, so I would be all right. My government would make sure of that.

I was interrogated many times during my stay in Camp X-Ray, and that was where I heard the word al-Qaeda for the first time. Whenever they referred to a training camp they would say 'al-Qaeda camp'. Or, if they referred to a third person, they would say 'al-Qaeda member'. I asked them what al-Qaeda was, but during my whole time in Camp X-Ray the question was dismissed or left unanswered. I had heated debates with interrogators on this point. I refused to agree with them, to allow them to put words in my mouth. Not knowing what al-Qaeda was, and because of the interrogators' insistence in using this term, I always said, 'No, it was not an al-Qaeda camp' or 'I was not a member of al-Qaeda.' The interrogators even had to teach me how to pronounce the word 'al-Qaeda' properly.

Interrogators would become so furious when I corrected them on this issue that they threatened me, alluding to the beatings I had endured before my arrival or mentioning the IRF teams in the camp. It was a case of 'say what we tell you to say' and 'believe what we tell you to believe'.

As time passed, the threat of 'special treatment' and psychological conditioning took its toll. The interrogators wore me down so that when they said, 'So when you attended the al-Qaeda training camp . . .' I would answer the question without denial or protest. I became too exhausted to argue. I allowed the interrogators to frame my words and say anything they wanted. To be honest, I was already petrified and subdued by the time I arrived in Guantanamo. This was the purpose of the mistreatment, and their programs were carefully crafted, run by presumably the world's best and backed by limitless resources. They used these programs to their full advantage, and I cooperated as a result.

My knowledge of armed struggles in South Asia was exclusively confined to Kashmir – I knew practically nothing of Afghanistan. This also gave the interrogators an edge in their suggestive, manipulative theories, confusing me through intimidation, having me accept their version of the 'facts', even though what they claimed was not how I understood the situation on the ground in Kashmir, Pakistan and Afghanistan, having personally been there.

Further on, namely at Camp Delta and beyond, some interrogators would take the time to explain what al-Qaeda was. They claimed there were two al-Qaedas. In one version, it was a global terrorist organisation with thousands of members everywhere, patiently waiting to wreak vengeance on an unsuspecting civilian population. They referred to this as the 'propaganda al-Qaeda'. In the other version, it was an elite club with no more than fifty members of Egyptian descent, between the ages of forty to fifty years old. These fifty or so members were said to be ex-military officers and politicians who were disappointed with how the Egyptian government had conducted itself during the wars with Israel in the 1960s. In response, they left their positions and went underground to form an organisation that would attempt to overthrow the government and run it according to their principles.

Some interrogators would espouse both versions, while others would stick to one. My US civilian attorney, Joshua Dratel, whom I would meet years later, is known to have some knowledge on this subject. He leaned towards the 'elite club' version. As I have already explained, I saw no evidence to suggest that a global terrorist network existed.

The word 'al-Qaeda' was first used publicly by the Bush administration in January of 2001 in an attempt to prosecute Bin Laden for the terrorist attacks on the US embassies in Kenya and Tanzania.[51] They wanted to prosecute him in his absence in the *Jamal al-Fadl* case, the former Bin Laden associate who defected to the US and testified that Bin Laden was the head of a global terrorist network. Bin Laden needed to be painted as such in order to fit into the legislation used at the time to prosecute leaders of organised crime, such as the mafia. So, along with this case came the notion of a network of 'terrorist cells' and 'sleeper cells'. Before this, the term al-Qaeda was unheard of. Apparently, Bin Laden himself didn't even use it until the US government had bestowed it upon him.[52] Therefore, we can be forgiven for not having heard the term 'al-Qaeda' prior to September 11.

I am not saying that terrorist groups don't exist. I believe that there are some very angry and dangerous groups of people out there who have committed grave acts, including Bin Laden and the September 11 attacks. But I don't believe that prior to September 11 they were all connected as a structured global network controlled by one man.

Interrogators had conspiracy theories about al-Qaeda and September 11. One of them folded a US$20 note in a particular way so that it looked like two tall buildings on fire and said, 'Look, the Twin Towers.' He had a good laugh about it.

The first and only book allowed at the time into the heavily controlled camps of Guantanamo that detainees were allowed to read was a novel about the assassination of a US president. In this story, no-one saw who the assassin was, despite the murder taking place in public. It was captured on a security camera, however, and US government insiders digitally changed the real killer's identity – one of their own – to an Afghani government official and played the tape continuously on US television. After a year, the public was angry enough to support a war against Afghanistan and the troops went in. The main theme of the plot was that the whole assassination was staged (a 'false flag' operation) so certain shadowy insiders could destroy a 'terrorist' network hiding underground in Afghanistan. I found it a very strange choice of literature to give us under the circumstances and considering that it was approved by the military authorities. It was passed around during the first few weeks of arriving in Camp X-Ray to those who could read English.

I was threatened on numerous occasions during my interrogations in Camp X-Ray. On one such occasion, maybe six weeks into my time there, I was interrogated by three civilians. Two of the civilians were white guys, while the third, who sat silently in a corner, looked to be Arab. After a few minutes of general chitchat, they produced a hand-held video recorder. On the

screen was a still shot of a man lying on a bed with a white
sheet pulled up to his chin, while the surrounding walls and
everything else was white. His entire face, however, was horribly bruised, a mix of black and blue that stood out in stark
contrast to his surroundings. I was sure I was looking at a dead
man. When I asked if he was dead, the Arab in the corner spoke
for the first time. With a really hateful expression, he said, 'If
you don't cooperate, we will send you to Egypt. You can find
out if he's dead and experience how it happened.' He conveyed
it would be a hellish and painful destination.[53] I knew he was
serious and the thought scared me, as I'm sure it was intended
to. After this threat I was taken back to the cage.

The main physical danger during daily life in the camp was being
IRFed. Sometimes MPs would pretend that a detainee they were
escorting, especially at times of restraint removal, had resisted
or lashed out aggressively. In response to this imagined slight,
the MPs would strike the detainee with hard blows, sometimes
ramming him into the concrete. They seemed to look for any
opportunity to physically assault us – and definitely appeared
to enjoy doing so. IRF teams have smeared faeces on detainees,
sprayed pepper spray in their eyes (one detainee lost vision in one
eye due to such an attack), shoved detainees' heads into toilets,
sprayed high-pressure hoses up their noses to simulate suffocation, and broke bones.[54]

   It made for a very dangerous environment. The savagery of
the beatings was something I'd expect to see out the front of
a pub late at night. The worst thing about this was there was
no-one to complain to, no-one who could stop this from happening to us. Even those in charge, whom you would expect
to act responsibly, endorsed such action. It was about 'softening us up' for interrogation, a continuous struggle to show

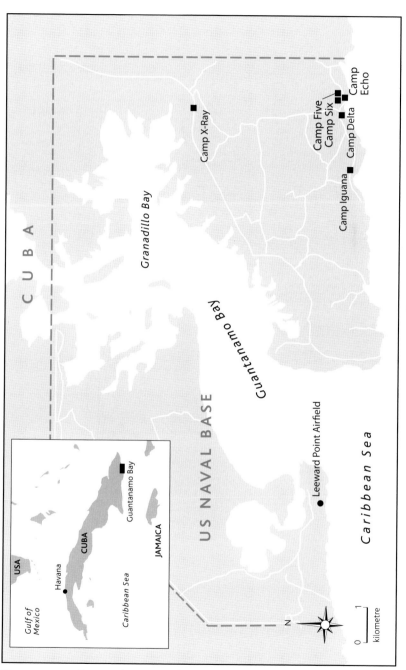

Guantanamo Bay and surrounds.

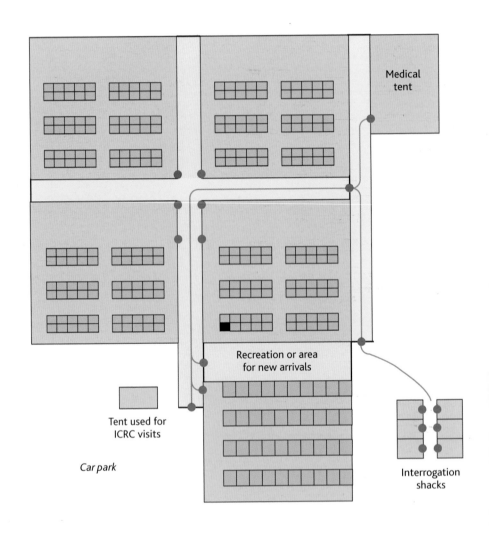

Medical tent

Recreation or area
for new arrivals

Tent used for
ICRC visits

Car park

Interrogation
shacks

Camp X-Ray with my cell highlighted.

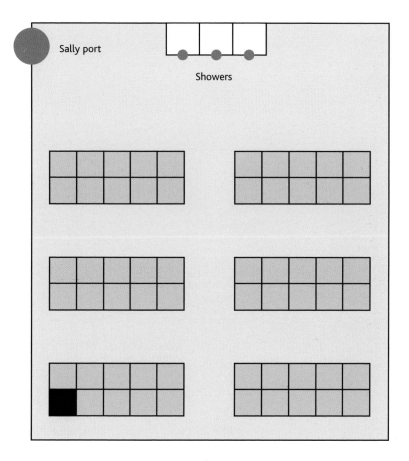

My section within Camp X-Ray.

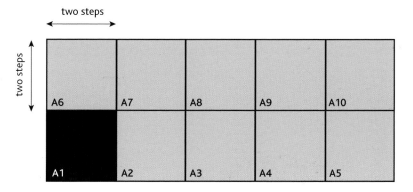

My block and cell.

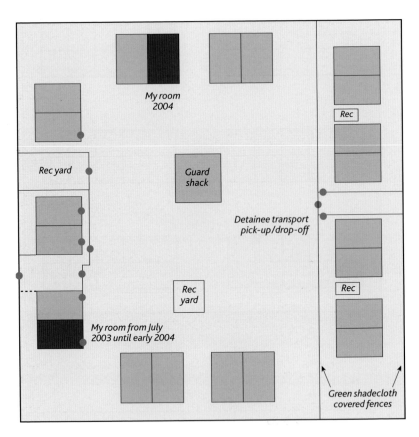

Camp Echo.

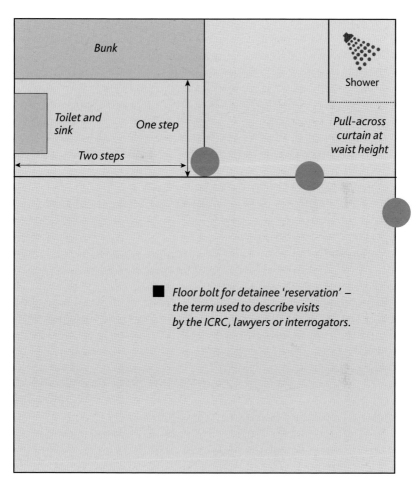

Bunk

Toilet and sink

One step

Two steps

Shower

Pull-across curtain at waist height

■ Floor bolt for detainee 'reservation' – the term used to describe visits by the ICRC, lawyers or interrogators.

Camp Echo cell.

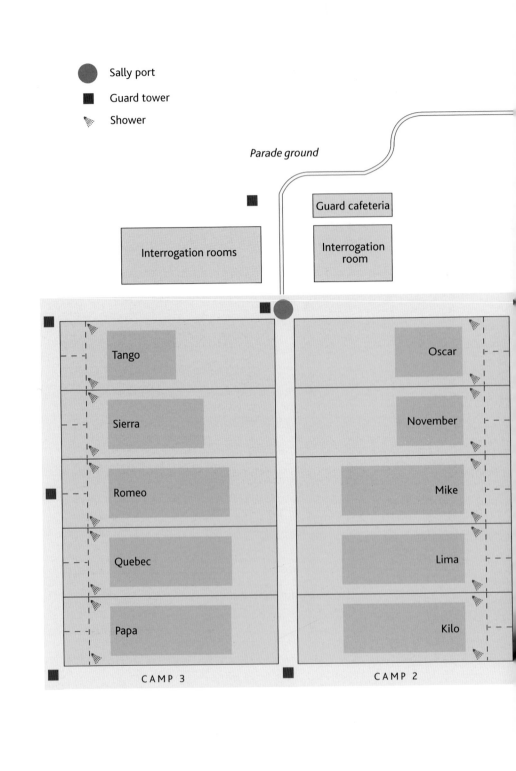

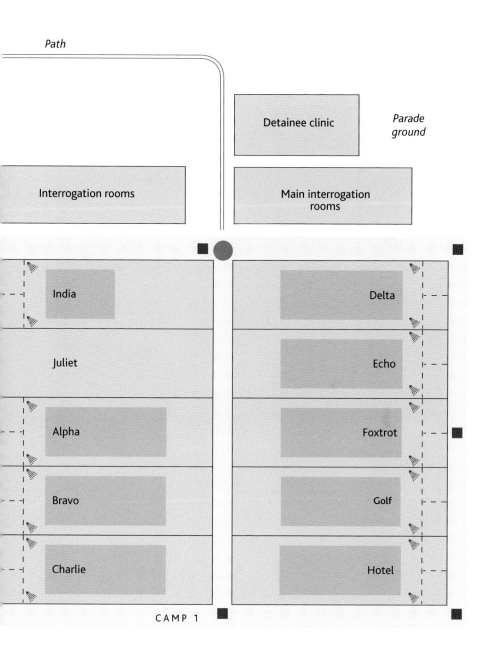

Camp Delta.

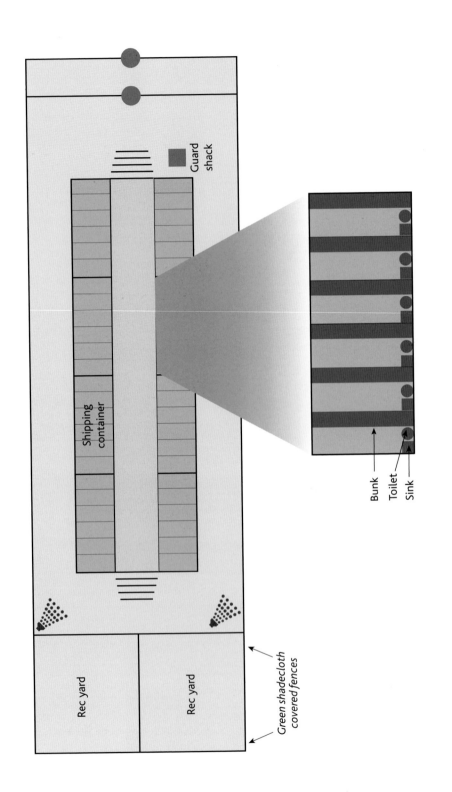

Bunk

Toilet

Sink

Shipping container

Guard shack

Rec yard

Rec yard

Green shadecloth covered fences

A block with enlarged individual shipping container in Camp Delta.

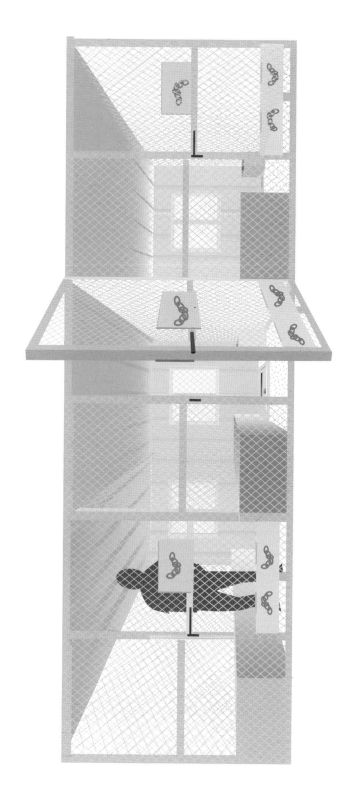

Camp Delta cages. A cage is one-sixth of a shipping container – my home for years.

Me in primary school.

Fishing as a young teenager.

Working at Numery Station in my mid-teens, near the Simpson Desert, Northern Territory. (Photos © David Hicks)

Track work at Aomori, Japan.

Kosovo Liberation Army (KLA) training camp in Albania.
(Photos © David Hicks)

The group I trained with in Albania.

Saluting the NATO flag during a ceremony at the KLA camp, Albania. (Photos © David Hicks)

Recognise this shot? Some media claimed this is me in combat. Others went further to claim this is me in Afghanistan, aiming at US or Australian troops.

This is the full photo – nothing but a boys' trophy shot with empty weapons from a storeroom in Albania. (Note the slippers.)

One of the many examples of political cartoon satire in the
Australian media during my detention. (Cartoon by Nicholson from
The Australian, www.nicholsoncartoons.com.au)

Protest march in Sydney, 2006. (Photo courtesy David Harvey)

Australian Lawyers Alliance CEO Eva Scheerlinck (front) with
protesters gathered at the Uniting Church in Sydney, 25 March 2007.
(Photo © Newspix/Britta Campion)

Dad protesting from within a cage in New York City, 28 July 2003.
(Photo © Getty Images/Eric Malema)

Aloysia and me on our wedding day, 1 August 2009.

Me with my family in 2010. (Photos © David and Aloysia Hicks)

'who was in charge'. The more a detainee tried to resist or help himself, the more extreme action the MPs employed, which only increased as the years passed.

Another injustice were the times we were set up for punishment. Apart from the concrete slabs we lived upon, the ground within the blocks was covered in small, white gravel. This gravel was too far from the cage walls for our hands to reach, yet guards would place little bits of wire offcuts (which had been lying around due to the recent construction) under the stones up against the concrete edges. They would return a few minutes later, unearth the wire and accuse the nearest detainee of having nefarious designs to escape or maim. This was used as another excuse to send in the IRF team to give us a hiding. It's interesting, in hindsight, to see the extent to which the soldiers went to justify their actions. Why didn't they just beat us without playing silly games? These beatings and other activities were systematic and ordered from above, not the result of low-ranking MPs looking for ways to have some fun.

We had one victory in our block thwarting these set-ups. On one occasion, a detainee a few cages down from me had been taken to interrogation. I saw a female MP, who was searching his empty cage (a 'shakedown', as they called it), take his toothbrush and hide it under the gravel. While I was stressing about what I could do, the Muslim chaplain entered the block. I was able to call him over and explain what had happened. He went away and spoke with the MPs working the block. When he left, the female MP came back over, recovered the toothbrush and placed it back in the cage. When the detainee returned, nothing happened to him, luckily.

The various chaplains who were assigned to the camps were fundamentally good people. They did try to help us, and the fact that time and again they were moved on and replaced is proof that they went in to bat for us. They were disgusted by what they witnessed and often complained. One chaplain once told me that he himself was constantly watched. Other soldiers took notes of what he said during prayers at the soldiers' mosque. They kept a list of all personnel who were Muslim, anyone who attended the mosque and prayed. He said American Muslim soldiers at Guantanamo were treated as possible traitors. This attitude culminated with the arrest of a Muslim chaplain in 2003 on fabricated charges of spying.[55] He was eventually acquitted. There never was another chaplain after that.

There were other reasons for being IRFed. The overalls we wore had slits at the hips that would normally allow a wearer to reach into his pant pockets. We were given nothing to wear underneath, and when detainees bent forward during prayer, naked skin would be exposed where it was not permitted in Islam, especially during prayer. To remedy this, some detainees wrapped the towel around their midsection while in prayer. This was against the rules, and if a detainee would not stop praying when he was yelled at to remove the towel, the IRF team was sent in to punish him. Usually the detainee would have finished praying by the time an IRF team arrived, but I remember a day when an MP entered a cage on his own while the detainee was still praying and had his forehead on the ground. The MP began to ram his head into the concrete, but the detainee ceased his prayer and out-manoeuvred the MP, getting the better of him. The MP screamed and barely made it out of the cage without the detainee following. This disrespect shown to Islam caused an outrage among detainees, and the defiance began. Stopping prayer before its completion, unless for a very valid reason, especially at the orders of a non-Muslim, is not acceptable in Islam. This was only one of many religious aspects that the US military often ignored or openly violated.

The worst IRFing I witnessed involved a Bahraini detainee. Early one afternoon, he made some jokes that elicited laughter from the majority of detainees in our block. In response, the IRF team was sent in. Before they entered the cage, they ordered him to lie facedown on the concrete, which he did – he even placed his hands behind his back for cuffing. Sergeant Smith, who was to enter first with the shield, threw it to the side instead and ran in, jumping high into the air. He was in full riot gear, including knee pads. Smith tucked his feet up behind him and landed with full force onto the detainee's upper back with his knee pads. We all heard the crack. The next two MPs entered quickly and crisscrossed their bodies over his, pinning him to the floor while wedging their feet into the wire fence halfway up the sides. The last two MPs to enter remained standing, kicking him continuously with their boots.

In the meantime, Sergeant Smith had grabbed the detainee by the hair with both hands and began lifting and slamming his face repeatedly into the concrete. After twenty or so blows, Smith then used one hand to hold his face, cheek-down, to the concrete. With his other hand, he pounded his exposed cheek. The detainee looked lifeless by the time they had finished with him. They put the restraints on, picked him up and carried him away. Then, as I had seen in the past, the blood was hosed and scrubbed away with a brush.

Many other soldiers had been standing around the outside of the cage while this attack took place. I said to one who was not far from me, 'Are you seeing this?'

He replied, 'I don't see anything,' and walked away.

As with all such beatings and general IRFings, this event was filmed.

The beating occurred only days before we were moved to the new camp. The ICRC filled us in on his condition. If I remember correctly, he had a few broken ribs, a broken wrist and a broken nose. He rejoined us some weeks later, and I saw his bruised face, his arm in plaster.

I considered myself lucky because Sergeant Smith often threatened to do something similar to me; he was just waiting for a time when he would escort me somewhere. I knew he was serious, because just about every time he handled a detainee he would make an excuse to harm him personally or call in the IRF team. Thankfully, and due more to luck than anything, he was never given that opportunity with me.

As previously mentioned, the military had nominated a Muslim chaplain to be on-site full time. This was after we had been there for a month or so. He was able to arrange Qur'ans for all detainees who wished one, and for the call to prayer to be announced over a loudspeaker five times a day. This seemed to enrage the military personnel in general, and hostility towards detainees' religious practices increased. The soldiers created more disturbances during times of prayer, and there were numerous instances of Qur'ans being kicked or thrown about during cage searches. On more than one occasion, Qur'ans even ended up in the buckets of urine and faeces. Then there were silly things the MPs did, like throwing handfuls of pork bits into detainees' food or playing Don McLean's 'American Pie' over the loudspeakers. During one of the forced plane transportations before arriving in Guantanamo, Bruce Springsteen's 'Born in the USA' was played loudly as the surrounding US soldiers sang in unison. Ironically, they must not have known that the song contains lyrics criticising America's involvement in Vietnam.

Sleep was a major issue in Camp X-Ray, and would remain

so for all the years I was in Guantanamo.[56] Camp X-Ray was illuminated so brightly, with so many floodlights, that night was turned into day. As time passed we did not have to produce our identification armbands every hour, thanks, I believe, to the ICRC. Nor did we have to show our toothbrushes; they had taken them away. However, the officers came up with a new rule that was just as bad: we were not allowed to have our hands or faces covered at any time. When we slept at night, they could not be covered by the single sheet provided. However, this is not as simple as it sounds. Once I had managed to fall asleep, my hands often acted as a pillow, because we did not have one. I would be woken by a soldier kicking the cage and screaming as loud as he could, only centimetres from my face, 'Show your hands' or 'I need to see skin.'

It was madness – and a horrible way to be woken. If I did manage to keep my hands and face exposed while I slept, which takes some training and discipline, I would be disturbed by the kicking and screaming directed at another detainee nearby.

By around late February 2002, things were different from when we first arrived, when all of us had been beaten into quiet and robotic submission. Some of the detainees were now gaining confidence and strength due to the weight of the injustices and the length of our imprisonment. Time and again, techniques were employed to recreate those early days of capture, when we were malleable and frightened, though some detainees never lost their spirit and remained defiant to the end. The initial shock that detainment has upon the detained is exploited by captors; it is a time for interrogation and breaking spirits. This window of time is outlined in the current US Army Field Manual[57] and is seen as an opportunity not to be missed – a detainee's strength will return.

Captors strive to prolong that period of vulnerability and recreate it in cycles.

The first hunger strike also occurred around this time, labelled by the military as a 'riot' because detainees yelled and screamed and kicked their cages. With typical overkill, the day shift and afternoon shift were summoned to back up the night shift by surrounding the camp with armed Humvees and soldiers. It looked like a whole battalion was bearing down on us.

After this event, a general went around the camp with a translator, hearing detainee grievances. The main theme was that we wanted information, more meaningful and uncensored contact with family, better conditions, religious tolerance and, ultimately, to be released. From then on, every Friday, the general gave a speech over the loudspeakers. He talked of a new camp with better facilities and that the sooner we cooperated and revealed all our information, the sooner we could go home to our loved ones. Each Friday during these announcements he promised we would be moved to this new facility before the next Friday, though he broke that promise numerous times. Journalists were invited to listen to these announcements and, depending on where we were positioned, we could see them just outside the camp's perimeter.

I asked my interrogator about this new facility. He claimed that we would have ocean views from our windows, the interrogation rooms would have coffee machines and we would be able to help ourselves. He also said that detainees would be housed according to their language group, and I would find myself with a number of English-speakers. The point: this new facility would be some improvement on Camp X-Ray. I would have to wait to see about that.

Nineteen

Cassel: If the President deems that he's got to torture somebody, including crushing the testicles of the person's child, there is no law that can stop him?
Yoo: No treaty.
Cassel: Also no law by Congress. That is what you wrote in the August 2002 memo.
Yoo: I think it depends on why the President thinks he needs to do that.

> Doug Cassel, Professor of Law and Director of the Center for Civil and Human Rights, Notre Dame University, with John Yoo, author of the torture memos, December 2005

A DAY ARRIVED when two or three yellow school buses drove into camp along the dusty track. The windows had been replaced with sheets of metal, allowing passengers zero visibility. The camp began to bustle as armed military personnel positioned themselves in every corner and teams of escorts marched about, jingling with the three-piece suits they carried. One block of detainees was escorted directly into the waiting buses. Other detainees from mixed blocks, including me, were then escorted to the now empty block to wait for the buses' return. I suppose this period was exciting, because something major, something different, was happening. There was about to be a change of scenery, we hoped a change in circumstances – for the better.

When the buses returned, I was chained with a bag secured over my head with tape. Then I was guided onto the bus and locked to the floor. When we began to move, I could hear other detainees in chains around me. Some of them wriggled about, and were struck in the back of the head and screamed at for their troubles. To avoid being hit, I remained as still as I could, but I soon learned that no matter how carefully I followed orders, I was to be struck and screamed at anyway.

It was a short journey and the bus came to a sudden stop. I could hear the movement of other detainees – chains rattling, feet scraping – before hands gripped my arms tightly and yanked me up from the floor. I was led off the bus and ordered to halt. The tape and bag were removed from my head. I was disoriented. The Muslim chaplain was standing in the bright sun to greet me. Before I could gather my thoughts, I was led through two lockable gates called a sally port. Again, there were fences covered in green shadecloth and lots of razor wire. A square, white sign hanging by the gates I entered read: 'C Block'. Once through the gates, I stood before a long, narrow structure. It looked to be a hybrid between a cage and an enclosed building, like ATCO portables. I was escorted into this structure and down a hallway.

Detainees were on both sides of this walkway, housed behind diamond wire. I was not taken far into Charlie Block, as it was called, when I was directed into an empty cage on my right. The restraints were removed, and I was left alone to absorb the new environment and chat with fellow detainees. This was the new facility we had heard so much about – Camp Delta.

The most obvious fact about this facility was how small the cages were: one step wide, two steps long. The whole thing was constructed of metal. A metal shelf about half a metre off the ground to sleep on was crammed into this small space, along with a sink and a hole in the floor for a toilet. The entire enclosure must have been no bigger than an average suburban toilet, the floor space definitely smaller than a double mattress and twice as small as the cages at Camp X-Ray. The worst realisation was that we were now all being housed in shipping containers.

Civilian contractors had welded four shipping containers end to end and replaced one of the long, newly created front walls with diamond wire. Diamond wire was also used to internally divide this enclosure into twenty-four cages, meaning each shipping container could contain six detainees in a manner the authorities described as 'single-occupancy cell'. This long, narrow, twenty-four-cage structure was raised off the ground on cement blocks opposite another four shipping containers. A raised platform between the containers allowed enough room for a soldier to walk along and inspect detainees. This whole contraption was then covered in white panels and roofed, giving the appearance from the outside that we were housed in clean, comfortable, fabricated buildings, hiding the metal shipping containers and the internal forest of diamond wire in which we lived.

Down some steps, out the back, were two cupboard-sized cement boxes used as showers. A bit further again, through two gates, were two large cages, enclosed by cyclone fencing, twelve steps by twelve steps each, with a cement floor. These were the 'recreation' cages. The whole lot was then surrounded by the ever-present shadecloth-covered fence, and beyond that armed guard towers pierced the skyline. Like Camp X-Ray, this camp was also under construction. On arrival, only enough blocks had been built to house about two hundred detainees, though after another year Camp Delta would house just over 800 at its peak.

These blocks were our whole lives for years at a time, the sum of our existence. There was nowhere else to go – except interrogation or hospital – and there was nothing else to do but sit in these toilet-sized metal cages and wait.

Usually four, sometimes five, soldiers would work each block at one time. The highest ranking soldier on the block would be an E6, or staff sergeant. Most of the time an E5 sergeant was in charge. There were always two E4s, or 'specialists', and then one E3 called a Private First Class or PFC. The highest ranking soldier that would tour the camp was the E9, known as a sergeant major, or officers such as captains and lieutenants. On very rare occasions, a general would show up. Any soldier ranked under PFC was rarely seen working with detainees.

There were some things I quickly noticed about Charlie Block. Though one of my neighbours spoke English, I was not close enough to the others to communicate freely. Up until that stage I had naively given my interrogator the benefit of the doubt and I was now furious at how confined Camp Delta turned out to be, especially at the pathetic little room I found myself in.

During that first day in Camp Delta, I put in a request to see my interrogator and was escorted to see him the next day. I was led out through the sally port, past where the bus had deposited me the previous day. Directly to my right was the boundary fence of Camp Delta (Charlie Block was at the far end of the camp). Beyond that were a few hundred metres of grass, then a cliff. Beyond that was the Caribbean Sea – and freedom. I was not blindfolded as I was led through the camp, which gave me an opportunity to assess my new surroundings. As mentioned, only a few blocks were complete at the time. Elsewhere, construction was under way. We walked up

a large, gravelled driveway, passing sally ports of other completed blocks: Alfa, Bravo, Delta, etc. Eventually, we came to
a large, double-locked guarded gate. Once we passed through,
we had left the part of the camp where detainees were held,
though we were still inside a high-security facility.

This next area comprised portable ATCO air-conditioned
buildings. I did not know what services they provided, though
in time I would learn that one of these buildings was used to
receive and distribute detainee food, another dealt with MP
food. There was a detainee medical clinic, and the rest of the
buildings housed interrogation rooms.

I was made to turn right and enter one of these buildings.
Inside, it was cool and dark. As I walked along the hallway
military personnel exited and entered the many doors with
solemn expressions. The atmosphere harboured something
bad, something nasty. The building itself was oppressive.

I was able to catch a glimpse in one of the many rooms
as I was marched along the hallway – clearly a mistake made
by someone too slow to close the door. Inside was a mass of
electrical cords, computers and video-recording equipment. I
was turned left into the very next room. My usual military
interrogator, plus two men I did not recognise, were waiting
inside. The next thing I noticed was a huge, one-way reflective mirror that took up most of one wall. I thought of the
recording equipment next door and the behavioural analysts
undoubtedly gathered with pen, paper and crackpot theories,
all staring at me expectantly. I was weary. This was not like
Camp X-Ray or other previous interrogations. This felt more
staged, more foreboding.

The familiar interrogator started to apologise about how
things were and said they would 'improve'. He then explained
he had to leave the island on a mission and that I would not
be seeing him again. The interrogator's associate, who had

remained quiet until now, said they had a proposal for me: they would place me next to the various English-speaking detainees over a period of time, and I was to milk each one for information and report it back to the interrogators. If I agreed to do this, I would be allowed fifteen minutes with a lady from the Philippines. I instantly refused and requested to be sent back to my cage. For the first time during this interview, I saw hate on their faces as they ordered the MPs to escort me back to Charlie Block.

Prostitutes, drugs and other such activities were apparently on the menu as possible incentives to gather information. However, they were the wrong offerings for these customers. Islam gave detainees strength to resist. Interrogators tried hard to make them waver in their faith, interrogation theory suggesting that you should try to isolate a detainee and offer him temptations, playing on his desires, especially any known past vices.[58] The assumption was that all men are human and if the detainee wavered or, even better, actually sinned, then the detainee's faith would unravel along with his source of strength. He would then break and be ready for moulding into whatever the interrogator desired. Having spent so long on the island and knowing what took place there, I believe it happened, but only about ten or so times out of 800 detainees.

Whether a detainee would be offered such an incentive as drugs and prostitutes, or any other type, would depend on the circumstances. The main factor seemed to be how cheaply you sold yourself in the beginning. For example, if you agreed to cooperate for a burger or a cigarette, you could not demand something of a higher value at a later date. If you did, interrogators would just leave you out in the cages for weeks or months at a time. That way the detainee would eventually wear down, break and agree to resume cooperating for the incentive they had in the past. Those detainees who held out for long periods of time – not cooperating and resisting 'enhanced interrogation techniques', also called *torture* – could name their price short of freedom if they chose to cooperate. Others would have broken for different incentives. The interrogators had the authority to arrange anything. Many detainees remained defiant, though, demanding their rights and a day in court to challenge allegations and prove themselves innocent.

I admired the strength of many detainees. Some of them had still not cooperated by the time I left Guantanamo, after five and a half years, even in the face of torture. I will explain what 'cooperation' means later – it doesn't necessarily mean 'giving up what you know'. It's more like, 'Say what we tell you to.'

I had been back in Charlie Block for only an hour or two after this attempted interview when escorts came to move me. I was about to learn one of the pathetic games interrogators played if you did not cooperate. They thought to punish me by relocating me to Alpha Block, where none of the detainees spoke English. The interrogators appeared to have used this block to gather together the angrier detainees, the ones developing aggressive mental health issues as a result of their treatment in captivity. The interrogators knew I would not be able to communicate with anyone and that it would be frustrating. And it was.

Months passed before I was taken to interrogation again. I had quite a shock when I was introduced to my guests. It was an Australian delegation consisting of ASIO, the Australian Federal Police, and a representative from the Australian embassy in the US, a woman. I was excited, thinking it was time to go home, but they quickly doused my hopes. I was told that this was not a consular visit – if I had any complaints or requests, there *might* be time to address them later. They told me they had come to conduct an interview regarding my activities overseas. Then, without asking for my consent, a tape recorder was placed on the table and they began a more formal introduction. When they asked if I would participate in an interview, I refused. They didn't seem to be expecting that answer and turned the tape recorder off. They claimed they were there to help me, to see if I had broken any Australian laws, because if I had they would be able to get me out of Guantanamo and back to Australia. On the other hand, if I didn't participate, they would never know if I had broken a law or not and would be unable to do anything for me. I would have to remain in Guantanamo indefinitely.

The speaker then added that the US would like me to cooperate. I believe it was then that the ASIO representative said the US would not be happy if I refused, that I would remain behind and they would be powerless to help. He said this in an ominous manner, which was probably the biggest incentive to talk. The thought of remaining in the military's hands for years to come, in this place, scared the hell out of me. The treatment that I had experienced and witnessed always lingered near the forefront of my mind. It was also no comfort to imagine being left behind by my government indefinitely, as that is how I interpreted those comments.

The past treatment did temporarily give me the courage to speak up, however. I told them everything that had happened: the beatings, the privations, and the disrespect. But I was dismissed with, 'You're in their custody, not ours. There is nothing we can do about that.' It is sad for me to reflect back and see how compliant fear had made me. Instead of causing a scene, I was easily silenced because of my fear of 'angering the

Americans' and suffering some variety of punishments later on. I meekly dropped the subject.

They had one last attempt to convince me to cooperate in an interview: they produced an esky full of food and drink, and topped it off by placing a full packet of cigarettes on the table. They said it would be a shame to throw it all out, because they had brought the provisions for me, but I would have to agree to the interview to enjoy any of it. Arseholes! Again, the offer of food and drink may not sound like much of an incentive, but when you have been kept in a cage – and a rusting metal one at that – in the hot Cuban sun, purposely starved, the biggest and best meal of the day being half of a cold MRE nearing the end of its seven-year use-by date and given only warm water to drink for months on end, it is a huge incentive. After all this talk about going home, and the sight of the esky, I agreed to the interview. They placed the recorder on the table and began again. When they asked this time why I had changed my mind to participate I hesitated. All I could think was, *Don't piss off the Americans. Don't piss off the Australians – you want them to take you home, right? Don't get smart or you'll have to pay for it.* Fear is a great weapon. I answered the question by simply saying, 'I changed my mind,' and even that felt rebellious.

The interview began mid-morning and lasted until late in the afternoon. At one point they told me that under the cir-cumstances I could not have a lawyer present. I ate, drank and smoked as though I never would again. The interview resumed the next day for a similar length of time. When it was over, the embassy employee asked if I had any requests she could submit to the US on my behalf. She did not mention the mistreatment of detainees, and I did not push the point. Thinking it would be a waste of time, I only requested to be moved to a block where detainees spoke English, claiming I was unhappy in

Alpha Block. The last thing they said to me as a group, besides goodbye, was that based on the interview they could see no breach of Australian law. Nevertheless, they would continue to look into it. They then added something about passing on my regards to my family for me. And they were gone.

It seemed my request worked. The day after the Australians had left I was moved to Delta Block. There were no Westerners here, but a number of detainees could speak reasonable English. I took advantage of this and occupied my time trying to learn the various languages different detainees spoke. This block was positioned so I could see beyond the green fence. A new building was being erected next to the camp. This gave rise to speculation on what it might mean for us, but it would eventually turn out to be only a new detainee hospital. In an environment where one searches for any indication of being released in the near future, seeing such long-term projects disturbed morale.

Speculation and theories were a maddening part of our existence. We were kept in strict incommunicado with the outside world and not allowed to know the time, date, year or any other information to orient ourselves. This allowed the interrogators to create a new reality for us, one where they manipulated and controlled what we thought, knew and believed. This bizarre world became normal for us with the passing of years. They were also extremely strict about what was said to us. The MPs working the blocks were often threatened with severe punishment if they told us anything, even the time. The interrogators did such a good job twisting our thoughts that one plane load of detainees swore they were in China. It took at least a month after their arrival for the other detainees to convince them otherwise. We were starved for information, so we always clutched at straws. Our knowledge consisted of rumours, false leads and largely incorrect information. Whenever a detainee returned from interrogation he would report on all that had been discussed. We would then spend days analysing the interrogator's every word, looking for hidden meanings and clues to our fate. Other information came from the ICRC, guards and pure speculation. Detainees would scream this information from block to block, from shower to shower, and rec yard to rec yard. For years, it was a mentally taxing obsession.

While I was in Delta Block, the first large-scale protest took place throughout the camp. Information arrived at our block through detainee word-of-mouth that a Qur'an had been kicked across the floor by an MP during a cage search and that another Qur'an had been dropped into a toilet hole shortly after. Before this information reached us, a mighty commotion alerted us to trouble. First, we heard one block erupt into yelling and the sound of the metal cages being kicked. Then another block joined in, and another, and another. Once hundreds of detainees were involved, spread between ten or so blocks, the noise really was deafening. The welding was substandard and in some cages the metal beds began to fall apart, along with some sinks and taps. The guards were concerned about bits of metal that detainees could acquire from the breakages. Such large-scale disruption had not occurred before in Camp Delta, and the MPs didn't know what to do. There were so many things to monitor at once, between all the noise and damage.

One of the ways the guards dealt with the situation was to introduce pepper spray into their arsenal. It had not been used in Guantanamo until that day, and it took us by surprise.

The MPs ran through the blocks, spraying as many of the detainees who were kicking their cages as possible. Because we did not know what was going on, many detainees were caught unawares and sprayed in the face. Once an hour or so had passed, multiple IRF teams blitzed the camp, working hard as they entered cage after cage, punishing the detainees who were making the loudest noise and forcibly searching for bits of metal. The last tactic the soldiers employed was to play a reading of the Qur'an very loudly over a PA system that had been fitted throughout the camp. It seemed to work. People began to relax and eventually the situation returned to normal.

Things were not quite the same after that incident. There was a desperation in the detainees' struggle against their captors that escalated as the years passed, resulting in terrible abuses – and eventually death.

During that period of mid-2002 in Delta Block, I observed the detainee in the cage opposite grapple with his sanity. He attempted to communicate with the guards working the block. Not understanding Arabic, they ignored him. This angered the man and he began yelling. Instead of summoning an interpreter, the MPs summoned the dog handler, who arrived at the block with his German shepherd. In an unusual manoeuvre, they opened the detainee's door without restraining him first, and challenged him to come out and take on the dog. The detainee refused. Later in the day he wrote something above his window in Arabic using toothpaste. He then rolled up toilet paper into a thin rope and stuck it onto the toothpaste, outlining the words more clearly. When the MPs saw this, they ordered him to take it down. He refused, so the MPs restrained him and entered the cage themselves to remove the writing. Returned to his cage, he desperately hacked into his arm with a small sliver of metal. Blood pooled in the crook of his arm, which he used as ink to rewrite the words with his finger. When the guards noticed what the detainee was doing, they took him away. I do not know what became of him; I never saw him again.

For some reason, I had it in my head that I could be returned to Australia by August of 2002. No promises were given during the interview with the Australians, yet I could think of no reason they wouldn't send me home. I thought about the interview often, especially during times when hope was hard to find. I had set a mental deadline: if I was still languishing without information once August had passed, I would accept that I was in a hopeless situation, my eventual repatriation in doubt. I continued to wait patiently in Delta Block. As the weeks passed since the interview I was not even interrogated, which I took as a good omen. Then one day in early August I was escorted out of the block. My heart was racing with excitement, thinking I might be taken to a waiting plane. I was turned into the interrogation buildings instead. As my hope waned, I told myself that I might receive the news of my departure there. I was placed in a room with a military guy I had not seen before. Bursting with optimism, I pestered him with questions. He claimed not to know anything, except that I should be moved from Delta Block in the near future. To a desperate mind that sounded hopeful: my plan for release was still on track. Otherwise the interrogation seemed to have no purpose and was over quickly.

Within days of that interview, MPs arrived at my cage, ordering me to get ready to move. I was chained in the usual manner, but this time I thought, *This is it, I'm going home.* I was even more sure of this as I was led out of the camp altogether. As we exited the main gate for the first time, I turned to look back and could only shake my head in disgust at the sign hanging on the fence: Camp Delta, Camp 1, Camp Justice – Honour Bound to Defend Freedom. Yet behind that gate I could see shipping containers, shadecloth-covered fences, razor wire and guard towers, the whole sad scene coated in a thick layer of brown-grey dust. Even though the cages were more open-aired than enclosed, there was a faint smell of hundreds of unwashed bodies, something the guards often complained about. So much for America's brand of freedom.

I was placed in the back of a green John Deere Gator utility vehicle, which also gave me hope. One guard drove while the other sat in the back, using an arm to lock me in. We drove along the front of the camp for a few hundred metres in the buggy until we reached another gate with a sign that read 'Camps 2 and 3' with the same freedom-and-justice propaganda. We had watched this camp being built for the last few months and knew it had just opened. It wasn't what I was expecting, but I was not dismayed. We went through the numerous gates, the keys of which were about thirty centimetres long so they could not be lost or hidden were detainees lucky enough to come across one, and turned left into November Block. This twenty-four-cage structure was called 'Isolation'.[59] The room I was placed in was a metal box, as were all the rooms in November. There were no windows, no natural light. If it hadn't been for the eerie, soft-red glow that emanated from a protected globe, it would have been darker than night. A cold blast of air constantly streamed in from a hole in the roof. I didn't know what to think, but doubted this was the path to home.

I asked the guards working on this block why I was there. They responded that it could be punishment, or just the standard introduction to Camps Two and Three. When I asked how long I might be in there, they replied possibly weeks. One of the guards then asked if I would like him to inquire about my status to the interrogation department and I said yes.

In response to this query, I was taken to speak with the new interrogator I had seen prior to the move. He apologised for my being in isolation and claimed it was a mistake. He would rectify the situation quickly. The guy was full of it. After spending about ten days in November Block, I was taken out into the glaring sun, holding my garbage bag of belongings that always accompanied me on a move (iso-mat, blanket, sheet, etc.), and led to the last block at the back of Camp Two – Kilo Block – on the opposite side of Charlie Block in Camp One.

It had taken a few months, but I was back on a block with some of the British detainees. I could not physically *see* most of them, but if we yelled we could communicate. That was surely the intention. It would have made the MPs' job easier to write down what we discussed and the various ideas we came up with to pass the time. By this stage some detainees had discovered microphones hidden in taps and gaps around the windows. The interrogators compiled a file on each individual detainee. This file contained the minute details of our personalities – our weaknesses and strengths, likes and dislikes – a list that could be used against us for interrogation purposes. Guantanamo was run like a big laboratory where various physical, psychological and medical experiments were conducted.

I had not been in Kilo Block for long when interrogation resumed, this time with a new military officer I had not seen before. I had to start from the very beginning and go through my story again and again. The weather had become extremely hot, and the cages were beginning to rust badly. The water out of the tap, the only drinking water, was warm and the food situation was desperate. My average weight is around 81 kg, but I started to lose noticeable weight in Kilo Block. I began my time there around 72 kg and, very soon my weight was down to 58 kg.

*

It was in this block that I began to lose the small amount of hope I had been clinging to. August 2002 had come and gone, I had been here eight months yet here I was, with the haunting realisation that I could be here for years. The deployment of guards that had been with us since Camp X-Ray were gone. In their place was a fresh batch of soldiers, paranoid as hell about how 'dangerous' we were, brainwashed by their recent training and propaganda. This meant I had to again endure open-mouthed gawkers saying, 'Are you the Australian mercenary? I hear you can do spinning kicks and kick the roof. Will you show me?' Such ridiculous propaganda was still worrying me, because it was making me out to be something I wasn't. It certainly wasn't a flattering characterisation that would aid my mission to return home, but in the years to come I became too burnt out to care any longer. That was a major difference between us and the MPs. Because they were rotated out every six months to a year, they always remained fresh, excited and adrenaline-filled, while we grew weary and aged. Near the end of my stay in Guantanamo I would look at fresh-faced teenagers who carried on as though everything was still new and exciting, the whole time knowing that I had been in here longer than he or she had been in the military. I knew more about their training, rank system, future opportunities and their job at Guantanamo than they did. It was depressing.

The next batch of soldiers to come work the blocks in 2003, the second deployment to Guantanamo, would have their nametags covered by sticky tape. The first deployment had not done this. When some of them had been there long enough to relax a bit, I learned some answers to why this was. They had been told that if detainees discovered their names, they would also discover where they lived in the US and who their family members were, and then use their 'terrorist connections' to have them killed. Most guards on the blocks believed this. The real reason was that the higher-ups had become frustrated by detainees complaining to the ICRC about the abuses they suffered and identifying the perpetrators by their actual names, making it difficult to dismiss such allegations. By the time the superiors realised this, detainees had practically memorised the MPs' names anyway, so this new procedure of hiding identities did not begin until the new fresh batch of soldiers arrived. It's interesting to see the extent to which the higher-ups went to deceive not only their own people, but also the detainees and the world.

Sitting in that hot, rusty cage wore me down for many reasons, one of which was the local wildlife. The increase in food resources, now that hundreds of detainees and thousands of personnel had moved in, created a veritable population explosion in many species. It began with swarms of ants. They made their way into the cages, carrying eggs between their pincers, swirling about in huge numbers in patterns on the floor, attempting to establish nests. As a group they made a huge, grotesque body. Then came the mice. They also swarmed into the shipping containers in near-plague numbers. They were constantly scampering through my cage and became so bad that, whenever I managed to fall asleep, they would yank the hair from my head, probably to line their nests with. I tried to solve this problem by killing them quickly. It was definitely not something I wanted to do. I have seen the media attempt to make me look sadistic for killing them, as if it was for entertainment. That was not the case at all. The question that should have been asked is, what were mice doing in my living space? And with the mice came snakes. Long, skinny pythons would pop up in pursuit of the mice through the gaps in the floor where two shipping containers met. They would then follow them down to the next gap, six cages along. It made for interesting times.

Military medics often gave detainees tablets, injections and took blood samples.[60] While in Kilo Block, this program of forced medication intensified.[61] The most common excuse for the injections was immunisation against various strains of flu or for tetanus and testing for TB, but further reasons were not always given. Refusal was not an option: either you gave your arm voluntarily or you were physically subdued. Because of this, most detainees offered their arms. However, there have been reports since my release citing evidence of medical experimentation in Guantanamo.[62]

The medics began to give about half of us tablets and the rest injections every second day. At first we consented to what we were told was flu medication. Detainees receiving tablets were the first to rebel. They were given a certain colour and shaped tablet one day, then something totally different the next – presumably for the same reason. The detainees became suspicious, and when they refused they were quickly IRFed and forced to take the medication.

I was given an injection. Within an hour or so I couldn't help but huddle in a corner of the cage. Physically, I felt comfortable, even though it was an odd thing for me to do. In the back of my mind I knew it was strange, but as long as I stayed in that corner I had no real thoughts at all. When I tried to move from that position, whether to eat or go to the toilet, I became extremely agitated and nervous. I would quickly resume my huddled position. Getting the slight shakes was another side effect of this medication. Some time on the second day I began to feel normal again and came out of the corner. I knew I had acted unusually but, because most of that period was a blank in my mind, I could not decide if the injection was responsible.

I think it was the day after, when I began to feel normal again, that I was given another injection. I was scared and pleaded for them not to, but I was threatened with an IRFing if

I did not cooperate. A majority of detainees were being IRFed by then for refusing medication, so I just surrendered my arm, thinking that the needle might snap off in my shoulder if they jabbed me during a beating. I was quickly aware of the results. I went straight to the corner again and curled up but, unlike last time, I was under no illusions about what was happening or why. I tried to fight this chemical reaction but was power-less. My mind was clear and alert, and I could identify my behaviour as abnormal, but my body would not listen to my mind. I had no control and remained in the corner, despite wanting to move. This time around the experience was very distressing. All I could do was wait for the effects of the medi-cation to wear off a full day later.

Once again it was the ICRC that saved us. This period of forced injections and pills coincided with another visit from the only group of people on that island who did not wish us harm: the ICRC. Before I was given a third injection, MPs came and escorted me to an interrogation building, where I had a private interview with an ICRC employee. I pleaded with him to do something about these medical experiments. He told me that nearly every detainee he had seen so far had reported the same program and its effects. Almost instantly after that interview the injections and tablets were stopped, and I did not have to endure another injection. Instead of nearly daily doses, it went back to the normal – at least one injection every two months, including having blood samples taken.

I experienced two other health incidents in Kilo Block. One morning I woke with blood on the side of my face. It had been leaking from an ear while I slept, accompanied by a whistling sound. Later in the day I was taken to the clinic where I was told my eardrum had ruptured. I asked how such a thing could occur while I was sleeping. A doctor responded that I either had my ear up against a loudspeaker or I had been banging my head against a wall. I told him those explanations seemed unreasonable and shed no light on the mystery, nor did it help us prevent it from occurring again. He said, 'Don't go banging your head against walls,' and dismissed me.

A short time later, a groin pain I had been experiencing recently became so severe that I put in another request to see a doctor. After an examination I was informed that I had a double hernia. I agreed to be booked into the hospital for an operation, but this would take a week or so. The detainee hospital in those days was still a complex of tents, a bit like *M.A.S.H.* I was led into one of these tents, where each of my limbs was unexpectedly chained to the bars on the side of the bed. I could not move about or sit up. I was stuck on my back like some captured animal. When I asked the doctor about this, he said it was standard procedure and that I would remain chained like that for my entire stay in the hospital. I began to think of the recent injections and pictured them filling me with any substance they desired without my being able to prevent it. I asked the doctor if I would be receiving any injections or medication other than what was needed to perform the surgery, and all he said was, 'You will get what we give you.' I took this as a yes and panicked, complaining that I did not want the operation, asking to be returned to my cage. I was surprised when they agreed and further relieved when I was unstrapped from the bed and returned to Kilo Block.

The pain increased, however. The hole in my stomach lining became so large that when I stood up my intestines bulged out to the size of a golf ball. I could only stand for a few minutes before the pain became unbearable. If I sat down, my innards retreated and the pain disappeared. Another 'treatment' was to stick two fingers into the hole before I stood up. This method allowed me to stand for longer before the pain forced me down, but it was impractical, so I accepted defeat, took a risk, and requested to see my interrogator.

I told him of my need for an operation, which I'm sure he was already aware of. I explained how I had been strapped down, and my fear of being injected with harmful substances against my will. He asked what I wanted, and I said assurance and protection from experimental injections. He guaranteed such protection but stipulated that I would need to return the favour at his request, otherwise I would have to go it alone. I hated him for taking advantage of me, but that was one of the realities of Guantanamo: interrogators controlled every aspect of our lives, from the vital to the mundane, whether receiving letters from home or having a shower. However, he was good to his word on this occasion.

The very next day I was taken for surgery. It was good timing because the permanent hospital that I had seen being built a few months before from Delta Block had just been completed – no more tents. I was awarded the honour of christening the facility. All four of my limbs were strapped to the bed as before, but only for the first day; after that they were kind enough to strap only two opposing limbs, allowing me to sit up in bed and to scratch myself.

I was in Kilo Block for the first anniversary of September 11. Not surprisingly, the higher-ups made an issue out of it, preparing their soldiers for something 'dangerous' from us. Of course, nothing happened at all – it was not even mentioned among detainees – though the same cannot be said for the US. Mid-morning, jet fighters swooped over Camp Delta. They shot out over the ocean, turned around and made another pass. They flew so low that they would have been, literally, within a stone's throw. The two jets performed about six fly-bys before it was over. A few days later, when I was taken to interrogation, I asked what the

commotion had been about. My interrogator looked at me
and gloated, 'Were you all scared?' and expressed seething
anger when I explained that it was pretty cool because it
gave us something to look at to break the monotony. It was
like a free air show.

There were other ways the US military displayed their hardware. Every two months or so, the soldiers would take part
in live firing exercises, either in the camp itself or just outside
the perimeter fence. One of these exercises involved a floating
target in the shape of a ship positioned a few hundred metres
offshore in front of the camp. Mortars and large-calibre weapons were used on these occasions, which of course were very
loud. The other exercise, if that's what it was, consisted of
guards in the surrounding towers within the camp firing off
full clips in turns. They were expended in the air or directed
out to sea, and I wonder if this, too, was intended to intimidate
us. These sessions of live fire were only performed during daylight and lasted for an hour or two, giving us the impression of
being in, or close to, a field of combat.

Throughout Camp Delta loudspeakers could be found in each
block, on guard towers and fixed in other strategic places.
Towards the end of the year, 2002, these speakers were used
to deliver announcements to detainees. There were hundreds of
us from around forty nations, so every announcement began
in English, and was then followed by the main half a dozen
languages spoken by the detainee population. They went something like this: 'Some of you have spoken the truth and told us
all you know. Some of you have cooperated, but still not told us
all you know and have not been truthful in all areas. Some of
you will never leave here. For those of you who have cooperated
fully, you will return to your families and loved ones. Some of

you still have more to tell your interrogators. The sooner you tell us the truth, the sooner you will go home. And those who refuse to cooperate . . . you will stay here forever.' There was a strong emphasis on loved ones and family.

Once the announcements began, they were played every few days. It gave me great hope to hear them. I was sure I would be one of the first to go home, right up the top of the list. I thought about my interrogations, how I had always cooperated and told the truth. I considered the fact that I was an Australian citizen; I had not committed a crime; I did not have a criminal record back in Australia; I had done nothing wrong. I had never been more sure of anything: I was going home.

I was bursting with anticipation, then, when the announcement changed to mention that today, for the first time, they would be releasing some of us. Today! That was me for sure. *Some* of us would be going home – plural, a group – no way I wouldn't be in the first group. I kept looking for a reason they would deny me – I couldn't find one. Today, my time had come at last.

I was even more overwhelmed and shocked at how fast things were moving when I saw a large group of military personnel enter the block only minutes after the announcement, some wielding TV cameras. My cage was halfway down the block on their left, and the party was approaching. Then they were directly outside my door. I was ready to receive the good news, when they opened the cage door of my neighbour, an Afghani, instead. Reserving my emotions, I watched him shake hands with the soldier who opened his door. He was handed a change of clothes and his personal effects from when he was kidnapped. The soldiers made a show of the release, even allowing him to shake hands with fellow detainees through their bean holes on his way out. The party followed the Afghani out of the block and did not return.

As the minutes passed, information was yelled out to our block by detainees next door that another two Afghanis had been released. One was in his fifties, as the first detainee had been. The other poor soul was in his late nineties and could only shuffle along with the assistance of a walking frame. Even so, the MPs chained one of his wrists to the frame, while another two held him with the four-point contact. I had seen him before, and while it was sad and disgusting that he was even in Guantanamo, it was also humorous to see two young, burly guys escorting a thin, fragile old man, as if he would suddenly thrash his walking frame about in a life-threatening manner. I wondered how he survived the transportation to Guantanamo.

Once the party had departed the block I tried to keep my spirits up, but it was useless. It felt naïve to remain hopeful as the hours passed with no more releases other than the three Afghanis. It was a bitter blow to my morale and began the long deterioration of my mental health and wellbeing. I began to view my existence with a dark pessimism. My hopes, dreams, despair and disappointment took me on an emotional roller-coaster. The injustice and lack of understanding or knowledge of why all this was happening to me began to erode my sanity.

In the weeks following the releases, the loudspeakers continued to drone the same mind-numbing, desensitising information until eventually a new element was added. It went something like this: 'A new camp is being built. It will be modern and comfortable. You will be able to pray, sleep, eat and play sport together. Some of you will be moved there soon. Those of you who have cooperated and truthfully told your interrogators everything you know will be selected to be moved to this camp. If you qualify, you will be moved there to wait for a plane to return you to your loved ones, families . . . This new camp will be the last stage and destination for those of you who are selected to be released.' This new information generated positive speculation among some detainees, while others unsurprisingly met the news with scepticism. Overall, the information was largely ignored, then forgotten.

During mid-December 2002, I was eventually informed by escorts holding the now-familiar garbage bag that I was being moved. It was good that I did not hold any hopes, for I was only moved next door to Lima Block. Within days of the move, however, all occupants of Lima Block were moved to Camp One. The shipping containers of Camp Delta had become so degraded and rusty that civilian contractors were called in to rectify the problem. There were a large number of civilian con-tractors employed in Guantanamo. The whole camp, one block at a time, was being re-welded, modified and given a coat of paint. First, we were moved to Charlie Block, then across the way to Hotel Block, then back to Charlie Block, eventually returning to Camp Two and Lima Block. All of these moves were executed within a week or two.

Ramadan fell during this period, and detainees had to par-ticipate whether they wanted to or not. We were given half a cold MRE at about 5 am, before sunrise. Then at sunset we were given three dates each with which to break the fast. We then had to wait until about 8 or 9 pm, sometimes even later, to receive a 'hot' meal. The meal consisted mostly of rice, the serve so small it could fit in one hand. The higher-ups referred to all meals over the years as being 'culturally appropriate'. It was a very difficult period to endure. The chaplain at the time saw this and complained on our behalf, but it was a purpose-run program to starve us and then have us wait a long time for a meal. Between eating the three dates and the hot meal four or so hours later, Arab detainees who had not cooperated so far were taken to interrogation. They were placed in special rooms – half kitchen and half lounge. In these rooms, beautiful Arab women made and served large, hot meals, truly cultural meals, the type mother used to make. These meals were placed under the nose of the starving detainee, while an interrogator tempted him to give in and eat. Because this program required detainees to be literally starving, the whole camp had to suffer. Whether you were Arab or not, or had cooperated or not, we were all subjected to the same program.

Twenty

*'I know of no other country which treats its enemies like the
US does . . . I am enormously proud of what we do.'*

General Geoffrey Miller[63]

BY THE TIME I HAD SETTLED BACK into Lima Block, Ramadan
and its difficulties were over and the year 2003 had begun.
Unfortunately, that wasn't the only thing to begin. General
Geoffrey Miller had just taken over camp operations at Guantanamo. No intelligence of value was coming out of the detention
camps, and his mission was to squeeze and wring anything and
everything out of us by shaking the place up a bit.[64]

One of the first visible changes was the introduction of a
'levels system'. Level One allowed the most 'privileges', meaning
that the items we already had would not be taken away. There
was also another level called 'Level One Plus', which allowed
a detainee to have 'special' items provided by interrogators.
This might be a toothbrush, shampoo, soap, a whole roll of
toilet paper instead of the usual four squares, an extra sheet or
blanket, perhaps a book. Level Two, on the other hand, would
have something taken away from the few items we were used
to having, Level Three even more. Level Four detainees were

only allowed a pair of shorts. Anything more than a pair of shorts was now classed as 'comfort items'. We were no longer entitled to toilet paper and such necessities – even guys with false limbs had them taken away on Levels Two, Three and Four. It is hard to comprehend how at times we were required to use the bathroom without any toilet paper, not allowed any soap to wash our hands and then expected to eat with our fingers. All of this was perfectly acceptable to our captors.

It was an arbitrary system that determined what level a detainee would be on, dictated by our 'behaviour' or the whims of the interrogators. But, realistically, it was always the interrogators' call. MPs took all orders from interrogators. Only the general could contradict them, and only occasionally prevail. On the ground, it did not appear that there were ever conflicts over detainee abuse, only in areas where a detainee might be said to benefit. If an interrogator gave too much freedom as an incentive for cooperation, it might be 'endangering troop safety'. Or a conflict could arise if an interrogator did not want a potentially cooperative detainee 'disciplined' and risk isolating him, because of an action the general would not tolerate.

Many detainees were deemed to have still not 'cooperated' with interrogators by early 2003. There were also rumours that some detainees had been asked to sign 'confessions', which most of them had refused. This lack of cooperation is what motivated a new wave of interrogation techniques to be unleashed upon us.[65] A number of interrogation rooms were converted into torture chambers. They comprised four main ingredients: stress positions, temperature extremes, erratic lighting and noise.

Imagine: two soldiers come to your shipping-container cage and they strap a three-piece suit on you. You are led into a dark room and short-shackled to a ringed metal bolt in the floor.

You cannot sit, lie down or rest. At first it is uncomfortable but then the position quickly becomes painful. It is quiet and dark, and the temperature starts to rise or fall. Whichever way it swings, it continues to become more extreme until it is unbearable. Then the room will switch to the opposite extreme, and you are left for hours either sweating, nearly passed out from the heat, or shivering desperately from the cold.[66] The room could remain dark or become bright enough to hurt your eyes. Continuously flashing strobe lights seemed a favourite. A combination of the three is always a possibility. That gives you some idea of what we endured.

To add to this experience, sound was also employed – often extremely loud rock music, really heavy stuff. Sometimes CDs like 'Bob the Builder', with all its mechanical noises, or recordings from TV were used. A preferred choice was the 'meow mix' from a TV pet-food advert. I even heard croaking frogs. You could be chained painfully to the floor, freezing cold, strobe lights going mad and tooting steam trains reverberating in your ears, then pounding in your head, then resounding through your whole being – hour after hour. You could be *really* unlucky and have to remain there for a day or two. You might have one session now and then, but you would be more likely to suffer daily doses over weeks before being allowed any respite.[67] FBI reports confirmed that detainees were left for twenty-four hours or more in these torture chambers. Another issue was not being able to go to the toilet; it was humiliating. One guy was so traumatised that when the interrogator came in the next morning he had pulled all of his hair out, strand by strand.[68] I personally experienced the stress positions and temperature.

Other, 'lesser evils' were used to break wills and ensure cooperation. Operation Sandman was a sleep-deprivation program in which a detainee could be moved every hour for weeks on end, never given a chance for meaningful sleep or the right to refuse to participate.[69]

There were also new, innovative ideas for punishments. Instead of just losing all 'comfort items', a detainee might find his room sealed up and a can of pepper spray pumped in. It was common not just to be sprayed but drenched with an oil-based pepper spray, then carried into a freezing-cold shower that would disperse the oil over the entire body, intensifying the burn. Next, you would be placed in an isolation block with the reddish glow: November, Oscar or India blocks. These would be pre-chilled, and you would stay for a day or two before your clothes dried and the burning ceased.

Even the guards began to employ psychotic practical jokes, such as pepper spraying detainees' toilet paper.[70] This overhaul of new treatment was like a licence to all personnel working in the blocks to do what they liked to detainees without worrying about consequences. Conditions had always been bad at this US naval base, but with General Miller it definitely got worse.

We learned about these new techniques slowly. At first there were rumours of such-and-such a technique being done to so-and-so in a different block elsewhere. Then the rumours became more frequent and localised until, even if it wasn't happening to you personally, it began to happen to those around you on the same block, possibly even your neighbour. At least half the detainee population was exposed to these torture rooms and sleep-deprivation programs – possibly even more because some detainees would not discuss what had been done to them.

I was to learn that torture was an embarrassment for many, depending on their cultural background and often because it was of a sexual nature.[71] I met a man who would be one of the first six detainees chosen for military commissions, along with me. We spent a long time together, and he eventually shared something personal with me. He lifted his trouser legs to expose a number of large, deep holes in his calves. The skin looked as if it had been melted at the bottom. He told me he had been electrocuted. I asked if he had shown the injuries to his lawyers and what they had said about this. He had not shown them – and he never would – because he was embarrassed by the experience. I encouraged him to report the incident, but he would not budge, explaining that it was shameful to admit what had happened to him. I owe him an apology for making it public now, but I think it's vitally important that all abuses are exposed. The US military will get away with many cruel acts, especially the more serious physical ones, because some detainees will not openly discuss or report them.

Once these abusive techniques had become part of the daily routine at Guantanamo, other, even sicker, stories began to circulate.

A detainee's mother passed away in 2003. The interrogators thought that they would inform him. He was taken to a torture chamber and chained to the bolt in the floor. As the strobe lights lit up his surroundings, he was shocked to discover that the ground and walls were covered with pictures, either of a pornographic nature or the macabre – corpses, blood and guts – taken from a highly offensive internet site. Each time the room was bathed in the strobes' glare, these images were hideously revealed. As the minutes passed, he noticed someone standing in a corner. This mysterious individual was dressed as the grim reaper, complete with scythe. Once he had been spotted, the costumed man came forward and said something like, 'Your mother is dead and sucking Satan's cock in hell,' and continued to taunt him. Unsurprisingly, this detainee went mad. This inexcusable event was quite a big story among military personnel and they discussed it openly and often. Even subsequent deployments, years later, knew of the story. Of course, we detainees did as well.

Another detainee was chained to a chair while a female interrogator taunted him by touching her breasts and rubbing them on his back. Frustrated that the detainee would not respond, she left the room. When she returned, she placed her hand down the front of her pants. She then pulled it back out, covered in menstrual blood, and wiped it across the detainee's face and down the front of his shirt. She then left the room saying, 'Have a fun night in your cell without any water to clean yourself.' Interrogators turned off his water so he could not wash the 'blood' off. The US government has admitted the event and even defends the action, saying it was only 'fake blood'.[72]

We also heard stories of detainees who had been chained to the floor in interrogation booths. They would then have American and Israeli flags wrapped tightly around them while being taunted with photographs of Muslims who had been killed by foreign military forces. They would be left alone for hours, still wrapped in the flags, the visual images left in front of them.

It was around the time of all this madness that my interrogator asked if there was something I would like, within reason, so I asked for a book. I thought back to my early days, searching for something I would enjoy and something that would help pass a lot of time. I asked for *The Lord of the Rings* trilogy, a good, escapist read that would last a few weeks. A few days later I was returned to interrogation. As I entered the room I saw a book on the table. To my disappointment, it was not *The Lord of the Rings*. After a few minutes of meaningless chitchat, the interrogator pointed to the book. I had a look at the front cover and saw a kid on a broomstick; I said I didn't want to read it. My response elicited anger and frustration and, in a rare show of courage at that time, I argued back. I refused to take the book.

The next day the interrogator actually came into my block. This was almost unprecedented. Six detainees may have interrogators with six different names to hide their identity, but it is really the same interrogator. To show his face in front of so many detainees at once risked giving the game away. On this day, however, he entered the block with some of his associates and threatened me with physical punishment if I did not take the book. I began to protest, but he said I had no choice – I would have daily 'special treatment' until I read it. Scared and bewildered, I accepted the book.

The book turned out to be the first Harry Potter novel. The story was okay, but I felt it was in my interest to tell the interrogator I did not enjoy it. I had that opportunity a few days later when I informed the block guard I had finished reading the book, as I had been instructed. When I told the interrogator what I thought, he said 'good', and passed me another volume. 'This is number two, and there's still more to come.' I couldn't believe it, another one! But I knew the seriousness of my situation if I refused. I read the second book. Crackpot ideas were always being devised and implemented by teams of people who worked with the interrogators.[73] The Harry Potter one is weird – how could being threatened with torture if I didn't read the story of a boy wizard not be? But you can rest assured that someone had a serious, premeditated reason. I wonder what J.K. Rowling thinks? After I had read the second book, numerous other copies were handed out to all detainees who could read and understand English. I was just the first guinea pig in this bizarre experiment. The Harry Potter books remained in English, but as time passed many other books were distributed to detainees in Arabic, Pashto, Urdu and other detainee languages. They were largely children's books about Mickey Mouse and other cartoon characters, stories meant for preschool children.[74] Harry Potter was even publicly reported to be the 'most-requested book' in Guantanamo by a US government spokesman.[75] What is up with that?

Once 2003 was under way and I had settled into Lima Block, the loudspeaker announcements increased concerning Camp Four. By then detainees had largely dismissed its existence, and interrogators were having a hard time selling the idea as an escape from the daily brutality and enhanced interrogation techniques being used in Camp Delta. To try to solve this, interrogators spread rumours that two detainees from every block would be taken to where Camp Four was being constructed. They wanted us to see it with our own eyes and spread the word among detainees. I was one of two chosen from my block to go.

In true and familiar propaganda fashion, the authorities could not help but make this a ceremonial event. They had me dress in white clothes when orange was the only colour seen so far in Guantanamo. This would soon change, because Level One began to be issued tan uniforms with white T-shirts. Instead of the usual three-piece suit, only standard handcuffs were applied, joined to the waist by a velcro strap. Even the guards were more relaxed as I was escorted in the green Gator buggy without a blindfold. We drove to Camp One, through a new hole in the fence behind the clinic, then arrived at the site next door to Camp Delta. Only one building in Camp Four had been completed by that stage.

Nearby foundations suggested another three identical buildings were to go up. The perimeter fence had been erected, indicating what the overall size of the camp would be, including a very large rec area centred between buildings. A dozen or so important-looking, high-ranking officers were present, standing at attention in a half circle. One of them commenced the briefing, explaining that to be selected for this camp meant to be selected for release. Then he continued on about how humane, comfortable, relaxing and wonderful the camp would be, but he spoke as though he did not believe his own words. I was also unimpressed by the camp as I scanned my surroundings. I was told – ordered, actually – that when I returned back to my block I would spread the word to as many detainees as possible about how good this camp would be. When he finished, he asked if I had any questions, but what I asked concerning day-to-day procedures only angered him, so I was bundled back into the John Deere Gator and returned to Lima Block.

I spread the word that the camp existed but that it did not look good. I told them how ten or so detainees would live in one very small room, all having to share one toilet and sink, which would be a battleground first thing in the morning and at prayer times? It had a large recreation yard, but we would only have access to it for an hour a day; the rest of the time we would be locked down in the small room with no windows, cameras watching our every move. I was taken to interrogation. They looked surprised when I raised my complaints and said I wouldn't go there if given the chance.

A few months later, Camp Four was ready and the news was announced with much fanfare. It was on a Friday, Jumma in the Islamic calendar, a holy day equivalent to Sunday in Christianity. We were told that each Jumma a number of detainees would be chosen to go to Camp Four and begin the process of release, starting that day. A small group of military personnel would enter a block with a large, transparent plastic tub. The cage door was opened without restraining the detainee first, who was presented the tub with a handshake and a smile. The lucky detainee changed into white clothing, had the velcro cuffs applied and was allowed to shake hands with other detainees through the bean holes on his way out. The detainee then disappeared on the back of a Gator in a cloud of dust.

This performance was repeated each Friday when ten or so detainees were chosen from Camp Delta to go to Camp Four. Interestingly, these events were all filmed by a low-ranking officer. The weekly transfers occurred over a ten-week period, until the camp was close to its maximum capacity average of 100 detainees. All transfers then ceased, the propaganda came to an end and Fridays went back to normal. The fanfare of that event never took place again, even when transfers later resumed.

For the first time a large segment of detainees had been truly isolated from the main body, leaving the 600 or so of us in Camp Delta waiting anxiously for news of their fate, so as to judge our own. But for a long time no-one ever returned to tell the tale. All we could do was speculate on what was happening over in Camp Four. What would our futures hold? This event had captured the interest of all detainees. Only a few remained unconvinced that the release of everyone had possibly started.

One day a Camp Four detainee was sent back to Camp Delta. On arrival, he was hidden away in November Block, but we were not robbed of the valuable opportunity to learn what had happened. He yelled loudly enough so that his voice carried to the nearest 'normal' block. What he had to say then entered the detainee information bank: all we had been led to believe about Camp Four was a lie. While some little things were better, it was not much of an improvement and no-one was really going home at all. He said that Camp Four was nothing more than a new version of the old camp and the latest interrogation ploy.

As time passed more detainees started to return, while a few guys from our camp were sent to Camp Four to take their place. For weeks we had all hopelessly searched for reasons, patterns and similarities between the lucky ones that were selected for Camp Four and ultimately their release. We needed to know what they had done to qualify so we could follow suit. The big question was: how does one get picked for release; what do we have to do and say? Such questions became redundant anyway when we discovered that the promise of release was false. Five and a half years of detention would convince me that there is nothing a detainee can do himself to be released, whether through correct behaviour or cooperation. We could never find a pattern, nothing ever made sense. For example, there were *some* detainees who were understandably very angry about what had been done to them. They were very vocal about their illegal detention and torture, and how they would kill as many Americans as possible in retribution if they were ever released. Yet, even with those displays of anger, those types of detainees were released in the years to come along with the quiet, well-behaved and cooperative ones. It made it all the more perplexing for us. These days, I can more confidently cite political decisions that are responsible for a detainee's release – or not – from Guantanamo.

The speculation about Camp Four turned out to be correct – it was just another camp and not one step closer to home. Interrogators were just experimenting with a new environment for their manipulation program. Most detainees never trusted interrogators again after the Camp Four experience, let alone the torturous and cruel treatment they continuously put us through.

Twenty-one

'There is nothing against you. But there is no innocent
person here. So, you should confess to something so you can
be charged and sentenced and serve your sentence and then
go back to your family and country, because you will not
leave this place innocent.'

US interrogator to Fouad al-Rabiah[76]

'We understand that nudity is used as a technique to
create psychological discomfort . . . Even if this technique
involves some physical discomfort, it cannot be said to cause
"suffering".'

Steven G. Bradbury, Head of Office of Legal Counsel,
Department of Justice, in a memorandum to
John A. Rizzo, General Counsel, CIA[77]

DURING THE MONTH OF MARCH 2003, I was moved from
Lima Block to Mike Block next door. I was positioned between
a couple of guys from the UK. At the back of this block was
a Bosnian surrounded by empty cages. We were the closest
detainees to him. He was being told to sign a false confession, which he refused to do. In order to persuade him, he
was receiving two eight-hour sessions of interrogation within
a twenty-four-hour period every day. The guy looked a mess.

He said they had been submitting him to this for weeks before we came along. He was neither eating nor sleeping, and he confided in us that he had to endure being stripped naked and dragged about on the floor during interrogation. The rest he kept to himself.

The three of us watched as he was removed from his cage and marched out of the block every day and night. He was taken away fully clothed, then literally dragged back hours later. He was so exhausted he was unable to walk. We could see he had been undressed, because he was often returned with only his pants on, and they would be inside out. He was really taking a beating. Not only could we see him battling to maintain his sanity, he looked to be battling to stay alive. He was so skinny, sickly and weak, yet they kept on abusing him. For those of us observing, we knew such a sustained campaign could be launched against any of us at any time. I'm sure we all shared the same thought: *how long could I last?*

Around this time a rumour surfaced that MPs had killed a detainee in India Block, the isolation block in Camp One. There was outrage and detainees protested in what little ways they could. Those who had foam cups urinated in them and threw the contents on passing MPs. Many detainees spat on guards whenever they had the chance. The first large-scale hunger strikes began. There were threats of mass suicide, and the worry and concern expressed by the guards and interrogators at this threat gave detainees a sense of control. Many detainees refused to leave their cages for any reason, including orders to attend interrogation. In order not to look weak, the military always sent in the IRF team to remove the detainee by force. If twenty detainees refused in a row, or more as was often the case, two or three IRF teams would operate simultaneously, taking out all twenty detainees, one after the other. Sometimes an entire block would refuse and get IRFed,

followed by another block, requiring IRF teams to move from
block to block until the whole camp was involved.

These were really serious beatings. Lightweight detainees –
unfit, slow and malnourished – would fight with all their
strength against these five- or six-man teams fully suited in
kevlar, face guards and full-length shields. The detainees gave
it a good go and would get terribly pummelled and seriously
injured. Yet, amazingly, some of the detainees would keep
resisting, never backing down, getting IRFed until they passed
out from pain or exhaustion. I had never seen such strength
of heart, mind and spirit. Such courage is not a quality I
possess, especially during that period of my life, yet many of
the detainees did. They rebelled and resisted until the camp
resembled a combat zone. To keep up soldier morale after an
event such as this, some soldiers were even awarded purple
hearts, which I think is a good example of the propaganda the
soldiers received.

For the duration of the resistance, 700-odd detainees would
resist sleep, sometimes for two or three days, continuously
banging and kicking various parts of their metal cage until
they found the noisiest. Once identified, and such a part always
existed, they made as loud and constant a din as possible.
Apparently this racket could be heard some kilometres away.
It was amazing how long detainees as a whole could keep up
the banging without a break. Many times it didn't cease. In
the end, the military would cut the plumbing into the blocks.
This prevented water from being thrown on guards, stopped
detainees from being able to wash pepper spray off themselves
and sped up detainee fatigue by dehydration. It also interfered
with their prayers. Guards would then close up blocks and fill
them with multiple cans of pepper spray, releasing them into
big industrial fans set up at the front of the block. Then it was
just a matter of IRFing detainees again and again and again,

until they couldn't stand up any longer, with the day and night MP shifts playing tag team. Guards could rest and refresh between shifts but for detainees it was a long, continuous struggle. After two or three days even the strongest detainees collapsed in a heap, not stirring again for twenty-four hours or so. Even the soldiers would use the first day or two after such an incident to recover and leave the detainees to sleep.

With the rumour of the death in India Block, this was probably the biggest protest so far. From then on detainees did not care any longer about niceties or following some script for release. By then Guantanamo was seen for what it was, and detainees no longer had anything to lose. These kinds of protests often happened in response to some injustice: someone being IRFed unfairly, Islam being disrespected in some way, someone being seriously hurt in interrogation.

The general himself began using the loudspeakers to reassure the population that the detainee in question was not dead. He was recovering in hospital. The injuries sustained were at his own hands, an unfortunate and terrible accident . . . He claimed the military was not responsible for the detainee's misfortune – he had hanged himself with his sheet. He was already clinically dead when the soldiers first got him down, but was now in a stable condition in hospital.

The few detainees who had watched and listened to what happened told the rest of us a different story. The MPs filled the detainee's enclosed isolation cage with pepper spray. When the IRF team entered, they found the occupant standing on the metal bunk at the back of the room. They grabbed his ankles and ripped him down. As he fell, he hit the side of his head and landed on the floor. The MPs then beat him, after kicking him first. He was carried outside and taken away.

Whatever had caused his injuries, the detainee was in hospital and would be chained to the same bed for years.

He could not talk, feed himself or go to the toilet unassisted. He twitched and shook uncontrollably. Because of this, the MPs nicknamed him 'Timmy', apparently after Timmy in the cartoon *South Park*. I would see him on odd occasions when I attended the hospital in the years ahead. It was sad to see a man reduced to the state of a dependent baby. *Which one of us would be next?*

Needless to say, this was an extremely frightening time in a dangerous environment. Every day I witnessed or heard some act of unrestrained violence.[78] I couldn't understand how one human could treat another in such a way. I was a nervous wreck and not coping well. I constantly feared for my safety, found the daily living conditions tough, and I could not help at times being concerned about my life. I am not proud of how I performed during this test of my character and constitution. I was determined to save myself from the punishments that were wearing away my physical and psychological health. So I tried bargaining with my interrogator.

After having been reduced to a shadow of my former self, I begged for it all to stop. I admitted that I was a broken man and that I did not have the strength to go on. I waved the white flag. The interrogator gloated as he accepted my defeat and dictated the rules. I was promised total protection from the physical punishment being dished out, besides a few other things, in exchange for full cooperation. Once a week I would be taken to a place nicknamed the Love Shack by US personnel. The Love Shack was a large room within the interrogation facility set up to resemble a comfortable lounge room – an environment designed to create longings for home. It had a plush carpet, cushy lounge, flatscreen TV, entertainment system, ornaments and paintings on the walls. I was allowed to stay in the Love Shack for the duration of one DVD. This granted me an escape from the shipping containers and the hostile environment for two or three hours every week. During that time, I attempted to enjoy the unlimited cigarettes, real food and drink other than warm, desalinated water, but it really felt like I was consuming my own soul. I became addicted to those few hours of normalcy. Back in my cage I was allowed to keep soap, shampoo and a full roll of toilet paper.

Those products helped improve my level of hygiene, which had a positive albeit superficial impact on my morale. But the strongest influencing factor behind my surrender was an instinct to survive, a selfish determination, no matter how precarious the promise, of avoiding the long-suffering pain of detainee existence. While recalling this, I have had strong flashbacks where I relive the experience of that time: how it felt and how it impacted on me. In hindsight, I can see that I had lost my sense of self.

I had become a stranger to myself, a product of the inter-rogation methods I had endured for over a year now. A goal of interrogation is to repeatedly break you and then put you back together until the parts can be manipulated. You become the interrogators' creation. This may sound melodramatic to someone who has not been subjected to such institutional-ised brutality, but it will sound all too familiar to victims of torture. Such manipulative and soul-destroying programs are not conducted ad hoc – an exact science has evolved through experimentation over hundreds of years. The memory of what I have described depresses me deeply to this day. It does something to the soul; it felt like something had died inside me. Having suffered under those conditions, I would never judge a person's behaviour or decisions made under similar circumstances.

My end of the bargain was that I had to verbally repeat my story, agreeing with anything they added, even when they dic-tated my thoughts, beliefs and actions incorrectly. They also fed me things to say about other detainees as well. I did so obediently, even though I knew they were all lies. I struggled terribly with this and hated every minute of it, especially when they brought up other detainees. I searched desperately for the courage to resist and renege on the deal. I had no recourse. I had crumbled and was fully theirs.

All those fabricated stories relating to other detainees, most of whom I had never met pre-Guantanamo, many I had never even seen before, quickly reached the ears of the FBI, who until then had never shown an interest in me. In an interview with the FBI, they asked about the statements I had given to the military, especially all of the contradictions. I expected them to know about the manipulative process the military interrogator used to obtain the information and could not understand why they kept pursuing these lines of inquiry. After a few interviews I asked what they wanted, and then it dawned upon me that these people might be viewing my statements as factual. I told them I couldn't remember what I had said – the plot lines had become too numerous and complex. That half of what I had said was directly dictated to me, the other half was from my imagination. This declaration perplexed them and, after a few minutes of private consultation among themselves, they asked me what had been happening between me and the military interrogator. They did not look impressed. It was refreshing, almost amusing, to see a hint of professionalism – they obviously didn't appreciate the military's run-around. Interestingly, I did not see that particular military interrogator again. He and the Love Shack suddenly disappeared without explanation, and I feared that the 'protection' would go the same way. I waited daily to be taken to the torture chambers.

A number of weeks passed before my interrogations resumed. When they did, it was with a new military interrogator I had not seen before. To my horror, he turned out to be the one who ordered the Bosnian to be stripped naked and dragged about for hours every day.

To add more stress to the daily camp program, some detainees caught wind of the agreement I had entered into with my previous interrogator. I had been up-front with a neighbour on this issue, attempting to get some advice. Instead, he became angry and yelled out what I had told him in confidence. This caused quite a disturbance and a number of detainees on my block were abusive and yelled threats. Other detainees minded their own business, I suspect because they had fallen into the same trap. Many detainees were eventually forced to sign false confessions or make statements that were untrue. Other detainees openly defended me, asking for patience and wisdom. It was the voices of unreason that prevailed, however, bombarding me with hostile words, adding to the discomfort of camp life.

Apart from those few reasonable detainees who continued to speak with me, a chasm widened between me and the population. Interrogators capitalised on my isolation, indirectly inviting me to forget the detainees and side with them – not that I would ever view them as allies. While interrogating other detainees, the interrogators would allege that I was a mole and make leading suggestions: 'Why did I have shampoo and toilet paper?' Turning detainees against one another was not just a divide-and-conquer technique, it was also used as another means to obtain false statements, ones made in anger, out of spite, or revenge. The situation was tense among us on Lima and Mike Block, and it steadily increased until I was moved back to Camp One. I was there for a week before being transferred. After several of these movements, I returned to Mike Block in Camp Two. The hostile voices had quietened while I was away, and they ignored me upon my return.

*

Around this time, I and some other detainees were able to get hold of a pen and paper. Dreaming of home, I decided to draw a map of an old fishing spot in Adelaide. I stuck it on my wall with a bit of toothpaste. Later that day, I was taken out for a shower, and upon my return the map was gone. That night I was taken to interrogation. There were two men, the usual interrogator and another whom I hadn't seen before. He stared at me the whole time menacingly. The interrogator produced my sketch and accused me of drawing an escape map, complete with guard towers. It took a long time for me to explain how ridiculous that was – the 'map' was really a fishing spot back home. He said that he would check on the internet whether the place existed – if he found it, he would not hassle me again. I never did hear about that map again.

After listening to my story, the detainee next to me drew squiggly lines above a small circle on a piece of paper and stuck it on his wall, just as I had. He called the guards over to his cage and said, 'Look at this. What do you think it is?'

The guards responded, 'Get it off – you can't have that up there!'

He persisted, asking them, 'What is it?' He then lifted up his T-shirt and pointed to his sixpack, saying, 'This!' We all laughed at the bewildered guards.

One ordinary day, some time in May 2003, I was taken to interrogation. I was surprised, however, when I was led to the Love Shack. As I entered, three civilian men stood to greet me. They wore the biggest, friendliest smiles and warmly shook my hand in turn, a gesture that had never happened before. It had quite an impact on me. Their jovial demeanour charged the air with a hint of celebration. They asked me to sit and had the restraints removed, another novelty. Then an abundance of food and drink was spread before me. Cigarettes, a lighter and an ashtray followed. I was told to relax and enjoy myself; they had some great news.

After some idle chitchat, they said a decision had been reached regarding my situation – I would soon be going home to Australia. They congratulated me profusely. The positive vibe was catchy, and I accepted what I was hearing as the truth. For half a day we did nothing but eat, drink and smoke. After the way I had been treated for the last year and a half, it felt like a party.

Towards the end of the day, they proceeded to share more detailed information with me. Before being released, I would need to sign a statement. Within a week of signing, I would be moved to the island's naval brig, where conditions would mirror a federal prison. I would be able to use a gym, basketball court and spend long hours outside in the sun. I would have access to music, books and magazines. Conditions would be clean, and I would be able to maintain my personal hygiene. I could also smoke and, best of all, I would no longer be exposed to the interrogation techniques or 'the games', as they put it. They said there was no need for me to be treated in that manner any longer, and that they would now have sole control over me. They would visit daily, making sure I had everything I needed and that I was getting access to all the available benefits. They looked me in the eye and said they had been able to secure permission for me to stay in the brig until it was time to return to Australia – never would I see another detention camp again. They finished by saying that the very latest I would be released and returned to Australia was August of that year, leaving me only three more months in Guantanamo, at the most.

I was furious, however, when they told me I would have to sign a document. It's one thing to agree to something verbally, but quite another to sign an agreement, especially considering the contents of the document they produced. When I said I would never sign, they asked me to hear them out first. They suggested we should all return tomorrow and go over the document together, while enjoying more food, drink and cigarettes. I would have some say in its contents and amendments could be negotiated so that all parties were satisfied. 'Wait until tomorrow, see what you think, no harm in looking,' said these government salesmen. They also added that I should be grateful that the powers that be had taken the time to resolve my case; to be released was a privilege because all other detainees at that time were not being offered the same opportunity. Plenty would rot in Cuba for the rest of their lives.

When I still ummed and ahhed, they said I could sign now and go home, putting this nightmare behind me. If I refused, I would just be sent back to the camp, to conditions that slowly sucked the life out of me. I would have to suffer interrogation, MPs, a hostile environment and antagonistic detainees. They said I would be offered the same opportunity, the exact same statement, six months later with no changes anyway, so why not get it over and done with now. I thought about it for a long time and came to the conclusion that there wouldn't be any harm coming back and having a look. At the very least, I would get another day out of my cage to eat, drink and smoke. I agreed to see them tomorrow.

The following day began in much the same way. I was then handed the document. Looking at it closely, the first thing I noticed was the way it was written in the first person, as though I had typed up the document myself. The second thing that struck me was its outrageous contents. Furious, I threw it down onto the table in disgust. I refused to read the entire document and went to leave. The three men panicked and worked hard to regain the upper hand. They asked me not to be hasty and to recommend changes. They spent the next few minutes in damage control and, against all my instincts, I picked up the document and began reading again. Up to this point I had said whatever I was told and allowed my thoughts to be manipulated. But seeing those thoughts expressed in a concrete, written format, ready for my signature, was a shock. A voice in my head said, *If I was going to write about what happened, it would not look like this. Why would I sign that?* When I said this out loud and asked for the opportunity to do it myself, that choice in freedom was denied.

It was a four- or five-page 'confession', which contained the most outrageous assertions. If I was smarter, I would have left it how it was. Some parts were so ridiculous that others would surely have seen it for what it was: a trumped-up piece of nonsense, written by someone – clearly not me – who had little knowledge of the subject matter or didn't care. Unfortunately, I proved to be my own worst enemy, as I often did throughout my Guantanamo ordeal. Instead of leaving sections that would have exposed it as a dubious confession, I attempted to educate them and gave them a helping hand. For example, I suggested that they shouldn't refer to Tabligh as one of the most violent and extreme political organisations in the world.

I then argued and negotiated the allegations, disputing the way some points were misleading, such as the word al-Qaeda being peppered throughout the document and suggestions that I was a member of such an organisation or at the least knew that it existed. They also wrote that I agreed with al-Qaeda's ideology and that I harboured great love for the terrorist organisation and their actions. I then challenged other falsehoods, such as the allegation that I did not wear a military uniform at any time in Afghanistan, which would bolster their claim that I was an unlawful combatant.

In some areas they took my advice, such as the false claims made against Tabligh. In other areas, they would not budge, such as the matter of the uniform and other cunningly worded phrases. One of them had a small laptop, upon which the changes were made before printing off amended copies. I hated everything about this process: the document, the people I was with and myself for being involved. What I hated most of all was the realisation that I was going to have to sign the confession regardless of how it painted me or, as it suggested, how I painted myself. This cold reality reflected my limited options. I was reprimanding myself for exposing my weakness a month or two earlier, when I had said to the military interrogator that I was broken and had had enough. I virtually advertised that the time was ripe to offer confessions for signature.

By the afternoon I was unable to negotiate any more changes from these con men who disregarded fairness and truth. I was not at all happy with the confession but, when it came to the crunch, I signed. The most important goal was getting myself out of there and back to Australia. I was so desperate to leave the island that I probably would have signed anything. When we were finished, they said that I would be moved to the brig in about a week, but until then I was to return to Mike Block.

A week passed. I was taken not to the brig, but back to the Love Shack. Instead of the three who were present for the confession signing, I was met by someone else. He apologised for the delay, asked me to have patience and then sent me back to Mike Block. I relayed news of the confession to some detainees but, because of my previous problems, this information was taken the wrong way and they started hurling abuse all over again. At the end of the second week I was returned to the Love Shack, and again asked to have patience. I complained about attitudes on the block and asked to at least be moved elsewhere if I wasn't being relocated instantly to the brig. My wish was granted and I was moved back to Camp One.

*

I was transferred to Echo Block, and what I learned about neighbouring Delta Block disgusted me: it was now officially known as the Crazy Block among MPs. They were using it to house those detainees – about forty at the time – who had developed mental health issues and could no longer function normally. In my opinion forty is a large number, considering we had only been on the island for seventeen months. Then again, I'm surprised there weren't more given our conditions and treatment. I wonder how many detainees lost their sanity after three or four years? At the time of writing, some have been there eight years.

Interestingly, from what I understood at the time, a large percentage of those forty detainees were individuals who had been overly submissive to their interrogators. Some of them had been known to say things like, 'I am not a terrorist. Instead, I am an enemy to your enemies, to all detainees. I am not one of them or like them. I am like you. I will do anything you ask of me.' Some of them thought it was a way to convince their interrogators to believe their innocence. And when interrogators encouraged them, they thought this sycophantic approach was succeeding and went further. I know of one guy who went to extremes to try to convince the MPs that he wasn't Muslim. He requested pork and alcohol; he asked for music and always talked about sex. When the soldiers stood to attention every sunrise and sunset and saluted during their reveille, he would even salute along with them. When detainees around him prayed, he would make lots of noise, and insult God, Mohammed, Muslims and their families to their faces.

He and others like him thought they were doing the right thing to get released, that the interrogators actually *liked* them and believed they were innocent, and I would bet they all were innocent. Because they opened themselves up so completely and were willing, enthusiastic participants in these experiments they were manipulated sadistically. These detainees were examples of how interrogators would push their psychological mind games way beyond the limits considered safe, without regard for detainee safety. Their minds snapped.

The nightmarish noises that came out of Delta Block were disturbing. It was a frightful reminder of what I could become if I was not mentally strong enough. Losing my ability to reason, my very identity, and to have my brain wiped clean and replaced with a twisted stranger's was a much scarier prospect than the worst physical torture, which I could maybe recover from in time. To become like some of the Delta Block inhabitants was a life not worth living, as far as I was concerned.

For hours at a time, detainees would scream like donkeys, monkeys and creatures unknown, or hammer out droning, mesmerising rhythms upon the metal bunks. At times it sounded like a zoo, at other times like a perverse party. The most sickening part of this operation was that the MPs specially hand-picked to work this block actually encouraged this behaviour. They would stand around, laugh and egg them on, while medics kept them full of antidepressants like Prozac. The medication and encouragement fuelled the detainees' madness. I can remember the Bahraini detainee, who had suffered the horrific beating back in Camp X-Ray, yelling out to me from the rec yard, 'Come and join us – just try to kill yourself.' He ended up attempting suicide at least ten times before he was released. One time, while during a lawyer's visit, he was left alone so he could use the toilet. When the lawyer returned, the detainee had cut himself and was sprawled against the wire, smeared with blood.

Interrogators occasionally used these detainees for their dirty work. They would take false statements from these guys or just get them to sign confessions against other detainees.

One of them used to yell out that he was 'off to the restaurant' when being escorted to interrogation, boasting that he paid for the food in made-up stories about us. Some of these guys would be sent out into the blocks, placed in among a group of detainees to verbally abuse them or bang the metal cage as the others tried to sleep – anything that would generate anger. Whole blocks would erupt into chaos because of these manip-ulated souls, who would then be returned to Delta Block once their mission was completed.

In the years to come I would witness the worst example of someone having lost their mind while I was in hospital. This particular detainee would insert his fingers into his anus, then remove them and place them in his mouth. He masturbated chronically and played with his urine and faeces. Apart from this, he was constantly wriggling about and making strange noises. He was fine on arrival, the same as any one of us, but his mind slowly withered away. He was now unable to func-tion and would need a high level of care if he ever re-entered society. The scariest thing was that it could have happened to any of us.

At the end of June 2003, at least a month after I had signed the confession, MPs eventually arrived with a garbage bag for my few belongings, indicating I was to be moved. I was told I was moving to a special location, which I was so relieved to hear. I was tired – really tired. The camp had become an evil and dangerous place. Detainees were now paranoid and sus-picious; some were losing their minds. Our little world, this fish-bowl existence, was slowly changing us. We knew for the rest of our lives, or at least for a very long time to come, we would have to scrape to gain our sanity back. We were hav-ing something indescribable forced upon us, and there was no way to avoid the all-consuming, damaging effects. It felt like my life was being saved when I was moved from Camp Delta, like I had been pulled from a sinking ship. With a sigh of relief – and my last remaining shred of hope – I climbed into the back of an ambulance-turned-prisoner-transport vehicle and was driven away to an unknown fate.

Twenty-two

*'We have no capacity to try Mr Hicks because he did not
commit an offence against . . . Australian criminal law.'*
Former Prime Minister John Howard[79]

I SAT SQUASHED BETWEEN TWO SOLDIERS, blindfolded and
ear-muffed, for a brief five minutes. Hot air, dust and sunlight rushed in to embrace us as the doors were flung open on
our arrival. Soldiers' fingers wrapped tightly around my arms,
guiding me along a path I could not see as gravel crunched
underfoot. I could feel the full strength of the sun beating
down, then the relief of cool shade, as I was guided up four
wooden steps. I knew I was in an enclosed and mostly empty
room before the blindfold was removed. When my sight was
restored, I was in an average-sized square room. A wall of diamond wire ran down the centre from floor to ceiling, dividing
the room into two halves. On one side, where I currently stood,
was a single chair and a small table for the guard. The other
side, also divided into two parts, was for me. One section contained a shower, the first real shower I had seen for years.

The other section was an exact replica of the Camp Delta
cages (one step wide by two steps long), apart from it not being

a shipping container. It also contained a real toilet – granted, it was a metal one without a lid. When I was led around into this section and had the restraints removed, a door separating the cage and shower was closed and locked. An MP could open and close this door from outside in their half of the room, which was part of the daily program. My time was spent living in this quarter of the small room, though I was already used to the cramped space from the Camp Delta cages.

This room had no windows, so I could not see any natural light. Instead, artificial light glared down from the ceiling twenty-four hours a day. Only when the guards came and went could I tell if it was day or night outside. There was an exhaust fan used to keep the humidity down. However, it made a maddening, droning noise. Big, green mould spores spread across the ceiling like some alien creature from a horror movie. There was an air conditioner to help keep temperatures down. The house had a corrugated iron roof, and during the few power shortages I felt how hot it could get without it.

Unfortunately, the air conditioner was sometimes set to freezing by sadistic individuals or used under orders to add to my discomfort. I would be in thin clothing, barefoot, in a metal cage. The guards wore multiple layers of clothing, sometimes even thermals, and could go outside now and then to thaw out. All the while, as the hours passed, I would get colder and colder and was sometimes laughed at for how much I shivered.

There were two lots of recreation periods in this camp. When the middle door was opened to allow access to the shower, it was usually left open for an hour. This added a two-step wide by a two-step long space to the cage area to pace about in. I was almost able to walk four steps in one direction before having to turn around – the biggest living space I had been kept in yet. There was also a recreation yard outside, though it was a poor excuse for one. It was no more than four or five steps square – a cyclone fence cube. I was only allowed to use this rec yard in the night-time. This meant I would not see the sun for the next sixteen months. Eventually it took lobbying from my lawyers for me and other detainees to be able to take recreation during daylight hours. It was not completely dark out there in the night. The camp was lit up with the usual floodlights, some fixed and some portable, which were more than adequate to illuminate my new surroundings. This camp reminded me of *Hogan's Heroes*. There were eleven buildings set out in a rectangle, all facing a single glass structure in the middle. This was where the highest-ranking soldier was stationed, along with two or three other lower enlisted, and was referred to as the Guard Shack. All camp operations were run from this central point. The rest of the soldiers working in the camp rotated from building to building, keeping a close eye on detainees. My room was one of two within the building, meaning this camp – Camp Echo – could house twenty-two detainees.

It had only just been built, and I was the third detainee to be transferred there. Neither I nor the main body of detainees had heard about this camp previously. Besides Camp X-Ray and Camp Delta, Camp Echo was the third camp I was aware of. For the first few minutes upon my arrival I kept thinking, *This is not the brig*, and I kept telling my escorts that there must be some sort of mistake. Of course I was ignored. When the escorts had left and it was just me and a lone guard in a chair on the other side of the diamond wire staring at me, I gave him a hard time about the brig until he lost patience and told me to ask my interrogators.

As much as I didn't like to admit it, I told myself that I had probably been screwed over and there was no mistake: this green, painted metal cage was probably going to be my new home. I asked the guard if he was going to keep staring at me, and he said there would be someone sitting in that chair twenty-four hours a day, writing in a big, green book what I was doing every fifteen minutes, whether sleeping or using the toilet. A lot of green books were filled during the time I spent in Camp Echo, but they wouldn't make interesting reading.

Even though I had not been taken to the brig, I was still relieved to be out of Camp Delta. This new environment was not as intense and hostile, and I relaxed a little for the first time in quite a while. I was also able to gain a little hope and confidence; it was a time to gather what strength I could find. The guards working the camp at the time of my arrival were nearing the end of their deployment. The hype and propaganda of the mission had all worn off by then, and they were generally happy and relaxed because their freedom was near.

They were flouting rules and began taking magazines and laptops into the rooms. Staring at us staring at them must have been boring, to say the least. It was definitely boring for us. Some of them positioned their computers so I could watch movies along with them from behind the diamond wire. This was the first time I had seen a laptop computer. If I was lucky, I was given a magazine to read. These acts of kindness and the odd normal conversation with the guards also helped improve my state of mind.

Even so, I was still very much physically and mentally exhausted, and inevitably my belief in Islam was eroded. I stopped praying and no longer took part in religious observances. This is not because of anything to do with the religion itself or the people. I enjoyed the years I had spent with Muslim people. I found them to be very kind, and they had shown me another side to life. I believed that what was happening to the Muslims of Kashmir and other places was atrocious; I had wanted to help them, to see them live in peace and security. However, by this time I had been so broken that I just wanted to resume the life I had before venturing overseas and put everything else behind me.

After I had been in Camp Echo for a month or so, an Australian government representative came to see me, accompanied by an unidentified American. She read from a sheet of paper, and what she said was hard to comprehend. I hardly heard her words as she informed me that I had been chosen to front a military commission. It was the first time I had heard of military commissions or any type of 'legal' proceedings. I was in a daze; her words were a faint voice somewhere in my subconscious, their meaning and implications stunning my senses. I couldn't believe that after all this time, after all I had been through, this was all my government had to say to me. What about being released? What happened to going home?

Then I was snapped back: 'The Australian government has been able to secure a guarantee that you will not face the death penalty.' *Death!* I laughed out loud. Why would there be any talk of *death*? I could not stop laughing – I think I went a bit mad. I don't remember anything else, except that I was soon on my own again with a guard staring at me. She returned later that day to inform me that I would be assigned a lawyer. This would be the first lawyer I would have seen in the two years since being detained. She then asked about my general welfare. I cannot remember everything I told her, just what bothered me most at the time. I had lost a lot of weight, including muscle mass, back in Camp Delta. After my chest had disappeared, I was left with two golf-ball-sized lumps behind each nipple.[80] They were very sore to touch and caused me discomfort if I slept on my stomach. I had been complaining to the medics for the last few months to have the lumps examined but had always been ignored. I mentioned all this to the representative and stressed that I was afraid that they might be cancerous.

Within days I was transported to the hospital. After a quick

examination I was informed by a doctor that they could sur-
gically remove the lumps if I consented, which I did. I was
to go into surgery later that day. After I was chained to the
operating table and the anaesthetic had been administered,
I noticed an overweight man with salt-and-pepper hair and
beard dressed in civilian clothes enter the room. Everyone else
was in medical attire, and I remember wondering what he was
doing there – and then I passed out.

It is very difficult to explain what happened next, because
it was surreal and something I had never experienced before.
During the operation, I remember regaining a degree of consciousness. My brain registered that I had just received an
injection with an oversized needle in the spine at the base
of my neck, and that it was responsible for my awareness. It
was most unusual, like a bizarre dream, an entirely foreign
mental dimension. I then felt trapped, pinned to the bed and
vulnerable.

The only way to describe what happened next was that I
felt an evil spiritual presence enter my body. This *thing* did not
feel human as it penetrated a private, spiritual place so deep I
never knew it existed. It was a horrible feeling. This presence
was trespassing against my will and violating my soul, my very
being. I felt that it was intent on harming me.

As this process continued I felt the presence become frustrated. It disregarded my safety and inflicted internal damage
in a way I can't explain. The best analogy I can think of is a
thief going into a house. He begins by looking around calmly,
stealthily, searching for something in particular. But when he
cannot find what he is looking for and begins to run out of
places to look, he becomes desperate and angry and starts to
throw open drawers. He slashes open cushions and mattresses,
generally trashing the place. This presence was trashing my soul
in frustration, not being able to find what it was looking for.

I felt psychologically and spiritually raped. It was the most horrible, disturbing experience of my life. Out of all the nightmares and horrible memories I have today, the worst are grounded in that experience and involve some form of forced medical experimentation, something I am very paranoid of now.

When I regained consciousness from the operation, I had a throbbing pain at the back of my neck. Later, back in my cell, I found a lump where the pain was, a lump that is just discernible today and which I believe I will have for the rest of my life. A few months after this event, I was able to ask my US military defence lawyer, Major Mori, his opinion, and described the civilian I saw before passing out. He was not surprised and said that, while he did not personally know the civilian, he knew him to be an interrogator: if someone was to do as I described, it would be him.

I was never told what the lumps in my chest were, or if they were cancerous. And because they refuse to release any medical records, I will never know.

A new group of soldiers had begun their deployment by this period of 2003. In their own words, they told me that a small handful from each company working on the island – those who openly questioned orders, broke the rules and were known ratbags – were sent to Camp Echo as punishment. Troublemakers from all over the island and from different companies had been gathered together to form a temporary unit. Instead of a punishment, they saw the Camp Echo mission as a potential holiday and enjoyed their deployment. Their relaxed and open-minded attitude was good news. The effects of the usual military propaganda wore off more quickly; they were willing and able to interact and engage in conversation

in a relaxed, reasonable manner. I even became friends with
some of them. The Echo contingent came from all over the US,
from the northern and southern states, including offshore ter-
ritories like the Virgin Islands and Puerto Rico. They were all
different in their own way, some good and some bad, but they
were all *human*.

It took a while to build trust, but a lot of MPs would come
to see our situation for what it really was. When two people
are locked in a room together every day for months on end, it
should be no surprise that they will come to know each other
on a personal, profound level. It was unrealistic of the higher-
ups to expect their soldiers to remain cold-hearted and never
speak with detainees under those circumstances. One common scenario used to persuade MPs not to communicate with
detainees was, 'You start off by talking to a detainee, then he
makes you his bitch and he's got you doing all types of things
for him. One day you'll be giving him candy and the next day
you'll be opening the door and letting him out, getting yourself
and your battle buddies killed.'

These MPs asked intelligent questions and pieced together
bits of information. It was interesting to watch them struggle with what they had been told to believe, as they started
to doubt the whole 'War on Terror', whether it was the current mission in Guantanamo or elsewhere. I noticed erratic
patterns on how they handled this transformation depending
on different ethnic and cultural backgrounds, where they had
been raised and their social status. Some behaviours were consistent enough to allow for certain generalisations. It seemed
to be African–American MPs, especially those who had come
from poorer areas, who held more liberal views. They were
more resistant to the military's heavy-handed messages than
the others. I guess they might have identified with oppression
and injustice.

The propaganda the guards received lasted for the duration of their deployment in an attempt to counter the doubts
and moral qualms that inevitably crept in. This brainwashing
included such arcane techniques as showing trailers of men in
orange clothing and sporting big beards killing innocent American people for five minutes before and after every movie shown
at the military's local outdoor cinema. They even had T-shirts
in the 'gift shop' that dehumanised us, likening us to animals.
One pictured a rat in a turban, orange jumpsuit and shackles
that read 'Guantanamo Bay: Taliban Lodge', and another had
six shackled rats in the orange jumpsuits that read 'al-Qaeda
sixpack: Guantanamo Bay'.[81] Desensitisation was a major
weapon against humane thoughts. They were never allowed to
refer to me by name, only as Detainee 002. The propaganda
worked so well that I saw some new MPs shake so badly while
applying or removing handcuffs that they dropped the keys.

However, once they had been working with detainees for
a while, they saw we weren't dangerous – we were nothing
more than average people. Some felt embarrassed for fearing
an average Joe Blow in a cage, for losing confidence and doubt-
ing themselves. Then they felt betrayed by the military and
their superiors for having made them feel that way. I had more
than one guard open my cage door while I wasn't restrained
and no-one else was in the room. They did this in defiance of
those who told them they could not have done this without
being hurt or murdered, or that half a dozen soldiers needed
to be present any time a cage door was opened. There was risk
in their rebellion: if they were caught, they would serve years
behind bars themselves.

Some guards, regardless of background, were traumatised
by what they saw at Guantanamo and what they were ordered
to do there.[82] In their own words, there were a lot of military
combat counsellors on stand-by to help MPs get through the

job. Some guards openly questioned orders, some refused certain missions. The majority did as they were ordered, only to break down afterwards. Because Camp Echo required me to spend a long time alone with soldiers, I often had glimpses of their private life, which they would share with me openly and in detail. My opinion, for example, had even been sought on more than one occasion by guards who were sharing their relationship problems with me – male and female. One time a male soldier suddenly began to sob and moan. He kept repeating, 'Look what I've become.' It took him a few minutes to calm down. I asked what was wrong. He told me he was upset because of what he had just been doing to another detainee. He would not elaborate on what that was and eventually asked me to forget about it and stop asking.

The human contact during this time helped me along. I met some really good people, whom I enjoyed spending time with, and I was able to have long conversations about everyday topics. Some soldiers apologised on behalf of their government for what was happening to me and the other detainees. Other guards shook my hand through the bean hole and wished me luck, told me to keep my chin up and offered other such words of encouragement as their deployments came to an end. Plenty of soldiers said they believed our treatment and the whole situation was wrong. Many announced that, as soon as their time was up, they were gone and never returning to the military. These statements formed a common theme. Some of these soldiers were barely old enough to be out of school. The only reason they joined the military was to have their college tuition paid for. They had never intended to go overseas and fight. They were reservists and had been guaranteed by their recruiter that they would not be deployed. Most of the thousands of soldiers who went through Guantanamo were reservists.

*

Because Camp Echo consisted of one detainee and one guard in an enclosed room behind closed doors, if I was lucky some kind guards would allow me to eat their leftovers. I was still underweight and constantly searching for food. To be starving and have to smell real food and watch it being eaten was a difficult experience. If I was *really* lucky, I would be given a pinch of chewing tobacco. We had to do all of this without the higher-ups finding out, and some fellow soldiers would quickly snitch if they heard or saw acts of leniency. The guards should have been rewarded for showing some kindness and humanity. Instead, they were punished and the aggressors rewarded.

The guards who enjoyed hurting detainees and assisting in the weird interrogation techniques usually, but not always, came from the ranks of the active units, rather than the reservists. They were also usually the ones who claimed they had joined the military so they could experience war and kill their enemies. Their definition of 'enemy' could be very broad. But I am still, and always will be, very thankful for those guards who offered little, but very risky, acts of kindness. Many at that particular time helped me in their own way. Of all the so-called 'forbidden' things that took place between the guards and me, none of them breached or risked national security. No harm was done, only good. The higher-ups should remember this while detainees are still currently in Guantanamo.

The rules in the camp dictated that no soldier could talk at any time to a detainee, even responding to a hello. Only giving orders or asking a necessary question were not classified as talking. Giving a detainee actual information was a serious disciplinary offence. When a medic was overheard telling a detainee about the Muslim chaplain being arrested by the military while he was back in the US mainland on holiday, he had to face court proceedings. I'm sure others faced prison time or had their pay docked while being demoted.

Notwithstanding this oppressive incommunicado program and censorship, I did learn bits of information. I first heard about the war in Iraq around the end of 2003. I also learned about another two camps. One was called Camp Foxtrot, and I could see it next door from inside Camp Echo. I could also see that, externally, it was designed the same way that my camp was, practically a mirror image. I had never met a detainee who had been to Foxtrot or had heard of anyone having been to the camp. What went on there and who went remained a mystery to detainees. I was never able to find out from MPs either. However, in recent times an ex-guard has informed me that the CIA used this camp to monitor us through the hidden bugs that were in our rooms in Camp Echo.

The other camp was called Camp Iguana. It was built upon a cliff by the seaside and was used to house the child detainees. A handful of young people, some no older than eight, were taken to Guantanamo.[83] In later years, Camp Iguana would be used as a place for detainees to meet with their lawyers.

Twenty-three

'One by one, the terrorists are learning the meaning of American justice.'

George W. Bush, State of the Union Address, 28 January 2003

'Detainee was reminded that no-one loved, cared or remembered him. He was reminded that he was less than human and that animals had more freedom and love than he does. He was taken outside to see a family of banana rats. The banana rats were moving around freely, playing, eating, showing concern for one another. Detainee was compared to the family of banana rats and reinforced that they had more love, freedom and concern than he had. Detainee began to cry during this comparison.'

Interrogation log of Mohammed al-Qahtani

SOME TIME IN DECEMBER 2003, after two years in detention, the camp staff sergeant brought a phone into my room. I had not seen a phone since I was a free man and was not sure if this was some type of joke. He said an assigned military law-yer would ring, and I was to wait and answer it myself. When it rang I answered with some apprehension. The voice on the other end identified himself as Major Mori of the Marine Corps and, if I chose, he would be my acting lawyer. I agreed enthusiastically, hoping that I would get some answers at last. He said he would come to see me soon and asked if there was anything he could bring. I instantly answered, 'Food and cigarettes.' I was to be the first detainee in Guantanamo to see a lawyer. The release of detainees had not begun yet, aside from the three in Kilo Block, so this was a momentous occasion.

The only reason a lawyer was allowed to see me was so Mori could help negotiate a plea deal. The interrogators knew they had succeeded in training me and that I was ready. What they didn't count on was that there was still a little bit of fight left in me and, more importantly, that Mori was a good man – he slowly undid the spell I had fallen under.

Some of the programs I was subjected to in Guantanamo came from a text known as the KUBARK manual, which has been described as 'the most comprehensive and detailed explanation in print of coercive methods of questioning'.[84] The KUBARK manual sets out procedures used by North Korea during their conflict with the US to extract false confessions for political purposes. Thirty-six US airmen – high-ranking, well-trained, patriotic officers – first wrote, then spoke on Korean state television what seemed to be voluntary 'confessions', after two years of almost purely psychological manipulation and torture, about how their mission had been to wipe out the civilian population with bacteriological weapons. These men's experiences were studied on their arrival home after the war. US intelligence organisations wanted to know how such committed and loyal servicemen could have been manipulated to claim such allegations against their own country. In order to prevent it from happening again, they learned the techniques.

It was a long two weeks before Major Mori appeared in my room at Camp Echo. And, amazingly, an Australian had come with him. He introduced himself as Steven Kenny, a lawyer from Adelaide. He was retained on behalf of my father and happy to act for me pro bono. I was overwhelmed to listen to Steve's report on my family, with whom I had not had direct or meaningful contact up until that point, bringing messages of love and hope. He had literally come straight from my father's home. It was hard to comprehend that travel from there to here was actually possible, but he was proof. They had brought letters, books, photos and other much-appreciated nick-nacks from my family. Eventually, I was able to concentrate on the job at hand and spent the rest of the day informing Steve and Mori of my story before Guantanamo and all that had passed since.

On the second day, Steve obtained permission to bring in a real steak, which he had cooked. It was still in the pan and cut into bite-sized pieces because I was not allowed to have a knife, even a plastic one. My mouth watered as I consumed my first real fresh food in two years. After eating, I continued my story and then they shared some information of their own. They told me of how my father had gone public in an attempt to inform the Australian people of my plight. I could not hold back the tears when Mori showed me a photo of Dad standing in a wire cage, dressed in orange, on a main street in New York. I still become highly emotional today when I see that truly amazing photo. I then heard how Bronwyn, whom my father was married to before my mother, had begun a support group called 'Fair Go for David'. Her daughter, Stephanie, my half-sister, and a favourite uncle named Chris, were involved in the group. They wrote to politicians, organised public rallies, doing whatever it took to raise awareness and get me home.

I was then shown the other side of the public debate, such as media reports of what the Bush and Howard administrations had been saying about those of us detained at Guantanamo. Donald Rumsfeld described us as the 'worst of the worst'. The

Australian Attorney-General at the time, Daryl Williams, said, 'You have to be realistic about the nature of the threat that the prisoners who have been transferred to Cuba represent. They have been trained to be terrorists and to act in accordance with the objectives of al-Qaeda. That makes them about as dangerous as a person can be in modern times.'[85]

I couldn't believe it. It was also surprising for me to see how much attention my predicament was generating. I had never dreamed that a prime minister of Australia would ever say my name, let alone do so publicly. My fate in Guantanamo had become such a media focal point that I was overwhelmed and unable to comprehend it. Then there was the media's own language concerning me. It was hateful and demonising; it suggested I was guilty of something but did not specify what. The stories were trashy, sensationalist and unprofessional, hardly hard-hitting journalism. It was a case of trial by media; I was already convicted without proof, without the benefit of the presumption of innocence.

The lawyers then attempted to explain that a court action begun in my name, but had later become known as the *Rasul v. Bush* case, was pending in the US Supreme Court, where we sought *habeas corpus*, a writ allowing a prisoner the right to challenge their detention. I had already been confronted with too much information over a two-day period to absorb any more and at that stage did not comprehend the legal implications. Besides, I was not interested in court actions; I only wanted to go home. So I was shattered when they said they were leaving the next day and would return in the new year. I honestly thought that the lawyers would stay and visit me daily until everything was resolved. It was really hard to swallow Mori's words when he said the legal process would still take some time yet and I would have to hang in there.

I could not comprehend why events were unfolding this

way. After two years, and a lawyer's opinion, I still had no definite answers, no date – not even a rough guess of when I would be released. All the hope that these new friends brought was quickly extinguished. Before he left, Mori asked what I would like him to try to change about my daily living conditions. I blurted out 'food' without even thinking. Skinny and weak, I was at my wits' end with hunger. It was only the scraps the guards slipped me that kept me going. I begged Mori for anything extra; a daily MRE would be fine. 'What about the guard food?' he suggested, and I could only laugh. I was very upset when I said goodbye to Steve and Major Mori. They left, taking the year 2003 with them, and I began my third year in Guantanamo with no definite end in sight.

I witnessed a miracle in the days following the lawyers' departure. The camp staff sergeant passed me a menu and told me to pick what I wanted. I was confused and had to ask what he meant. From now on, he said, I would be eating from the guards' menu. At the beginning of each week I was to pick what meals I wanted for the coming week. Needless to say, this was like Christmas. Since being in Guantanamo, each meal consisted of an average of twenty flat *teaspoons* of food with a piece of very old fruit and a slice of stale bread. I wrote an exact menu of the meagre portions, spoonful by spoonful, and still have it today.

The lawyers came and went, each time remaining for a day or two. As time passed I met my US civilian lawyer, Joshua Dratel, and the paralegals on the team, Susan and Elizabeth. I also met another lawyer representing the large civilian firm Jenner & Block in the US. Mori was my most important contact with the outside world, and he would remain the central figure in the legal team. His regular visits dispelled the interrogators'

hold and slowly unwound the years of psychological entrap-
ment. He was energetic and always infectiously positive, yet
kept his enthusiasm tempered with the daunting realities we
were up against.

For the next few years Mori would come and visit every six
weeks on average, even if no work was to be done, for the sole
purpose of allowing me human contact and to keep my morale
up, which was a constant battle for both of us, but the damage had already been done. While the initial visits and flood
of information from home was uplifting, I soon began to slide
back into depression. What Mori did for me, however, was
invaluable; he is a courageous man with a big heart.

Some people have expressed surprise that a Pentagon-
elected US Marine became such a staunch advocate for me.
From my understanding, Mori deeply believed in the Uniform
Code of Military Justice (UCMJ) and was a proud advocate
of the courts-martial system. Mori was disappointed, outraged even, at the departure from this code and system for the
bizarre, newly created military commissions that contradicted
the principles he upheld. Then there was the way in which we
were being treated, and how so-called evidence taken under
duress would be admissible.

Mori was told he would be meeting the 'worst of the worst'
and representing an evil character responsible for the death
of Americans. Instead, he met me. After getting to know me,
spending months, then years, exhaustively investigating my
case, he felt the American people, Australians and the world at
large had been deceived and lied to. It went against his beliefs
and faith in the military culture and country he loved and
served.

Having access to lawyers allowed me other privileges. Mori
obtained permission for me to keep real soap and shampoo
in the cage. When guards entered the enclosed room, they

no longer screwed their faces up at the stench, even though the clothes I wore remained smelly. I would eventually come to have a toothbrush and real toothpaste. I had five or six books that I quickly read and reread. Mori provided me with a detainee-approved pen (a high-security pen, a little transparent, flexible bit of rubber) and some scrapbooks so I could begin to prepare my defence, if it came to that.

Even though I was now on a new diet and slowly regaining weight, the medics allowed me to drink one bottle of the weight-gaining drink Ensure per day. Other detainees in the camp were also on Ensure because of how much weight they had lost. To help stockpile the drink in the camp, medics brought a fridge and happened to place it in my room, out where the guards sat. This gave me the occasional opportunity to drink more than one Ensure a day. For a very short time I had Mori stock the fridge with food and drink during his visits. After he had left, the friendly guards would pass me what I wanted, but this was too much for the E6 and he quickly put a stop to it.

In February 2004, I was moved to a different room on the other side of the camp. Apart from going from the door of my room to a transport vehicle, this was the first time I had seen the sun in nearly eight months. As I was escorted across the camp a guard called me Casper on account of my paleness. When the ICRC visited, they could tell if a detainee had been denied sunlight for long periods by how dark his hair had become since their last visit.

The ICRC had campaigned for windows to be installed in the rooms of Camp Echo. The request was granted and contractors installed very narrow, heavily frosted slits where the guards sat. They allowed no natural light in, but I could finally tell if it was day or night outside without having to look at the five-millimetre gap under the main door.

It may have been some time in March when Mori arrived with the news that shocking photos showing detainee abuse in the Abu Ghraib prison in Iraq were circulating in the media. It proved that US troops were torturing their prisoners, and people began having second thoughts about stories of abuse in Guantanamo.[86] The military initiated multiple internal investigations and, because of my past complaints of mistreatment, I was interviewed by one of these teams. The investigations were really about clearing the military of responsibility, so it was no surprise when some months later they reached the conclusion that my complaints were unfounded.[87] The Australian government came under the spotlight at that time and responded by saying that I was a supporter of the Taliban and had never complained of mistreatment at any time prior to the Abu Ghraib photos being released. This, of course, was completely untrue. Prime Minister John Howard, Foreign Minister Alexander Downer and Attorney-General Philip Ruddock released public statements that they had received 'assurances' from the US government that I had been treated humanely.[88]

What they *didn't* know was that Mori had done his own investigating into my treatment aboard the USS *Peleliu* and *Bataan*, including the land facility where I had been beaten for eight or so hours. Because Mori was a marine, and it was the marines who had custody of me during that period, he was able to get inside information and spoke with the soldiers who had actually seen me at the time. Because lower enlisted soldiers were receiving punishment over the Abu Ghraib scandal, Mori found a bunch of low-ranking marines who were quick to point the finger in an attempt to avoid becoming involved and punished. Mori was able to obtain statements from six different soldiers, all of whom confirmed the beatings and profuse spitting I described earlier.[89] I also wrote an affidavit describing some of the treatment I, and others around me, had suffered.[90]

However, back in Camp Echo I was having other troubles. My letters from home were being heavily redacted. Sometimes entire pages were blacked out so I could not read them at all. I wondered why they even bothered giving them to me. Other letters had too many redactions to be of use: 'The baby now has *blank* teeth. John has turned *blank* years old. We have moved to number *blank* on *blank* street,' and so on. Words of encouragement, news, information and love were blacked out at the bottom of letters. Anything Mori wished to bring into the room had to first go through inspection and censorship. This meant food, shampoo, letters from my family and all the legal paperwork, even defence-strategy material. A lot of books my family sent were denied: *Catcher in the Rye*, *To Kill a Mockingbird* and books on Australian history, to name a few. All refusals were justified under the umbrella of 'national security'. Interrogators once personally brought me a letter that contained the sad news that an aunt had passed away from cancer. They sat in silence, watching me read, and then asked if I would like to talk with them about it. A nice gesture if they meant well, but they would have surely taken advantage of my grief had I accepted.

While in this second room in Camp Echo, I was told that I would be allowed to receive a phone call from my family. This was to be the first official phone call made by a detainee in Guantanamo. There had been rumours among detainees for some time that two or three other detainees had been allowed to make unofficial, clandestine calls. One was rumoured to have been the prince of Bahrain, the others I think may have been sons of politicians, and possibly a second prince. I was taken to an interrogation room in Camp Delta with Major

Mori, where several antique telephones protruded from a large, black box. I was given a lengthy lecture on the rules. They dictated what I should say: I am fine, how's the weather, etc. The list of what *not* to say was much more exhaustive. I could not describe camp procedures, the camp layout, detainee treatment, any day-to-day matters, whether concerning myself or other detainees – not what we ate, how long or how often we showered or any other such mundane, ridiculous information. This was all done in the name of camp security, and soldier and detainee safety. The officer lecturing me said he would be on one of the other phones – if I said one word out of line, he would hang up and I would never be allowed a call again. It was further explained to me that my family would be in a government building in Adelaide. From there, the call would be diverted to another government building in Canberra, then sent to a government building in Washington, and eventually end up in the interrogation room in Camp Delta. Someone would be listening at each diversion point, ready to sever the connection if necessary. This system made for a time delay between Dad and me, making conversation confusing at times, but it gave the military and others confidence that nothing could get in or out that they thought inappropriate. Mori was to listen on another handpiece to advise me on what to say, which questions not to answer and subjects to avoid. The officer claimed that my father had been given the same instructions, though, much later, Dad told me no-one had said such things to him.

It was hard to believe that I was really speaking to my dad – I was overwhelmed – but the officer had already ruined the importance of this occasion and robbed my happiness upon hearing my family's voice. Dad had lots of understandable questions, but Mori kept shaking his head at me not to answer, and the officer kept threatening to hang up. All I wanted to do was tell my father the truth of what was happening to me and the others. To be robbed of this opportunity deepened my depression. I felt intimidated and afraid for the entire phone call. Other than when Dad alerted me to the latest football news, which was quite momentous because Central District had gone on to win a streak of unprecedented premierships, I spent the rest of the time saying, 'Sorry, Dad, I can't answer that', or 'Sorry, Dad, we can't talk about that.' It was amazing to speak to him, and I greatly appreciate having been given the opportunity, but the military knew how to spoil any hope or happiness I could have found in it. Every so often, as the years passed, I was allowed to make more of these calls – maybe five all up out of the five and a half years I was in Guantanamo. I would eventually speak with my mother, Bev, Stephanie, Uncle Chris and others, all under the same intense procedure.

It was during my time in Echo that I was accused of attempted escape. One day I was having a conversation with one of the guards, whom I had known for a while. We had many long chats and got on well. I told him that I knew a way to open the door to my cell. He asked me to show him. I used the toothbrush that Mori had got for me to push the padlock sideways, which allowed the bolt to be moved enough to open up the door. We both had a laugh about it. Then he told me that he could manipulate it so I couldn't do it; he placed two padlocks on the door. After three or four hours passed, we had forgotten all about it. The staff sergeant walked in to see the two padlocks and asked why they were arranged like that. The guard panicked and said that I had demonstrated how I could open the door – it was faulty. In desperation, he tried to convince him that I was doing the guards a favour by show-ing them the flaw, for it would apply to all the other cages in that camp. The sergeant classified the incident as an attempted escape and made the guard fill out a report. I then had every item confiscated, except for the clothes I wore and the thin mat to sleep on. It took three or four months to get everything back.

The guard did as ordered but refused to use the words 'attempted escape'. The sergeant threatened that if the guard didn't comply he would be disciplined – but he would be rewarded if he did. After five or six attempts at representing the truth, he ended up adding the sergeant's wording. However, the guard also took statements from two other guards who were working in the camp that I didn't attempt to escape at all and that he was threatened to change the report. The staff sergeant ended up losing his job in the end due to many such instances of incompetence, and the other soldiers in the camp celebrated his departure.

Around this time a curious thing happened – all of the female MPs disappeared. I asked where they had gone and was told they were training for a new mission: female prisoners were being brought to the island, and only female guards were to work with them. The female guards returned some weeks later, and I never heard about the matter again. US personnel taking women as captives distressed me – I could only imagine what interrogators would do to them after seeing what they did to us men.

In early June 2004 I received bad yet ridiculous news. For the first time I had been formally charged. My legal team and I had always wondered if it would happen, because they didn't think that the US government could charge me with anything, and it turned out they couldn't. Instead, they created a whole new system. The charges were baffling: conspiracy, attempted murder by an unprivileged belligerent, and aiding the enemy.[91] This news was a blow to my psyche because it would slow down the process of my release. What was even more disheartening was that my own government openly supported these newly created military commissions, which meant I would be tried by military tribunal rather than a regularly constituted court. It was the only Western government in the world to do so (though Canada has since joined that short list).

Mori explained that conspiracy on its own is not a recognised war crime; it accompanies and helps describe a crime only. Someone had to conspire to actually 'do something', which I had not, nor was I alleged to have. The attempted murder charge was bizarre: the US government was suggesting that being an 'unprivileged belligerent' in itself was a crime. First, the term 'unprivileged belligerent', alleging I was not recognised as part of a national military and had no right to participate in hostilities, was newly created and did not exist under law. Second, the question of whether I was 'privileged' or not wasn't an issue; it is the nature of one's actions that matter. The mere participation in hostilities is not illegal. Civilians have the right to engage in hostilities under international law. Besides, I was not alleged to have personally engaged in hostilities or to have injured or attempted to injure anyone. The government even admitted I did not fire a single shot. They seemed to be suggesting that I went to the frontline with an *intention* to engage in hostilities and associated with people who attempted to injure others by directing small-arms fire in the general direction of the Northern Alliance, who were allies of the US and others, and that meant that I was attempting to murder them. In another example, prosecutors argued that while I was detained in Guantanamo in 2002, the Taliban were engaged in hostilities in Afghanistan and that I should be held responsible for their actions. It did not matter that I had never met these people, was unaware of their activities, and that it was occurring thousands of kilometres from me.

Aiding the enemy is a US federal offence, but not a law of

war offence. One has to be a US citizen, owing an allegiance to his country, and then fight against the US or assist others in doing so to be eligible to be tried. The American government claimed that because I was an Australian citizen, and Australia is an ally of the US, I owed an allegiance to the US. This was a thin line of reasoning. The only country who could try me for aiding the enemy was Australia, but the Australian government admitted I had broken no Australian law.[92]

That is an explanation, in layman's terms, of the charges. But, regardless of the charges being incorrect or non-existent under the law, the strongest nation in the world, who had total control of me and snubbed their nose at the rest of the world and international law, was charging me anyway.

About two weeks after being charged, near the end of June, the US Supreme Court ruled in the *Rasul v. Bush* case. We had won and Guantanamo was brought under the jurisdiction of the US courts. We could now proceed to challenge our detention in US federal courts.[93] Another detainee, who had also been charged and slated for military commissions, got in first and began to challenge the US government. This case became known as the *Hamdan v. Rumsfeld* case. This good news countered the bad news two weeks earlier: one minute we were celebrating and hopeful, and the next wallowing in doom and gloom.

The proposed military commissions were being condemned by a number of governments, legal experts, many organisations and concerned people around the world.[94] So far, six of us had been picked for prosecution, and four of us had been charged: two from Yemen, one from Sudan, two from the UK and me. The two British citizens had not been charged because their government was opposed to the system. The UK Attorney-General,

Lord Goldsmith, publicly asked for them not to be put before
the commissions, saying they could not provide full and fair
trials – the standards were far from acceptable.[95] The UK government even publicly condemned Guantanamo, calling it a
'shocking affront to the principles of democracy', and a senior
judge labelled it a kangaroo court that made a mockery of justice.[96] This was the general consensus throughout Europe. The
conditions at Guantanamo were now widely known; even the
stories of severe abuse and torture were acknowledged as fact
as more proof slowly emerged. The commissions themselves
were being opposed from all angles.

Even though they were called military commissions, they
were not modelled on past accepted commissions.[97] They
were entirely new and governed by ad hoc, fluid rules that
constantly changed to benefit the government. Many of these
rules had not even been decided upon or were chosen at the
last minute. The usual legal procedures and protections did
not apply, such as the right to a speedy trial, being read your
rights, having access to a lawyer, etc. The prosecution, judge,
jury – even defence – were all military personnel and worked
on behalf of the same government – a government that denied
detainees the assumption of innocence by publicly stating we
were all dangerous terrorists, the 'worst of the worst', and
would eventually be found guilty. There was no independence
within the system. Even prosecutors quit, saying the system
was flawed and rigged to secure convictions. On 2 October
2005, Colonel Morris Davis, who was assigned to prosecute me, was in a meeting with the General Counsel of the
Department of Defense, William Haynes. During that meeting, Haynes said that the military commissions would be the
'Nuremberg of our time'. Davis responded by saying that at
Nuremberg there were acquittals, which gave them legitimacy
and validated the process. Haynes responded, 'Wait a minute,

we can't have acquittals. If we've been holding these guys for so long, how can we explain letting them get off? We can't have acquittals – we've got to have convictions.'[98]

The appeals process went through the same chain of command, and even if a detainee was found to be innocent, the President could override the verdict anyway, or the detainee could be held indefinitely as an 'enemy combatant' and never be released. The odds were heavily stacked against detainees.

Other procedures were also unfair. We were kept in conditions that did not allow us to adequately prepare a defence. There was no meaningful privacy between attorneys and clients, so the prosecution would always be one step ahead. Not only were all of our legal documents photocopied, but the rooms were monitored with video recorders and listening devices. The defence teams comprised two, maybe three, people and were allocated a pitiful budget. The prosecution teams had dozens of people working around the clock with a bottomless purse. A detainee could be removed from proceedings at any time and not be allowed to know the allegations or evidence against him. If defence military personnel were privy to such information, they were never allowed to disclose it to their clients.

Coerced evidence was permitted, including statements gained through torture. If the prosecution wanted, the defence was not allowed to cross-examine witnesses, to see them or even know who they were. Even triple hearsay was allowed. (For example, 'Bob told me that John told him that Mike is a terrorist.' Therefore, Mike is a terrorist.) Basically, the prosecution had a blank cheque to do what they liked, to make up the rules and change them as they saw fit – anything to secure a conviction. The list goes on, and it is all on the public record.[99]

Interestingly, no US citizen was held in Guantanamo or had to face these military commissions. The US government admitted that the system was second-rate and not appropriate for one of their own. In other words, every other nationality was inferior and therefore fit for second-rate justice. By supporting the commissions, John Howard was conceding that to be Australian was to be undeserving of the rights Americans extended to their citizens. I don't believe that, as I'm sure other Australians don't. Howard had the cheek to suggest I was unpatriotic, un-Australian; I would say his stance in allowing an Australian to face a system of justice inappropriate for an American and accepted as second-rate was unpatriotic.

It was a smart move by the US not to allow its citizens to go to Guantanamo or face commissions. It would have been a different story in the US had an American been involved.

In response to the *Rasul* case, the international condemnation of the photos that came out of Abu Ghraib and increasing pressure to justify the war in Iraq, the Bush administration passed *The Detainee Treatment Act of 2005*. The Act prohibited the use of cruel, inhuman and degrading treatment against detainees in US custody, no matter where they were held. However, there was a sinister twist. The Act's definition of torture did not comply with the internationally accepted definition of torture. It also included a provision that prevented any detainee from ever challenging their detention in a US court, so it legalised indefinite detention. And in a final masterstroke of illegality, the Act prevented the prosecution of any US official or military personnel for their use of torture, cruelty or degrading treatment.[100] They were effectively letting themselves get away with war crimes.

In 2005, after some FBI agents became disillusioned with the treatment they witnessed, an investigation was held into a number of events, revealing, among other atrocities, that Camp Four detainee Mohammed al-Qahtani was forced to wear a bra with a G-string on his head. He was tied to a leash and made to perform dog tricks, subjected to a number of strip and cavity searches, and stood naked in front of female interrogators. He was then required to dance with another man while being told he was a homosexual and that his mother and sister were whores. Of course, this wasn't the worst of it. He had pictures of September 11 victims taped to his clothes, was given enemas, made to urinate on himself, refused sleep and food, and routinely humiliated. The recently un-redacted Church Report, which was commissioned by the Secretary of Defense to investigate allegations of abuse, found the behaviour of military personnel 'clearly abusive, and clearly not in keeping with any approved interrogation policy or guidance'.[101]

I was now having periodic consular visits from Mr Tucker, an employee from the Australian embassy in Washington. Even though I knew the Australian government used these visits as an excuse to tell the public how well I was being looked after, that I was in high spirits and good health, I liked him. I knew he was privately distressed by what he saw and tried hard to improve my daily living conditions. He was actually successful in some areas.

I was having a terrible time with lower-back pain[102] and relentlessly complained to guards, medics – anyone who would listen – but nothing ever happened. It probably pleased them to hear I was in pain. The cages were not designed for long-term use, but I had lived in them continuously for years. There was nowhere to assume a stress-free posture and I was in constant agony. Mr Tucker was able to arrange a small table and chair, which greatly helped my posture during times I was allowed to write. I was allowed to have more books and eventually ended up with a library of about forty. It was even arranged for me to continue with my schooling via a correspondence school in Adelaide. I was able to hold on to these privileges long enough to complete Year 11 Maths and English. Because I had nothing else to do, I completed a semester's work in ten days. It was getting the paperwork mailed to and from Guantanamo that was time-consuming. Of course, the Australian government milked those few concessions for all they could as an example of how 'humanely' I was being treated and how well it was looking after one of its citizens incarcerated abroad – despite ignoring the illegality of the whole situation.

A moment approached in late August 2004 that I both dreaded and anticipated: it was time to front the military commission. The dread came from having this procedure forced upon me – I wanted nothing to do with it. Hundreds of other detainees didn't have to be subjected to this ordeal, so why had I been chosen? Some detainees had even been released by then, despite having been accused of deeds much worse than I was. I had always assumed I would be one of the first released. I could never have foreseen that I would be singled out from hundreds of others and publicly paraded about as a terrorist, complete with horrible accusations, especially when I had left Australia to help disadvantaged people. I was meant to have stood up to oppressors, not be accused of being one.

Why I had been chosen to front the commission was baffling to my legal team and me. Theoretically, the US government would need to begin with a strong case, with a real terrorist who had committed serious crimes. They needed to gain support for the detention system and to use this detainee as an example of the kind of devious characters it had held during the War on Terror. The first case had to be a show-stopper. To use me was to risk discrediting the system. If I was one of the worst, if I had committed some of the most heinous crimes, what would that say about the rest of the detainees? The only explanation we could come up with was that because John Howard had openly supported Guantanamo and the commissions and publicly condemned me, it was too late to turn back – he now had to justify his comments and decision to leave me there. The interrogators also knew that I was broken.

One might think that I would be concerned about the commissions, obsessed with the potential seriousness of the outcome and the impact it could have on the rest of my life – I might never taste freedom again. Instead, all I could think about was getting out of my cage and experiencing a different routine, different food, different clothes, faces, atmosphere, environment – any disruption to the monotony. These are typical thoughts for someone who has spent years in isolation with very little to do. It shows the psychological disadvantage one is placed in, and how far one can become detached from reality, no longer able to see the bigger picture, consumed instead with day-to-day survival.[103]

But what I looked forward to the most was the opportunity to see, touch and speak with my family. I had been told that the Australian government had secured permission for Dad and Bev to come over for the proceedings. It was not guaranteed, but I might even be allowed to meet with them privately. I was assured the Aussies would keep pushing for that. It seemed amazing that I would be able to tell my dad things that I had never been able to in letters or get past the strict censors, and I was sure he had important news to give me.

On the morning of the hearing Mori arrived early at Camp Echo. We had breakfast and then I changed into a suit that he had bought me. I really wanted to stay in my detention clothes so the rest of the world could see how I had to live every day, but Mori thought I should wear a suit. It was a cheap $100 special made in Cambodia, not the expensive Italian-made suit the Australian media and a former military prosecutor claimed that I demanded.[104]

Mori left to go to the commission buildings, and I waited patiently for escorts. They shackled me with a three-piece suit and bundled me into the back of an old ambulance, then it was a half-hour drive to the commission building. I was led into a back room while a military photographer took endless shots with a blinding flash, no doubt preparing some sensationalist headline: 'Dangerous terrorist goes on trial'. I was chained to the floor and surrounded by six or so guards. Mori then burst into the room with the news that I was allowed to meet my family briefly before the hearing. He returned shortly, asked the guards to leave, and said, 'Are you ready?' I already had tears in my eyes as Dad and Bev entered the room. We hugged and cried together, and did not break our embrace for some time.

I was still chained to the floor throughout our entire time together. Despite the emotional reunion, I could not shake a persistent voice that kept reminding me that we didn't have long and I needed to get down to business. As quickly as I could, I relived the early days of my capture and ran through all the treatment that had taken place up until the present. I then pressed them for any and all news, making the most of this amazing moment before I was sent back to confinement, unable to communicate face to face for the years that would follow. It was the first time since my capture that I could truly believe what someone told me, without any doubts, imaginary or not. Before I knew it, our time was up. I was on my own again with six guards before Mori returned and said we would be entering the commission room in a couple of minutes.

It was the strangest feeling as I was unchained and stood up.

I knew something big was about to take place: the world would be watching, and in this coming show I would play the star villain. The thought sickened me. I was led out of the room and into a passageway. Both sides were lined with soldiers all the way to the big wooden doors at the far end. Everything transpired in slow motion as I walked along – I could have been walking to the gallows for all the impact it had on me. The only noise was the clacking of my hard, leather-soled shoes in the passageway. The soldiers in their rows looked like display ornaments, reminding me of life-sized suits of armour lining the halls of stone castles. Each moved their face to look at mine as I passed. I made it to the end and the cuffs were removed. Two waiting guards placed tense hands on the doors, staring at the other two guards who were to escort me in.

I brushed myself down and straightened the front of my suit. I nodded that I was ready and took one step forward as the guards swung the doors open wide. I had gone from a narrow, silent corridor to a large, noisy room. Inside was the world, and filled with people who belonged to that world. I hadn't just come from a silent corridor, but from a cage, a hostile environment, years in isolation. The interrogators' manipulation had changed the way I saw my surrounding environment. Compared to the people present, I felt like an alien from another planet. Because of my daily situation, I had adapted and the surreal had become my 'normal'. I had forgotten what it was like to be human, and it was this world, these people, who had become strange. I couldn't summon the courage to scan the room with a clear vision. I had been told previously where my family would be positioned, and the crowd was a blur until my eyes rested on Dad and Bev. I gave them a nod, unable to summon a smile given the situation, and took a seat next to Mori. Everything was blocked out except for the panel members in front and the prosecutors to my right.

I have no real memory of the proceedings. It was something I did not enjoy, so I probably blocked it out. The reunion with my family had been a mix of bliss and sorrow because of the conditions it had taken place under. I was emotionally drained. Later that night, back in the solitary cage of Camp Echo, I ran through everything that had happened. Dad and Bev's faces were still clear in my mind: every touch, every word spoken. I had to convince myself that our meeting had actually happened and kept replaying the scenes over and over. I was filled with a new hope, but also a new pain, an acute awareness of injustice and how cruel people could be.

It was, and is, hard to comprehend how people can mistreat others for no reason other than some political purpose; my whole family was punished and made to suffer, not just me. The conflicting emotions I experienced later that night when I was alone made me wonder if seeing my family had been a bad idea and worsened my depression, but deep down I knew it was a good thing, especially for them. Not that it would matter. As the days piled on weeks and then months passed, that short time spent with Dad and Bev faded and no longer seemed real. The memory became more like a dream, lost in the jumbled recesses of my disoriented mind.

Twenty-four

'More hideous crimes have been committed in the name of obedience than have ever been committed in the name of rebellion.'

C.P. Snow[105]

IN RESPONSE TO LOSING THE *RASUL* CASE in the Supreme Court, the US government made a poor attempt to rectify one of the judges' opinions by implementing a procedure called Combatant Status Review Tribunals (CSRT). While the US government claimed detainees were not entitled to or protected by any law in the world, international law experts said the US government should have granted detainees POW status at the very least, until that protection was confirmed or they were proven to be covered by other protections. No-one can remain outside the law, yet the US government claimed detainees were. When a person is apprehended within a combat zone they are either classified as a POW or a civilian under the Geneva Conventions (GC). If the detaining power disputes the prisoner's status as a POW, they are placed in front of an Article 5 Tribunal. It comprises a panel of three military officers. If the prisoner claims POW status and the detaining power cannot prove otherwise, even if there is only the smallest doubt, he shall enjoy the protections of the Third GC. If it is proven he was not a lawful combatant, he shall be treated as a civilian under the Fourth GC. Depending on allegations, if any, he shall then be tried under international law or a sovereign nation's domestic criminal laws. Either way, the prisoner falls under at least one legal jurisdiction and his treatment is dictated by at least one set of rules. There are no blank cheques as the US government claimed it enjoyed.

In the *Rasul* case, the US Supreme Court mentioned the government's failure to adhere to these wartime procedures and the doubt cast on detainees' status in its decision. In an attempt to create some straws to clutch to in future court proceedings, the US government, in an unprecedented act, established the CSRTs so it could claim it had satisfied the court's requirements and detainees had now been given a legally acceptable status. Unfortunately, though, that status was 'Unlawful Enemy Combatant', also something unprecedented and unheard of. It was all about the US refusing to recognise us as POWs, denying us the protections and procedures of existing laws, including the Geneva Conventions and all other international and US domestic treaties, so as to subject us to their newly designed and constantly changing 'laws' that applied to us and no-one else in the world.

Detainees were marched to a hastily set up room in a trailer and stood in front of three officers. Instead of a presumption of innocence or recognising POW status as a starting point, the proceedings began by introducing the detainee as an Unlawful Enemy Combatant, that is, being a member of the Taliban or al-Qaeda and guilty of fighting US troops and/or being involved in terrorist activities. The detainee was then told to prove otherwise. To navigate these proceedings, detainees were provided with a 'representative', who was also a US military officer. Unlike with a lawyer, detainees did not enjoy any confidentiality with these individuals, who had to disclose all information a detainee shared with him, which could be used against him in later proceedings.

The CSRTs were like trial runs for the government to see what a detainee's defence would be. In a later Federal Court hearing, CSRT transcripts were made public to show the farcical nature of these hearings. A detainee would be accused of something and he would ask to hear the evidence in order to dispute the allegations. Time and again, detainees were told they could not see the information the government relied on to make its allegations. When detainees asked how they could dispute something they had not seen or make an argument against something they didn't even know about, the officers would say, 'We are here to ask questions, not you. Since you have no argument against these allegations and have nothing to say in your defence, we find you to be an Unlawful Enemy Combatant.'[106]

In one Federal Court case, the government argued that a particular detainee from Germany had been found to be an Unlawful Enemy Combatant based on information in one paragraph that had been redacted. When the judge asked why that material had been censored, the government responded that their entire case relied on that one paragraph and that it also contained information classified under national security. Since there was nothing in the un-redacted information to suggest that the detainee had been involved in belligerent or terrorist activities, the redacted portion was revealed. Instead of incriminating evidence, it stated that US and German intelligence had both concluded that he was innocent on all counts and should not have been arrested. The judge was furious and ruled in the detainee's favour, blasting the government for abusing national security as a justification to lie and deceive. The government just apologised and claimed it was a one-off mistake. The judge questioned the hundreds of other redacted transcripts relating to other detainees and wondered what secrets *they* were hiding. The case would ultimately result in the tribunals being determined illegal.[107]

Mori warned me not to take part in these CSRT proceedings without him being present, whenever my turn came. I usually had a rough idea when Mori would return to Guantanamo, and so I presumed it was him when I was told one day to get ready for visitors. I was shackled, led out of the cage and secured to the ringbolt in the floor. When the door opened it was not Mori but three or four strangers. They identified themselves as 'representatives' involved in the CSRT procedure. They then began by reading the allegations against me for being an Unlawful Enemy Combatant and asked how I pleaded. I said 'not guilty' and added I would not cooperate further unless Major Mori was present and until then could they please leave the room. They spent the next ten minutes trying to convince me to tell them what my defence strategy would be in the military commissions. They eventually gave up and left, claiming they would return. Mori did not arrive and I began to worry. A week later the CSRT group returned and once again spent fifteen minutes trying to prise defence-strategy information out of me.

Mori eventually arrived a few weeks later and was not surprised to hear what I had to say. He was meant to have come as planned, but as he went to board the plane in Florida he was refused entry. The military claimed there was a hurricane off the coast and all flights had been cancelled. Mori quickly discovered there was no hurricane and that other flights were still going back and forth to the island. When he confronted those preventing him from travelling, he was simply told he was not allowed to see me at the time. Mori suspected that my CSRT was probably taking place after months of waiting, and he came as soon as they allowed.

Hurricanes were an issue during the three- to four-month annual season. Every year Guantanamo would be put on alert a number of times but, lucky for us, a mountain range not only created a rain shadow, it also deflected the brunt of the storms. Even though hurricanes often raged around us, I heard it had been many years since one actually ravaged the base. I use the word 'lucky' because I had the evacuation procedure described to me in case of an emergency – it sounded like a nightmare. At least once a year a hurricane threat was taken seriously enough that the first few stages of the evacuation procedure were implemented. First, detainees would be served MREs for every meal because the kitchens were closed. Next, the soldiers were removed from the guard towers. When the block guard shift was finished, they would sleep nearby, at the ready, instead of returning to their quarters. One year, the guards were to sleep in the empty cages next to us after their shift, but they only stayed for about four hours because the high-alert warning was downgraded. The last emergency procedure that we could see, though many others probably occurred outside the camp, was the gathering of every three-piece suit, ready for evacuation.

It was what they meant to do with us that I dreaded. We were to be moved at the last minute to old bomb shelters some-where on the island. Four to five detainees would be bolted to the same ring in the floor. The three-piece suits would have to remain on us the whole time we were down there – eat-ing, sleeping, using the toilet in buckets in front of each other. We would probably have stayed down there like that for three or four days, which I'm glad never happened. This procedure would have affected only Camp Delta, as the other camps were considered hurricane-proof. Detainees knew that if we all refused to go when they tried to evacuate us at the last minute, the soldiers would not have enough time to forcibly drag us along, and they would have panicked. It would have been an interesting situation.

Now that commissions had begun, Mori and I looked at the main piece of evidence the government was relying upon: a document written by another detainee, which he called a diary. It was a brief autobiography containing lots of damning comments about me. Some were so bizarre, in fact, that the whole document suggested the author was not in a clear state of mind. Mori said it didn't matter if the document was clearly a fabrication, because the commissions were set up in a way to allow any ludicrous allegation to appear factual. The panel members as well as prosecution could and would deny us a chance to cross-examine the author, whether he was a prisoner and easily accessible or a free man. Mori was afraid that the detainee might have made a deal with interrogators for incentives, possibly even for his release. I actually knew this detainee and told Mori not to worry – there would be an explanation for his madness.

The detainee would be released long before me and went public with an explanation that did not surprise me.[108] For weeks interrogators had subjected him to rigorous cruel psychological conditioning, including sleep deprivation, combined with daily injections. He claimed these unknown chemicals caused one of his testicles to swell painfully. This detainee knew I was in the same camp, and interrogators convinced him I was in the room next door, which I was not. They instructed the neighbouring detainee to bang innocently on the wall as a means of saying hello. The author of the diary was convinced by interrogators that it was actually me banging, and that I was directing my anger at him.

Interrogators had him further believe that I was producing

documents at the time that would send him away for life, and that I had agreed to testify and lie in the commissions because I apparently hated him. It was all untrue, of course. They convinced him that the only way to save himself was to bring his own false accusations against me. By the time the interrogators had finished playing with the poor guy he was a total mess and did not know what was going on, since he had started writing the diary at their insistence. It was only when they stopped the injections because of the side effects it was having on his testicle that he realised what he had done. Interestingly, this occurred not long before I was charged.

The above is a very typical example of the type of miscarriage of justice that is to be found in Guantanamo, and I would say that much of the so-called evidence has been obtained through torture, lies, deceit and any other underhanded way.

Those detainees who spent time in the Crazy Block but could still function were moved to Camp Echo, where they enjoyed such activities as music, TV and cigarettes. In return for these privileges, they had agreed to go to the commissions as witnesses, where they had been assured they would not have to face the accused or be cross-examined by defence counsel. Strange as this may sound, the prosecution controls those commission rooms – if they don't want something to happen, it won't happen.

To highlight this, in years to come when I was moved back to Camp Echo before my release, I could see and communicate with detainees in the rec yard. One of the guys I talked with almost daily decided to open up and share his private information with me. He was one of those detainees who had agreed to testify with made-up stories in exchange for privileges. He was also one of those who thought the Americans legitimately liked him for doing so and was motivated by their encouragement. I had seen him smoking in the rec yard, an act generally regarded as impossible, and had glimpsed a massive flat-screen TV in his room.

He told me of another two detainees within Camp Echo who had agreed to give false evidence as he had. I also saw these two in the distance. They shared one house, had outside access all day and played loud music late into the night. They were too far away for me to communicate with, though. I told the guy in the rec yard that he was mad for agreeing to give them false evidence, not just on principle but for his own release. The commissions could be going on for many years and, because interrogators were relying on his false testimony, he also might have to stay for many years to publicly lie about others. Meanwhile, hundreds of detainees were being released, who could now do whatever they wanted – not just smoke and watch DVDs.

The guards who had shown me some shred of humanity, with whom I had watched DVDs and enjoyed long conversations, were at last finishing their deployment and about to leave for home. It was sad for me to say goodbye to some of these guys – we had spent a lot of time together and I would miss their company. I knew there would be lonely times ahead. Things were about to radically change, and in the worst possible way.

The incoming deployment of guards were unfriendly and acted like arseholes. In time these guards would learn we weren't who their superiors claimed we were, as they all eventually did; however, I was too tired to go through the six-month process of building trust and seeing the propaganda wear away until we could relate on some level. I simply had no interest in this new group. But whether I was interested or not wouldn't matter.

The higher-ups had caught wind of the relationships

developing in the Camp Echo rooms between guards and detainees. They knew they could not change or control the situation if they continued to place two people together in such close proximity for so long. To solve this problem, the guards were removed from the rooms completely and cameras were put in their place, protected behind a plastic dome bolted to the roof directly above my head. From then on, I might only see another human being for twenty minutes within a twenty-four-hour period. When the last deployment left it was as though they were never replaced.

At first the camera was an annoying intrusion, watching me eat, go to the toilet and sleep. At that stage I was able to blame the soldier controlling it, knowing there was an actual person at the other end, an extension of the human eye. But as time passed, my perception of the technology changed – the camera took on a life of its own. It became animated: a malevolent imp squatting on the roof, always watching, always listening. I had epic mental battles with the stupid thing; goosebumps would run along my spine under its evil, unblinking gaze.

On my own, day after day, in a cage within a room with no natural light, the years of hardship hit me all at once. I deteriorated more quickly in the following few months than I had in all the years I had spent there so far.

In the shipping containers of Camp Delta we were always in full view of each other: sleeping, eating, using the toilet. We lived in close proximity, right in one another's faces, each restricted to his own little personal space of metal.

In Camps Five and Six, though I could not see other detainees unless I stood up at the door, at least once a day there was an opportunity to say hello, maybe have a decent chat and hear the latest news from the detainee grapevine. Even on days when I did not see or speak with anyone, I could still 'feel' the detainees around me, the energy and the noise. That bit of privacy the two camps provided was an advantage over Camp Delta. Even though I still had the comfort of knowing I was not suffering alone, the strength derived from numbers was not as strong as it was in the shipping container environment.

In Camp Echo, there was not even any energy for reassurance. Nothing. No indication that anyone was near – just this intense, consuming sense of being alone. I felt like the sole occupant of an entire universe, and the infinite isolation was maddening. I truly felt I was flirting with the realm of the insane.

During my time in Camp Echo I took advantage of the table, chair, pen and blank exercise books I'd been given, which I miraculously still have today. I wrote two novels: one was 150 pages long and the other 350 pages. I also wrote short stories, poems and accounts of my experiences since detainment. During this time, while I was struggling with my sanity, I had a moment of clarity when I was able to see myself objectively, in the third person. I could analyse my situation and environment, including the impact it was having on me. While I was in this state, I picked up my pen and wrote down the essence of what I saw and felt:

The mind has become extremely sensitive to its surroundings, delicate; much too delicate. Noises, light intensity, words one may hear, all trigger emotions, thoughts – positive or negative – placing one in a certain mood.

A bright light may make one feel exposed and naked, frustrated and restless, whereas a dim light is more soothing and comfortable. Natural lighting is most positive. A green painted room relaxes; white, agitation.

Enclosed spaces (Camp Echo) is an evil environment. The world instantly becomes a small existence. The humming of the fans makes it even smaller. At least when they're off one

can hear the outside noises – vehicles, birds, people – allowing the mind to drift outside the room, expanding one's
world.

But the oppressive atmosphere is crushing, suffocating;
it eats away at the mind, destroying it. Then when the door
opens and the natural light floods in, all the evilness retreats
before it and for a moment all seems normal, as though a
great weight has been lifted. But when it closes again, as it
always will, the demons rush forth from their hiding places
and it is worse than before.

The three demons: anger, depression, insanity; the worst
enemies, forever encircling like hungry vultures. Their
weapon? Inactiveness. Thinking is one's weakness, so is
sleep. Together they launch savage attacks whenever one's
defences are down. But sleep is beyond one's control.

A defence is to live in fantasy, blocking out the reality
around one's self. But sometimes one will stop what he is
doing, look around, realise where one is, viewing one's conditions as an outsider would, everything seen clearly, and
the demons win again.

Another defence is to become mad, a release from
thoughts and emotions, for if one is mad he no longer cares
or even realises his predicament, oblivious like a child.

Twenty-five

'Told detainee a dog is held in higher esteem . . . Began teaching detainee lessons such as stay, come, and bark, to elevate his status to that of a dog.'

Interrogation log of Mohammed al-Qahtani

LATE IN THE AFTERNOON on an October day, after having spent sixteen months in isolation, the guards came to tell me that I would be moving to Camp Delta. This was an amazing statement. I thought I would never see Camp Delta or another detainee again. I was sure the guards had made a mistake, but they assured me they were correct. At around 10 or 11 pm I was told to have my stuff ready and, sure enough, escorts came, blindfolded and secured me, and led me out to a transport vehicle. Within half an hour the blindfold was removed and I was indeed back in Camp Delta.

I was greeted by other detainees, which was a very strange sight. They had brought the six of us nominated for military commissions to Papa Block located in Camp Three. Almost two years later and I was back opposite Kilo Block. It felt like a lifetime since I had been in this place; times had changed and I was now possessed of a different mind-set. So much had happened since I was last in Camp Delta. I had seen lawyers, been to one lot of commission hearings, received information and had a general idea of what was happening in Guantanamo and the outside world. I had seen a different side to the guards, had many strange experiences, spent months in isolation, used a telephone, and had even seen and spoken with my family. I had definitely come a long way.

Out of the five other detainees with me in Papa Block, two were from the UK, one I knew previously from Camp Delta long ago, the other I had never seen before but felt I knew well because the guards had talked about him for years as they went back and forth between our rooms in Camp Echo. On arrival I asked if I could be escorted to the British guys' cages to say g'day. I was escorted to see the guy I already knew, who also happened to be the author of the incriminating diary. I had yet to learn the reasons behind the stories he used against me and, as I shook his hand and said hello, he began to cry and apologise for what he had written, offering a quick explanation.

It was past midnight by the time we were all settled in our cages, which were close enough together to communicate, and we talked until the sun brightened the sky, the first sunrise we had witnessed in a very long time. On the chance we could be separated again at any moment and sentenced to another stretch in isolation, we exchanged information as quickly as possible, cross-referencing everything our lawyers and others had told us, searching for any hint that we might not be able to trust those who fed us our information. We looked for contradictions in our knowledge and understanding of the situation. Most importantly, we hoped to find any information we had not heard before, no matter how small or trivial.

All this analysing came down to one question: when were we going home? Because we had been isolated from other detainees for so long, it took three or four days of constant talking before we exhausted ourselves and each other. This socialising and exchanging news was good for all of us, and a relief for me personally after the struggles I had been having in Echo.

It was Ramadan when we were moved back to Camp Delta. Some detainees, particularly one fellow in our group, refused to talk with me because I was no longer practising or following religious duties. He was furious, yelling, screaming and carrying on, ordering other detainees to excommunicate me. Not all detainees, and none on our block, listened to this advice or accepted his reasoning. I could not help but think that those who did listen were poor missionaries for their religion and only pushed me away further from Islam, while they probably thought that their hardline stance would bring me back into the fold.

One of the first things we noticed as the days passed was the level of detainee harassment in the camp. Comments disrespectful to Islam were announced over the loudspeakers, especially at times of prayer. Derogatory statements were made daily about Mohammed and Islam in general.

After a few days I was able to speak with the author of the false diary in more detail, and I explained how the prosecutors were planning to use his statements against me. He was willing to be interviewed by my legal team to explain his coercion officially, but my team, up until that time, always had their requests to meet with him denied, which was extremely frustrating. I asked him if he could describe, on some scraps of paper he had in his cage, the treatment he had received at the time of writing the diary and why he had made such allegations, as well as the general profile he had created of me. At the time, I had his diary in among my legal paperwork, and I read some of his more damning comments aloud because he could not remember what he had written. This allowed him, word by word, to address those exact points in the document he was creating on my behalf. We then needed to deliver his own signed words to my lawyers, for nothing could have been more important to me, other than my release.

With no other choice, we asked one of the guards to pass along an envelope containing the diarist's explanations to me. He agreed, but as soon as the paper was handed over to him he ran off with it. After a lot of complaining by Major Mori, the prosecutors, whose hands the envelope ended up in, surrendered it to my legal team. It didn't matter in the end because, as mentioned earlier, the detainee was released and went public anyway.

By the beginning of November 2004 it was time for me to go to the commissions once more. We were still in pre-trial hearings and, similar to last time, I did not involve myself in the legal proceedings on the day. I paid great attention to motions and preparations prior to the hearings and the outcomes after, but on the day I was only concerned about seeing my family. Two family members were allowed to attend hearings at one time but, if it hadn't been for the kindness and generosity of the Australian public, they might not have been able to afford what was an expensive round trip and might not have seen me at all. On this occasion, funding was sufficient for one family member to attend, and happily it was my half-sister Stephanie who came.

The commissions went for three days this time, instead of just one, and I was grateful that the authorities allowed us to spend time together on each of those three days. Just as it was with Dad and Bev, it was overwhelming when Stephanie and I first saw each other and hugged. We visited each morning before hearings commenced, and sometimes we were allowed to eat lunch together. We also got to say goodbye at the end of each day before I was returned to my cage. Three days is long enough to become accustomed to spending time with a loved one, so saying goodbye to Stephanie was probably harder than the first time with Dad and Bev. At least on that occasion, when the commissions were all over until the next round, I had fellow detainees to return to – not just the watchful imp that lived on the ceiling in Camp Echo.

However, it quickly became apparent that there might not be a next time. The *Hamdan v. Rumsfeld* case had progressed and a federal judge had ruled in Hamdan's favour.[109] The military commissions were deemed illegal and the judge also put a stay on the commissions pending appeals. Hamdan was ordered to be returned to a normal block, rather than one where detainees were segregated for specific purposes. The government appealed this decision but the military commissions would now be postponed for the following year or longer, at least until the Supreme Court decision, if it ever went that far. The commissions would never begin again if the Supreme Court upheld the federal judge's decision. This stay of proceedings benefited all of us; for me it meant no more commission hearings in the near future – and hopefully never again.

Mori and I discussed this development. It was cause for hope and presented a realistic chance for me to go home. So many people had been pointing out the faults of the military commissions, and now a US federal judge had joined that condemnation. So far the Howard government had accepted the inadequacies of the commissions, but by this point Howard openly stated I must be dealt with in a timely manner.[110] This delay meant military commissions would not proceed for the next year, maybe two. We knew the Howard government could turn the situation into a political win for them by bringing me home under the pretext that the US was moving too slowly, and that the commissions were an unacceptable venue for an Australian citizen. The waiting game began.

In early 2005 two more Australian lawyers, David McLeod

and Michael Griffin, joined the team. They were both extremely capable and lived up to their impressive resumés. David was a group captain and Michael a colonel in the Australian military and had knowledge of international law and the rules of conflict, areas of expertise essential to my case. (Michael would be awarded the Order of Australia medal in 2009.)

Also in early 2005, one of the British guys from my block was transported to Camp Echo for a lawyer's visit. These visits could last for two or three days, and we would sleep at Camp Echo without returning to our assigned camp until the visit was completely finished. On the second day that he was gone, the other British citizen from our block was also moved to Echo. However, he was told to take all his stuff and, while the escorts were present, they also took all the items of the other guy who was already in Camp Echo, suggesting that he, too, had now been permanently moved. I was shaking with excitement. There was another British citizen in the next block over, and within minutes he yelled across to us that he was also being moved to Echo. Then almost straight away we heard that the fourth and last British citizen was to follow. I was beside myself that they were possibly being released.

Mori had always believed that if the last of the British citizens were released then I would also be released – beyond a doubt. I needed confirmation about the Brits but I could not get it. No detainees knew what was happening and neither did the guards on the block, though they probably wouldn't have told me anyway if they did. I felt I would go insane from the lack of knowledge: was I going home or not? My skin was prickling in anticipation of escorts arriving any minute to whisk me away to Camp Echo.

These four British citizens were the last European nationals

left in Guantanamo. Over a year ago, there had been forty or
so citizens from France, Spain, Denmark, the United Kingdom,
Sweden and Germany in Guantanamo. Some time earlier, the
European Court of Human Rights, which exercises jurisdiction over all European nations, handed down a ruling that
Guantanamo was an essentially illegal operation and delivered a strong recommendation that all European nations who
had citizens in Guantanamo should take every step possible to
have them released and sent home. It was another favourable
outcome that I did not advantage from, and more proof for the
Australian government that Guantanamo was unacceptable to
civilised nations.[111] Instead, it was one more occasion in the
long, sorry saga that separated Australia from the other Western nations. If Australia had a human rights Act, or another
form of legislated human rights protections, I would have been
going home at the same time as the British guys.

By lunchtime on the day the Brits had been moved, I was
truly exhausted as the countless unanswered questions rushed
about in my head. I harassed the afternoon shift when they
first began, but my hopes were soon dashed by the simple,
stock response 'I don't know', or the slightly more elaborate,
'I don't know anything. I wake up, come here, go back to my
barracks, go to sleep, then start all over again.' Once the afternoon shift had settled in, I was taken to the outside rec yards.
As I was pacing around the cage, obsessing about the Brits,
the sergeant who was sitting on the step watching me looked
around secretively and waved me over.

I knew he was going to put my mind at ease, and I was
so grateful that I could have kissed the man. He had my full
attention as he whispered, 'The Brits and the other Australian
are being released.' I instantly threw up. No news had ever
produced such a violent reaction from me before; my spirit
had just been crushed in the most traumatic way. I couldn't

move or speak; my soul was screaming in anguish. The sergeant panicked at my reaction and pleaded for me to pull myself together or the other soldiers would know something was up. 'What about me?' I kept asking. 'Was anything said about me going home?' He hung his head when he replied 'no' and recommended I go back to my cage. I tried to be brave as I was escorted back into the block and had a cry when I was alone, completely unable to understand the logic of my being left behind.

Ever since day one I, like all detainees, lived with the hope and expectation of being released any time, any day. It is an exhausting and mentally draining way to exist but that was the reality of Guantanamo and the reality of indefinite detention. A soldier could suddenly come to your cage and say, 'You're going home.' As tiring as carrying this expectation was, it also kept us going. Now, however, for the first time, despite having been charged before, this was the very first indication that I was not going to be released in the near future. I now knew I would not be released unexpectedly. Logic told me that if my government had been considering bringing me home, they would have just done so while the plane was arranged to take the other Australian home. That was a very difficult reality to accept. It was a scenario that had my legal team just as baffled as me.

This was the worst day of my life. No event had ever made me feel that way before, and hasn't since. From the time I threw up I could taste blood in my throat for the following two or three days. Something died inside me at that moment and I became obsessed with killing myself, the only way I could think to finally end this relentless nightmare that kept intensifying with the passing of time.

Twenty-six

'Our enemies are innovative and resourceful, and so are
we. They never stop thinking about new ways to harm our
country and our people, and neither do we.'

George W. Bush
Washington, DC, 5 August 2004

MR TUCKER HAD MOVED ON from the Australian embassy in
Washington, and a new official now performed the consular
visits. He came to Guantanamo as consul-general to assist
with the other Australian's release and paid me a visit while
he was in the neighbourhood. I did not like this new consular
official and how he conducted himself during this visit. To add
insult to my predicament, he would not answer when I asked if
he was there to assist in the other Australian's release. Instead,
he handed me a calculator – I was still doing the correspondence schoolwork then – and said that it should keep me going
for some time to come.[112]

Shortly after the others had been released, the remainder of
us were moved to the other end of the camp. We were placed in
Tango Block, which comprised only four shipping containers
and could hold twenty-four detainees. However, we were the
only three in there.

One of my earlier memories of this time was when I was

343

being transported to Camp Echo to see Mori. As usual, I was blindfolded and had the three-piece suit on. The guards grabbed me as if I was a battering ram and drove my head into the door twice before throwing me against the wall of the inside of the van. When we made it to Camp Echo, they threw me out of the van and I fell to the ground. When I told Mori, I showed him the marks on my arms where they had cuffed me tightly. I was furious. He complained on my behalf but, of course, nothing was done to the offending guards.

During my time in Tango Block, I decided how I could put a stop to this endless nightmare and decided I would use a razor blade. We usually had an opportunity to shave once a week. During the early days we could only shave in the shower, but I was eventually given permission to shave in my cage. The razors were of poor quality and may have been safety razors because they were only a few millimetres wide and had flimsy edges to make it difficult to apply downward pressure without bending them. At shaving time a razor and reflective paper were passed through the bean hole and the guard watched while I shaved. When I was finished they would collect the items.

As the weeks passed the guards became tired of watching me, and they would walk off and return after five minutes. As more weeks passed they became slack and did not bother collecting the razor until the end of the shift. I knew if I was going to obtain a razor I would have to wait patiently – it was only a matter of time. I started to leave the razor in a position where the soldiers could not see it as they walked past my cage, like behind the flap of the bean hole. If they approached and asked for the razor, it did not look like I was trying to hide it. It took a long time, but eventually the day-shift guards swapped with the night shift without asking for the razor. At last they had forgotten, and I had what I needed.

I then asked the next shift for nail cutters. It worked the same way as shaving but if I cut my nails up against the door, the bottom bean hole prevented them from seeing what I was doing. The soldier kept walking away and coming back to check on me, making my task all the more easy. Every time he left I quickly used the nail cutters to eventually free the razor from its plastic housing. I flushed the broken bits down the hole in the floor and hid the razor in among my legal papers.

I had it all planned out. It was a very complicated procedure that required a lot of effort and planning – I was, after all, in a maximum-security detention camp. A successful suicide was virtually impossible and required the type of long-term, obsessive planning that I had engaged in for months. I was desperate; there was no other way out. I also knew I could not fail. Others who attempted suicide and failed, including self-harmers, ended up in a refrigerated metal box with only a pair of shorts on, which I found ironic. I would end up in a worse situation and be even more driven to commit suicide, instead of being treated in a humane manner and given professional help.

When everything was ready to go, the next question was, when to do it? Since day one, Mori always came to see me with good and bad news. There was always something to be equally depressed and hopeful about. I made a pact with myself that the first time Mori came to see me with only bad news, then I would go ahead with the plan. Until then, the plan would rest in my mind and the razor among the papers. Years later I was told by a psychologist that because I had lost control of every aspect of my life, this plan gave me a sense of control, that I still had a say in my destiny.

Instilling a sense of hopelessness and inertia was a part of Guantanamo policy. The belief that the interrogators control-led every aspect of detainees' lives gradually took hold. This shift in authority was so important that the pinnacle of success was to have a religious detainee believe that the interrogators even decided if he should go to heaven or hell. It was not surprising that a detainee devised an equally extreme measure to retain some sense of self-determination, that they still had a trick up their sleeve to surprise their captors. And having been there myself, I can attest that it works: it gave me a sense of satisfaction in an environment of hopelessness to know that I still had an emergency escape plan.

I did receive some hopeful news while I was in Tango Block. Three prosecutors had written emails to their superiors that were somehow leaked to the media. The prosecutors had resigned, claiming they had witnessed criminal conduct in the military commission's prosecution office and that the commissions were rigged to secure convictions.[113] They also said that evidence supporting the detainees' innocence was destroyed and that false evidence was created to implicate them.[114] Damning conversations were quoted, and one prosecutor complained, 'I lie awake worrying about this every night.'[115] I was sure the Howard government would not be able to ignore such unambiguous evidence – if they didn't know that the proceedings were going to be unfair, they surely would now. Even highly respected members of the Australian Defence Forces and the New South Wales Director of Public Prosecutions were saying that it was 'patently obvious' that the military commissions process was 'wrong', 'un-objective' and 'fundamentally flawed'.[116] Former Governor-General Bill Hayden also accused Howard of being a 'servile accomplice' to the inhumane treatment and lack of justice.[117] Former Chief Justice Sir Gerard Brennan called Australia 'morally impoverished' by its acceptance of the handling of my case, and hundreds of lawyers and judges condemned the lack of due process.[118] I was shocked, then, when the Howard government dismissed these damning emails and again asserted its belief that the system was fair.[119] If they could not be swayed by revelations that had come from the prosecutors themselves, I had to stop kidding myself and accept that my government *did* know what was really going on; they just went along with Bush's policies.

Another source of hope was discovering that while I had been in Guantanamo the British government had passed a law that allowed a person whose mother had been born in Britain to be eligible for citizenship, instead of just their father. Because the British government was opposed to Guantanamo and the commissions – and had secured the release of all their citizens – if I could obtain British citizenship then the UK government, unlike Australia, would not only prevent me from facing the unfair system of military commissions, but also have me released. I was desperate now, clinging to anything. We began the application process.

We also had the *Hamdan* case moving through the US court system, which gave us another reason to be hopeful. So far we were in front, and we believed that the Supreme Court justices would rule according to the law and not by political persuasion. If so, the military commissions would be abolished.

Unfortunately, there was always some event that conspired to snatch away any hope, such as when my legal documents were stolen. While I was still in Tango Block I had come back from a shower and noticed a book and some paperwork missing. The guards admitted to taking the book, but not the papers. The book was about illegal interrogation techniques adopted by the US during the War on Terror, called *The Torture Papers*. I had had it for a year, and one of the editors was my US civilian attorney, Joshua Dratel. The military claimed it contained information I was not privileged to view. However, it was the papers that worried me. I had spent days writing down the various legal options I had, depending on what moves the US government made. It was part of my defence strategy.

I hated how they could just take what they wanted. Wasn't I already disadvantaged enough? I felt like a boxer who had been completely tied up, thrown in the ring and expected to fight – not to mention my opponent was three times my size, had trained for years while I had been kept in isolation, fragile and undernourished. And to top it off, he was on performance-enhancing drugs while I had been given a mouthful of sleeping tablets. What chance did I have? It makes you wonder what they were afraid of for me to be disadvantaged so severely. My innocence was obviously not an option.

Camp Delta had been a frightening enough environment for me in 2002 and 2003, and 2005 was no different. Whereas detainees had once fought back and the atmosphere had been infused with resistance, I could now feel desperation and exhaustion: the detainees were on their last legs. Now and then I heard them in surrounding blocks moaning. These detainees were crippled with pain and their treatment filled me with fear and anger.

The cages in Sierra Block next door had been converted into perspex cubicles. It was used as a punishment block and detainees sweated by day and shivered in the early hours of the morning.[120] The only item they were allowed was a single pair of shorts, sleeping directly on the metal floor. Often I heard them being IRFed, and they would yell out that their boxes were being filled with pepper spray.

One new, mind-boggling technique the military had devised to torture detainees was the 'noise machines'.[121] They had taken chainsaws and removed the blade so that it was only the compact engine. It was then placed in a small frame welded together especially for this purpose and left on full revs right outside the detainees' cages. When it ran out of fuel they just refilled it and kept it going. Soldiers could easily pick up these contraptions and move them about. At times I had even heard soldiers whoop, as if it was great fun. There were also smaller engines in frames that looked like whipper snippers with the long shaft removed.[122]

In the early days the camp authorities went to great lengths to give the appearance of humane conditions, as much as circumstances allowed, whenever the ICRC was on-site. The food would improve slightly, clean linen was dispensed, those who wore only shorts had the usual items returned. General harassment ceased. The harsher interrogation techniques were put on hold a week or so before their arrival. Sometimes the military would set up display rooms, as they did for the media, which did not reflect the reality of conditions in Guantanamo. They even asked the more pliant detainees to speak positively about camp procedures and general treatment while being interviewed. None of this fooled the ICRC, however, and they were never allowed access to all detainees.

As time went on, the authorities did less and less to hide their activities. By 2005, they arrogantly continued their harsh policies right in front of ICRC employees. I saw ICRC members walk through the camp while the noise machines were revving away and say something to the guards. When I had my interview with them during that visit, I asked them what they thought of the devices. They said their first tactic had been to argue for the detainees' health. When that didn't work, they changed tack and highlighted the damaging effects it would have on the soldiers' hearing. To solve that problem, the guards were issued disposable earplugs and industrial earmuffs, and went right on with business as usual.

The military and interrogators had forced detainees into a desperate state, so it is no surprise that they took the only recourse they could think of to protest their treatment. Two to three hundred detainees would hunger strike at once. They would overflow the hospital and cause the medical staff grief by a shortage of beds. Detainees began by hunger striking for three days, then a week, until a month became common. As the years passed detainees trained themselves to go longer and longer without food. This ability, coupled with a growing desperation, enabled detainees by 2005 to hunger strike for 100 days straight, only consuming fluids. Whenever I saw other detainees in Camp Delta, they looked so skinny and sick. They suffered a lot of health problems from this extreme deprivation, including serious heart problems.

However, the military would never allow themselves to be beaten and have detainees get their own way. The soldiers were determined to show detainees who would always win – and met detainee desperation with their own extreme measures. Detainees were force-fed and made to suffer as much as possible in order to discourage them from hunger strikes. Detainees were strapped into a chair, described by its manufacturers as 'a padded cell on wheels' with arms, legs and head secured tightly with straps.[123] A large tube is then painfully forced up through the detainee's nose and down into his stomach, without the use of anaesthetic. A can of Ensure is then instantly pumped through the tube at a dangerous rate, until the detainee feels that he will burst. Next, he is given a laxative. Usually a nappy is used, and as the days pass the urine and excrement creates a rash that spreads across the body. If this occurs, the detainee is strapped to a hospital bed and treated until the rash is gone, then he is strapped back into the chair and the procedure begins again. The tube is pulled out and replaced each time the detainee is force-fed, instead of just leaving it in there. The tube is sometimes passed from one detainee to another without being cleaned of the other person's bile, blood and mucus.[124]

I compiled a list of all of these sadistic practices while I sat stuck in Tango Block.[125] I felt I was living on borrowed time, that I would go mad at any moment. There was also a list of little things that tested my patience. My body had been deteriorating for three and a half years and was getting worse, so I began running on the concrete in the outside rec yard. I had to do this in thongs, and was forced to run in tight circles, so there was always pressure on the inside leg. After a few weeks of running I heard a crack in my foot and experienced acute pain. Within days it turned black and swollen. It took weeks for it to return to normal, and when I began running again my other foot cracked.

I was sent to the clinic on that second occasion and told I had stress fractures from running in such a manner in flat shoes. I asked for supportive shoes and was denied, and I was not given painkillers or a walking stick or crutches to take the pressure off my feet. What was I meant to do? The conditions forced upon me were destroying my health – I had tried to do something about it on my own initiative but made things worse. 'You're not meant to be healthy or comfortable,' was the reply.

Sometimes we had to wear the same clothes for a month or longer and, when the clothes were eventually changed, the smell of the previous detainee was strongly infused in the new ones. It took a couple of weeks for my own sweaty smell to replace the stench of the other detainee. When I complained about this I was laughed at. Many detainees were having problems with ingrown toenails, including myself, apparently due to not wearing shoes and being flat-footed. The toilet hole in my cage floor was constantly blocking, and the flush would get stuck. As a result, my cage flooded with sewage – faeces floated about in two inches of dirty water – and I had to walk about in it with untreated open wounds on my big toes. The room flooded this way at least once a week.

This was how things stood when the consular official returned for a visit. I don't remember how I managed to get my list of complaints into the room, but I did, and presented it to my visitor. I was angry and fed up with the circumstances and went on about the noise machines, sewage in my cage and everything else, including brandishing my feet with their bleeding, infected wounds. He took the list and said he would pass it on, but he was clearly not impressed.

Another issue on the list was how I had been left to urinate on myself while being short-shackled, or just plain shackled, in the interrogation rooms for hours. This was very common for all detainees; some had also been forced to defecate as well. I was left in a stress position for hours when I was made to wait in the interrogation rooms before or after an interview. Sometimes I would just be taken to the interrogation room, shackled to the floor for half a day to a full day, then taken back to my cage without having seen anyone. It was demoralising and humiliating, especially if I had to keep wearing my soiled pants till the next time the linen was changed.

I was very angry about this and everything else at the time of the consular visit. When he entered the room I pointed to large, dark stains in the carpet behind me in the corner. I asked him if he knew what it was, and when he showed no interest I asked him if he couldn't smell the strong odour of urine. Then I started explaining how I had been left unattended and had no choice but to urinate in the corner. I asked him whether he thought that was acceptable treatment. It was all very frustrating.

The very next day after the consular visit, escorts came into Tango Block and said, 'You're moving to Camp Five.' Things were getting worse. I had never been to Camp Five, but had heard plenty about it. It had a reputation as the worst camp on the island, and I had always dreaded going there since I had heard of its construction during the days I was in Camp Echo. I had hoped to avoid it – and thought that I would. Reluctantly, I filled the garbage bag handed to me and surrendered my limbs for shackling.

Twenty-seven

'All too often arrogance accompanies strength, and we must never assume that justice is on the side of the strong. The use of power must always be accompanied by moral choice.'

Theodore Bikel

'These are among the most dangerous, best trained, vicious killers on the face of the Earth.'

Former US Secretary of Defense Donald Rumsfeld[126]

IT WAS NEAR THE END OF 2005 when the transport vehicle left Camp Delta, skirted the perimeter of Camp Echo and stopped outside the notorious Camp Five. The compound's brooding presence caught my attention because it was the first real permanent structure I had yet seen in Guantanamo and closer to what I imagined a real prison would look like. Its design was three, two-storey wings, radiating out from a central hub. Walking from the van to the front entrance, I saw a squat bronze plaque to my right, commemorating the completion of the building's construction and the various parties involved. I was marched quickly with my head forcibly diverted from the direction of the plaque, but I saw Halliburton and Kellogg, Brown and Root (KBR) among those responsible. Interestingly enough, they are companies once directed by former US Vice President Dick Cheney.[127]

I watched myself in the huge one-way mirror as I approached the front entrance. The image I saw was of a puffy, pasty man secured in chains, surrounded by soldiers, two of them gripping him with four hands. This approaching image fractured in the centre and parted to the sides, revealing a dim, cool, cavernous interior. Directly in front was central control lording it over a two-storey chamber, and ultimately the entire complex. Around the perimeter of this cavern at ground level stood three big red doors, preventing access to the wings beyond, where I was destined to join the other destitute bodies. Camp Five looked like a technological marvel compared to the primitive padlocked cages of other camps, with its electrically operated doors commanded from central control, down to the uniform accessories worn by the soldiers. But the sci-fi atmosphere made the experience more cold and impersonal – I felt more lonely, depressed and helpless than ever.

One-way mirrors abounded in this camp, and to see a full-length version of myself was a curiosity. Only small pieces of reflective paper allowed at shaving time gave detainees an opportunity to examine their tired, stressed features. The reflective paper was not always available, and some detainees never shaved, which meant some people had not seen themselves for years, making it an unsettling experience when they eventually did. The only other opportunity to catch one's reflection was in the one-way glass of Camp Delta's interrogation rooms, but the physical persuasion of two soldiers' hands forcibly dictated the direction of our vision as we entered and exited, and once chained to the floor the reflective glass could be too high.[128]

I was led to one of the big, red, reflective doors, which a guard opened upon request from central command. A hallway lined with other red doors was exposed, each harbouring a detainee; a stairwell at the far end led to more detainees above. I was escorted to the first room on my right, which was generous in size compared to the cages of other camps (two steps by three steps compared to one step by two steps). It was white and had the usual bunk and sink, plus an upright metal toilet (minus the seat). There were two strips of strong transparent material in the door, allowing me to see out into the hallway. This was not always possible, because the soldiers had two magnetic strips cut to size for covering these windows on occasion. There was also a slim, frosted window in the back wall above the bunk, similar to the ones in Camp Echo. The one in this camp seemed to let in a little more natural light but was still impossible to see out of. Four very long fluorescent globes akin to spotlights beamed down upon me twenty-four hours a day, making it extremely bright and extremely difficult to sleep at night. Above the sink near the roof was an air vent that issued a consistently strong and very cold blast of air. Detainees, including myself, were forever plugging the many little holes that made up the thirty-centimetre square grate with toilet paper, only to have it removed by soldiers during room searches. If the grate wasn't plugged and blocked, I literally shivered – there was nothing worse than being denied toilet paper.

We all complained about the air vents; some detainees even went on hunger strike for no reason other than the cold temperature and the adverse effects it was having on their health. It was that bad, but nothing was ever done because the whole point was to make us uncomfortable and undermine our health.

Camp Five had a really nasty atmosphere and energy about it, which I believed made all who dwelled within its walls – guards and detainees alike – a little mad and melancholy.

Besides a few books and some legal paperwork, I had lost all other privileges when I was moved to Camp Five, such as the table and chair. One of the guards asked me what I had done, because I had apparently 'pissed somebody off' and Camp Five was my punishment. I replied that I didn't know but suspected I was being punished for complaining to the consular official. The message was clear: 'Appreciate what you have and your general treatment, because we can always make it worse.'

Until I was moved to Camp Five I had engaged in some form of daily exercise within the cages over the years. It had become an extremely important tool in my battle against depression and physical deterioration. There was not a lot I could do in a cage the size of a toilet, but I always managed something: push-ups, sit-ups, stretches. Depending on the guards, I had been allowed to tie sheets and towels to the diamond wire to assist in these exercises. My favourite was to fashion a pull-up bar out of a sheet. I was unable to exercise in this manner in Camp Five. The guards even told me to stop exercising whenever they saw me, ridiculously claiming that I was training to assault them. This was a huge interference with my daily routine, and I stopped exercising altogether.

The suicide plan that had taken me months to develop in Camp Delta would have been impossible to carry out in this new environment. I spent my initial days in Camp Five trying to devise an alternative plan, but I could not think of anything. I threw the razor away. Losing that sense of control over my destiny and no longer exercising plunged me into depression.

Camp Five could boast one positive attribute that no other camp shared: hot water. In all the years in all the camps in Guantanamo, I only had cold showers. This was not so bad during the day in summer, but during the night and coolish weather it was freezing. In Camp Five, however, to stand under the hot, soothing flow for the allocated five minutes was luxurious. The camp could also boast another trait: the smallest outdoor rec yards.

There was a lot of open hostility and harassment from the guards at Camp Five; even simple orders were screamed. Their worst policy was making us sleep on our backs with our faces towards the lights. I tried many ways to shield my eyes from the brightness. We were not allowed, and never had been allowed, to use a sheet or blanket to cover our faces. Instead, I tried placing a piece of clothing over my eyes, such as shorts, but was yelled at to remove them. A year or so before, I had been issued a pair of glasses because of the effect the diamond wire was having on my vision. In Camp Five I tried to take advantage of these glasses by folding a square of toilet paper so that it covered the inside of the lens without any of the paper sticking out of the sides and alerting the guards to what I was up to. I was able to get away with this for a few nights until they confiscated my toilet paper. I tried to reason with them, pointing out that shaded glasses did not prevent them from seeing my face, but then they took my glasses and ordered me to stare at the lights. Even when I closed my eyes, the lights were bright enough to penetrate the lids. I was still getting chronic headaches at this point, so I was taking anti-inflammatory painkillers every day to try to curb the pain in my head, as well as my back.

Then I tried something that, to my surprise, worked. My hair was just long enough to hang over my eyes, so I tousled it to look like any normal morning hair. It didn't always stay in place but it was thick enough to block out the light, and I was never screamed at to remove it from my face. I figured the soldiers looked past the hair because it was already strewn about my head, and not conspicuous like using sheets or toilet paper for cover. Once I had discovered this secret I stopped having my hair cut.

I spent this period at Camp Five poring over the books Mori had provided on international law, the laws of war and the Geneva Conventions. These texts were interesting and enabled me to play a part in strategising my defence. But I also found the information frustrating because it highlighted just how much I was being denied due process.

While I was in Camp Five the British citizenship case proceeded. I won the first court case and the government appealed. We went back to court and I won the second case as well. If the government wished to appeal again, there was only one more court to go: the House of Lords. It seemed obvious that I would win at that hearing as well, and the government would be forced to intervene on my behalf as it had for its other citizens. Instead of the government appealing, I was moved to Camp Echo for a day and presented with British citizenship around 9.30 am. Then at about 2.30 that afternoon my citizenship was revoked.[129] This manoeuvre meant that to have my citizenship reinstated I couldn't appeal directly to the House of Lords – I had to take a detour through various tribunals first. Even though I looked set to win, the British government had just bought itself over a year, instead of the two or three months before it would have had to face the inevitable. They hoped that a resolution would have come about by then. This particular manoeuvre through the tribunals caught me off guard, but once it had sunk in I was not surprised. I was disappointed, but it was just Guantanamo, where nothing went my way. The resistance of the British government to intercede on my behalf is understandable. It had been a nightmare for them to negotiate the release of their citizens and had caused some unease between both the American and British governments. They also did not wish to embarrass the Australian government by having to secure my rights after Howard had abandoned me, arguing I was not entitled to UK citizenship.

The hostility towards detainees in Camp Five was always evident. I often heard IRFings taking place or detainees in other wings banging their sinks and toilets, protesting some unjust treatment. On one occasion I witnessed the detainee in the cell opposite get IRFed. He had flooded his room and pushed the water out under his door into the passageway. He then covered the two window strips on his door with toilet paper, preventing the soldiers from seeing in. When the IRF team arrived and gave him an ultimatum, he removed the toilet paper and surrendered himself for shackling.

He was removed from the room while soldiers entered to inspect. I watched him make fun of the IRF team, pretending he was scared of the six armour-clad soldiers. When the room inspection was complete and he was led back inside to have the shackles removed, he headbutted one of the soldiers. Out in the passage with the IRF team was a film crew, a translator, an officer and a medic. The officer said, 'Get him,' and the soldiers moved out of the way to allow the IRF team to enter. This detainee was small and skinny and still shackled in a three-piece suit, yet I watched him out-manoeuvre the six soldiers and begin to fight back, actually getting the better of them for a short time. It was gutsy and inspiring to witness, but he was inevitably overwhelmed and punished. As they removed the shackles they twisted his arms and squeezed every pressure point, making the detainee scream.

A few days later I heard another detainee scream. This time the cries belonged to a teenage Canadian citizen, who had a room in my wing.[130] He was taken to the interrogation room, on the opposite side of the passage to me, next door to where the previous detainee had been IRFed. I could not see what was happening in there but the Canadian was screaming out, '*Why?* What are you doing this for? What do you want? Help!' in between long bouts of gut-wrenching screams that echoed in the empty passageway. I could hear chairs scraping against the floor and soldiers grunting as the Canadian was brutalised. The treatment must have gone on for an hour or two and seemed to have no purpose other than to hurt him.

Then, on 9 June 2006, three detainees were found dead in Camp Delta. The military labelled the deaths as 'an act of asymmetrical warfare' and 'manipulative self-injurious behaviour'.[131] Every detainee, no matter where they were on the night, had an opinion on whether it was suicide or murder, and those opinions were evenly divided. My own opinion at the time was that the deaths were possible suicides. I know from experiencing camp procedures how desperate one can become. However, evidence continues to be released pointing to suspicious activity.

Recent reports suggest that the detainees were interrogated in a secret camp before their deaths, called Camp No, which is run by a civilian organisation (CIA or Joint Special Operations Command). According to two former guards, it is called Camp No because, 'No, it doesn't exist.'[132] Army Staff Sergeant Joe Hickman, who was posted on a guard tower that night, reported that he saw the transport vehicle dropping off detainees at Camp No on the night of the deaths at around 8 pm. At 11.30 pm the van returned, dropping 'something' off at the clinic. When Hickman arrived at the clinic, he found a distressed medic saying that 'three dead prisoners' had been delivered. Hickman recalled the medic saying that they had died because they had rags stuffed down their throats, and one of them was severely bruised. Davila, another guard present, corroborated the story, saying he had spoken with navy guards who said the men had died as the result of having rags stuffed down their throats.[133] In a press conference, the media was told it was suicide. But according to Scott Horton, the journalist who interviewed the guards, the following morning the warden, Colonel Mike Bumgarner, told the guards that they all knew three prisoners in the Alpha Block at Camp One committed suicide during the night by swallowing rags, but the media would report that they had committed suicide by hanging themselves in their cells. He advised them on the importance of not undermining this official report by speaking out of line. He reminded the servicemen that their phone and email correspondence was being monitored.[134]

Also raising concerns about the official suicide story is Human Rights Watch, who released a press statement raising suspicions that full, un-redacted reports into the deaths have not been released.[135] The families of the men have been calling for an independent investigation since the suspicious deaths occurred.[136] One family ordered an independent autopsy when the body was returned to them. The report found that organs essential to the investigation had been removed, such as the pharynx, larynx and throat. Toenails and fingernails were cut so short that no DNA could be taken from the bodies.[137] The evidence pointing to foul play continues to mount, especially considering the 'enhanced interrogation techniques' sanctioned at the time. Whatever happened, the truth about those deaths and the subsequent ones, for there have been two others since, is still to be revealed.[138]

A week or so passed before the news of the deaths reached us in Camp Five, but it made sense when it did. On the day it occurred, every detainee in our camp had every item confiscated.[139] With no explanation the guards rushed my room, as well as everyone else's, and left me with nothing except a pair of shorts. For a whole week, I slept directly on the concrete floor and froze in the glare of the lights. When a week had passed, the others and I were given a T-shirt and pants, but had to continue to sleep directly on the concrete floor. A few days later the iso-mat was returned and so forth, so that after a month most items had been given back. It was a very difficult, testing time.

If I had had a way to end it all, I would have carried it out. However, I adopted a different approach. For the first time I decided to hunger strike. My theory was that if I did not eat for long enough I would become so weak that I would sleep my time away, oblivious to my surrounding environment and what I was being made to endure. I could no longer tolerate the waking moments and needed to escape. I lasted thirty days on liquids alone and lost a lot of weight. It was a visit from Mori, the smell of the McDonald's he brought, the news he relayed concerning the *Hamdan* case and the fact that most personal items had been returned that made me decide to eat again. Another visitor around the thirty-day mark was the Australian consular official. He dismissed my hunger strike as nonsense. I really disliked this man. I had stopped eating for myself, not to get attention. In fact, my hunger strike was largely secret so I wouldn't be punished for it. I still accepted the meals – I just flushed them down the toilet. The consular official had no idea of the consequences of a hunger strike, nor did he seem to care about the environment I was in. The man was inexperienced with the types of policies and practices found in Guantanamo or their effects on the mind and body. Mori, on the other hand, could tell by the smell of my breath, loss of weight, lack of ability to concentrate and because he paid enough attention and took enough interest in me to notice. It was then that I decided never to meet with the consular official again.

The British citizenship case had been an exercise in hope and frustration, especially while the government continued to fight and look for loopholes in my claim as I continued to win. As with many other situations, the experience had been a whirlwind of emotions with always the same destination in mind – getting out of Guantanamo and going home. But this was eclipsed by bigger news around the end of June, when the long-awaited outcome of the *Hamdan* case was announced by the US Supreme Court. Hamdan had won, so all detainees had won![140] The court pronounced the military commissions as illegal; they were gone and our invented charges dissolved along with them. It was a great relief and a time for me to be hopeful; I was now facing the most realistic chance ever of going home. The Australian government could no longer ignore the warnings concerning the military commissions – it was a real told-you-so moment. All eyes were on Howard. What would he do? Would he accept that he was wrong, that he had supported one of his citizens being subjected to a system now proven to be illegal by the very country that invented it? How could he continue to leave me there and insist that the Americans were responsible enough to deal with me through some form of legal hearings? Another anxious waiting game began.

While the significance of all these recent events – the hunger strike, being punished for detainees' suicides or murder, the outcome of my British citizenship case and the *Hamdan* decision – hung over me, escorts came to my room and said I was going for a ride I would soon appreciate. I wondered what they meant. I forget exactly what was said, but as I was being led to the van the two soldiers hinted that my release was imminent. Once we were seated in the back, I began to ask questions but they kept being evasive, deepening my belief that I was about to learn about my release. They would not elaborate, and I was surprised upon arrival that our destination was an interrogation room in Camp Delta. I was seated and handed a phone with instructions to answer it when it rang; by then I was fully convinced that they were allowing my family to give me the good news first.

When I answered, Dad was on the other end, and after the initial pleasantries he began to give me the footy updates. I was expecting him to cry out that I was going home, so a growing dread hijacked my emotions. I did not take well to talk of football and interrupted, demanding, 'Do you know anything about me coming home?' I received the usual answer – 'I don't know' – and became angry, not at Dad, but at myself. I had allowed myself to be fooled by the soldiers once again. I had given myself over to an illusion. I was furious about the deception and went on about the detainee deaths and our subsequent punishments. Phone calls usually lasted twenty minutes, but on this occasion I was left to rave for an hour. No doubt the authorities learned a lot about my state of mind that day, and analysed it to their advantage.

When all of these events had passed, the days began to blur together. I was back to eating normally and had a few books to help pass the time. One of those books was on yoga. I had first seen it in Camp Echo, but every time I had tried a pose I agitated the pain in my lower back. Now in Camp Five, due to boredom and a determination to heal my back, I began to practise the poses slowly and build up my strength so that I was able to complete three yoga sessions a day without hurting myself. As the weeks melded together in this way, I remained hopeful of going home, considering commissions and the charges that had been pending against me for a long time were now gone. I knew with each day that passed I was one day closer to going home. In a way, time was on my side. Without the commissions, Howard had less of an excuse to leave me there. But too much time put my sanity at risk. Who would give in first, Howard or me?

During this period President Bush had one of three decisions to make: release us; take us to a properly constituted court, such as courts-martial or the federal courts; or tweak the old condemned system, ignoring the rulings of his own court, and brazenly plough ahead. There was a chance he would choose the last road, but it was doubtful – it was thought Bush had more respect for his own legal system and would not openly rebel against the justices now that their final decision on the matter was made clear. So as I sat in my cell I did not let that potential outcome destroy my hopes.

In October of 2006 Bush played his hand, exposing his regime for what it was. He chose to ignore the US Supreme Court and the mounting public pressure, which had grown since the revelations of the secret prisons.[141] Of the many reasons the commissions had been ruled illegal, one was that Congress had not sanctioned the system. This was the area Bush addressed. With a Republican-dominated Congress, Bush had them pass the *Military Commissions Act 2006*, which gave Congressional authorisation for the use of military commissions.[142] However, Bush did not address any of the other jurisdictional or procedural defects, including the retrospective charges, and announced that the still illegal commissions would go ahead.

Theoretically, the charges against me could be filed again and the military commissions process would start all over. If so, it was reasonable to assume that my own government would again uphold the American system. It seemed so unfair that a predicament that had been resolved a long time ago, and which I never expected to see again, would once more have such a damaging impact on my life.

Because of this change of events, I spent one whole afternoon squatting at my bunk, writing down all my thoughts on paper. I brainstormed all the possible scenarios. I imagined myself having to spend many more years in Guantanamo fighting the commissions and charges, and so for the first time on paper I wrote down the option of pleading guilty on the condition that I would be released to Australia very quickly and enjoy certain daily living conditions until my departure. Such a decision would be a last resort, but it did present the quickest way off the island if I was charged again. I had already spent just short of five years on this island, living a surreal, forlorn existence. About fifty-eight months, or around 1700 days – I was physically and mentally approaching a rapid end.

Over the years, since I had been in contact with Major Mori, the prosecution had offered plea bargains, albeit unreasonable ones. From my point of view, there were always positive outcomes on the table anyway, so there was no incentive to even talk with the prosecution. I had not committed a crime or been accused of such. There were no victims, no criminal activities had been in the planning, and the US government agreed. Despite these facts, in the early days, pleading guilty meant serving twenty years in prison; as time went on it dropped to ten. In the weeks preceding the Supreme Court *Hamdan* decision, the prosecution, knowing they would probably lose, was desperate for convictions and dropped it to two years, the lowest it had ever gone.

As I was writing down my various thoughts that day, including my demands if I ever accepted a plea deal as a means to escape, I noticed that the guards kept looking into my room more than usual and showing an interest in what I was doing. When I had finished, I stacked the paper together and stretched out on the floor. Soon after, the soldiers demanded I get up and shackled me. They searched my room and picked up my legal notes. I alerted the soldiers to what the papers were and asked that they be put back. Instead, I was ignored and the papers were confiscated. When I was unshackled and back in the cell, I demanded to know what was happening to my paperwork that was supposedly private and protected by client–attorney

privilege. I was told to relax, that it was just being photocopied, and I would get it back soon.

Apart from the obvious reasons such an action would cause
me distress, what worried me the most were my notes about
pleading guilty. I could picture Prime Minister Howard receiving a briefing and being told, 'Hicks is ready to throw in the
towel, just wait a little bit longer.' If Howard was about to
announce my release, he would definitely cancel those preparations now with the intelligence, in my own handwriting, that I
was considering pleading guilty. I felt that it would be my fault
if I was not released.

In the following days I made another show of writing, making sure the soldiers saw me. I wrote down things I hoped
would dispel the idea that accepting a deal was on the cards:
if they were relying on me folding, they would have to rethink
their plans. I wrote as if it was a continuation of the plans
they had photocopied and that I was full of strength and confidence. If it didn't work, at least it helped make me feel better.

A day or so after, when I was in the shower, I watched a
soldier enter my cell through the large, reflective pane in front
of me. He pulled a small gadget from his pocket upon entry;
I had a clear view that it was, in fact, a camera. It made me
feel better that they had a copy of my staged notes. I noticed
from that time forward that they began photographing all
my written notes, so I didn't keep any more legal documents
in my room.

It was around this time that some guards admitted to a US
Marine Corps sergeant that it was common practice to beat
detainees, including punching them in the face, withholding
mail and removing 'privileges' for no reason.[143] The sergeant
stated that they laughed and boasted about how common it
was. The statement was taken to the inspector general at the
Department of Defense, but no action was taken. It was leaked

to the press, however, and the pressure increased for the image of Guantanamo to be revamped.

For the previous weeks we had heard from the guards that a new camp, called Camp Six, had just been completed, and that the detainees from Camp Five would be the first to be transferred there. I had also heard about this camp from my lawyers, the ICRC and the information detainees brought back from their lawyer's meetings. All reports were positive, such as two detainees per room, all-day mingling permitted inside a common area with the cell doors left open, wet weather outdoor rec area and another uncovered outdoor rec area the size of a football field. It sounded suspicious and we remained sceptical.

Then, without warning, all the detainees in my wing were handed garbage bags and told to prepare for transportation to Camp Six. At a guess, this would have been early morning in the first days of November 2006. We were taken from our cells one at a time, and transported in a green Gator without being blindfolded. We travelled a few hundred metres between camps in the sun until we arrived at an inconspicuous doorway set in a huge bleak-looking, concrete wall. Once inside this enormous structure we walked down long cement passageways before coming to a double door. These doors swung open to reveal a huge cavern, three maybe four storeys high. This was one of a number of chambers, or 'bays' as they were referred to by military personnel, which were to house detainees within this sprawling facility.

Twenty-eight

'The United States is committed to the world-wide elimination of torture, and we are leading this fight by example.'

George W. Bush during the United Nations day
held in support of victims of torture, 2003

THE BAYS OF CAMP SIX WERE DESIGNED so that twenty-four cells made an 'L' shape with another twenty-four cells above. This created a forty-eight-celled, two-storey structure. Within the arms of the 'L' were metal tables and chairs bolted to a cement floor. On the far side of the tables and chairs from the cells were two showers. The inner cell walls were thin sheetmetal, forming a single, prefabricated box. Some cells had single beds and other cells, like mine, had bunk shelves to sleep on. Like Camp Five, the metal rooms in Camp Six were pumped full of cold air, but there was nothing we could do about it in this new camp.

The propaganda the military had publicly spread concerning the 'humane conditions' detainees would enjoy in Camp Six again turned out to be a lie. Twenty-three-hour lockdown was still the policy. Our cell doors were never opened to allow us access to the tables and chairs in the centre of the bay, and we were told outright that we would never use them. The wet weather outdoor rec area had been sectioned into six very small yards surrounded by walls two to three storeys tall, preventing the sun from reaching detainees except for the two hours in the middle of the day. The main outdoor rec yard, which was to be the size of a football field, had not been completed, and we were told it never would be. This change of plans was blamed on a disturbance in Camp Four.

A few months before, I heard that soldiers had fired rubber bullets at the detainees in Camp Four, which resulted in a protest. In Camp Six we were told we could not be trusted and needed to be punished. There would be no improvements to living conditions – not that it had ever been their intention.

The bay resembled a stone cavern, which intensified every noise. Within a twenty-four-hour period all detainees had to go to rec and shower twice, or at the least have a cell search. Because of the way in which it was conducted, it was maddeningly impossible to sleep during that time. For the following twenty-four hours we were not allowed to come out of the cells. But this did not mean it was a time to sleep and recover from the previous twenty-four hours' din. If soldiers could not achieve eye contact with a detainee while he observed him through the perspex slits, the soldier would slam the door until the detainee startled from his sleep and moved to look in their direction. When the soldier achieved eye contact, he then moved to the next door. Three guards paced the cells on a regular non-stop circuit, waking us at least every ten minutes, sometimes more often. Even if I was lying on my bunk, already staring at the door then directly in the soldier's eye when he appeared, I had to move a part of my body to prove I wasn't dead. This exhausting madness went round and round, day after day.[144]

As had been the case for years, the daily necessities were performed so that even *they* were a form of punishment. We were rushed to the shower, yelled at to hurry while we were in there, often had the water turned off before we could wash the suds off, then rushed back to our cells. We were rushed to rec, rushed to shave and change linen – every opportunity was exploited to harass us. It became old after a while.

Events like mealtimes in a prison setting are usually looked forward to because it breaks the monotony and gives one something to do for a short period, in addition to satisfying hunger. But food itself had become a form of punishment. Meals such as green, powdered scrambled eggs would be served along with oranges so extremely freezer burnt that no moisture was left. Hard-boiled eggs were first cooked and de-shelled on the US mainland, deep-frozen and reheated months later at Guantanamo, leaving the whites the consistency of leather. All hot meals were cooked in thick oil, and if they were served cold the entire meal solidified into a single gooey conglomerate. In Camp Six, the soldiers used to put our hot meals in front of a large air-conditioner duct for a couple of hours before serving, which made it practically inedible. Not even the simplest pleasure was allowed to relieve us from the constant hardship, but only used to exacerbate. Even today, if I could, I would just take a nutrition pill and be done with it.

For some bizarre reason the authorities started to give detainees selected news articles each week. These printouts from the internet were always in English and only available during rec time. This news consisted of soccer updates as well as political news. Since my time in Tango Block, weekly propaganda posters designed by the military were hung throughout the camps in the rec yards, including in Camp Six. One of the posters showed Saddam Hussein hanging from a noose.[145] We had read about Saddam's execution in the printouts, and detainees had heard the news from their lawyers, so we believed what we saw. In large Arabic script angling across this poster was what someone translated to me as, 'Saddam refused to cooperate with lawyers and look what happened to him. This could be you.' Some detainees took this as blackmail to get them to cooperate with lawyers, and they rebelled by becoming even more defiant in refusing to speak with legal counsel.

For years there had been a small, core group of detainees who spent their time lecturing others at the top of their lungs. They dictated how detainees should interpret events and react to interrogation techniques. They encouraged hunger strikes. They demanded detainees never talk with guards, especially to engage in idle conversation and laugh with them. They ordered detainees never to cooperate with interrogators and claimed the ICRC was working for the military. Even lawyers should be avoided because they were really interrogators in disguise. This last claim had some merit to it because military interrogators had been known to pose as lawyers and, on one or two occasions, even as the ICRC. The military was notorious for posing as FBI agents, especially on occasions when enhanced techniques were being used. This concerned the FBI enough that they went public, explaining these were not their agents and they did not use torture.[146] The detainees who promoted such views were few in number, and not all detainees paid attention to them, but around 300 detainees often listened and followed their advice.

I came to know one of these angry and mistrustful detainees well, because he was a member of the 'first six' chosen for military commissions, and we had been together since Papa Block. One day when we were in neighbouring rec yards in Camp Six, he confronted me and shared a story I had been unaware of. He began by telling me that he was a member of al-Qaeda and that out of the 800-odd detainees brought to Guantanamo in the early days, only about twenty had actually been al-Qaeda. He said he and only four or five others were still in

Guantanamo at that time, because the rest had been released with other detainees.

Before I could ask, he claimed that the US knew who they were all along, but released them anyway for political purposes he was not interested in sharing. He said these twenty or so individuals had established an intelligence network among detainees; they knew who everyone was, who was cooperating with interrogation, who was not and other related information. He said most of these al-Qaeda figures were still in Guantanamo when the US government first announced the six who would be facing military commissions. They took great interest in this, curious to see which 'brothers' were being prosecuted. My name had caused them some confusion because they had never heard of me before and did not know who I was. They had a laugh at the US for its line-up of 'al-Qaeda' suspects, and then forgot all about commissions and related issues.

However, as the years passed, it was always my name being publicly associated with the commissions. I was always the one being pushed forward to go first, and it was only my government that spoke publicly in favour of commissions and how I must go before them. He claimed this brought me to the attention of al-Qaeda because they could not figure out why I had become so 'high profile', and it seemed certain that out of hundreds of detainees it would be me who went first, accused of being someone and something they knew not to be true. He kept saying it was suspicious that I had been the first detainee allowed to meet with a lawyer, the first detainee to be allowed to ring his family, the only detainee whose family had actually been allowed onto the base to meet with me, despite some other detainees having been to a military commission by then. And now I was to be the first again for these new commissions. He challenged me by asking me to explain why I had become the public face of commissions and why I was always being pushed to go first. I had no comeback for that, no answers to satisfy him, no answers at all. I just didn't know – and I still don't. There was nothing I could say.

Then he informed me of his theory, claiming to speak on behalf of the other so-called al-Qaeda members. The only reasonable explanation was that I was an agent on the payroll of the US government, and possibly my own government, and that I was going to eventually go in front of a military commission and say guilty. By doing so I would help legitimise the commission system and the US government would use my cooperation and acceptance in its Federal Court hearings, namely the Supreme Court, to justify their use and then condemn and prosecute a heap of detainees after me. I would then return to Australia and quietly disappear with my fortune while innocent men were convicted by an unjust system. He went on further to threaten me, saying some detainees who had already been released would make contact with their local underground mujahedeen movement and put out the word that I must be assassinated. He said that to volunteer to live in Guantanamo for so long and to help the US government harm Muslim people by helping legitimise the commissions was really going out of my way and must be taken very personally by them.

I listened to this with amusement because of how ridiculous and ironic it was, yet I was also concerned that what he had to say about assassinations might have been true. Here I was, detained on allegations of belonging to an organisation I had never heard of, while a proclaimed member of that organisation was threatening me with death for being an employee of the US government! It was madness, and it shows how irresponsible it was of the Australian and US governments for having publicly made those ridiculous allegations, and the media for entertaining them.

When I reported this discussion to my legal team they dismissed it as nonsense and said the detainee in question was a 'wannabe' who would say anything to get attention from the US and try to infuriate them, to hurt them with words, because it was the only power left open to him. There was also the possibility that he just wanted to be famous in his own lands, to be known as a member of the shadowy al-Qaeda network. Over a year before, while we were in Papa Block, the detainee in question would request the highest ranking soldier on duty, the E9 sergeant major, to come to his cage. I then listened to him go on and on about al-Qaeda and supposedly sensitive previously unknown information, implicating himself from every ingenious angle. At first the sergeant major would nod profusely and take copious notes – I even remember him sweating profusely, standing to attention, very professional and polite. However, he came to see what was happening, or someone told him he was being played, and eventually stopped coming altogether.

The detainee in question was more than likely all talk. In any case, while I have not forgotten the threat, it also does not occupy my daily thoughts. But I wonder what he thought when in the end I did say 'guilty', which was not long after our conversation, just as he predicted I would; if he then truly believed I was an actual plant, to justify the use of military commissions. I wonder if this clinched the theory for him? I did this only a month after he had confronted me, and in reply I said I would never say guilty, no matter what.

This was not the only time I had been accused of being a spy. In May 2007, independent journalists interviewed former Guantanamo detainee and former Taliban ambassador to Pakistan, Mullah Abdul Salam Zaeef. During this interview, he commented that, 'All the people, including me and the Arabs, we're thinking he was a spy.'[147] He went on to say that I was not a 'true Muslim', and basically, I was never one of them. The US military prosecutors must have conveniently forgotten about this interview. Here I was once again, accused of being a member of an organisation which thought I was a spy for the US. The other frustrating fact about all of this was that here was a high-ranking Taliban official, whom the US classified as an enemy, yet who was freed without charge, and I was still there!

Also at the time, the former chief spokesperson abroad for the Taliban was attending Yale while I was imprisoned in Guantanamo, being accused of providing support for the Taliban.

Twenty-nine

'If it were not for injustice, men would not know justice.'

Heraclitus (540 BC–480 BC)

I STILL HAD NOT BEEN CHARGED after three months of wasting away in Camp Six, and as each day passed the likelihood of my release increased. There was a congressional election, which resulted in the Democrats regaining the majority for the first time while Guantanamo had been in existence, meaning there was a chance they would not allow the Republican *2006 Commissions Act* to proceed.

I had developed a new problem in Camp Six: stomach pains. If I consumed either food or water, the resulting pain was excruciating. My stools were shaped and coloured to suggest that something was terribly wrong. I was suspicious about this pain because it had occurred after I had reported a used bandaid in one of my meals. I knew that the kitchen contractors were asked about it and my tired, suspicious mind pictured the cooks putting some form of powder in my food – enough to cause pain but not seriously endanger my health. The medics found a tablet for me that worked like magic. No matter how much pain I was suffering, not long after taking just one of these tablets the pain completely disappeared. I had to take the tablets for four or five days before the pain completely stopped of its own accord, only to have it start all over again after one or two days of being pain-free.

Around the beginning of 2007, I was told I had a visitor from the Australian embassy in Washington. I had refused to see the Australian consular official since being punished for speaking with him about the conditions back in Tango Block, but I was told on this occasion I could not refuse or I would be IRFed. I was surprised when I entered the interrogation room to be met by a man I had not seen before. He introduced himself as an Australian embassy employee and said that he was on a consular visit, yet he spoke with a heavy American accent. Everything he said sounded false. I quickly reached the conclusion that the man was not from the embassy at all, an assertion he strongly denied when I challenged him. I was not in the mood and became very angry, accusing him of being an impostor. I did not believe what he had to say and refused to talk with him. Back in my cell I took the visit as a good omen. I thought it might have been a final test of my strength before they made the decision to release me: was I on the verge of giving in or not? A few days later, when my lawyers complained about this deception, the authorities insisted the man in question had not posed as an Australian consular official.

This belief in my imminent release was bolstered a few days later when John Howard went public and set the US a deadline for the first time. He said that if I wasn't charged by February, he would request my release. The deadline was only weeks away, and I did not believe for a moment that the US was going to charge me in time. In the five and a half years, this was the most convinced I had been of receiving news of my imminent release.

I would learn years later that at this time, on 9 January 2007, Colonel Morris Davis received a phone call from Jim Haynes asking how quickly he could charge me. Coincidentally, this was a day after US Department of Defense and Department of Justice officials met with Australian government representatives to discuss my case. Colonel Morris Davis testified to the House Armed Services Committee that he was unable to charge me at the time because the *Manual for Military Commissions* had not even been drafted yet. In other words, there was nothing to define the elements of an offence; he could not charge me when there were no rules outlined to establish guilt. Haynes ended the conversation by telling Colonel Davis that they had to get the case going and that he would 'move the manual to completion as soon as possible'.[148] Davis also said that I should never have been charged. This phone call, as well as continual political interference in my case, led to Colonel Davis resigning in October 2007.

Colonel Davis further explained in an interview:

To charge someone, there are elements of the offence that the prosecution has to prove, and those are laid out in *The Manual for Military Commissions*. That document had not been published on January 9, 2007, so I had no elements of proof to look at to determine what to charge David Hicks with. Yet I'm getting a call from the general counsel saying, 'How quickly can you charge him?' We eventually charged him on February 2, along with Omar Khadr and Salim Hamdan. But, again, if you look at the timing of it, Susan Crawford, who is the convening authority, wasn't appointed until, I believe, February 7. So, here we are charging people five days before there's a convening authority to refer charges to, which I think to a reasonable person just doesn't make much sense.

Also, the regulation for trial by military commissions, which is kind of the deep-in-the-weeds details on how the commissions are conducted, wasn't published until late April 2007, which was after the David Hicks trial was completed. So we didn't even have the regulations written at the time we prosecuted David Hicks.[149]

At about 4 pm on 2 February 2007, a medic came to my cell as usual to prescribe my stomach pain medication. Instead of the tablet, however, he produced a small bottle of a mixed liquid and told me to drink it. I asked what it was and he called it a 'G.I. cocktail', saying it would be good for my stomach. Without thinking, I swallowed the liquid. I don't know what it was, but the stuff was very strong because within ten minutes I couldn't stay awake any longer. Very little time had passed when I was woken by a loud banging on my cell door. I was very drowsy and had difficulty comprehending what was happening, but I could make out a large group of people looking in at me. One of them addressed me: 'I am here to formally charge you. I can read the charges here or we can go to a private room.'[150] What he had said registered in my brain, but I was too drowsy to be emotionally affected by this disastrous revelation. I managed to stand up while they shackled me and was escorted to an interrogation room. Two men read the new charges, but I could barely stay awake and was returned to my cell without any of it sinking in. All I cared about was sleeping.

Not long after this, I was visited by the Australian consular official, and I told him about the cocktail and how it affected me. His conclusion was that I had exaggerated, once again. He claimed to have seen the list of ingredients; it only contained a bit of Benadryl. So my complaint was dismissed as usual.

As the days passed I could remember what had happened, but

I was hoping it was a bad dream. Deep down I knew when Mori came he would confirm what my groggy mind suspected. Mori arrived within a few days and went back through the second lot of charges with me so I understood their nature: Attempted Murder and Providing Material Support for Terrorism.[151]

Mori then relayed a message to me that had originated in Australia. John Howard told one of his staffers who told Mori to tell me that under no circumstances would he let me return to Australia without my entering a guilty plea. Mori added that he was not surprised, because Howard needed to justify leaving me in Guantanamo for all those years and supporting the military commissions, despite the opposition and court rulings. I believed John Howard. He had proven to be a stubborn character; time and again he had dismissed the damning evidence and placed all his faith in the US getting it right. There had been numerous opportunities in the past when he could have brought me home and turned the situation around to make it look like he was taking a tough stance against the lack of due process and denial of a fair trial, but he never did. He was determined to have his way; he had bet everything on the one outcome. I suppose in his view the political damage was already done in Australia: he was a man who had invested too much into an inflexible policy. I accepted that my five and a half years of hopes had been for nothing, and in the end Howard had won. After all those years of surviving and waiting, I truly believed I was only days away from being released; now these new developments guaranteed I had many more years to go. I was shattered.

Mori and I discussed these developments. He was of the opinion that there might still never be trials because the US government did not particularly want to go ahead with them. Pre-trial motions, on the other hand, were a good way to promote their propaganda and show how dangerous and evil we were meant to be without actually having to prove it. They could also counter any positive media the detainees received. For example, the recent five-year anniversary of detention at Guantanamo[152] garnered global sympathy in recognition of the plight of the detainees. Then in the following weeks charges were laid and the US government went global, utilising the charges to remind people of what type of 'evil characters' were being held in Guantanamo. The young Canadian detainee was charged shortly after me, and Mori thought that had been done so it would not look like I was being singled out, not that it helped much.[153] Our final conclusion of what was to come was that there would be a round of pre-trial motions in an attempt to derail support for me through negative publicity. Yet when it came to the crunch and it was time to progress to actual trial, an event would occur to halt proceedings and I would go back to rotting in my cell, possibly for years to come.

All I knew was that there was no way I could go on living in Guantanamo under such oppressive conditions, and I gave up the will to continue. Over the last few months in Camp Six I had begun to contemplate a new means of successfully suiciding because I knew I could not go on much longer. Suicide in Camp Six, like in Camp Five, was virtually impossible, but I decided on a method that I was convinced would be foolproof. Mori had come at last with no positive news and, even if he had, it would not have sustained me. For the first time my mind was set; the decision was made. I just needed to decide on when.

Mori told me that the first round of pre-trial hearings would be within a month. I knew that family could attend, and I decided I would wait to see Dad first. I asked Mori if he could ask him to attend, but he said it would be better to wait – the first pre-trial hearing would only be for the day. At a later stage, when we had begun to argue motions, the hearings would last for two or three days. Because my family had limited money, it would be wiser to wait until a later date so I could spend more time with them.

Mori wouldn't promise to ask my dad to attend the coming hearing, which caused me great distress because I knew I wouldn't be able to hold on any longer. Luckily, the ICRC came for a visit and I stressed the importance of how I really needed to see my family at that first hearing. They promised to tell my dad that I wanted him to come no matter what. My plan was to say something meaningful to Dad without giving my intentions away, so that in the days following his return to Australia, when he heard the news of my suicide, he would realise that I had actually said goodbye.

It was around this time, 23 February, that US Vice President Dick Cheney visited Australia. It was only after my release that I discovered that a former Cheney staffer confirmed in *Harper's Magazine* that it was during this meeting that Cheney interfered directly to have a plea deal struck. I was yet to find out about this deal and what it contained.[154]

The time arrived for me to return to the military commissions on 26 March. Therefore, I was relieved to see that Dad and Stephanie had come. We spent some time together at the beginning of the day but I had decided to give my subtle hint at the time of our goodbye. There were so many things I wanted to say in front of the judge, while the world was listening. I had written a list of all the disadvantages preventing me from defending myself. I wanted to make demands concerning my daily living standards so that I might have had a better chance of fully concentrating on the proceedings, and not being so preoccupied with sleep, food, avoiding harassment, being afraid of having all legal notes confiscated, etc. It was a long list and one I wanted the world to hear. Instead, I said nothing and had my defence team sacked so that only Mori was left to represent me.[155] My US civilian attorney Josh Dratel was sacked by the judge because he had refused to sign an agreement stating he would abide by the commission rules. The problem for him was that no rules existed on paper at the time, and the judge could not answer when Josh inquired what those rules would be. He was being asked to sign a blank cheque and he rightly refused due to his ethical and professional principles. This event and the sacking of my legal team occurred near the end of the first day of proceedings but by then it was just a show for the media that had gathered, because by then we had already signed an agreement.[156]

I was able to spend a late afternoon adjournment with Dad and Stephanie and, unsure whether I would have another opportunity to see them, I considered it was time to say goodbye for the last time. I was getting ready to impart my coded farewell when Mori rushed excitedly into the room and shoved a document in my face. Dad and Stephanie left and Josh and my Australian lawyers entered. The document was a plea deal. All I had to do was plead guilty to the Material Support of Terrorism charge and I could actually get out of Guantanamo within a promised sixty days. The absurd Attempted Murder charge would be dropped. I would have to serve seven months in an Australian prison, but my lawyers were already aware that the Australian government would allow me to serve that time in an Adelaide jail so as to be near my family. The Australian government wanted me to accept this plea agreement more than anyone else.[157]

It was a heart-wrenching decision to throw at me at that time. It tore me apart and massively interfered with the course of action I had already committed to. I had to think what pleading guilty to a terrorism offence would mean for me personally; it was something the Australian media would never let me forget. There was the anguish of giving in after a mammoth five-and-a-half-year struggle. I had been so close, and Howard had given a deadline, yet it had all been snatched away. To say I was guilty was to give in to Howard and show him that all the unconscionable deference he had shown the US government had been the correct policy. All the lawyers were in agreement that the deal was the quickest, most realistic way to get off the island, and seven months in an Australian prison would not be difficult to endure after surviving in Guantanamo. The most important goal for Mori was getting me out of US military custody and under the umbrella of an actual, proper legal jurisdiction, which would have been anywhere in the world outside of Guantanamo. I did not make a decision straight away and asked for Dad and Stephanie to come back into the room so we could discuss the situation. I also asked my lawyers if they could try to secure time served as part of the deal or lessen the prison sentence.

While I was still discussing the options with Dad and Stephanie, the lawyers returned to report that they could not get the sixty days in Guantanamo or seven months in Australia reduced, and the five and a half years I had spent in custody so far would not count towards any sentence – I would not get time served. The deal had already been arranged between Howard and Dick Cheney during the Vice President's visit to Sydney.[158] The Australian government had said publicly in the past that I should get time served; however, being released or serving less time than I was being offered meant that I would have been free before the completion of the approaching Australian elections scheduled later that same year. The prosecution had also been cut out of the process, rendering them obsolete.[159] It was Susan Crawford, the appointing authority and a political appointee, who mediated between my legal team and the politicians. She had never served a day in the military, and many US armed services officers were appalled at her appointment by the Bush administration.

Susan Crawford, after negotiating with my lawyers and saying no to serving less time, agreed to allow me to enter an Alford Plea if I chose, as an incentive to cooperate.[160] Under this US legislation, a person can plead guilty without admitting to the act they are accused of. In other words, contrary to media reports, I did not 'admit' or 'confess' to providing material support to terrorism; I pleaded guilty without accepting guilt to the charge so I could return home. To plead guilty was really saying that the system was unfair and I could never win, not that I ever provided support to a terrorist organisation.

I had two choices: take the Alford Plea and face all ramifications and consequences that would follow, or return to my cell, resign myself to hopelessness and follow through with my suicide plan. I looked my father and sister in the eyes and thought of all that they and many others had done for me. I knew the great pain my death would cause them, and I decided I couldn't go through with it. I knew that if I got out of Guantanamo at that stage, there would still be a chance for me to heal the physical and psychological damage to a point that would allow me to function and lead a relatively normal life. But if I was to stay any longer, I was afraid the resulting damage would be irreparable – it would not even be worth being released. I took a deep breath, the silence in the room was intense, everyone was focused on me, knowing the answer was about to be revealed. Regretful and relieved, I said, 'I'll sign.' My lawyers launched into a flurry of activity and left the room while Dad, Stephanie and I embraced and cried, knowing that it was over at last.

From my understanding of what I had agreed to, the maximum sentence the jury could impose was seven years. Whether I received the maximum or less, all incarceration time would be suspended except for nine months. The maximum amount of time I could continue to spend in Guantanamo was the following sixty days, though there was nothing in the agreement to stop the governments from arranging to have me returned to Australia instantly. I would then spend the remainder of the sentence in an Australian prison. Entering into this agreement brought certainty, but what it ultimately left me with was a suspended sentence of six years and three months. Even though I wanted to be – and should have been – released as a free man like the hundreds of others before and after me, this agreement meant I had a further nine months without my liberty, and then I would have my freedom.

There are other parts of the plea 'agreement' that were outrageous but I had to agree to if I wanted to get out of Guantanamo and return to Australia, such as a one-year gag order in which I could not discuss any aspect of my detention, treatment or anything to do with my story with the media from the moment of my plea.[161] This meant that the gag order would still apply for the first three months after my release from Yatala Prison in Adelaide. I also had to agree to fully cooperate with Australian and US law enforcement officials for the rest of my life. I would assign all profits and proceeds related to my story to the Australian government, even if I was to receive compensation for torture, mistreatment, illegal imprisonment, etc. I had to agree that I was not forced or 'coerced' into pleading guilty and that I had never been illegally treated by any person or persons while in the custody and control of the United States government. I had to waive all rights to appeal or 'collaterally challenge' the conviction. I also had to acknowledge that the US has the right to arrest me as an Unlawful Enemy Combatant if I ever leave Australia again. These are just some of the injustices I had to agree to, though there are others.

When my family and I said our final goodbyes, we had the novel opportunity of saying, 'See you soon.' I then had to follow through on my part of the bargain. I thought I was pleading guilty to the one charge and that was it, but after I had said the magic word I was informed there would be a 'statement of facts', where I would have to keep admitting guilt to a series of details. I was not happy about this and protested, but I was told that if I did not go ahead with it then the deal would be forfeited. With heavy reluctance, I did what was required of me. Technically, I was convicted for every terrorist act worldwide since 1989.

I hated saying 'yes, sir' to everything during the staged commission. As I played along, I questioned why I was not defending myself. I couldn't understand that after all those years, when I was standing in front of the world's media, while I had a voice, that I did not expose the injustices that had occurred over the years. On more than one occasion I paused, almost having the courage to say 'no, sir' and to vocalise what I really thought and knew. Being so submissive at that time, when I should have been strong, still haunts me today. And then there was Mori's sentencing speech. Privately, we argued about whether to participate. My point was that we had done enough and there was no need to volunteer a further illusion of guilt or acceptance of the system. I asked him not to say anything, the deal was already signed and there was nothing to gain. But he had a mad idea that if we toed the line and played along there was a very real possibility that I would receive less than the maximum sentence, even time served. As always, I agreed, but I didn't contribute or say anything and left it up to Mori because I just couldn't participate. The plan didn't work, but I only have praise for Mori. I will always be grateful to him, and we will always be friends.

I did not return to Camp Six after these proceedings, instead I spent my last fifty days back in Camp Echo in the exact same cage I had lived in before. Ironically, now that I had been through the show trial and pleaded guilty, the pressure

was off. I had no more stomach pains. The door separating
my section from where the guards used to sit was left open. I
had access to the whole room, an unheard-of freedom, and I
passed the hours thinking about my days in that camp, in that
same room. It was a time to reflect on my past five and a half
years, knowing that this time I was actually going home. I did
not experience any harassment from the guards and was even
allowed chewing tobacco in my room, as long as Mori paid
for it. Another novelty was that if I had the door separating
my space from the guard's area shut and locked, then the main
door to the room was left open, allowing pure, natural light to
flood in. Times were certainly different. Of course the dooms-
day mentality I had adopted over time caused me to stress
those last fifty days away by thinking that I'd been double-
crossed. I kept picturing a soldier offering some excuse why I
couldn't be released and that I'd be stuck in Guantanamo, this
time with the guilty stigma attached.[162] But for the first time
events played out the way they were meant to.

The sixty-day deadline was near when Mori and the Australian consular official arrived in Camp Echo to complete
some paperwork. I had to sign more forms, this time for the
Australian government, stating that everything I had said and
done regarding the plea deal was voluntary and that compe-
tent lawyers had advised me and I fully understood all the
consequences. I was told I had no choice because if I refused
to sign these new extra documents the Australian government
would not take me. The consular official threatened me with
this himself and Mori agreed and said I had no choice. I did
not want to sign anything or have anything to do with the
commissions or plea deals, but my fear of being left behind
was great. Once again I was forced into doing something I did
not want to do.

After all this unpleasantness Mori passed me a bunch of

cards and letters passed by censorship, all well-wishes from the Australian community. Those kind and motivating words were a great boost to my strength and morale. He also had the news I was waiting for: I was to be released in two nights. It was only then that I truly relaxed and believed I was going home.

Just after dark, two soldiers entered my room carrying civilian clothing and told me to change. Then they shackled me and I was led out of the room after I had privately said goodbye to a place where I had spent so much of my life. I was escorted out through the main gate of the camp and into a waiting van. We drove for a while then performed a few tight manoeuvres, before we came to a stop. I was sitting in the back between two soldiers, a medic opposite, unable to see out of this sealed section to know where I was or what was happening. I then felt the van bob up and down and recognised the rhythm of an ocean swell, a feeling I had not experienced for years. We were on a barge, and I remembered Mori saying that to reach the airport you had to cross water. The next leg of the trip was short before the van came to a stop. This time the back doors were flung open and I was unexpectedly assaulted by the loud roar of plane engines.

I stepped out of the van and saw two lines of soldiers forming a passageway between the back of the van and the base of a flight of stairs about thirty metres away, which led up into a waiting plane. This human corridor was bathed in a strange purple glow, and beyond the light was an unnatural darkness. What I didn't know at the time was that these purple globes highlighted me to all observers, while preventing me from seeing beyond the first row of men. It was a strange and exciting feeling as I walked the gauntlet of soldiers, slowly approaching the transport that would take me home. When I came to the stairs, I was greeted by two South Australian correction officers from Adelaide's Yatala Prison.

They yelled over the top of the waiting plane's roar to a nearby marine to remove my shackles, and I had a moment of satisfaction to see the marine's concerned face; he asked if they were sure. *Real people from the real world*, I thought, as the marine removed the three-piece suit with an expression that said, *Don't blame me if you get hurt*. Mori, who had requested to accompany me back on the plane, appeared out of the darkness and said disappointedly that his request had been denied. He apologised and we shook hands, knowing we would see each other again. Accompanying me on the plane besides the two correctional officers would be my Australian lawyer, David McLeod, someone from the Australian Federal Police and a few others. Mori stepped back into the darkness and then, feeling that this was a great moment in my life that I would never forget, I slowly climbed the stairs, step by step. When I reached the top I made myself stop and turn around. I looked down at the crowd below and, without surprise, saw just how many soldiers the purple lighting had shielded from view – and all of them were staring up at me. I looked into the distance at the lights, buildings and dark expanses of night – parts of Guantanamo that had always been so close, yet I had never seen or even knew existed. I savoured the moment, determined to absorb it. I had fought for and dreamed of my exit for five and a half years; I did not wish to forget it. One of the Australian officers told me to move, snapping me out of the moment and back to the job at hand. I quickly absorbed the crowd below, shook my head at the sprawling throng, spied Mori and gave him a nod, then turned around and entered the plane. The doors were closed and Guantanamo was no more.

Thirty

'Freedom is what you do with what's been done to you.'
Jean-Paul Sartre

AFTER A BRIEF STOPOVER IN TAHITI TO REFUEL, where I was allowed to get off and stretch my legs, the plane landed mid-morning at RAAF Base Edinburgh in the northern suburbs of Adelaide. I was taken through arrivals and then placed in the back of a prisoner transport vehicle parked inside an enclosed building. I was pleasantly surprised to see windows in my back section of the van, which meant that I would be able to watch my progress through the streets of Adelaide on the way to Yatala Prison. It was going to be my first glimpse of my old home since 1999. After waiting alone for an hour, the driver and a few others climbed in the front and the roller door to the outside world was opened. The first thing I noticed were police motorbikes and a few cars. As we drove out into the open more cars fell in behind, and by the time we were on our way the convoy consisted of at least fifteen cars and six motorbikes. I was amused at the lengths to which the state government was going just to make a point – and how different this was from the cages of Guantanamo.

It was bewildering to watch the motorbikes speed ahead of the convoy and block approaching side streets, divert traffic and keep the way clear for us. I thought it was all too much when they actually got off their bikes inside the Gepps Cross intersection and stopped all traffic. I wondered what the public thought as they watched this oversized convoy cruise past with my bewildered face at one of the many windows.

I was surprised at first because I didn't expect such an over-reaction – I had come to expect such dramatisation from the US, but surely not Australian law enforcement. The longer I thought about it, it did make sense. They were just continuing the charade, keeping alive the illusion that all this security was necessary to contain the 190-centimetre, 140-kilo, professionally trained, foaming-at-the-mouth David Hicks. I would be told in the near future that the state police had been against such a lavish waste of resources and had wanted to transfer me quietly without the convoy and subsequent circus. Those in charge and those who needed to know, knew I was not a threat, unlike the hardened criminals they often dealt with. However, the South Australian Premier Mike Rann had apparently insisted that my arrival be dealt with in such a showy fashion, ignoring the cool-headed professional advice of the police. I was told he wanted to show the larger cities of the eastern seaboard that Adelaide could pull its weight when it came to international affairs. Maybe demonising me also scored him some political points.

On arrival at Yatala Prison, I had to be processed, and the manager made a comment that it wasn't every day you saw the federal Attorney-General's signature on an arrest warrant. There needed to be a warrant to create an illusion that I was being imprisoned legally, because without the warrant there wouldn't have been justification to incarcerate me. I was then taken to G Block, the high-security isolation wing, where I would await my release on 29 December, seven months away.

There were certainly some differences between Guantanamo and Yatala. In Yatala, I was not just able to have cigarettes and matches, but was able to smoke in my cell whenever I wanted, which was a huge freedom of choice, though perhaps not the healthiest one. There was a canteen from which I could order small amounts of food and drink, which I could also keep in my room and consume as I saw fit. I was able to order protein powder to try to regain the weight I had lost. I was able to change my clothes daily and have regular hot showers. I could send out and receive unlimited letters, all of them unredacted (but still photocopied). I was able to make two or three phone calls a week, though I was treated differently from the other prisoners and had some trouble in this area. I could actually enjoy weekend visits, a luxury for myself and all my family after the years of forced separation. Amazingly, I did not have to sell my soul for any of these privileges.

Then there were the more profound differences between Guantanamo and Yatala. If I was to come out of my cell in Yatala for any reason, it would only be between 8 am and 4 pm. After 4 pm, it was guaranteed that I would be left alone in my cell until the morning. There was no reason for me to be fearful or constantly on edge, expecting to be taken out of my cell any time of the day or night. As time passed, I lost the fear of being tortured; I no longer feared for my safety. There was no longer any temperature manipulation, disturbing noise or other bizarre and cruel programs. This new opportunity to relax, enjoy the stability of a routine and feel that I had some knowledge of what was happening around me and to me, was a luxury after the constant chaos of Guantanamo.

During the second half of my stay in Yatala, a few AFP officers came to see me. They asked if I would participate in an interview and I agreed. They started off by asking a few mundane questions and then produced a document that they asked me to sign. I read the document and was outraged that it was basically a mirror image of the plea agreement I had to sign to get out of Guantanamo. It was even worded as though I had written it myself. I refused to sign and the interview came to an end. These AFP officers came another three or four times while I was in Yatala and attempted to pressure me into signing the same document, claiming they just needed to wrap up my file. If I signed they would disappear and I would never hear from them again. They even resorted to indirect threats by reminding me of the Guantanamo plea agreement, where it states that I would cooperate with the police for the rest of my life – to break any part of that agreement risked having to return to Guantanamo to serve the suspended sentence. This is why I have not agreed to an interview again, because they have always tried to get me to sign papers.

After seven long and short months, the day of my release arrived. I may have been back in Australia for some time but my ordeal had not ended, and it would not until I was free. On a psychological level nothing had changed. I had still not had a chance to seek help and begin rehabilitation to recover from the long years in Guantanamo.[163] Everything was still fresh. I was still living one long, continuous experience. While I had remained a prisoner in any capacity, I would not have been able to put it all behind me and move forward. To finally see this nightmare end, to begin the healing, was the greatest anticipation of all.

I was surprised with myself the night before I was to be released. I was expecting not to be able to sleep, yet I followed the same routine I had for the last seven months. I woke the same as I always did and cleaned the room spotless, as was the rule before 8 am cell inspection. I convinced myself, and I had become good at mental discipline, that I might not hear anything about my release until late in the day and that it might not even occur until the next day. I promised myself not to annoy the guards with questions, not to be anxious and make the day a long, stressful one.

Therefore, I became impatiently excited when guards let me out of the cell – even before the 8 am inspection – told me to have a shower and change into clothes supplied by my family instead of the usual prison garb. I had only been back in my cell for a few minutes, trying hard to be casual, when I was asked to come out again. Then, before I even had time to absorb what was happening, I was being released. It was all very low key. I was expecting paperwork, procedures and to have to be moved to another area. Instead, I was given my property and told to follow one of the guards outside.

He led me to a building next door where Dad and Bronwyn were waiting. It was all very surreal and overwhelming, and I had to fight back the tears. The strangest part was probably standing among normal people as a normal person, after six years of isolation. For the first time in years, I was not wearing chains or being told where or how to stand. I then stepped out into the sun a free man and into a waiting car.

We drove at walking speed along the Yatala driveway and passed a large group of media. Most of their faces were hidden behind cameras and flashes of light, except for the odd one who burst forward from the pack wearing an expression of desperation, screaming unintelligible sounds. After them, on the corner of the main road, I was greeted by a group of people wishing me well for the future. Compared to the media they looked relaxed, happy and non-threatening. I would like to thank those people for coming out and supporting me, for sharing such a memorable moment. Then for the next hour or so I witnessed firsthand the impressive plan my family and friends had strategised.

Once we were out on the road, we had a police car in front and one behind – and a dozen or more cars driven by journalists further behind again. Even though they reported I was traumatised and needed some quiet time with family to recuperate, they were determined to harass me anyway. We were also being followed by five helicopters – all media. We drove through a neighbouring suburb where the streets were narrow with a long line of intrusive cars. As we negotiated a roundabout the police car behind stopped and blocked the road, preventing the media from following.

We then turned a corner and sped off – and we were free. I was passed some clothes and a cap and told to change quickly. With the helicopters still above, we drove into an underground shopping centre car park. Following orders, I left the car wearing new clothes and, while still under cover, entered the shopping centre. I walked straight through and exited the other side. A stranger approached and passed me a leather jacket, a helmet and told me to get on the back of his motorbike, and three bikes took off through the traffic, undetected by the helicopters. We eventually arrived at another underground car park where I jumped off the bike and into a car, and into another set of clothes. I was now with Stephanie and free of the media, completely anonymous on a fine Saturday summer morning.

We drove directly to a beach somewhere around Henley and Grange. I stepped out of the car spellbound; it was a moment I could never recreate. After years of having a wall always a few feet in front of my face, I was now staring at an expansive, placid blue ocean and its infinite horizon. My sister had even thought to bring shorts, and I ran down the beach, sand between my toes, and dived into the clear salt water. I swam and splashed about, and even had a quick chat with a fellow bather who had no idea who I was or what I had been through, no idea that an hour before I had been in isolation in a high-security part of a prison. It felt so good to talk to someone, one fellow human being to another.

We then drove to Stephanie's house, where I enjoyed a beer in the company of my brother-in-law, Graham, and basked in the freedom. We received reports that the media was camped out the front of other family members' homes, but the only place they had not thought to look was Stephanie and Graham's.

Upon release I was subjected to a control order requested by Ramzi Jabbour, the AFP's former counter-terrorism chief who has since been criticised for his lack of objectivity and unprofessional handling of the Dr Haneef case,[164] the Indian physician wrongly accused of aiding terrorists. Control orders are a newly created, very intrusive and unnecessary invention of the AFP and Howard under the draconian anti-terror laws created after September 11.[165] The control order placed a range of restrictions on me for twelve months.[166] I am only the second person in Australia to have been subjected to one.

I did not contest the control order or defend myself in the proceedings for a number of reasons. First, I had just undergone six years of torture and solitary confinement; I was mentally and psychologically unprepared to face the world for the first time in a public courtroom. My reintroduction back into the real world needed to be done quietly, in privacy with my loved ones. The first hearing for the control order was due while I was still in Yatala. I wanted some time to recover as a free man before I faced such a circus. Second, I was advised that I should not make waves and just let the government get away with this one – if they applied again, then we would fight it. And finally, I was just tired. I had had enough of rigged court proceedings, of having ridiculous allegations levelled at me publicly. I just wanted to get on with my life.

Among the provisions of my control order was that I had to report to a local police station three times a week, and then later, after a court amendment, twice a week. The biweekly check-ins made life very difficult. Normally, when someone has to report in to a police station, they are on parole for a crime. Because I had not been charged with any crime in Australia, and had never been in the past, there was no charge number. This meant that I had to sign a piece of paper to prove that I had reported in because I wasn't on the computer system. The local police thought the whole thing was ridiculous. They were always pleasant to me and my family.

The judge ordered the check-ins for a Wednesday and a Saturday. This meant that I could not go away for the weekend or go on a holiday because I had to check in to the nominated police station. I did plan to spend the first few days after my release in a quiet country location. There was a daily curfew between midnight and 6 am, later changed to between 1 am and 5 am. This meant that I had to be within a specified and approved premises between those hours. This may not sound so bad on the surface, but it made it very difficult to reintegrate back into society and caused much inconvenience to me and my family. If I wanted to stay at Dad's house, or anywhere for that matter, as all the family wanted to spend time with me, I would have to put an application in to the AFP, in writing, a month or so before I actually wanted to go somewhere. It took a long time for approvals to come through. It was stressful trying to arrange my life and I had to second-guess my future; sometimes I did not receive approval until the night before a planned trip.

During the control order period, I was even too afraid to go to the late movies for fear that it would run over and I would not arrive home in time for the curfew. Whether I was going out for dinner or to a mate's house for a barbecue, I had to always keep my mind on the time; I found it hard to enjoy the moment. It also interfered with other simple things, like fishing. I could not go fishing overnight or travel to reach a spot for sunrise, the best times for serious fishermen.

There was flexibility, but arranging changes to my control order was impractical and made my life very difficult.

Another infringement was that I could only use one mobile phone and one landline; both were monitored and had to be previously approved by the AFP. The penalty for me using a non-approved phone, or a breach of any part of the control order, was five years' imprisonment. I was also only allowed to use one approved computer, but the AFP weren't able to sort out a system, so for twelve months I was unable to use the internet or read emails.

Overall, the control order had a significantly negative impact on my mental health. I was still effectively in custody; it was an extension of my trauma and interfered with my psychological rehabilitation. It was often a case of one step forward and two steps back along my road to recovery. Only when the AFP decided not to renew the control order, which expired on 21 December 2008, was I able to begin proper counselling with positive results. The control order was a complete waste of valuable resources and manpower, and totally unnecessary.

There was no media outside the house during the first day of my release, but because it was a Saturday the control order required me to report in. The media obviously knew that out of the limited police stations within Adelaide, it was Port

Adelaide where I was required to report. The media was positioned in large numbers in front of the station, complete with satellite dishes, making normal entry impossible. With the help of the police, I was able to enter the station from the back and get away again without being detected.

Sunday passed peacefully and when Monday came I had to report in once again. On the way to the police station, Graham and I were tailed by a car and, suspecting it to be a journalist's, we turned around and returned to Stephanie's. Dad called soon after to inform me that a journalist had called and said, 'I know where your son is,' and informed him that they were the ones who had just followed me. The journalist claimed that she wanted the best for me and was willing to do a deal. If Dad and I allowed her and a photographer to take a picture of us together so they could claim the scoop, they agreed not to ask any questions. Not that I would have consented to an interview because I had no interest in talking to the media. Besides, a gag order (separate to the control order) and the threat of five years' imprisonment prevented me from speaking to them anyway. In return they promised to stop staking out the house and following me around; they also would not inform other members of the media where I was staying. Because I was confident that they were the only ones who had found me and knew where I was staying, I grudgingly agreed, or rather Dad did on my behalf. When the negotiations were complete, I watched the journalists leave from behind the curtains of a front window, and only then did I emerge for the second time that day to attempt to report in.

Within a few hours the photo was finished and I was back at the house. It seemed the journalists were good to their word because I was able to enjoy New Year's Eve without being harassed. There were fireworks at midnight down the road at the beach, but because of the control order I had to watch them from the front garden. The curfew was still midnight at that stage.

By lunchtime the next day, however, the media was swarming out the front, parking illegally, harassing the neighbours and causing a general disturbance. They were even offering cash to the neighbours who lived in two-storey properties if they could set up their cameras in the rooms that offered views into Stephanie's backyard. No neighbours cooperated and some even rang the police, who came out more than once to issue fines for illegal parking and warnings for trespassing. I was lucky because the neighbours and those in the surrounding community are lovely people. I had no need to leave the house that day and watched all of this mayhem from behind the curtains. I wondered how they had all found me, and the obvious answer was that I had been double-crossed. I could not see the journalist among the loitering horde, but I'm sure I spotted the photographer looking sheepish, and I wondered how much he had been paid for disclosing my whereabouts.

The following day was a forty-degree Wednesday, a check-in day, leaving me no choice but to give my location away to the masses who were holding a twenty-four-hour vigil out the front. They had locked themselves inside their air-conditioned cars or were lazing around and sweating beneath the summer sun on the footpaths and neighbours' lawns, looking bored. That soon changed when, without warning, I took a deep breath and walked out the front door. The unruly mob leapt to their feet and chased after me, casting aside all decent behaviour. I made it to the car by looking straight ahead and blocking out everything happening around me. Safely buckled up inside, we left for the police station, dragging journalists and photographers along behind.

Their unprofessional behaviour continued as I entered and exited the police station, and as we returned home some of them raced ahead at a dangerous speed, determined to catch me before I disappeared inside, placing pedestrians in danger before screeching to a stop. The game was up and I expected them to remain camped outside for days to come, but by that night the street was empty and it was safe for the local children to come out and play once more.

While I had been in Yatala my children had come to visit on a few occasions. Once the hide-and-seek game with the media was over, I went to see them for the first time in years as a free man, and we began to re-establish our relationship. When we all got together for that first time, their mother told them in front of me the truth surrounding the circumstances of our break-up. I was thankful for her honesty. After I saw my children, I then caught up with other members of my family, including those I had not seen for years, and then came my friends. In so many areas of my life, I had to start over from scratch. I had no clothes, so I went shopping for a new wardrobe. When the AFP raided the homes of my family members years before, they took everything, including all identification, and what identification I had at the time of being rendered the Americans kept for themselves. This left me with no way to prove who I was, so I then had to apply for a hundred points worth of identification.

I then arranged to tackle a long list of physical health issues. First came the comprehensive blood test. Because of how puffy and sick-looking I was, and my concerns about forced medication in Guantanamo, my family had requested that I have an independent full medical exam in Yatala Prison when I first arrived back in Australia. This request was always denied, and only eight months after leaving Guantanamo was I able to have my first tests. I was told prior to the tests that too much time had passed for any past nasty substances to register, and the results were negative for anything insidious.

X-rays exposed a fracture in my right hand from when it had been kicked and crushed by military-issue boots. Scans of my lower back revealed three herniated discs and six facet joints suffering active arthropathy. My teeth were yellow, rotting and in desperate need of cleaning and maintenance. Recently, one tooth that had to have a root canal in Guantanamo has had to be completely removed due to dodgy dental work. There seem to be others that are fractured, but that is still ongoing. The dentist says the fractures may be due to grinding my teeth during sleep, especially while experiencing nightmares. An osteopath diagnosed that hard blows to the right side of my face, combined with continued stress that tightens the muscles around my skull, resulted in an aching jaw that cracks very loudly numerous times a day.[167] Even my kidneys have been left riddled with stones, one of them reaching 1.3 centimetres in size. The doctors I saw in Australia also thought the stones might be from trauma, such as receiving hard blows to that part of my body, or even possibly the large amounts of unknown medication I was forced to take. I eventually had my stones blasted, and once I had passed them they were analysed. The results suggested that long-term dehydration had created them.

Regarding my psychological health, I began counselling upon release and will probably continue to receive help long into the future. I have improved in some areas. In the early days, there were occasions when I had to get up and practically run out of restaurants while attempting to have dinner with family and friends. On one occasion, I was even unable to *enter* a restaurant. The crowds and noise were too much, and I suffered anxiety attacks. I have come a long way in that regard, but I can still have bad reactions; even simple socialising can be quite a challenge.

An interesting and common effect of isolation is losing the ability to talk and explain oneself sufficiently. Even the few guys I had spoken to in Yatala who had spent a year or more in isolation noticed this effect. It is most notable when you attempt to engage someone in conversation, such as during visits. It is not unusual to forget words and have a complete mental blank, no matter how hard you try to remember. Everything becomes a big, confusing muddle. The word you're searching for is often right on the tip of your tongue, but nothing comes out, and it only gets worse as time passes.

I had forgotten social etiquette, what is polite conversation or not. I am told I can sometimes come across as quite gruff and rude. I have a problem with screwing up my face and looking angry or sad when I'm actually happy. At times I cannot help but become defensive and argumentative, always ready for another hostile interrogation session. My beautiful wife is in the process of teaching me how to smile again, especially in photos, and with her love and that of my family and friends I am learning how to function again.

Worst of all are the nightmares that still haunt me. They usually involve having to relive past experiences, like seeing myself kidnapped and detained again, and are accompanied by overwhelming feelings of hopelessness and vulnerability, knowing no-one can help me. The worst dreams are those involving medical experimentation and torture too horrible to describe, a long-term consequence of the chemically induced questioning I was subjected to, as well as other enforced medications. Unfortunately, I have not been able to tackle all of the ongoing physical problems due to finances. Other foreign governments have set up services for their returned detainees, but the Australian government has not. Some of the medical costs are prohibitively expensive, yet there are not many services available to assist me. It is only thanks to the kindness of a few people who have sacrificed their own time and money that I have been able to attend to some of these problems.

As the weeks passed I saw new electronic gadgets for the first time. Mobile phones that took photos, even moving video, and were small in size. DVD players, Xboxes, MP3 players, flat-screen televisions, iPods, BlackBerries, Facebook and other such new modern marvels.

Within two months of being released from Yatala I began part-time work, taking my counsellor's advice that I should limit my hours and not 'jump in the deep end'. At first, this work involved the propagation of seeds and cuttings of local native plants in Adelaide. Later, when I moved to Sydney, I continued general wholesale nursery work part time for nearly two years, before advancing to a full-time managerial position in early 2010. Until now, Guantanamo has left me with a host of loose ends that represent a full-time job in itself, as my poor wife knows very well, being run off her feet all day dealing with the baggage I've been left with. My family and I are looking forward to the day I can leave most of this behind and commence as relaxed and normal a life as possible. The long period of working part time also allowed me to write the first draft of this book and complete a few self-edits, a mammoth task that has taken an average of forty hours per week for two years, including sitting up until 3 am on some occasions. I'll be lucky to have any hair left by publication.

This book has been important on two fronts. Covering the past has been cathartic for me, even though some of it has been very emotional and upsetting to relive. Telling my story will assist in my ambition to move forward, putting the past behind. Also, I think it was important for me to tell my own story in my own words – fully, truthfully, openly and in detail. So many others have attempted to tell my story for a host of reasons, I believe mainly for financial and career gain, when they have never *known* my story, never met or spoken with me.

Since my return to Australia, the situation surrounding Guantanamo, and the so-called War on Terror in general, is constantly evolving. The political bedrock has shifted: the Howard government was replaced by the Labor government, and Bush's Republican regime has been replaced by Obama's Democrat administration. Guantanamo has been publicly recognised by the US government as a facility that must be shut down due to the lack of international support and credibility, and steps are under way to ensure that eventually happens.[168] Further evidence has emerged that the majority of us detained were innocent. Former Chief of Staff to Colin Powell, Colonel Lawrence B. Wilkerson, gave testimony that former President Bush, Dick Cheney and Donald Rumsfeld all knew that the majority of us in Guantanamo were innocent. He stated that the Bush administration thought it was 'politically impossible' to release us. He went on further to say that the Bush administration didn't care that there were innocent people locked up – that the end justified the means. In other words, they were concerned that it would be one big embarrassing exercise to admit the truth. He admirably concluded his testimony by saying, 'I served in an administration that tortured and abused those it detained at the facilities at Guantanamo Bay and elsewhere, and indefinitely detained the innocent for political reasons.'[169]

In an important admission, the Obama administration (including the Justice Department) has publicly acknowledged that the military commissions under the 2006 Act, the system I was forced to plead guilty under, was fundamentally unfair and unfit to provide just trials.[170] To remedy this, the

2006 Commissions Act has been replaced with the *2009 Commissions Act*,[171] rendering my conviction and subsequent plea deal, in the view of my US attorneys, null and void. The manufactured offence I was convicted of that was created by the Bush administration, Material Support for Terrorism, has also been recognised as not being a legitimate war crime. Before the *2009 Commissions Act* was passed, the Senate Armed Services Committee heard testimony from US Assistant Attorney-General David Kris and Defense Department General Counsel, Jeh Johnson, acknowledging that the offence should not be included in the *2009 Commissions Act* because it is 'not a traditional law of war offence'.[172]

To further the embarrassment for the US administration, seven prosecutors have resigned or been reassigned due to ethical concerns of participating in the flawed military commissions system.[173]

More evidence has come to light about the treatment and policies impacting detainees in Guantanamo. No-one can now claim that we were not tortured. Susan Crawford, who was the convening authority, admitted that they tortured Mohammed al-Qahtani.[174] It has also been revealed that detainee statements the interrogators knew to be false were used for CSRT hearings, reinforcing the fact that torture was used to extract false confessions.[175] There has been the release of some more 'Torture Memos' in 2009: a leaked ICRC report into the torture of '14 high-value detainees', as well as a CIA Inspector General's report that revealed a number of horrific abuses, including interrogation with weapons, such as I was subjected to.[176] In response to the CIA Inspector General's report, US Attorney-General Eric Holder has appointed a special prosecutor, John Durham, to hold a preliminary investigation into a small number of abuse claims and the CIA's destruction of video evidence.[177] At the time of writing, documents released under FOI reveal Jose Rodriguez, then head of CIA clandestine services, saying 'The heat from destroying is nothing compared to what it would be if the tapes ever got into the public domain . . . They would make us look terrible; it would be devastating to us.'[178] Unfortunately, the bulk of us have been forgotten.[179]

Thankfully, Spain has begun criminal prosecutions against Bush officials, namely the men who attempted to legally sanction torture.[180] The Spanish investigation has found evidence of waterboarding, detention underground in total darkness for three weeks, deprivation of sleep and food, blows to the testicles, detainees being 'inoculated . . . through injection with a disease for dog cysts' and the smearing of faeces on prisoners.[181] Italy has convicted twenty-three CIA employees *in absentia* for their involvement in the rendition program and the kidnapping and torture of an Italian citizen from the streets of Italy.[182] A host of reports have been released pointing to the systematic nature of the abuses at Guantanamo and the fact that they were devised and sanctioned at the highest levels of the Bush administration, not just perpetrated by a 'few bad apples'.[183] More and more guards and ex-Bush administration officials and agents are coming forward, condemning the use of torture because it just didn't work: it only created more hatred.[184] I believe more evidence will come to light regarding the illegal conduct during those years, and I hope that high-ranking civilian and military officials will be held accountable. More recently, the UK has said it will conduct an investigation into its own officials who played a role in the torture and illegal treatment of its citizens detained abroad during the War on Terror.[185]

As far as due process goes, for the 176 men still remaining in Guantanamo at the time of writing, the illegality of the system was once again exposed in 2008 when the *Boumediene v. Bush* decision was handed down.[186] Importantly for detainees, the decision meant that Congress could no longer suspend *habeas corpus*; the government was shamed into allowing detainees to challenge their unlawful detention. As of now, thirty-one out of forty-one detainees have been cleared for release, providing further embarrassment for the US, especially since they claimed all of the people in Guantanamo were dangerous killers. The Pentagon has announced that around thirty-five detainees will be charged (not many out of the 800 'worst of the worst') and that 'roughly' fifty will be held indefinitely without charge or trial.[187] It is time Guantanamo was closed down, along with the rendition program, indefinite detention, and the current methods of interrogation.

On a personal level, I still currently have the illegal conviction, suspended sentence and plea agreement hanging over my head; however, I believe this also will be eventually addressed.

I don't judge those people who hold a negative attitude towards me, considering the rubbish that has been heaped on me in the media and by the former government. However, despite those negative opinions, there are some facts my detractors must swallow. During my time overseas, and at any and all times during my life, I did not engage in acts of terrorism, support acts of terrorism or make plans for a terrorist act. The groups I trained with were not al-Qaeda or any other terrorist group – I had not heard of al-Qaeda until Guantanamo. While overseas, I was not aware of any group or any person who committed acts of terrorism or was aware of someone planning acts of terror, personally or in general. This includes the fact that I did not engage in training for acts of terrorism, whether hijacking, bomb-making, targeting civilians, etc. I did not confess to supporting terrorism.

I have never killed anyone or attempted to. I have never hurt or injured anyone during my travels, nor did I try to. I did not threaten anyone or cause someone to be afraid or concerned for their wellbeing. At no time did I steal, destroy or damage someone else's property, nor did I attempt or plan to. At no time during my overseas sojourn did I commit a crime against someone, create a victim or even inconvenience someone. I did not betray Australia by fighting against any Australian or American troops at any time. There were no US or Australian troops on the ground in Afghanistan while I was there. No-one dead or alive can make a claim against me, seek revenge or say that I wronged them in some way. No-one requires an apology from me. I have never broken any international, US or Australian law.

Any and all inconvenience, namely directed at my family, was brought about due to my incarceration and treatment, and that was at the hands of others. It was the US who broke international law by imprisoning and torturing me and disregarding established laws, including the sanctity of due process. If I was suspected of having been involved in criminal activity, I should have been arrested following legal protocols and dealt with in a timely manner by the law – everything that has passed since the end of 2001 need not have occurred. It was the Howard government who was responsible for knowingly leaving me in those cruel and inhumane conditions for so long, allowing the situation to get out of control and for making my ordeal a high-profile event for what they must have considered political advantage. Again, none of that needed to have occurred. If someone is to blame or bear the brunt of negative opinions, it should be the former government for deceiving and misleading, wasting manpower and resources, and playing on people's fears to strip us of our freedoms through legislation that is apparently in our interests and for our own safety.

The way in which I chose to help others may not have been the wisest. I wish I had done things differently, but my motivations were of a good nature. I could have joined a humanitarian mission or been a reporter, giving the people a voice – and I should have. All I ever wanted to do was to help others. I saw the people of Kosovo and Kashmir no differently from my family and friends. The way these people from faraway lands suffered during the invasions and occupations of their homes affected me the same as if my own family and friends had been invaded, occupied and oppressed. To have seen fellow human beings suffer at the hands of professionally trained soldiers infuriated me and was the motivating factor to bear arms and risk my life to help them.

The situation in Kashmir is still continuing and has escalated since I was there. At the time of writing, September 2010, thousands of Kashmiris have taken to the streets, protesting Indian rule and the heavy hand of the security forces. Up to seventy people have been killed recently by Indian government security forces, and this number is expected to rise. This conflict over independence has been ongoing for many years, and I hope a speedy resolution bringing peace will come about soon.[188]

I have strongly rejected, and always will, any claims that I was a terrorist or supporter of terrorism. My personal definition of a terrorist is a coward and a murderer. A terrorist is someone who disguises himself as an innocent civilian and targets innocent, unsuspecting civilians in civilian areas.

A few months after my release, I moved to Sydney to receive some medical treatment. The kindness and support of Sydneysiders has been overwhelming. It is an amazingly beautiful city. I enjoy my work and I have met some great people and made some new friends. Everywhere I have been the public has been wonderful, wishing me well in passing on the street during the time following my release, especially when out with

Dad at his local shopping centre. It was not unusual to share tears and hugs with strangers overjoyed to see me home and reunited with my father.

Despite the ups and downs since beginning and adjusting to this new life, there have been many enjoyable times, and the most wonderful of those moments was marrying my beautiful and intelligent wife, Aloysia. She is studying for a doctorate and works for an international human rights organisation and is tireless in her life-long efforts to help others. She is a lover of animals (well, maybe not cockroaches and mosquitoes) and is a vegetarian. Aloysia has a heart of gold and has been a pillar of strength and very patient during my more difficult moments adjusting to my new life after Guantanamo. Aloysia was involved in the campaign to have me released and, in the process, became a friend of my dad. Dad played a large part in our evolving romance at the time. There is a very strong bond between us, and I love her dearly.

As time passes I am slowly able to put the negatives of the past behind and replace them with the positives of the present and hopes for the future. I am often asked why I haven't begun an action to sue the government.[189] It is because I have faith that the present and future governments will do the right thing by me, that truth will win out in the end. The Labor government knew that I was treated unfairly, and they continually condemned the Howard government for subjecting me to ill treatment and an unfair system. Former Prime Minister Rudd said in 2006, 'Hicks should be released . . . He will not be given recourse to a fair trial under the US military commission, however it is constituted. There will be no presumption of innocence. The evidentiary tests are poor. And therefore this is a question of basic civil rights and civil liberties for all of us.'[190]

And our Attorney-General, Robert McClelland, commented in 2003 that, 'The Howard government is devaluing our citizenship with its support for the trial of David Hicks by a US military commission at Guantanamo Bay because its practices are alien to Australians' expectations of a fair trial . . .'[191] He even called for an investigation into the allegations of torture I was subjected to and said I should be left alone to get on with my life.[192] However, there was also concern from within the Liberal Party about what was happening to me, namely how long the process was taking.

There are many reasons to be happy. It is wonderful to be married and to share my life with such an amazing person. I am looking forward to building a stronger relationship with my children. There is nothing better than spending time with my family, enjoying a meal together in private or just talking. I am lucky to experience and enjoy the little things that are easily overlooked – warm sunny weather, the happy songs of birds, little lizards running through the undergrowth – these all provide moments of tranquillity. I appreciate visiting the ocean or a slow-flowing stream surrounded by lush vegetation. I am also lucky to have a roof over my head, food in my stomach and great people around me: family, friends, associates, kind people offering assistance and well-wishers from the public. We all have a lot to be thankful for, and I hope I never forget the little, simple things in life that really matter.

Though the aftermath continues – the politics, media scrutiny, the divided opinions of a nation, the passions, the big players who became personally involved – the long, drawn-out saga is over. I was an uneducated northern suburbs Adelaidean, a nobody, who unknowingly stepped into a script that was coming to a climax, a story that would begin an impassioned chain of events in this country, and the world over. I could never have known the circumstances I would return home under as I left for Pakistan all those years ago, or what would become of my very first trip abroad to Japan, or for that matter a job advertisement in a newspaper which triggered all the events in the years that followed.

I do not know a word to describe how I feel when I go back over my story, revisiting the many crossroads of my life and how the situations around me played out. I got caught up in something huge, events now engraved in our history books. At times it is vividly real to me, at other times I can barely recall the memories.

I sit here on my own and in silence and look at photos of average men and women who rallied to my defence, dressed in orange T-shirts in solidarity, performing amazing deeds; the passion of the time is captured on their faces. I see a photo of my father dressed in orange in a cage on a main street in New York. In both of these examples I am reminded of what my predicament had become in Australia. Those events took place in a world I was isolated from. I still have trouble comprehending what that world must have been like. The protesters in those photos humble me and fill me with emotion, and I get a glimpse at how those times must have been, and it confirms the reality of what I lived through. It was not a dream, not a dream at all.

'True peace is not merely the absence of tension: it is the presence of justice.'

Martin Luther King Jr.

Recommended Reading

Amnesty International, 'Human Dignity Denied: Torture and Accountability in the "War on Terror"', 27 October 2004.

Begg, Moazzan. *Enemy Combatant: My Imprisonment at Guantanamo, Bagram and Kandahar*, Simon & Schuster: New York, 2006.

Burke, Jason. *Al-Qaeda: The True Story of Radical Islam*, 3rd edition, Penguin Group: London, 2007.

Centre for Constitutional Rights (CCR), '*Current Conditions of Confinement at Guantanamo: Still in Violation of the Law*', 23 February 2009. Report available at: http://ccrjustice.org/files/CCR_Report_Conditions_At_Guantanamo.pdf

Coll, Steve. *Ghost Wars: The Secret History of the CIA, Afghanistan and Bin Laden, From the Soviet Invasion to September 10, 2001*, Penguin Press: New York, 2004.

Danner, Mark. *Stripping Bare the Body: Politics, Violence, War*, Black Ink: Victoria, 2009.

Greenberg, Karen J. & Dratel, Joshua L. (eds) *The Torture Papers: The Road to Abu Ghraib*, Cambridge University Press: New York, 2005.

Griffiths, John C. *Afghanistan: A History of Conflict*, 2nd edition, Timol Publishing: London, 2000.

Margulies, Joseph. *Guantanamo and the Abuse of Presidential Power*, Simon & Schuster: New York, 2006.

Mayer, Jane. *The Dark Side*, Scribe Publications: Victoria, 2008.

Physicians for Human Rights, *'Broken Laws, Broken Lives: Medical Evidence of Torture by U.S. Personnel and Its Impact'*, available at, http://brokenlives.info/?page_id=69

Rejali, Darius. *Torture and Democracy*, Princeton University Press: New Jersey, 2007.

Reyes, Hernán. 'The Worst Scars Are in the Mind: Psychological Torture', *International Review of the Red Cross*, 89 (867), September 2007.

Rose, David. *Guantanamo: America's War on Human Rights*, Faber & Faber Ltd: London, 2004.

Sands, Philippe. *Torture Team*, Penguin Books: London, 2008.

Williams, Kristian. *American Methods: Torture and the Logic of Domination*, South End Press: Massachusetts, 2006.

Endnotes

Part One

1. It is estimated that around 100,000 Albanians were killed and 1.5 million people – the entire Albanian population – were displaced before NATO began its bombing campaign. For more information see, The Independent International Commission on Kosovo, *The Kosovo Report: Conflict, International Response, Lessons Learned*, Oxford University Press: Oxford, 2000; and Steiner and Alston, *International Human Rights in Context: Law, Politics, Morals* (2nd edn), Oxford University Press: Oxford, 2000, pp. 653–654.

2. Between 1999 and 2000, every conflict investigated by Amnesty International found that the torture of women, most often through rape, was used as a weapon of war. Rape is employed systematically to intimidate, humiliate, terrorise, extract information and contribute to 'ethnic cleansing'.

3. On 9 June 1999, the conflict between the KLA and FRY officially ended. Appallingly, between March and June of 1999, it is estimated that 863,000 civilians sought refuge outside Kosovo, and 590,000 became internally displaced. Evidence of widespread torture, rape, pillaging and looting was common. See, The Independent International Commission on Kosovo,

The Kosovo Report: Conflict, International Response, Lessons Learned, Oxford University Press: Oxford, 2000.

4.   Article 47 under Protocol 1 of the Geneva Conventions provides that a mercenary is any person who (a) is specifically recruited locally or abroad in order to fight in an armed conflict; (b) does, in fact, take a direct part in the hostilities; (c) *is motivated to take part in the hostilities essentially by the desire for private gain and, in fact, is promised, on behalf of a party to the conflict, material compensation substantially in excess of that promised or paid to combatants of similar ranks and functions in the armed forces of the party*; (d) is neither a national of the party to the conflict nor a resident of territory controlled by a party to the conflict; and (f) has not been sent by a State which is not a party to the conflict on official duty as a member of its armed forces (emphasis added).

5.   Article 47 of Protocol 1 of the Geneva Conventions provides that 'a mercenary shall not have the right to be a combatant or a prisoner of war', so, therefore, they are not lawful combatants. There are international protocols and UN resolutions that prohibit and condemn the use or training of mercenaries. However, these are not legally binding. Even the statute of the International Criminal Court adopted in 1998 establishes being a mercenary as a crime, but the state must be a signatory. See Leslie Green, *The Contemporary Law of Armed Conflict* (2nd edn), Manchester University Press: Manchester, 2000, p. 114.

6.   General Assembly Resolution 44/34, 4 December 1989. Currently, there are only thirty-two state parties and ten state signatories. Australia has followed the US and is *not* a state party. See, International Committee of the Red Cross (ICRC), www.icrc.org/IHL.nsf/INTRO/530?OpenDocument.

7.   Mercenaries are covered by the Fourth Geneva Convention, which protects civilians during times of armed conflict. However, if a country is a party to the 1989 *Mercenary Convention*, they must amend their national criminal law to treat mercenaries as criminals and therefore liable to extradition and trial. See Leslie Green, *The Contemporary Law of Armed Conflict* (2nd edn), Manchester University Press: Manchester, 2000, p. 117.

8.   For more information about the allegations and substantiated cases of Blackwater's involvement in murder, CIA torture and illegal trading and shipping of weapons, see Jeremy Scahill,

Blackwater: The Rise of the World's Most Powerful Mercenary Army, Nation Books: New York, 2007.

9. US contractors were given immunity under Iraq's domestic laws under the Coalition Provisional Authority Order 17. At the time of writing, the case involving five Blackwater guards who admitted to killing seventeen Iraqi civilians in 2007 was dismissed. Judge Urbina stated that the guards only gave the statements on the proviso that they would receive immunity, and under the threat of job loss. Now, the Iraqi Prime Minister has confirmed that he will attempt to prosecute them in Iraq despite the Coalition Provisional Authority Order 17. In another incident in January 2010, two Blackwater guards, Justin Cannon and Christopher Drotleff, each faced thirteen counts under the *Military Extraterritorial Jurisdiction Act,* including two counts of second-degree murder, one count of attempted murder and discharging a firearm during a violent crime. See, www.jurist. law.pitt.edu/currentawareness/contractors.php.

10. See, *Crimes (Foreign Incursions and Recruitment) Act 1978.* The legislation was amended in 2005 as a result of Australia's 'anti-terror' legislation.

11. It is important to acknowledge here the fact that history is often told with bias, and that my experience does not encompass the atrocities perpetrated by some members of the KLA against the Serbs. At no time did I ever hear of or witness any KLA soldiers committing war crimes, but I know now that some did. As with any violent conflict, there are victims on all sides, and it would be wrong of me to not mention them.

12. Kosovo unilaterally declared its independence in 2008. On 22 July 2010, the International Court of Justice (ICJ) upheld Kosovo's declaration of independence.

13. Many innocent civilians were massacred by the Indonesian troops when they invaded and occupied East Timor on 7 December 1975. It is estimated that around 200,000 people died during the occupation. Many in the Australian public and the international community were critical of the Australian government for its complicity in the years of violence and brutality inflicted on the East Timorese people, especially in light of the Timor Gap Oil Treaty, and its reluctance to hold the Indonesian government to account. East Timor finally gained independence from Indonesia on 30 August 1999.

14.   *The Howard Years* aired on ABC Television, 17 November 2008.
15.   Kashmir is a disputed region between Pakistan and India. After the partition of British India in 1947, the states of Jammu and Kashmir had the option of joining either Pakistan or India. The maharajah of Kashmir at the time rejected both nations and sought independence for Kashmir. The struggle for control has led to horrific human rights abuses and needless conflict. For more information see the International Crisis Group's website www.crisisgroup.org and Human Rights Watch, 'Everyone Lives in Fear: Patterns of Impunity in Jammu and Kashmir', September 2006, at www.hrw.org.
16.   LeT leader, Professor Hafiz Muhammad Saeed, interview with ABC America, reported in Amir Butler's 'Australia's Banning of LeT Raises More Questions', 17 November 2003, available at www.scoop.co.nz.
17.   LeT is reported to have grown into a terrorist organisation in the last few years. Before September 11, LeT was an arm of the Pakistani government. Since then, the Pakistani government has shut down and dissolved the group. It is reported that the name LeT was used by a new group of people. The US claims that this new group is linked to al-Qaeda, and the Indian government has blamed LeT for the Mumbai attacks. LeT's former leader repudiates any attacks against civilians. Providing 'material support' to the group became an offence under Australian law in March 2002; however, the Parliamentary Advisory Service notes that the government has never articulated the threat posed by LeT to Australia. Amir Butler from the Australian Muslim Public Affairs Committee stated that, 'It is difficult to see the threat that that Kashmiri independence group poses to Australian security.'

     For a profile of LeT, see, Jayshree Bajoria's article, 'Profile: Lashkar-e-Taiba (Army of the Pure)', 2 December 2008 at the Council on Foreign Relations website, www.cfr.org.
18.   It is reported that the CIA paid $200,000 a month and gave weapons to Massoud. For more information see, Steve Coll, *Ghost Wars: The Secret History of the CIA, Afghanistan and Bin Laden, from the Soviet Invasion to September 10, 2001*, Penguin Press: New York, 2004.
19.   Former US President Reagan made a commitment to support the anti-communist 'freedom fighters' in 1985. See, Thomas G.

Paterson, J. Garry Clifford, Shane J. Maddock, Deborah Kisatsky and Kenneth J. Hogan, *American Foreign Relations: A History, Since 1895, vol. 2*, 6th edn, Houghton Mifflin Company: Boston, 2005, p. 433.

20. See Nafeez Mosaddeq Ahmed, *The War on Truth: 9/11, Disinformation and the Anatomy of Terrorism*, Olive Branch Press, 2005, pp. 207–208.

21. John C. Griffiths, *Afghanistan: A History of Conflict*, 2nd edn, André Deutsch: London, 2001, p. 232.

22. Steve Coll, *Ghost Wars: The Secret History of the CIA, Afghanistan and Bin Laden, from the Soviet Invasion to September 10, 2001*, Penguin Press: New York, 2004.

23. John C. Griffiths, *Afghanistan: A History of Conflict*, 2nd edn, André Deutsch: London, 2001, p. 236.

24. *ibid.*, p. 184. Also, Thomas G. Paterson, J. Garry Clifford, Shane J. Maddock, Deborah Kisatsky and Kenneth J. Hogan, *American Foreign Relations: A History, Since 1895, vol. 2*, 6th edn, Houghton Mifflin Company: Boston, 2005, p. 499.

25. See, Hillary Clinton testimony to a subcommittee of the House Appropriations Committee, reported by Anwar Iqbal, Dawn.com, Saturday, 25 April 2009. Available at www.dawn.com. YouTube version also available at www.youtube.com/watch?v=X2CE0fyz4ys.

26. Steve Coll, *Ghost Wars: The Secret History of the CIA, Afghanistan and Bin Laden, from the Soviet Invasion to September 10, 2001*, Penguin Press: New York, 2004.

27. Robin Raphael in John C. Griffiths, *Afghanistan: A History of Conflict*, 2nd edn, André Deutsch: London, 2001, p. 236.

28. John J. Maresca, Capitol Hill testimony, Federal Document Clearing House, 12 February 1998.

29. The initial plans were drawn up by Enron before it collapsed due to corruption in 2002.

30. Michel Chossudovsky, 'Al-Qaeda and the "War on Terrorism"', Global Policy Forum, 20 January 2008.

31. Human Rights Watch describes Afghan women among the worst off in the world – violence against women is 'endemic' and the government fails to protect them from crimes such as rape and murder.

32. Jason Burke's excellent book *Al Qaeda* is the most knowledgeable, realistic look at what was happening on the ground in

Afghanistan and Pakistan, and in the world of militant Islam in general.

33. See BBC documentary by Adam Curtis, 'The Power of Nightmares: The Rise of the Politics of Fear', screened 3 November 2004. Transcript is available at www.daanspeak.com.

34. LeT leader, Professor Hafiz Muhammad Saeed, interview with ABC America, reported in Amir Butler's 'Australia's Banning of LeT Raises More Questions', 17 November 2003, available at http://www.scoop.co.nz.

35. Article 4 of the 3rd Geneva Convention covers POW status, including those belonging to a foreign volunteer militia. The regulation about wearing a distinctive insignia or emblem has been relaxed as a result of Article 44 of Protocol 1. See Leslie Green, *The Contemporary Law of Armed Conflict*, 2nd edn, Manchester University Press: Manchester, 2000, pp. 102–121.

36. Between 7 October and 10 December 2001, 2256–2949 civilians were killed by the US bombing campaign. The US deliberately targeted civilian areas by carpet bombing, not strategically targeting military sites as claimed. One of many quotes from on the ground said, 'The bombs are going on the wrong places. They don't damage any military headquarters, but they are killing innocent people.' They also targeted mosques: 'I saw it with my own eyes. [The mosque] had been hit at nine o'clock at night. And I saw for myself that many people had been killed.' Justin Huggler, a journalist, said, 'US bombing campaigns generally deliberately target civilian infrastructure. In this case, there are reports of power stations, telephone exchanges, and even a major dam being destroyed, with potentially catastrophic effects.' See, Justin Huggler, 'Carpet Bombing Kills 150 Civilians in Frontline Town', *The Independent*, 19 November 2001; and Professor Marc W. Herold's 'A Dossier on Civilian Victims of United States' Aerial Bombing of Afghanistan: A Comprehensive Account [revised]', March 2002. Available at www.cursor.org/stories/civilian_deaths.htm.

37. In 1995, Massoud's troops were responsible for massacres, raping and looting against Hazara in Karteshe. See, Human Rights Watch, '*Afghanistan, Crisis of Impunity*', July 2001, p. 22.

Part Two

38. It was during this period that the US military dropped leaf-
     lets over Afghanistan offering monetary rewards for handing
     over suspected al-Qaeda or Taliban members. This led to many
     innocent civilians being handed over by neighbours who held
     a grudge or poor farmers who wanted to feed their families.
     The leaflets boasted that men could have 'wealth beyond their
     wildest dreams'. Figures now reveal that more than 85 per
     cent of detainees taken to Guantanamo were sold for around
     US$5000 by Afghani and Pakistani mercenaries to US forces.
     Only a small percentage were caught 'on the battlefield' legally
     defending themselves against foreign occupation. See, Amnesty
     International, 'Bounties Paid for Terror Suspects', 16 January
     2007, available at www.amnesty.org. See also, Alfred McCoy,
     'The Outcast of Camp Echo: The Punishment of David Hicks',
     The Monthly, June 2006, p. 23.
39. The Obama administration has refused to release the many
     tapes and records of interrogations and other evidence of mis-
     treatment and abuse.
40. Sensory deprivation is used on detainees to instil a sense of
     fear, disorientation and cause dependency on their captors.
     In the 1950s the CIA funded a study into human behaviour
     and mind control in response to the Cold War. Dr Hebb of
     McGill University conducted studies on people to induce a
     state akin to psychosis by placing students in air-conditioned
     cubicles with earmuffs, gloves and goggles. Within twenty-
     four hours they began to experience hallucinations, and by
     forty-eight hours complete breakdown and disintegration of
     personality. Increased pain sensitivity and psychological stress
     have also been attributed to sensory deprivation. According to
     the KUBARK manual, sensory deprivation makes the detainee
     more susceptible to the interrogator. See Professor McCoy,
     'Hicks "Severely Damaged", Says CIA Expert', ABC *Lateline*,
     13 June 2006; and John Zubeck (ed.), *Sensory and Percep-
     tual Motor Process* and *Sensory Deprivation: Fifteen Years of
     Research*, Meredith: New York, 1969, p. 232; and Physicians
     for Human Rights, 'Broken Laws, Broken Lives: Medical Evi-
     dence of Torture by US Personnel and Its Impact', available at
     http://brokenlives.info/?page_id=69.

41.   Since September 11, the US has used as many as seventeen ships as part of the CIA's rendition program, including the USS *Peleliu*, as 'floating prisons'. Many believe that this is so that the numbers of those detained could remain secret. As well as this, the treatment that David endured clearly violated human rights protections. For more information, see www.reprieve.org.uk/ secretprisons; and www.guardian.co.uk/world/2008/jun/02/ usa.humanrights.

42.   Interview was joint Australian Federal Police (AFP) and ASIO team between 24 and 25 December 2001. They had been ordered to see whether there was evidence to prosecute David under the *Crimes (Foreign Incursions and Recruitment) Act 1978*. In their report, they (specifically Ramzi Jabbour, AFP) deny that David made any 'mention of any form of maltreatment'.

43.   Most detainees in US custody have alleged that they were either raped, threatened with rape, or anally probed. Sexual violence is a war crime. Sexual humiliation is used to induce feelings of humiliation and fear. Read about the sexual abuse of al-Qahtani in Joseph Margulies's *Guantanamo and the Abuse of Presidential Power*, Simon & Schuster: New York, p. 87. For more information about proven cases of sexual assault, see *'Broken Laws, Broken Lives: Medical Evidence of Torture by US Personnel and Its Impact'*; and Centre for Constitutional Rights (CCR), 'Torture and Cruel, Inhuman and Degrading Treatment of Prisoners at Guantanamo Bay, Cuba', July 2006, available at www.ccrjustice.org.

44.   It is contrary to international law to allow a prisoner to think that they will be executed. The ICRC complained to the military officials, saying, 'The detainees think they are being taken to be shot.' Apparently, military officials debated whether to tell the detainees the truth, but decided to wait until after the first round of interrogations. See, Joseph Margulies, *Guantanamo and the Abuse of Presidential Power*, Simon & Schuster: New York, 2006, p. 65; and David Rose, *Guantanamo: America's War on Human Rights*, Faber & Faber Ltd: London, 2004, pp. 51–53.

45.   'I still see the dogs in my dreams – that they are coming for me and are going to bite me.' Detainee describing the fear the dogs created for him upon arrival at Guantanamo. See, 'Hadyar's

Testimony' in *'Broken Laws, Broken Lives: Medical Evidence of Torture by US Personnel and its Impact'*.

46. From Department of Defense news briefing, conducted as the first prisoners were brought to Guantanamo Bay, 11 January 2002.

47. Also called ERF, Emergency Reaction Force.

48. The use of dogs to threaten and intimidate detainees can be traced back to France, Belgium and the concentration camps during Nazi Germany. In 2002, Defense Department lawyer Jim Haynes wrote a memo authorising the use of sleep deprivation, stress positions, nudity and dogs. An investigation into FBI allegations of detainee abuse (*The Schmidt Report*) found that 'military interrogators improperly used military working dogs during interrogation sessions to threaten detainees, or for some other purpose'. The use of dogs to intimidate at Guantanamo was such an effective technique that it was transported to Abu Ghraib, Afghanistan and Iraq in an approved plan to 'scare-up' prisoners. See, Darius Rejali, *Torture and Democracy*, Princeton University Press: Princeton, New Jersey, 2007; and, *The Schmidt Report: Investigation into FBI Allegations of Detainee Abuse at Guantanamo Bay, Cuba Detention Facility*, 1 April 2005.

49. Many Guantanamo interrogators (including psychologists and psychiatrists) were trained by Survival-Evasion-Resistance-Escape (SERE) instructors, or had experience in the Joint Personnel Recovery Agency (JPRA), which oversaw SERE training. SERE was a program designed to train military personnel who had been caught as POWs to withstand torture during interrogation if they were to be caught by a 'dishonourable enemy'. Military personnel went through a program of beatings, starvation, stress positions, being stripped naked and thrown into small cages for days. The SERE program was established after years of experimentation by the CIA and the other four branches of the US military. Jane Mayer points out that the SERE program was a strange way to try to obtain the 'truth' from detainees because it was founded during the Cold War and used against American airmen during the Korean War. Ideas for interrogation also came from the TV series *24*, which depicted a fictional character torturing detainees to get information about a terrorist plot. The Senate

Armed Services Committee Report outlines how the harsh interrogation techniques came about. See, Senate Armed Services Committee Inquiry into the Treatment of Detainees in US Custody; and, Jane Mayer, *The Dark Side*, Scribe Publications: Victoria, 2008, p. 158; Philippe Sands, *Torture Team*, Penguin Books: London, 2008, p. 73; and former soldier put through SERE training, David J. Morris, 'Empires of the Mind: SERE, Guantánamo and the Legacies of Torture', *Virginia Quarterly Review*, Winter 2009, available at www.vqronline.org.

50.   There was wide condemnation from the international community once the photos leaked showing detainees strapped down and wheeled around.

51.   See Adam Curtis's film *The Power of Nightmares: The Rise of the Politics of Fear*, screened on BBC 2, 3 November 2004. Transcript is available at www.daanspeak.com.

52.   *ibid.*

53.   Other detainees report being threatened with disappearance or that their families would be harmed if they didn't 'cooperate'. See, Physicians for Human Rights, 'Broken Laws, Broken Lives: Medical Evidence of Torture by US Personnel and Its Impact'.

54.   See Jeremy Scahill, 'Torture Continues at Guantanamo Bay', Truthout, 15 May 2009; and The Human Rights Centre and International Human Rights Law Clinic, 'Guantanamo and Its Aftermath: US Detention and Interrogation Practices and Their Impact on Former Detainees', November 2008, available at http://hrc.berkeley.edu.

55.   See, James Yee, *For God and Country: Faith and Patriotism Under Fire*, Public Affairs: New York, 2005.

56.   Sleep deprivation is used by torturers because it makes a person more suggestible, reduces psychological resistance and reduces the body's capacity to resist pain. Sleep deprivation was authorised under the 2002 Department of Defense Memo in the form of twenty-hour interrogations. The US military authorised sleep deprivation for its prisoners for up to seventy-two hours. See, Human Rights First & Physicians for Human Rights, 'Leave No Marks: Enhanced Interrogation Techniques and the Risk of Criminality', August 2007, p. 22, available at www.humanrightsfirst.org.

    The Schmidt Report found that, 'Military interrogators improperly used sleep deprivation against detainees.' See, *The*

Schmidt Report, Investigation into FBI Allegations of Detainee Abuse at Guantanamo Bay, Cuba Detention Facility, 1 April 2005 (Amended 9 June 2005), available at www.humanrightsfirst. org.

57. Many human rights organisations, including the UN, have been particularly vocal about the amended AFM due to the type of treatment sanctioned, especially 'Appendix M', which allows for prolonged periods of isolation. The objectives of this technique are to 'prolong the shock of capture . . . and foster a feeling of futility'. Amnesty International believes the AFM is 'not compatible with the international prohibition of torture or other ill treatment'. See FM 34-52 (*US Army Field Manual: Human Intelligence Collector Operations*, 6 September 2006), available at www.army.mil/institution/armypublicaffairs/pdf/ fm2-22-3.pdf.

58. See, *Army Field Manual*.

59. Solitary confinement is strictly prohibited under international law. It is a cruel practice that causes permanent psychological damage. The impacts can range from hallucinations, emotional damage, delusions and impaired cognitive functioning to anxiety and depression. Solitary confinement is outlawed under the Convention against Torture, International Covenant on Civil and Political Rights (ICCPR) and the Geneva Conventions. Camps Five, Six and Echo are considered solitary under international law; in other words, David spent the majority of his time in solitary confinement. See, 'The Istanbul Statement on the Use and Effects of Solitary Confinement', adopted 9 December 2007 at the International Psychological Trauma Symposium. Available at www.univie.ac.at; and Human Rights Watch, 'Locked Up Alone: Detention Conditions and Mental Health at Guantanamo', 9 June 2008.

60. Medical experimentation was outlawed under international law since its use in Nazi concentration camps. The history of US medical experimentation, for interrogation purposes, began with the MKULTRA program, which was enacted by the CIA in response to the Cold War. A number of biological agents and drugs were tested on people, including prisoners and prostitutes, to find substances that led to mind control and behaviour modification. See, Dani Veracity, 'Human Medical Experimentation in the United States: The Shocking True History of

Modern Medicine and Psychiatry (1833–1965)', 6 March 2006, available at www.scribd.com; and, Amnesty International Australia, 'Human Experimentation in Guantanamo Bay', 28 September 2009, available at www.amnesty.org.au.

61. Documented reports of detainees being given injections or other medications without consent can be found in Physicians for Human Rights 2008 report, *'Broken Laws, Broken Lives: Medical Evidence of Torture by US Personnel and Its Impact'*, p. 8.

62. Reports have surfaced confirming that a Department of Defense investigation into forced drugging of detainees has been suppressed, even though it was completed over a year ago. See, Jeffrey Kaye and Jason Leopold, 'Government Report on Drugging of Detainees is Suppressed', Truthout, 14 September 2010. And see, Physicians for Human Rights, 'Health Professionals' Ethics and Human Rights Violations Revealed in the May 2004 CIA's Inspector General's Report', August 2009. Available at www.physiciansforhumanrights.org.

63. Interview with David Rose, *Guantanamo: America's War on Human Rights*, Faber & Faber Ltd: London, 2004, p. 85. Rose notes that, while short in stature, Miller's favourite words were 'enormous' and 'enormously'.

64. Although these techniques were used before 2002, the military responded to General Miller's request by seeking legal approval for 'harsher' interrogation methods. They split the methods into three categories, the third category being the most brutal. The methods authorised included: stress positions, mock executions, solitary confinement, hooding and other forms of sensory deprivation, removal of 'comfort items', forced nudity, forced grooming, taking advantage of the detainees' fears (dogs), exposure to cold weather or water and allowing an interrogator to use 'a wet towel and dripping water to induce the misperception of suffocation'. See, Joseph Margulies, *Guantanamo and the Abuse of Presidential Power*, Simon & Schuster: New York, 2006, p. 97.

65. A Navy report remarks that, 'Guards and interrogators with JTF-170, who were under pressure to produce results, had begun using abusive techniques ... including physical contact, degrading treatment (including dressing detainees in female underwear, among other techniques), the use of

"stress" positions, and coercive psychological procedures.' See, Department of the Navy, memorandum for Inspector General, 'Statement for the Record: Office of General Counsel Involvement in Interrogation Issues', 7 July 2004, p. 3.

66. Using temperature extremes as a form of torture has been used for many years by many different countries. It was the Brazilians who switched from heat to cold cells in 1966. The 'cold cell', which was used in Guantanamo, was authorised in 2005 as part of the CIA's 'enhanced interrogation techniques', however, they had been used long before. The Haynes 2002 memo, signed off by Donald Rumsfeld, authorised this technique. See, Philippe Sands, *Torture Team*, Penguin Books: London, 2008, pp. 4–6; and, Darius Rejali, *Torture and Democracy*, Princeton University Press: Princeton, New Jersey, 2007, pp. 351–353.

67. These psychologically abusive techniques were used to disrupt sleep and disorient detainees. The CIA's KUBARK manual suggests that interrogations aided by the use of temperature extremes, noise bombardment and sleep deprivation are able to induce 'regression, psychic disintegration and feelings of helplessness that lower prisoners' defenses.' This, of course, leads to signed confessions and more malleable prisoners. For more information see, Physicians for Human Rights 2008 report, *'Broken Laws, Broken Lives: Medical Evidence of Torture by US Personnel and Its Impact'*; and Centre for Constitutional Rights (CCR), 'Torture and Cruel, Inhuman and Degrading Treatment of Prisoners at Guantanamo Bay, Cuba', July 2006.

68. Details of these torture rooms and other methods of cruel, inhumane and degrading treatment were released in the FBI emails that a court ordered to be released in December 2004. See, Amnesty International, 'United States of America: Guantanamo – Icon of Lawlessness', 6 January 2005; and, J.K. and G.W., 'Conservative Media Dismiss Gitmo Abuse as "Stressful", Ignore Gruesome First-hand Accounts', *Media Matters*, 16 June 2005. Available at www.mediamatters.org; and, Professor Alfred McCoy, 'Hicks "Severely Damaged", Says CIA Expert', ABC *Lateline*, 13 June 2006.

69. Operation Sandman is also known as the 'Frequent Flyer Program'. Salim Hamdan was subjected to fifty days of Operation Sandman. Mohammad Jawad, who was captured as a child,

was moved 112 times from cell to cell over a fourteen-day period. See, William Glaberson's article, 'Detainee's Lawyers Make Claim on Sleep Deprivation', 15 July 2008, available at www.nytimes.com; and see, ACLU, 'Major David J.R. Frakt's Closing Argument in Favour of Dismissal of the Case Against Mohammad Jawad', 19 June 2008.

70.   This was still being reported in 2009.

71.   Detainees in US custody in Abu Ghraib, Kandahar and Bagram (where many were taken to before Guantanamo) have reported being sodomised with broomsticks, a 'chemical light' or rifles. Other forms of sexual humiliation reported have been: parading men naked in front of female soldiers, forcing them to wear women's underwear and dance with other men, forcing them to undress in front of female interrogators and guards, touching their genitals or provoking them in a 'humiliating' way and forcing them to watch pornography. See, Army Major General Antonio M. Taguba's interview with Seymour Hersh, 'The General's Report: How Antonio Taguba, Who Investigated the Abu Ghraib Scandal, Became One of Its Casualties', 25 June 2007. Available at www.newyorker.com.

72.   For a full account from the translator present during the interrogation see, Eric Saar and Viveca Novak, *Inside the Wire: A Military Intelligence Soldier's Eyewitness Account of Life in Guantanamo*, Penguin Group USA, 2005.

73.   News organisations reported that an interrogator read a Harry Potter book to an inmate for hours in order to 'wear down the detainee'. See, Associated Press, 'Pols: Gitmo Conditions Have Improved', 27 June 2005.

74.   Keeping detainees in a 'childlike' state was considered advantageous to the interrogators because they were more suggestible and malleable.

75.   Richard Pindar, 'Harry Potter is the Most Popular Book in Guantanamo', *The Telegraph* (UK), 7 September 2009.

76.   *Fouad Mahmoud al-Rabiah v. United States.*

77.   Office of Legal Council Memorandum, 10 May 2005.

78.   Witnessing torture and violence can have the same psychological effects as actually experiencing the violence. Scientists have found that psychological manipulation techniques, such as deprivation, humiliation and forced stress positions causes more 'mental damage' than physical torture. See, Dr Metin

Basoglu, 'Cruel and Inhuman Treatment Causes More Mental Damage Than Physical Torture', 2 June 2009; and Hernán Reyes, 'The Worst Scars Are in the Mind: Psychological Torture,' *International Review of the Red Cross*, vol. 89, no. 867, September 2007. Also, see *JAMA* and *Archives Journals*, 'Psychological and Physical Torture Have Similar Mental Effects', *ScienceDaily*, 6 March 2007.

79.   2 August 2005. Available at www.pm.gov.au/news/interviews/ Interview1489.html.

80.   The same condition has been found in other detainees (including those held in Afghanistan) and may be attributable to hormones being administered. Chemical restraint has long been used to 'subdue' detainees, for example, by injecting anti-psychotic medication or putting hormones into drinking water. Administering female hormones into male prisoners is said to have the same effect by lowering levels of testosterone in the system and the levels of aggression. The lumps may be attributable to this change in hormones. See, Kathleen Auerhan and Elizabeth Dermody Leonard. 'Docile Bodies? Chemical Restraint and the Female Inmate', *Journal of Criminal Law & Criminology*, Chicago: Winter 2000, 90(2), p. 599.

81.   See, Amnesty International, 'Human Dignity Denied: Torture and Accountability in the "War on Terror"', 27 October 2004, pp. 25–6.

82.   Brandon Neely, Chris Arendt, Sgt Eric Saar and Terry Holdbrooks have been very brave and outspoken about what they saw at Guantanamo (thank you). See, Guantanamo Testimonials Project website http://humanrights.ucdavis.edu; and, Eric Saar and Viveca Novak, *Inside the Wire: A Military Intelligence Soldier's Eyewitness Account of Life in Guantanamo*, Penguin Group USA, 2005.

83.   Many children of so-called 'high-value detainees' have been kidnapped and tortured by US intelligence organisations and their agents. The children of the alleged mastermind of September 11 were kidnapped by the CIA in 2003. The CIA told the public, 'We are handling them with kid gloves.' Evidence of their terrifying ordeal has included interrogations using ants and other insects to coerce the children into providing information about their father. Many children remain missing, including the children of Dr Aafia Siddiqui, although her

twelve-year-old daughter turned up on her grandparents' door-step in 2008 after being left there by an American man. She has spent five years in US custody. For documented cases of the torture of children, see, Henry A. Giroux, *Heart of Darkness: Torturing Children in the War on Terror*, Paradigm Publishers, USA, 2010.

84.   The KUBARK Manual was drafted in 1963 and was intended to be used against foreign intelligence operatives and 'communists'. It was redrafted in the 1980s in response to US foreign policy in Latin America and renamed *Human Resource Exploitation Training Manual*. See, Joseph Margulies, *Guantanamo and the Abuse of Presidential Power*, Simon & Schuster: New York, p. 33.

85.   Daryl Williams, press conference, 14 January 2002.

86.   The techniques used at Abu Ghraib were first used at Guantanamo. General Geoffrey Miller was sent to Abu Ghraib to 'Gitmo-ise' it. *The Taguba Report* found the intentional abuse of detainees by: forcing groups of males to masturbate; forcing male and female detainees into sexually explicit poses for photographing; punching, slapping and kicking detainees; arranging naked male detainees in a pile; a male guard raping a female detainee; writing 'i am a rapest' (sic) on the leg of a detainee then photographing him naked and positioning a naked detainee on an MRE box with a sandbag on his head and attaching wires to his fingers, penis and toes to simulate electric shock; and taking photographs of deceased Iraqi detainees. See, *The Taguba Report*, 'Article 15-6 Investigation of the 800th Military Police Brigade', 2004. Redacted version available from www.npr.org/iraq/2004/prison_abuse_report. pdf; and, Seymour Hersh, *Chain of Command: The Road From 9/11 to Abu Ghraib*, HarperCollins: New York, 2004; and, David Rose, *Guantanamo: America's War on Human Rights*, Faber & Faber Ltd: London, 2004, p. 82.

87.   *The Church Report* was described by the American Civil Liberties Union as a 'whitewash' when only the executive summary was released in 2005. However, the deaths of two detainees in Bagram was 'accidentally' leaked in the report. The full un-redacted version was only released in 2009. *The Schlesinger Report* (2004) was another whitewash. The report found that out of 300 cases of 'reported' abuse in all detention facilities, only sixty-six were substantiated. The

report noted that, 'There is no evidence of a policy of abuse promulgated by senior officials or military authorities.' *The Schlesinger Report*, 'Final Report of the Independent Panel to Review DoD Detention Operations', August 2004; as cited in Karen Greenberg and Joshua Dratel, *The Torture Papers: The Road to Abu Ghraib*, Cambridge University Press: New York, pp. 908–975.

88. Former Prime Minister John Howard: 'Of course, and the man you refer to is a Taliban supporter. I find it strange that these allegations of abuse against Mr Hicks and Mr Habib have arisen only since the prisoner abuse scandal erupted in relation to the American forces.' As quoted in UNAA, *Unity*, 21 May 2004, available from www.unaa.org.au.

89. These statements are now in the hands of the Pentagon and are unobtainable.

90. The Hicks Affidavit, available at www.smh.com.au/news/World/David-Hicks-affidavit/2004/12/10/1102625527396.html. The full affidavit is not yet publicly available.

91. None of the charges are legitimate law of war offences. To convict someone of war crimes, the state parties must be at war at the time the offences were committed. All of the charges were retrospective; the US alleged that detainees committed the offences pre-September 11, which violates the US constitution, not to mention the notion of a fair trial.

92. 'If Hicks [was] to be returned to Australia, there is no, on my legal advice, there is no . . . crime under Australian law with which [he] could be charged.' Former Prime Minister John Howard, 4 June 2004. Available at www.abc.net.au/4corners/content/2005/s1494795.htm.

93. *Rasul v. Bush 542 US 466 (2004)*. The judge found that Guantanamo detainees have the right to *habeas corpus*. In response to this, the Bush administration passed the *Detainee Treatment Act 2005*, which removed the right to *habeas* claims.

94. Even in these early days, US military lawyers; the American Bar Association; the Australian Law Society and Lawyers Alliance; the British Attorney General, Lord Goldsmith; and scores of human rights groups such as Amnesty International, Human Rights First and Human Rights Watch all voiced concerns. Civil liberties organisations such as the ACLU, Australian Council of Civil Liberties and church groups (e.g. Australian

Catholic Social Justice Council and the Vatican) voiced major concerns over the legality and fairness of the process, as well as the welfare of detainees.

95. Lord Goldsmith. 'UK Calls for Guantanamo Closure: The Attorney General, Lord Goldsmith, Has Called for the Closure of the US Detention Camp at Guantanamo Bay', BBC, 19 May 2006.

96. Lord Falconer from the UK government condemned the system on a visit to Sydney. Lord Johan Steyn, a senior UK judge, made the statement, 'The term "kangaroo court" springs to mind. It derives from the jumps of the kangaroo, and conveys the idea of a preordained, arbitrary rush to judgement by an irregular tribunal which makes a mockery of justice.' See, BBC News, 'UK Minister Condemns Guantanamo', 13 September 2006. Also, Amnesty International, 'A Deepening Stain on US Justice', 2004, available at www.amnesty.org.

97. Helen Duffy, *The 'War on Terror' and the Framework for International Law*, Cambridge University Press: Cambridge, 2005, pp. 417–427.

98. Scott Horton, 'The Great Guantanamo Puppet Theatre', *Harper's Magazine*, 21 February 2008.

99. For more information see, Amnesty International, 'USA: Justice Delayed and Justice Denied? Trials Under the Military Commissions Act'; Australian Lawyers Alliance, 'An Analysis of the United States Military Commissions: An Unjust System', 1 March 2007; Human Rights Watch, 'Briefing Paper on US Military Commissions'; James G. Stewart, 'The Military Commissions Act's Inconsistency with the Geneva Conventions: An Overview', *Journal of International Criminal Justice*, 2007 5(1):26–38; and, Helen Duffy, *The 'War on Terror' and the Framework for International Law*, Cambridge University Press: Cambridge, 2005, pp. 417–427.

100. Human Rights Watch, 'Supplemental Submission to the Human Rights Committee During Its Consideration of the Second and Third Periodic Reports of the United States of America', June 2006; and 'Recent Developments: Detainee Treatment Act 2005', *Harvard Human Rights Journal*, vol. 19, Spring 2006. Available electronically from www.law.harvard.edu.

101. Vice Admiral Church wrote his report in 2004 on allegations of the abuse of detainees at Guantanamo. View the full interrogation log of al-Qahtani at www.time.com/time/2006/log/

log.pdf; and Steven Miles, 'Medical Ethics and the Interrogation of Guantanamo 063', *The American Journal of Bioethics,* 7(4):5; and 'Review of Department of Defense Operations and Detainee Interrogation Techniques', 7 March 2005, available at the ACLU website, www.aclu.org; and, Petty Officer 3rd Class John R. Guariano (USN), 'Myers Calls Guantanamo Torture Reports "Absolutely Irresponsible"', American Forces Information Service, 29 May 2005, available from www.globalsecurity. org.

Note: By 2005, there were 100 recorded deaths of men and women in US custody. General Richard B. Myers defended the deaths, saying that only 100 cases of detainee abuse had been substantiated and a closer look at the data recording prisoner abuse shows that, 'It is not systemic. It's not a policy of this government obviously.'

102. Back pain is associated with long-lasting restriction of movement, as well as physical trauma and stress positions. See, Physicians for Human Rights 2008 Report, *'Broken Laws, Broken Lives: Medical Evidence of Torture by US Personnel and Its Impact'*, p. 54.

103. Numerous studies have concluded that extended periods of isolation can cause significant psychological harm, including insomnia, confusion, hallucinations and psychosis. See, Human Rights Watch, 'Locked Up Alone: Detention Conditions and Mental Health at Guantanamo', 9 June 2008, p. 14.

104. See, Kyndra Rotunda, *Honour Bound: Inside the Guantanamo Trials*, Carolina Academic Press: Carolina, 2008; and, 'Hicks Dressed Like Wall-Street Banker', *The Daily Telegraph*, 11 June 2008.

105. C.P. Snow as quoted in Stanley Milgram, 'Behavioral Study of Obedience', *Journal of Abnormal and Social Psychology*, 1963, 67(4), p. 371.

106. For a great recreation of the CSRT hearings, see, *The Response*, a film created in collaboration with the University of Maryland School of Law and Venable LLP, Look at the Moon Productions.

107. Judge Green found that detainees were protected under the 5th Amendment of the US Constitution, which is the entitlement of due process. *In re Guantanamo Detainee Cases, 355 F. Supp. 2d 443 (D.D.C. 2005).*

108. Feroz Abbasi, 'The Lies I Have Propagated in My Handwritten Autobiography (May–June/July 2003 CE)', copied 21 November 2004 from the original.

109. *Hamdan v. Rumsfeld, 548 U.S. 557 (2006).*

110. At this stage the government's tone changed; they were now calling for David to be tried or they would seek his release. See Tom Allard, 'Hicks Could Be Home by Christmas', *The Sydney Morning Herald*, 15 August 2006. Philip Ruddock commented that David should be charged by November. The Law Council of Australia released a report of the Federal Government's position, which included public statements and policy directives. See, Law Council of Australia, 'The Australian Government's Position on David Hicks', 7 December 2006.

111. This was around the time of the leaked emails that revealed the military commissions were rigged. The pressure was mounting on the Australian government to investigate, not only the claims of abuse, but also the adherence of military commissions trial regulations to international fair trial standards.

112. At the time the consular official was supposed to be providing David with 'welfare' visits, he reported that David did not have any complaints and that he was 'in good physical condition', despite the obvious deterioration of his physical and mental health. See, Commonwealth of Australia: Official Committee Hansard, Senate Legal and Constitutional Legislation Committee, 16 February 2004.

113. Emails from Major Robert Preston and Captain John Carr. Captain Carr stated, 'I find a half-hearted and disorganised effort by a skeleton group of relatively inexperienced attorneys to prosecute fairly low-level accused in a process that appears to be rigged.' See, The Torture Report, www.thetorturereport. org.

114. General Geoffrey Miller claimed that interrogations were deliberately not recorded because it might provide evidence favourable to the detainees; however, every interrogation was filmed. Not only evidence to help detainees was destroyed, but also evidence of torture and ill treatment. See, Lt-Cmdr William Kuebler's comments, 'Pentagon Urged Notes Destroyed', BBC News, 9 June 2008; Glenn Greenwald, 'Mohammed Jawad and Obama's Efforts to Suspend Military Commissions', *Salon*, 21 January 2009; and Scott Higham, Joe Stephens,

Margot Williams, 'Guantanamo – a Holding Cell in War on Terror', *The Washington Post*, 2 May 2004.

115. Major Robert Preston stated that the commissions process was perpetrating a fraud on the American people and that the process was morally, ethically and professionally intolerable. See, Leigh Sales, 'Leaked Emails Claim Guantanamo Trials Rigged', ABC News Online, 1 August 2005.

116. Captain Paul Willee. When asked whether David would get a fair trial, his response was, 'Personally, I'd say absolutely not.' See, Tom Allard, 'Defence Force Lawyer Lashes Hicks Court', 2 August 2005; and Nicholas Cowdery, NSW Director of Public Prosecutions, called the Hicks case an 'unprincipled disgrace'. See, 'Lawyers Urged to Speak Out Against Hicks' Treatment', ABC News Online, 18 July 2006.

117. 'Hicks' Treatment "Cruel and Inhumane"', Reuters and AAP, 3 August 2006.

118. Judges included outspoken John Dowd and former High Court Judge Mary Gaudron. See, 'Ruddock Dismisses Criticism of Govt Handling of Hicks', ABC News Online, 3 July 2006.

119. Former Foreign Minister Alexander Downer (now working for the UN): 'We believe that the appropriate safeguards are in place to ensure that the trial is a fair trial.' Former Attorney General Philip Ruddock said that the US had been 'assiduous' in ensuring fairness. See, Norman Hermant, 'Govt Downplays Allegations Guantanamo Tribunals Rigged', ABC Lateline, 1 August 2005; and Tom Allard, 'Defence Force Lawyer Lashes Hicks court', 2 August 2005, available at www.smh.com.au.

120. Leaving people in 'sweatboxes' and subjecting them to temperature extremes has been used as a torture technique for centuries. In Vietnam, shipping containers left over by US forces were used to torture people in the intense heat of the tropical climate. The same technique has been applied in Guantanamo. An investigation into improper interrogations noted this technique: 'Military interrogators improperly used extremes of heat and cold during their interrogation of detainees.' See, *The Schmidt Report*, 'Investigation into FBI Allegations of Detainee Abuse at Guantanamo Bay, Cuba Detention Facility', 1 April 2005 (Amended 9 June 2005); Darius Rejali, *Torture and Democracy*, Princeton University Press: New Jersey, 2007, pp. 351–353.

121. Noise has been used by torturers to either mask sounds of others being tortured, such as when children's music was played by the Gestapo when beating Walter Bauer, or, when they are trying to disrupt sleep, terrorise or create emotions within the prisoners. In 2004, a US military official admitted that they made 'uncooperative prisoners strip to their underwear, having them sit in a chair, shackled hand and foot to a bolt in the floor, and forcing them to endure strobe lights and screaming loud rock and rap music played through two close loudspeakers, while the air-conditioning was turned up to maximum levels.' See, Neil A. Lewis, 'Broad Use of Harsh Interrogation Techniques is Described at Cuba', *The New York Times*, 17 October 2004; and Darius Rejali, *Torture and Democracy*, Princeton University Press: New Jersey, 2007, pp. 360–366.

122. Australian officials attributed the noise over the years to 'construction and equipment noise', after David submitted a complaint about not being able to sleep to Australian embassy officials. Letter to David McLeod from Simeon Gilding, Assistant Secretary Consular Branch, 23 March 2006.

123. View the Emergency Restraint Chair (ERC Inc.), or make your complaint at the manufacturer's website, www.restraintchair.com/diagram.htm.

124. For more information on force feeding see, Centre for Constitutional rights (CCR), 'Current Conditions of Confinement at Guantanamo: Still in Violation of the Law', 23 February 2009. Report available at www.ccrjustice.org.

125. A list of David's complaints was given to the Australian consular official, attached to a letter of 23 March 2006 from Simeon Gilding (DFAT) to David McLeod. Simeon Gilding from the DFAT acknowledged the list of complaints David handed over. The letter notes, 'As with all of our consular visits, our primary concern is to ensure Mr Hicks' welfare.'

126. 27 January 2002, US Department of Defense, news transcript.

127. Halliburton is a subsidiary of KBR. Dick Cheney was formerly the CEO of Halliburton. KBR was reportedly awarded a multi-million-dollar government building contract for Guantanamo. For more information see, Corporate Watch UK, 'Halliburton Plc.: A Corporate Profile', July 2003.

128. During interrogations, intelligence branches and BSCT teams (psychologists and psychiatrists) sat behind these walls to

provide information on the detainee's mental health, weaknesses and vulnerabilities. *The Kiley Report* confirms that medical personnel were utilised during interrogations. The ICRC called this 'a flagrant violation of medical ethics'. See, The Center for the Study of Human Rights in the Americas, 'ICRC: Analysis'; and, Kevin C. Kiley, *The Kiley Report*, 'Assessment of Detainee Medical Operations for OEF, GUANTANAMO, and OIF', Office of the Surgeon General Army, 13 April 2005; and Steven Miles, 'Medical Ethics and the Interrogation of Guantanamo 063', *The American Journal of Bioethics*, 7(4):5.

129. A letter was sent from the British embassy in Washington to David's legal team confirming that if he was granted citizenship then he would be deprived 'of nationality immediately after registering as British'. The letter was to arrange for David to be administered the oath and pledge in Guantanamo so that they could then revoke it. Letter from Alan Charlton to Charles Stimpson (Deputy Assistant Secretary, Detainee Affairs), 1 February 2006.

130. Omar Khadr was captured as a child and, according to humanitarian law, should have been rehabilitated if he was, in fact, a child soldier. His legal team have indicated that evidence clearing the young man has been destroyed purposefully. He is currently undergoing trial under the 2009 *Military Commissions Act*, although he has refused to participate due to the unfairness of the process and the military commission admitting evidence obtained under coercion. He has just turned twenty-four. See, Henry A. Giroux, *Heart of Darkness: Torturing Children in the War on Terror*, Paradigm Publishers: USA, 2010; and, Human Rights First, 'The Case of Omar Khadr, Canada', available at www.humanrightsfirst.org.

131. Rear Admiral Harry Harris: 'I believe this was not an act of desperation, but an act of asymmetrical warfare waged against us.' See, Andy Worthington, 'Murders at Guantanamo: Exposing the Truth about the 2006 "Suicides"', *The Public Record*, 18 January 2010; and, David Rose, *Guantanamo: America's War on Human Rights*, Faber & Faber Ltd: London, 2004, p. 64.

132. Army Staff Sgt. Joe Hickman and Specialist Tony Davila.

133. Scott Horton, 'The Guantanamo "Suicides": A Camp Delta Sergeant Blows the Whistle', *Harper's Magazine*, January/February 2010; and, Andy Worthington, 'Murders at

Guantanamo: Exposing the Truth about the 2006 "Suicides"', *The Public Record*, 18 January 2010.

134. *ibid.*

135. Scott Hall for Human Rights Watch, 'US: Release the Full Reports into Guantanamo Deaths', 7 December 2009.

136. Mahvish Rukhsana Khan, *My Guantanamo Diary: The Detainees and the Stories They Told Me.* Scribe: Victoria, 2008.

137. Amnesty International Australia, 'Another Death at Guantanamo', 3 June 2009.

138. There have been over 100 deaths of detainees in US custody (not including the five recorded deaths at Guantanamo), including Abu Ghraib, Bagram and other detention facilities. Twelve have been confirmed as being tortured to death by US military personnel, the CIA or its agents. Of all of the confirmed deaths, only twelve have resulted in minimal punishment or reprimand of any kind, and they have targeted only lower ranking soldiers. A Human Rights First report has pointed out that more people have been promoted since the deaths or as a result of abuse than reprimanded. See, Hina Shamsi for Human Rights First, 'Commands Responsibility: Detainee Deaths in US Custody in Iraq and Afghanistan', February 2006.

139. The NCIS, who was investigating the deaths, appealed to the court to remove all of the detainees' letters. The judge commented that the only evidence to suggest that the deaths were in fact suicides was drawn from media sources. Judge Robertson also noted that the Justice Department lawyers who argued the case went to 'great lengths' not to testify about the 'suicides' under oath. See, Scott Horton, 'The Guantanamo "Suicides": A Camp Delta Sergeant Blows the Whistle', *Harper's Magazine*, January/February 2010.

140. *Hamdan v. Rumsfeld 548 U.S. 557 (2006).* The judge ruled that the President had no authority to set up the military commissions and that they were illegal under both military law and fair trial procedures under the Geneva Conventions. The judge also noted that the structure of the commissions violated the Uniform Code of Military Justice (UCMJ) and the 4th Geneva Convention. Chief Justice Stevens noted that the Executive is bound to the rule of law and does not hold a blank cheque. For a good summary of the case see, Human Rights Watch, 'Questions and Answers on *Hamdan v. Rumsfeld*', available at www.hrw.org.

141. Former President Bush publicly admitted to the extraordinary
      rendition program and having secret CIA prisons in operation.
      He described the program as one that has 'saved innocent lives'.
      Bush claimed that there were only fourteen men in secret deten-
      tion but that they had now been transferred to Guantanamo Bay.
      These fourteen 'high-value detainees' were the subject of the CIA
      Inspector General's report that described abuses by CIA agents
      and their paid employees, such as Blackwater. The CIA agents
      told detainees that their family members had been raped. They
      placed detainees on racks and shackled them in painful positions,
      subjected them to mock executions, used painful pressure points,
      gave the men cold showers and placed them in front of air-
      conditioners for hours at a time, subjected them to water dousing,
      placed detainees in nappies and threw them to the concrete floor,
      left them in complete darkness for days at a time and placed them
      in 'sleep deprivation cells'. See, 'Bush Admits to CIA Secret Pris-
      ons', BBC News, 7 September 2006; and, CIA Inspector General's
      Report, 2004 (redacted version released August 2009). Available
      at http://media.washingtonpost.com. For a good history of the
      rendition program see, Jane Mayer, 'Outsourcing Torture: The
      Secret History of America's Extraordinary Rendition Program',
      The New Yorker: Annals of Justice, 7 February 2005.

142. For a good overview of the 2006 *Military Commissions Act*,
      see Human Rights Watch, 'Q and A: *Military Commissions
      Act* of 2006'. The UN Special Rapporteur on the Promotion
      and Protection of Human Rights while Countering Terrorism,
      Martin Scheinin, issued a statement raising concerns about
      the MCA. He said, 'The MCA contains a number of provi-
      sions that are incompatible with the international obligations
      of the United States under human rights law and humanitar-
      ian law.' See, Martin Scheinin, 'UN Expert on Human Rights
      and Counter Terrorism Concerned that Military Commissions
      Act is Now Law in United States', UNHCR Press Release,
      27 October 2006; and, in 2007 he made another statement con-
      demning the US for not allowing him access to Guantanamo
      and its clear breaches of the ICCPR (including trying people by
      military commission). Martin Scheinin, 'Preliminary Findings
      on Visit to United States by Special Rapporteur on Promotion
      and Protection of Human Rights while Countering Terrorism',
      UN press release, 29 May 2007.

143. Sean Alfano, 'Report: Gitmo Abuse "Common Practice"', CBS News, 6 October 2006.

144. Sleep deprivation is a very effective torture technique. The Committee against Torture (CAT) has noted that sleep deprivation used for prolonged periods constitutes a breach of the Convention against Torture and is primarily used to break down the will of the detainee. Sleep deprivation can cause impaired memory and cognitive functioning, decreased short-term memory, speech impairment, hallucinations, psychosis, lowered immunity, headaches, high blood pressure, cardiovascular disease, stress, anxiety and depression. For more information, see, Gretchen Borchelt, JD and Christian Pross, MD, 'Systematic Use of Psychological Torture by US Forces', *Torture,* vol. 15(1), 2005; and *'Broken Laws, Broken Lives: Medical Evidence of Torture by U.S. Personnel and Its Impact'.*

145. The US military claimed that the poster was provided for 'intellectual stimulation'. See, Peter Mitchell, 'Hicks Shown Saddam Death Photo', *The Daily Telegraph,* 2 February 2007; and, Tom Allard, 'Pictures of Dead Saddam Used to "Stimulate" Hicks', *The Sydney Morning Herald,* 3 February 2007.

146. Many agents (such as Jim Clemente) within the FBI were highly critical about what they saw, and a series of complaints were raised to their superiors and General Geoffrey Miller in 2002. An FBI member accused the military of criminal behaviour due to the 'harsh interrogation techniques' that were being employed. In response to the complaints, the army set up an investigation and the result is the *The Schmidt Report: Investigation into FBI Allegations of Detainee Abuse at Guantanamo Bay, Cuba Detention Facility,* 1 April 2005 (Amended 9 June 2005); and, Jane Mayer, *The Dark Side,* Scribe Publications: Victoria, 2008, pp. 202–205.

147. Sasha Uzunov, 'David Hicks Not a True Muslim', *Herald-Sun,* 17 May 2007.

148. Prepared Statement of Colonel Morris D. Davis, House Armed Services Committee, 'Hearing on the implications of the Supreme Court's Boumediene decision for detainees at Guantanamo Bay, Cuba', 30 July 2008.

149. Amy Goodman, 'Fmr. Chief Guantanamo Prosecutor Says Military Commissions "Not Justice"', *Democracy Now,* 16 July 2008.

150. *United States of America v. David Matthew Hicks*, Military Commissions Charge Sheet, 2 February 2007.

151. David was formally charged for a second time on 2 February 2007. A report into the legality of the charges found that, 'The suggestion that the offence of Providing Material Support for Terrorism under the MCA is merely a codification of an existing Law of War or an existing domestic law of the United States, and is therefore not a retrospective criminal law, is untenable. This is a recently invented and new war crime created with the passing of the *Military Commissions Act of 2006* on 17 October 2006.'

Former Prime Minister Howard used the opportunity to say that the charges mean that the military commissions system is 'fair and independent'. See, The Hon. Alistair Nicholson QC, Peter Vickery QC, Hilary Charlesworth, Andrew Byrnes, Gavan Griffith, Tim McCormack, Gideon Boas and Don Rothwell, 'Advice in the Matter of the Legality of the Charges Against David Hicks', 8 March 2007. ABC interview with Alison Caldwell, 'Howard Says Hicks Charges Show Military Commission is Fair', The World Today, 2 March 2007.

152. At the time of writing, it is the eight-year anniversary.

153. This was also confirmed in Colonel Morris Davis's testimony to the House Armed Services Committee. Haynes asked Davis to charge others as well as David in the phone conversation. This would have created the illusion of some legitimacy.

154. Scott Horton, 'At Gitmo, No Room for Justice', *Harper's Magazine*, 22 October 2007.

155. See Amnesty International USA: 'David Hicks Pleads Guilty on One Count. Amnesty International Observer Attends Arraignment at Guantanamo', 27 March 2007.

156. For an excellent legal analysis of the military commission proceedings, see, Lex Lasry, 'David Hicks v. the United States: Summary of the Report of the Independent Observer for the Law Council of Australia', 24 July 2007. His final conclusion: 'The "trial" of David Hicks, which took place in March 2007, was a charade . . . Australia's international standing and moral authority has been diminished by its support of a process so obviously at odds with the rule of law.' Tim McCormack's observations of the show trial are also interesting. See, Tim McCormack, 'David Hicks and the Charade of Guantanamo Bay', *Melbourne Journal of International Law*, 8(2), 2007.

157. At this point public pressure had mounted at its highest point, including Liberal Party supporters. A Newspoll found that 70 per cent of Australians wanted David to be brought home. See, 'Poll Finds Most Australians Want Hicks Home', ABC News, 14 December 2006.

158. See, Scott Horton, 'Gitmo: No Room for Justice', *Harper's Magazine*, 22 October 2007. There was also political interference coming from Alexander Downer. Declassified (although heavily redacted) documents obtained from the Australian Department of Foreign Affairs and Trade (DFAT) reveal that Downer told US officials, including Attorney General Alberto Gonzales, that, 'Australia wanted to see the case resolved as quickly as possible' in 2006.

159. Before Colonel Morris Davis blew the whistle and publicly stated that he was left out of the process, Alexander Downer spoke with an ABC reporter, rebutting claims of political interference: 'I mean, the plea bargain was negotiated between the defence and the prosecution in the context of the military commission process, and it was signed off on by the convening authority.' Minister for Foreign Affairs Hon Alexander Downer, MP, 'Transcription: Interview with Virginia Trioli – David Hicks', 24 October 2007.

160. Cornell University Law School defines an Alford Plea: 'Also known as a "best-interests plea", an Alford Plea registers a formal claim neither of guilt nor innocence toward charges brought against a defendant in criminal court. Like a *nolo contendere* plea, an Alford Plea arrests the full process of criminal trial because the defendant – typically, only with the court's permission – accepts all the ramifications of a guilty verdict (i.e. punishment) without first attesting to having committed the crime.'

161. General Hemmingway boasted to an Australian newspaper that he was the one who thought of the gag order: 'I just thought . . . it was time for Hicks to spend some time thinking about why he was where he was, and worry about publicity after that.' See, Mark Coultan and Penelope Debelle, 'Hicks Gag My Idea, Says General', *The Age*, 5 April 2005.

162. The US government retains the right to continue to detain someone indefinitely, even if they are found to be innocent.

163. For medical consequences of torture and cruel treatment see,

Human Rights First and Physicians for Human Rights, 'Leave no Marks: Enhanced Interrogation Techniques and the Risk of Criminality', August 2007, Appendix B.

164. See, the report of the Clarke Inquiry into the Case of Dr Mohamed Haneef, 21 November 2008.

165. For more information on control orders and other anti-terror legislation that has been recently introduced, see, Brian Walters, 'Terror Australis: How Australia's Anti-Terror Laws Put Us at Risk', *Lawyers Weekly*, 1 November 2009; and, Australian Human Rights Commission, 'A Human Rights Guide to Australia's Counter-Terrorism Laws'.

166. See Brian Walters and Neil McAteer, 'Note on International Human Rights Law for Counsel for David Hicks'; and, Special Rapporteur on the Promotion and Protection of Human Rights and Fundamental Freedoms while Countering Terrorism, 'Australia: Study on Human Rights Compliance While Countering Terrorism: Report Summary'. Australia is a party to the International Covenant on Civil and Political Rights (ICCPR), which provides that rights outlined in the ICCPR should be enshrined in domestic legislation. Many are not, due to Australia lacking a Human Rights Act. Many legal experts note that the two control orders imposed so far have been disproportionate to the actual 'threat' and have constituted a breach of the right to liberty and security of person, the right to privacy and the right to freedom of movement.

These restrictions are outlined in *Jabbour v. Hicks [2008] FMCA 178* (www.austlii.edu.au/au/cases/cth/FMCA/2007/2139.html)

167. Other detainees report having pain and problems with their jaws due to blows to the face. See, Physicians for Human Rights 2008 report, *'Broken Laws, Broken Lives: Medical Evidence of Torture by U.S. Personnel and Its Impact'*, p. 22.

168. President Obama signed three executive orders the day after he took office: 1. To close Guantanamo; 2. To end torture; and 3. To close CIA blacksites. From a human rights perspective, these orders still have loopholes. For example, rendition is still occurring on a 'short-term, transitory basis', which is up for interpretation, and practices under the Army Field Manual may constitute a breach of the CAT. The executive orders are available from the White House website.

169. Testimony by Colonel Lawrence B. Wilkerson, *Hamad v. Bush et al.*, 24 March 2010.

170. President Obama, 15 May 2009, 'Statement of President Obama on Military Commissions', Office of the Press Secretary, retrieved 19 May 2009; and Washington Correspondents, 'Obama Retains Bush Era Military Tribunals', AFP; and Bill Meyer, 'Obama's Support for Terrorism Charges in Dispute at Guantanamo Military Trial', Cleveland.com, 15 July 2009.

171. For an analysis of the new 2009 *Military Commissions Act*, see, Amnesty International, 'Trials in Error: Third Go at a Misconceived Military Commission Experiment'.

172. Senate Armed Services Committee, 7 July 2009. David Kris testimony available from www.armed-services.senate.gov/statemnt/2009/July/Kris%2007-07-09.pdf; and Jeh C. Johnson, www.armed-services.senate.gov/statemnt/2009/July/Johnson%2007-07-09.pdf.

173. Lieutenant Colonel Darrel Vandeveld resigned in 2008, and many have followed since.

174. Bob Woodward, 'Guantanamo Detainee Was Tortured, Says US Official', *The Washington Post*, 14 January 2009.

175. Fouad al-Rabiah brought a *habeas* claim to a US court. The judge ordered he be released immediately when she found that false statements made by al-Rabiah were used in his CSRT hearing that deemed him to be an 'unlawful enemy combatant'. See, Amnesty International, 'You Will Not Leave This Place Innocent: Admissions of Torture', 13 October 2009.

176. For a good summary of the four memos, see Amnesty International, 'The Torture Memos', 4 May 2009. The ICRC report on the treatment of fourteen 'high-value detainees in CIA custody' is available at www.nybooks.com. See also, Mark Danner, 'US Torture: Voices from the Black Sites', *The New York Review of Books*, 9 April 2009. The CIA Inspector General's report is available at http://media.washingtonpost.com/wp-srv/nation/documents/cia_oig_report.pdf, or a summary is available at www.amnesty.org.au/hrs/comments/21585/.

177. The CIA destroyed video recordings showing the interrogations of several men. Chairman, Thomas H. Kean and Vice Chairman, Lee H. Hamilton, of the 9/11 Commission, have accused the former Bush administration of obstruction due to their denying the existence of the tapes, and the alleged orders

from the administration for their destruction. John Durham was directed to investigate the tapes in 2008, then in 2009 was appointed special prosecutor to investigate the Inspector General's report. At the time of writing, two tapes previously thought to have been destroyed have turned up under the desks of CIA agents. See, 'Tapes Show Interrogation of 9/11 Suspect Binalshibh', BBC, 17 August 2010. For more, see Amnesty International, 'Special Prosecutor Appointed', 25 August 2009, available at www.amnesty.org.au/hrs/comments/21593/.

178. Zach Zagger, 'CIA Documents Reveal Possible Cover-up of Interrogation Video Destruction', *Jurist Legal News and Research*, 16 April 2010.

179. The Detainee Abuse Accountability Project, 'By the Numbers: Findings of the Detainee Abuse Accountability Project', April 2006 (vol 18:2(G)). The report found that US authorities have failed to investigate allegations, or have investigated them inadequately, and numerous personnel have been protected and spared criminal liability. At the time of writing, four UK detainees who attempted to sue the US government due to the torture and religious abuse they endured had their case thrown out of a US Supreme Court. The Obama administration argued that they were not entitled to be treated as 'persons' under the *Religious Freedoms Restoration Act*. The court reinforced a lower court's decision that the defendants were immune to prosecution because 'torture is a foreseeable consequence of the military's detention of suspected enemy combatants', and that, even if torture and religious abuse were illegal, defendants were immune under the Constitution because they could not have reasonably known that detainees at Guantanamo had any Constitutional rights. See also, Centre for Constitutional Rights, 'Supreme Court Refuses to Hear Suit Seeking Accountability for Guantanamo Torture', press release, 14 December 2009.

180. See, Marjorie Cohn, 'Spain Investigates What America Should', *San Francisco Chronicle*, 6 April, 2009; and, Amnesty International USA, 'Arrest Warrants Coming for 6 Bush-Era Officials in Madrid?', 31 March, 2009; and, Amnesty International Australia, 'Finally Accountable?', 6 April 2009.

181. Jeremy Scahill, 'Torture Continues at Guantanamo Bay', Truthout, 15 May 2009, available at www.truthout.org/051609Y.

182. See, 'Italy Judge Convicts 23 Former CIA Agents in Rendition
     Trial', *JURIST*, 4 November 2009; and, Amnesty International
     Australia, 'CIA Agents Convicted in Italy', 6 November 2009.
     Available at www.amnesty.org.au/hrs/comments/22051/.

183. See, 'Senate Armed Services Committee Inquiry into the Treat-
     ment of Detainees in US Custody' (full un-redacted report
     released in 2009). The report shows that the CIA were trained
     to use those techniques in early 2002 before any high-value
     detainees were even captured. The Bush administration always
     claimed that they were forced to ramp up techniques only after
     they had captured the high-value detainees and because they
     refused to talk. The report also claims that the Bush administra-
     tion may have pressured interrogators to use torture to extract
     false confessions and obtain 'information' that would link al-
     Qaeda to Saddam Hussein, and therefore serve as a justification
     for war. The report points to high-level Bush administration
     officials who were involved in the spread of torture techniques
     throughout US detention sites, especially Donald Rumsfeld. See
     also, UN Commission on Human Rights, 'Situation of Detain-
     ees at Guantanamo Bay', 62nd Session, 27 February 2006.

     The International Committee of the Red Cross took the
     unusual step of going public with its concerns about unlaw-
     ful and indefinite detention in 2003. See, Neil A. Lewis, 'Red
     Cross Criticises Indefinite Detention in Guantanamo Bay', 10
     October 2003. In 2004, an ICRC report was 'leaked' to *The
     New York Times* regarding the abusive treatment that they
     described as 'tantamount to torture'. See, Neil A. Lewis, 'Red
     Cross Finds Detainee Abuse in Guantanamo', *The New York
     Times*, 30 November 2005.

184. After describing a hellish list of torture techniques, the CIA
     Inspector General's Report concluded that the techniques did
     not stop any 'specific imminent attacks'. See, Mark Seibel and
     Warren P. Strobel, 'CIA Official: No Proof Harsh Techniques
     Stopped Terror Attacks', McClatchy, 24 April 2009. Terry E.
     Arnold, who was the number two counter-terrorism official in
     the US State Department believes that torture only increases
     terrorism. He also commented that people on the street knew
     what was happening in Abu Ghraib before the American media
     did, and that is why people took up arms in Iraq. See also,
     interview with George Washington Blog, 'Leading Counter

Terrorism Expert and Former High Level Official Slams War on Terror and Questions 9/11', 3 February 2009; Peter Finn and Joby Warrick, 'In 2002, Military Agency Warned Against Torture: Extreme Duress Could Yield Unreliable Information, It Said', *The Washington Post*, 25 April 2009.

Retired CIA 'Directorate of Operations', Milt Beardon, commented: 'The administration's claims of having "saved thousands of Americans" can be dismissed out of hand because credible evidence has never been offered – not even an authoritative leak of any major terrorist operation interdicted based on information gathered from these interrogations in the past seven years. All the public gets is repeated references to Jose Padilla, the Lakawanna Six, the Liberty Seven and the Library Tower operation in Los Angeles. If those slapstick episodes are the true character of the threat, then maybe we'll be okay after all.' See, Milt Beardon, 'The Truth is Out on CIA and Torture', *The Washington Independent*, 1 July 2009.

185. British Foreign Secretary William Hague has announced that a judge-led investigation will take place into whether the MI5 and other British government agencies were complicit in the torture and ill-treatment of its citizens in overseas prisons. However, the UK government has stipulated that to undertake the investigation detainees who have current claims against the UK government would have to drop their cases. See, Patrick Wintour, 'Torture Claims Investigation Ordered by William Hague', *The Guardian*, 20 May 2010.

186. See, *Boumediene v. Bush, 553 U.S. 723 (2008)*. For updated figures on detainee numbers see, 'The Guantanamo Docket', www.nytimes.com.

187. Charlie Savage, 'Detainees Will Still Be Held, but Not Tried, Official Says', *The New York Times*, 20 January 2010; and Amnesty International, 'Broken Promises: Indefinite Detention at Guantanamo Bay', 1 February 2010.

188. See, 'Two Thirds in Kashmir Want Independence', AFP, 12 September 2010.

189. A number of respected lawyers and international human rights organisations are of the opinion that the Australian government may be liable for war crimes under the Convention Against Torture (CAT) and International Covenant on Civil and Political Rights (ICCPR), for complicity in allowing David's torture

and inhumane treatment, not providing an independent investigation into the allegations of mistreatment, having Australian officials present for David's ill-treatment and leaving him in Guantanamo to be abused. See, 'UN Committee Against Torture Concluding Observations on Australia', May 2008, available at HRLRC (www.hrlrc.org.au); and Peter Vickery QC (Special Rapporteur, International Commission of Jurists, Victoria), 'David Hicks – Justice After Hamdan?', 14 August, 2006; and, The Hon. Alistair Nicholson QC, Peter Vickery QC, Hilary Charlesworth, Andrew Byrnes, Gavan Griffith, Tim McCormack, 'David Hicks – Military Commissions Act 2006 – Compliance with Common Article 3 of the Geneva Conventions, the Hamdan Decision and Australian Law'.

Also, the Australian government may have committed war crimes by contravening the Geneva Conventions, the Australian Criminal Code and ICCPR by allowing David to face an unfair legal system that applied charges retrospectively and not ensuring a full and fair trial. See, Peter Vickery 'David Hicks and Retrospective Criminal Laws', February 2007.

Legal experts also deem the charge Material Support for Terrorism to be illegal. See, 'Advice: In the Matter of the Legality of the Charge Against David Hicks', 8 March 2007.

The ICCPR also states that a person is innocent until proven guilty. The former Howard government contravened this on a number of occasions by stating that David was a member of al-Qaeda and was 'dangerous'. See, The Hon. Alastair Nicholson et al., 'Opinion: David Hicks, *Military Commissions Act* 2006, Compliance with Common Article 3 of the Geneva Conventions, the Hamdan Decision and Australian Law', 20 November 2006. A Statement of Claim was brought before the Federal Court of Australia outlining war crimes perpetrated by Howard and Downer in 2006.

190. Michael Gordon and Michelle Grattan, 'Leader Pledges to Bring Hicks Home Quickly', *The Age*, 14 December 2006.

191. Robert McClelland, 'Howard Lets Military Commissions Devalue Our Citizenship', media release, 9 July 2003.

192. Robert McClelland, 'Torture Allegations', Australian Parliament press release, 8 October 2003.

Acknowledgements

First, thanks to my family and friends for your support and understanding when I have been locked away typing and not available for you.

I would like to thank the team at Random House for helping me put this book together and for helping make it a fairly smooth process, especially my publisher, Nikki, and editor, Brandon. I have greatly enjoyed working with you guys. Cheers. Thanks to Richard for his recommendation. Thanks to James from Ice Cold Publishing for the illustrations and the map placed with pride and joy at the beginning of this book.

Thanks to Dick and Julian for your feedback, advice and endless support. Thanks to Tamara and the team at Gilbert + Tobin for their legal expertise and support through this process. Thanks to Peter for putting up with my impatience.

Special thanks to Lance for all of the late-night phone calls and your wisdom and experience in the many areas I have had to consider in this process, and especially for your friendship.

Thanks to Jim, who was kind enough to allow me to use his home while he was away on more than one occasion. That quiet and personal space was important. And thanks to Ron and Valerie for the use of your very beautiful hideaway to work on the last edit. Thanks to Pat for the time off work on the days I had to write and attend to related business.

And special thanks to my beautiful wife, Aloysia, who has shown a lot of patience and understanding, especially during the nights I kept her awake at 2 am with my banging around out in the lounge room while writing this book. After going through this process, I can understand why authors always make sure to acknowledge their partners. She deserves an extra-special thanks for all the endnotes, quotes and the list of recommended reading she put together. My book wouldn't be the same without all that hard work and countless hours researching and writing the references; I recommend people read them.

Aloysia would like to thank Jake L. and Katie, and we would both like to thank Erin.